Red Sabbath

The Battle of Little Bighorn

Robert Kershaw

Ian Allan

PUBLISHING

The battle began on Sunday – the Sabbath – 25 June 1876 and by evening Custer and every man in his battalion was dead. 'The sun went down that night like a ball of fire,' declared a 7th Cavalry Corporal. It was indeed The Blood Red Sabbath.

Dedication
To all our friends in South Africa

First published 2005
This paperback edition 2008

ISBN 978 07110 3325 2

Published by Ian Allan Publishing

an imprint of Ian Allan Publishing Ltd, Hersham, Surrey KT12 4RG.
Printed and bound in Great Britain by Mackays of Chatham, Kent

Contents

List of Maps and Diagrams...v
Introduction vi
Prologue ix

Chapter 1	**Red Cloud's war**..**1**
	The Fetterman Massacre 1
	Lessons...17

Chapter 2	**Clash of cultures**..**29**
	The frontier army..29
	The Indians...42

Chapter 3	**The war for gold**...**51**
	Catch them by spring..51
	First blow – debacle on the Powder River.........................60

Chapter 4	**'Find and fix' – converging columns** **69**
	Where are the Indians? 69
	Converging columns 77

Chapter 5	**Check on the Rosebud** **91**
	'Blind man's buff'..91
	'Like swarms of blackbirds'..99
	A hard fight...108

Chapter 6	**Where is the village?** **117**
	'Where the Indians are not'..117
	Approach march 128

Chapter 7	**Fatal decisions** **143**
	'Worms wriggling in the grass' 143
	Advance to contact..154

Chapter 8	**First blood**...**167**
	The vision fulfilled 112
	Dilemma in the valley bottom.......................................180

Chapter 9   **Divide to conquer**...**189**
                   The column of death...189
                   Buying time 202

Chapter 10   **So near yet so far** **211**
                   Sifting evidence 211
                   Calhoun Hill..218
                   So near yet so far...232

Chapter 11   **Red Sabbath** **239**
                   Weir Point, 1700-1745 hours...240
                   Calhoun's position, 1745 hours..243
                   Keogh's Ravine, 1750 hours 246
                   Conical Hill and the southern salient, 1800 hours................251
                   Last stands, 1815 hours...264

Chapter 12   **'What tomorrow might bring'**...**273**
                   The hill 273
                   'Forward' Terry..283
                   The aftermath 293

                   Postscript..301
                   Notes...317
                   Bibliography...331
                   Index...335

List of Maps and Diagrams

The Fetterman Massacre, 21 December 1866 11

The Wagon Box fight, 2 August 1867 21

Co-ordinating the campaign – General Sheridan's failure 85

The Battle of the Rosebud, 17 June 1876 101

The Battle of the Rosebud, 17 June 1876 107

'Blind man's buff': 119

Advance to contact 153

Custer's crucial decision points 165

Reno's valley fight, 25 June, 1500-1600 hours...188

Custer's dispersal of his command at the Battle of the Little Bighorn.............217

The Battlefield terrain today...252

Dispersal into final 'last stands'..257

Custer's tactical battle 261

The projected collapse of Custer's battalion..266

Reno-Benteen defence position, 25-26 June...284

The mystery of the 'unknown soldier' on the Rosebud.....................................304

Introduction

What is new or left unsaid about the Battle of the Little Bighorn, an engagement that has spawned so many and often opinionated accounts?

My research quickly suggested to me that the fight should not be divorced from that of the Battle of the Rosebud, which preceded it by eight days on 17 June 1876. The same Indians defeated Brigadier General Crook's column, far superior in soldiers to that of Custer, with fewer warriors. Both battles, because of the immediacy of Indian experience, are inextricably intertwined.

Any examination of the Battle of the Rosebud bears out the assertion that Custer's tactical conduct days later completely exemplified the sort of response that could have been anticipated from any contemporary cavalry commander of the day. If he had known the outcome of Crook's engagement he would have acted differently, but he did not. Crook's command was almost overwhelmed in the first few minutes of the action. The Indians did not run – on the contrary, they attacked. Crook divided his command as he had done during the attack on the Indian village at the Powder River months before, also unsuccessfully. Audacious and aggressive actions displayed by his cavalry commanders at the Rosebud met with near disaster.

Custer's defeat represented a total failure of US Army intelligence. The army did not know where the Indians were at the outset of the 1876 campaign, or how many they were. The Fetterman Massacre ten years before had demonstrated that Plains Indians, unlike any other on the American continent, could mass in sufficient numbers to overwhelm a number of companies of organised troops in open battle. This lesson was ignored. Even when the US Army at the outset of the 1876 campaign twice found the location of its key strategic Indian objective village in May, it took until late June to engage it. Nobody passed on information.

Recent archaeological research has revealed the gross disparity of the numbers and superiority of Indian firearms at the battle. The Indian aspiration to get them was galvanised by their losses at the Wagon Box fight during Red Cloud's War in 1867. Non-military analysts have logically and scientifically interpreted this archaeological evidence. Precise time and motion studies, such as that offered by Gray, are helpful to an understanding of the battle, but rarely is conflict so ordered. An intangible seldom included within many mathematical matrixes and premises put forward is the decision-making process. Accounts over the years appear permeated with a sense of inevitability, with the known outcome driving these logical formulae. Custer was human and had the opportunity to step back from the brink on a number of occasions, but chose not to do so. A closer examination of time and space relative to military factors such as geography and terrain, firepower, tactics and unit strengths provides interesting interpretations.

What became especially apparent to me was the one-sided ratio of cavalry to Indian casualties. This is at variance with heroic Hollywood interpretations of the battle, such as *They Died With Their Boots On*, of which I was a childhood fan. It appears that seven or eight of Custer's men perished for every Indian killed. Such an outcome suggests less a defeat than an unmitigated disaster. How could this be so? Do the known archaeological and other scientifically established facts bear this out? It is for the reader to decide.

Dr Jerold Brown, an author in his own right and Associate Professor of History at the Combat Studies Institute at the US Army Command and General Staff College at Fort Leavenworth, Kansas, especially assisted me in this book. In addition, Glenn Robertson, the Deputy Director, helped in organising with Jerold a British Army battlefield tour to a site I thought I would never be privileged to see. Dr Brown is an expert on this battle, having walked the ground on US Army 'Staff Rides' on countless occasions, and has the

innate ability to bring the events to life. I have incorporated many of
the ideas he and I bandied together over two joint visits in 2001 and
2002. He was also generous in uncovering and sharing a number of
lesser-known accounts of the battle. I hope that he may find this
book as useful to him in his teaching as his inspirational and
common-sense military interpretations were to me.

Jerold was able to give me an insight into the totally different
cultural perspective of the Plains Indians, whose mode of waging
war is lost if expressed in conventional military terms. They did not
plan but instinctively acted in concert, a product of their social
background, training and warrior development. This primeval
approach to warfare, coupled with outraged aggression at attacks
on their families, was sufficient on this occasion to tactically defeat
the US Army.

Every effort has been made to trace the source and copyright
holders of the maps and illustrations appearing in the text, and
these are acknowledged where appropriate. Many are my own.
Similarly I wish to thank those publishers who have permitted quotations of extracts from their books; these sources are annotated in
the notes that follow the text. My apologies are offered in advance
to those with whom, for any reason, I have been unable to establish
contact.

As ever, my commiserations go to my wife Lynn and sons
Christian, Alex and Michael, obliged to support yet another project
while the business in hand was actually to enjoy our stay in South
Africa.

Robert Kershaw
Pretoria, South Africa
January 2005

Prologue

'There never was a better day to die'

Red Horse, Minneconjou Sioux Chief

It was Sunday 25 June 1876, the Sabbath. Beyond the banks of the Little Bighorn River the ripple of gunfire was of an intensity never heard before. According to a surviving Crow Indian scout, the firing was a continuous roll sounding like 'the snapping of the threads in the tearing of a blanket'.[1]

There are no surviving white soldier accounts of Custer's battle at the Little Bighorn, but recent archaeological evidence suggests that they were probably taken aback at the extent of Indian firepower and not configured to face it. A multitude of heavy-calibre .50, .70 or .44 bullets tore through the dispersed ranks of surprised US cavalrymen. Whooshing and whining through long grass and sagebrush, tumbling bullets exploded into small clouds of orange-tinged dust or thumped and splatted into flesh. The impact of such a round striking the body can violently knock a soldier from his feet. Shock waves accompanying such a blow can virtually remove an arm or transform a leg into a bloody broken ruin. Civil War veterans on other parts of the battlefield later recalled rates of fire appropriate to the high-intensity set-piece battles they had fought 11 years before. Recruits were stunned. This was beyond their experience. Indians ran at the first contact. It was not meant to happen like this.

Archaeological finds and Indian evidence enable a sketchy outline of the nature of this desperate phase of the battle to be construed. As soldiers fell, gaps in already dispersed skirmish lines became ever

Red Sabbath

more apparent. Horses struck by this storm of fire reared violently, screeching and groaning at each new impact. Horse-holders, every fourth cavalryman in the line, were bodily lifted or violently jerked by their crazed charges. They were distracted from supporting the over-committed skirmish lines ahead of them. The majority of disorientated cavalry soldiers, not knowing what to do and unable to hear shouted commands from pitifully few officers and NCOs, uncertainly stood their ground. Standing in the open they were cut down with increasing frequency by the intense gunfire. Those belatedly realising the need for cover found it denied by arrows arching overhead seeking out their positions. The army had been trained to fight in lines and reduce opposition by weight of fire-power. Their savage and unconventional opponent did not oblige by forming up in a like manner. Skirmishing braves were almost impossible to hit, constantly bobbing and weaving and firing from behind any vestige of cover provided in abundance on ridgelines broken by sagebrush and grass-covered converging ravines.

Gunfire was not the only threat. Flights of arrows, black against a clear blue sky, hissed overhead and rained down on horses and troopers alike, eliciting groans and squeals of pain. Others streaked by on a flat trajectory with greater frequency than pistol shots. They struck with a shocking velocity that could punch through uniform cloth, flesh and even metal uniform buttons, grisly barbs protruding from the other side of torsos and limbs.[2] Shrieking Indians waved blankets above their heads and blew on high-pitched eagle-wingbone whistles, vaguely distinguishable and spectre-like in the swirling dust. Distracted and frightened cavalry horses broke away from their handlers and galloped, rearing and plunging, down the slope away from the fighting.

One white soldier fighting that day was Private Nathan Short, with C Company from the 7th US Cavalry Regiment. Aged 22 years, he stood 5 feet 7 inches tall, with grey eyes, a fair complexion and brown hair, having enlisted the previous October. An unremarkable soldier, he typified many serving in his regiment. Only six brief weeks of formal drill training had prepared him for his first battle. Enlistment at St Louis was a world away from the bizarre situation he faced now. He and his companions were unshaven with faces, v-necks and forearms badly burned by the sun. Dusty uniforms were threadbare and caked in dry sweat, causing some rotting seams to come apart. Civilian shirts purchased from army sutlers had superseded some of the uncomfortable uniform jackets. Trousers were often patched or strengthened in the seat or thighs with hessian from corn sacks. They had been campaigning in the field for weeks and looked more like irregulars than US cavalry. Dry leather on their faded boots was already beginning to crack. Fatigue and stiffness from days of hard riding and forced marches had slowed the reactions of some to seemingly drunk men. But like all soldiers, the urge to survive transcended fatigue. They fought hard.

Private Short's company task was rearguard to Lieutenant Colonel George Armstrong Custer's column of five cavalry companies numbering 210 men. They were attempting to block the screaming access of hundreds of Indian braves surging up a ravine from their massive summer encampment on the banks of the Little Bighorn River. A Northern Cheyenne leader White Bull recalled Indians 'struggling up the gulch northeast of the soldiers like ants rushing out of a hill'.[3]

When walking the present-day battlefield, one realises how little he would actually see and how collapse may have resulted. White markers indicating body positions offer a ghostly survey of the final disintegration. Dispersed at the front edge of the small hill was Lieutenant James Calhoun's Company, positioned astride and covering the main ravine approach routes to the rest of the cavalry column. The nearest element, Company I, commanded by Captain Myles Keogh, was dispersed in column and waiting beyond the spine-shaped ridge further to the north-west about 300 to 400 yards away. The rest of Custer's command, his headquarters and Companies E and F were at the end of this razor-backed ridge on another hillock about 1,300 yards from Short's position. It was difficult, if not impossible, to keep all the companies in view. Gunfire flashes and shadowy blue movement amid powder smoke were the only indicators enabling any sketchy outline of the cavalry force deployment to be observed. Red Horse, a 41-year-old Minneconjou Chief, described how:

> 'The dust created from the stampeding horses and powder smoke made everything dark and black. Flashes from carbines could be seen. The valley was dense with powder smoke.'[4]

Soldier leader groups could be typically picked out grouped around the silhouette of ragged company pennants waving forlornly in the gloom. By now it was apparent to many of the soldiers that they were dangerously dispersed, and vulnerable to aggressive Indian forays that sought, as in classic buffalo hunts, to cut out the weak and helpless. 'I never heard such a whooping and shouting,' exclaimed Red Horse describing the scene. 'There was never a better day to die.'[5]

The cavalry column, recoiling at the intensity of firepower directed at them, had lost the initiative. Grave markers indicate there was not an established defensive perimeter and neither were the partially mounted companies deployed in any form of offensive formation. A sudden counter-attacking cavalry foray, often conducted *in extremis* during the Civil War, was not an option against this unconventional foe. Manoeuvring for fighting space would steadily dissipate the battalion's firepower. Standing today on Nathan Short's position one accepts that he may have seen the additional deployment of a skirmish line south of the small mound occupied by Custer's headquarters, but he would have no idea of the plan. The new position at the southern extremity of Custer's command traversed ravine approach lines filling with Indians leading up from the river and the Indian encampment, dispersing the cavalry force even more.

At this late stage in the battle, Private Short, like his comrades, was staring failure in the face. He was a green recruit. Everything he had been told about the enemy was contradicted by events going on around him. Indians, he would have been assured, were lightly armed savages who ran before a protracted engagement. The Agency Indian 'loafers' that hung around the gates of the fort were singularly unimpressive. They were not comparable to the fearsome fighters he faced now.

Twenty or so C Company troopers had ridden down from the ridgeline directed by their commander, Captain Tom Custer, the regimental commander's brother. They were told to adopt positions on the right flank of L Company ensconced on the high ground to their left, later called Calhoun Hill. The different colouring of their horses would have made the deployment visible from some distance, C Company's light sorrels standing apart from L Company's bays. Fear-crazed mounts soon evaded their holders behind the skirmish lines and dispersed, reducing the mobility of the dismounted cavalrymen. Odd flecks of faded light blue and grey flannel-shirted soldiers would be difficult to pick out among the dirty green and light-coloured sagebushes and grass. An approximately visible line bent or blended with flurries of dust-besmirched activity as new groups of braves struck at its symmetry. Calhoun's rearguard was overwhelmed. Indian accounts speak of a buzzing sound that filled the air, as this occurred, like the noise of enraged bees pouring from a disturbed beehive.

The cavalry front faced a dilemma. What to do with the wounded now being dragged into pathetic little bundles? Soldiers from the other surviving companies occupying ridgelines in view of Calhoun Hill were in a position to uneasily observe as these forlorn piles were overrun by the approaching mass of shrieking Indians. Tomahawks and stone clubs rose and fell, dispatching the wounded in the gloom of battlefield obscuration. Whoops accompanied by groans and wailing pleas for mercy carried across on the still air. Soldiers watched intently as the wounded from C Company were mercilessly dispatched, drawing their own baleful conclusions about chances of survival.

Should the horse-holders, every fourth man, abandon their charges and move forward to engage in the firefight? Bugle calls were barely heard over the cacophony of sound. Shouted commands by officers and sergeants were muted by crackling and volley crashing gunfire. Who was directing fire, Short may have considered as he slid round after round into the increasingly hot and powder-pitted chamber of his lever action .44 Springfield carbine. Twelve rounds to the minute rapid fire does not last long without access to the saddlebag re-supply held by a horse-holder, possibly dead already.

Sergeant Finlay from Calhoun's company was dispatched earlier on horseback to break through the Indian cordon to reach Captain Benteen's battalion. His vital reinforcement was expected at any moment and would end their ordeal. With him was the pack train with supplies of additional ammunition, running perilously short. Indian accounts concur that many mounted soldiers attempted to escape. Finlay went down in visual distance of his fellows. An Irish immigrant and a tailor, he had made the buckskin jacket his commanding officer was wearing. His wife was pregnant back at Fort Abraham Lincoln with their third child.

Windows of opportunity permitting escape were rapidly closing. Short, alongside L Company, was separated from the nearest support, which was Keogh's I Company 400 yards away. He may have retrieved his horse and attempted a desperate breakout. Archaeological finds and Indian reportage confirm that fire was frequently directed at lone troopers attempting to escape, dodging and weaving around scattered groups of predatory warriors, howling and brandishing weapons as they sped by. Short rode a sorrel roan. Did he find a gap in the Indian perimeter amid obscuring clouds of dust and powder smoke?

Little Hawk, a Northern Cheyenne brave, may have been referring to C Company when he watched 'one company of soldiers' that 'went down toward the Little Horn'. He saw them dismount and engage the crowds of Indians moving up from the camp. They were overrun, and:

'One man who did not dismount rode away. He was riding a sorrel horse and Indians began to shoot at him, but they could not hit him nor overtake him. At last, when he was almost out of shot [range], a ball hit him and knocked him off his horse. He is the only man who has not a stone [marker].'[6]

Six weeks later General Terry and Gibbon's column was ferried across the Rosebud in the vicinity of Custer's earlier march to the Little Bighorn, carrying on the campaign. On 3 August 1876 Second Lieutenant Charles Booth of B Company, 7th Infantry Regiment, spotted the carcase of a horse alongside dense undergrowth on a sagebrush plain parallel to a line of cottonwood trees. An army-issue carbine lay nearby, in working order and with no sign of rust. Across the horse's neck was an unused grain bag of typically 7th Cavalry pattern. It was a sorrel roan and had been shot in the head.

Five days later a bullet-pierced body was detected 2 to 9 miles further up the Rosebud, in the direction Custer had previously travelled. It was face down beneath a perfumed wild rose bush. Reddish-brown facial hair still adhered to the skull. Beneath the body was a cartridge belt of US Cavalry pattern marked '7C' (7th Cavalry) and a waist plate belt buckle and three brass buttons. The skeleton was indisputably a soldier. A straw hat picked up was typical of those sold to members of the 7th Cavalry by regimental sutlers at the final bivouac on the Yellowstone River before Custer's departure. Inside the headband the owner had etched his company number. It was '50'. On investigation, Sergeant Kanipe, who survived the battle, confirmed that this was the number that had been assigned to Private Nathan Short of C Company, 7th Cavalry.

* * *

The story of Private Nathan Short encapsulates the many mysteries that surround the battle of the Little Bighorn. Discoveries at the site over the years have tended to raise more questions than answers. Oral Indian testimony claims that the battle with Custer 'took about as long as it takes for a hungry man to eat his dinner'.[7] Such a rapid collapse suggested an overwhelming surprise, but as no white soldiers survived we may never know. The debacle cost the

US Army 268 men, or just over 1% of its authorised strength in 1876. Although small in comparison to American Civil War battle casualty figures, it was the largest single military loss of life since that conflict. During the Indian wars the US Army lost 1,128 men in the Trans-Mississippi West, and the battle at the Little Bighorn accounted for almost a quarter of the total killed during this period.[8] By today's standards a loss of 1% to the British Army would mean 1,080 men, or 6,000 for the US Army. Government accountability would merit close scrutiny, as was indeed the case by an American society basking in the self-congratulatory atmosphere of its first centenary. Defeat at the hands of savages, such as the public read about in one-dime novels, was totally incomprehensible. Losses were sharply at variance with the normal twos and threes regularly reported upon in popular press accounts of frontier skirmishes. Five cavalry companies in Custer's battalion were wiped out to a man. The surviving seven companies split between Major Reno's and Captain Benteen's commands were given a severe mauling. Their casualty rate was 20% of the total, including 66 wounded, of whom six subsequently died of their wounds.[9] Custer's battle, it was assumed, had to have been a heroic last stand against enormous odds. A myth was perpetuated of a desperate struggle of Thermopylaean proportions.

For about a century this belief was sustained through William Cody's 'Wild West Show', illustrated by contemporary bar-room posters and Elizabeth Custer's zealous support of her husband's heroic image via books such as *Boots and Saddles* and Custer's own *My Life on the Plains*. The foe portrayed in these works was less the Indian, rather anyone pernicious enough to question the heroic status of the myth. This battle was fought in the courtroom of the Reno Inquiry and through numerous books and articles, which has resulted in a 'Custerama' cottage industry of literary output. Hollywood has been the greatest and most effective purveyor of the story. Errol Flynn played the indomitable buckskin hero in *They Died With Their Boots On*. He stands alone, sabre and pistol in hand, with the 7th Cavalry pennant fluttering as a backdrop, facing hordes of Indians to the strains of 'Gary Owen'.[10] The sheer drama of pending massacre with rescue almost but not quite at hand has thrilled cinema audiences within the western genre for years. Custerama went through various revisionary stages, with the American public questioning its military policies for the first time during the Vietnam War. The *Little Big Man* treatment of the defeat portrayed Custer as an unfeeling megalomaniac whose suicidal underestimation of the fighting competency of the Indian mirrored the same complacency based on racial superiority that was dogging US military success in Vietnam. *Son of the Morning Star* sought through a grittier portrayal of events to explain the debacle from both the Indian point of view and tensions within the Custer chain of command.

In 1983 a prairie fire at the Little Bighorn site provided an opportunity after decades of speculation for a more objective and scientific cleansing of facts. Extensive vegetation and bushland that had lain undisturbed for nearly a century was stripped clean by a fire that had a similarly sanitising impact on opinion. Archaeologists discovered some 9,000 artefacts, confirming evidence for the first time of substantial Indian firepower. Individual firing pin imprints could be computer tracked across mapped artefact findings, revealing previously unrealised clusters of Indian and military activity across the battlefield. Findings have added credence to oral Indian and Pictograph evidence that has been neglected or disputed for over a century.

An interesting parallel to the Battle of the Little Bighorn is the American experience at Mogadishu, Somalia, in 1993. It offers conclusions not dissimilar from those that emerge from Little Bighorn. On 3 October 1993 about 100 elite US soldiers were besieged by thousands of Somali irregulars. Eighteen US soldiers were killed in the ensuing action and more than 70 badly injured. Somali losses were estimated to be about 500 to 1,000. Both engagements, like the Terry/Gibbon and Custer column action of 1876, resulted from 'peace-keeping' operations in the context of modern-day Peace Support Operations (PSO). The US Special

Forces unit felt, like the 7th Cavalry, that it was technologically invincible and was about to 'seriously kick Somali ass'. Mark Bowden's authoritative work *Black Hawk Down*, describing the action, presciently identifies the battle norm applying to both engagements. 'War was always about to happen' but missions invariably fell short. Likewise the 7th Cavalry, given the chance to settle the score for previous Indian depredations, relished the opportunity.

Civilised states normally resorted to non-violent ways of resolving disputes, which assumed the willingness of everyone to back down. 'Here in the Third World,' Bowden explained, 'people hadn't learned to back down, at least not until after a lot of blood had flowed.' The envisaged US military raids were never going to alter generations of ingrained Somali inter-clan rivalry. The 7th Cavalry likewise did not anticipate serious resistance. The shooting down of the first US Black Hawk helicopter lost in the engagement on 3 October 1993 shocked the US Task Force leaders and robbed the Force of its sense of righteous invincibility. Bowden claims that this followed a series of intelligence failures by Washington. Officials were completely stunned by the size, scope and ferocity of the Somali counter-attack.[11] It is evident from the subsequent swift and total collapse of the 7th Cavalry battalion at the Battle of the Little Bighorn that it had experienced something similar. What happened to the biggest expeditionary force fielded by the US Army since the Civil War against a similarly unsophisticated foe? Its Commander's only misgiving was that his opponents might disperse before he could land the decisive blow.

Archaeological surveys have done much to verify previously disputed Indian testimony, but the battle site, frequently disturbed over the century, cannot provide authoritative forensic evidence as to what happened. By interpreting the available scientific data and assessing human behaviour against terrain studies, this book seeks to identify some conceivable truths.

Maybe it was Private Nathan Short who lay beneath the rosebush with a rusting pocket-knife and three copper pennies in his pocket.[12] If so, he had struggled 70 miles from the battlefield only to die in a riverside meadow beneath one of the sweet-smelling bushes that gave the Rosebud River its name. His was a lonely death in the shadow of the Wolf Mountains, 7 miles south of the Yellowstone River.

The Battle of the Little Bighorn, like the story of one soldier, Nathan Short, is not as it appears to be.

Chapter 1

Red Cloud's war

'Save the last bullet for yourself.'

Frontier byword

The Fetterman Massacre

The signallers on Pilot Knob, an isolated hilltop 4,900 feet high and just over a mile south of Fort Phil Kearney, watched the black snake wriggle hesitantly toward the snow-covered summit of Lodge Trail ridge, 5,000 feet high and 3 miles across the intervening valley. It was a clear day, piercingly cold on their lone summit, but visibility was good. The army column had left the fort about half an hour before. The time was now approaching noon on 21 December 1866, barely 18 months since the great Civil War between the states in America had drawn to a close. Using sema-phore, the flags on Pilot Knob had warned the Fort's commander, Colonel Henry Carrington, that the exposed wood train, cutting timber in the forested high ground to the west of the fort, had come under attack from Indians again. The 'pick-pock' of rifled musket fire could occasionally be discerned above the noise of the wind. After the technological revolution of innovations such as telegraph promoting prompt and efficient communications during the Civil War, it seemed ironic that the victors now stationed in the West had to resort again to flags.

The incident reported by the signallers was not unusual. Fifty-one different skirmishes had occurred often before their eyes since the fort's construction had begun the previous summer.[1] Mining prospectors drawn by the magnet of the Montana goldfields had utilised the new route established by John M. Bozeman between Fort Laramie, Wyoming, and Virginia City. The new Bozeman trail reduced the distance to reach the mines by 400 miles compared with other routes. It stretched more than 500 miles across rich hunting grounds used by the Crows, Northern Cheyenne and Dakota Sioux Indians. Widespread hostility had occurred in response, particularly with the latter, since April 1864. Attempts were made by the US Government, recovering from the worse conflict in its history, to negotiate a diplomatic solution with the Plains Indians. This achieved only marginal success and was not assisted by the gory massacre of an innocent Indian encampment at Sand Creek in 1864. Hostility appeared inevitable. Following Indian depredations along the Bozeman Trail, the US Government resolved to establish a chain of military posts along its length to protect travellers and quieten ever more vociferous civilian appeals for action and help.

The massive Union field armies of 1.4 million, mostly volunteers with about 80,000 regulars, were reduced to 54,000 by 1866. A limit of 75,000 had been declared at the war's end one year before.[2] This drastically reduced force was required to ensure the integrity and security of national frontiers with Mexico and Canada, police the recently subjugated Confederate states, and only thirdly to protect newly established western settlements and their extended lines of communications. Responsibility for the Bozeman Trail belonged to the Department of the Platte, whose headquarters in Omaha was commanded by Brigadier General Philip St George Cooke. The Department could field only 2,000 officers and men. A stockade constructed at Fort Reno, 169 miles north of Fort Laramie at the forks of the Powder River, by a column commanded by Patrick E. Conner failed to subdue the tribes. Colonel Henry Carrington led the 2nd Battalion of the 18th Regiment of Infantry up the Bozeman Trail in June to establish Fort Phil Kearney on the banks of the Piney Creek near present-day Banner, Wyoming, in July 1866. Smaller company locations were established at Fort

Reno and two companies at Fort C. F. Smith 91 miles north of Phil Kearney near present-day Yellowtail, Montana, to complete the picketing of the Bozeman Trail.

Fort Phil Kearney was established just south of the point where the Trail crossed the Big Piney Creek, and its site was of questionable tactical value, situated in a narrow valley surrounded on three sides by high terrain. Sioux and Cheyenne continuously dominated the heights and were able to observe all movement in and around the fort. The Bozeman Trail it was designed to protect passed over ridges out of sight of the fort to the north and south. It had water but its security depended on a regular supply of wood hewn from the foothills of the Bighorn Mountains to the west to provide fuel and building materials. Construction of the main post was of pine logs, comprising an 800 by 600 feet stockade standing 8 feet high. There was even a sawmill within the fort to cope with the staggering number of logs needed for its construction. The fort included a barracks and living quarters for troops and families as well as other mess, storeroom and hospital structures. Almost as much military effort was to be expended in building the stockade and protecting the woodcutting parties – an escort of 55 not including civilian contractors – as securing the Trail. Two weeks before, on 6 December, a combined offensive action against the Sioux threatening the wood convoy had resulted in near disaster, when an officer and sergeant had been killed and five men wounded. It became apparent to Carrington that the Indians were intent on decoying and ambushing part of his force and this is what nearly occurred beyond the Lodge Trail ridge feature to the north of the fort.

It was this feature that the column seemingly split in three parts was observed to cross from the lookout position on Pilot Knob and from within the fort.

Captain William J. Fetterman, the commander of the unit on the march aiming to rescue the woodcutting team, had arrived at Fort Phil Kearney only the previous month. Lieutenant George Grummond had accompanied him, and now commanded his cavalry detachment of 27 men from C Company, 2nd Cavalry, which included some mounted infantry and two civilian scouts. The remainder of this hastily thrown together force consisted of 49 foot-borne infantry from four different companies of the 2nd Battalion, 27th Regiment. Fetterman was growing increasingly impatient. Despite the fact that he had a small group of Indians in sight, there was a requirement to pause at the icy waters of the Big Piney to allow the infantry to remove their shoes and stockings to cross. The cavalry overtook them and pushed on ahead. The infantry were not at fault. In these sub-zero temperatures they could become incapacitated by frostbite with wet feet. In their haste to close with the Indians ahead, the cavalry, although riding flank protection, pulled steadily ahead of the walking infantry. Snow on the ground was patchy and was replaced by wind-blown sheet ice as they ascended Lodge Tail Ridge. Horses and soldiers slipped on the treacherous surface. The more experienced cavalry riders forged ahead of the struggling mounted infantry, who in time created another separate group apart from the infantry, forcing the pace as best they could on the slippery surface. The force still managed to keep close to the Indians who periodically halted with the pretence of checking their ponies' hooves. They visibly taunted the troopers, flapping their loincloths and exposing their bottoms in derision at the pace but always keeping about 300 yards ahead. Longer-range infantry Springfield muzzle-loaders occasionally brought a desultory fire to bear.

Fetterman was supremely confident of the outcome of the mission despite his close call with disaster on 6 December. His cavalry were armed with seven-shot Spencer carbines purloined from the fort's band. Captain Frederick H. Brown, the Quartermaster, was with him, without authority, reluctant to pass over the certainty of action despite his imminent departure on posting. His two civilian scouts, James S. Wheatley and Isaac Fisher, relished the opportunity to try out their newly acquired 16-shot Henry Repeater rifles.

The leaders of the column considered themselves men of action. Fetterman had been brevetted Lieutenant Colonel and cited for gallantry during the Civil War. Although Grummond was his junior, he had served as a Lieutenant Colonel of the 14th Michigan volunteers and brevetted Brigadier General of Volunteers. They were experienced combat officers enduring the frustration of lesser promotion opportunities in the demobilised Union armies and disdainful of their commanding officer Carrington. Despite commanding an Infantry Regiment during the war, Carrington had sat it out as a staff officer and aide to the Governor of Indiana. Although liked socially, there was some suspicion that he had used political connections to avoid combat. His lack of aggression in the last round of skirmishes had convinced his subordinates that he did not exercise command vigorously or effectively. Fetterman was convinced that he would demonstrate otherwise. Command of the column had originally been given to Captain James W. Powell, who had impressed Carrington during the 6 December skirmish by his competency and maturity in not falling for the Indian decoy ploy. However, Fetterman insisted on his seniority right and Carrington reluctantly acquiesced. Fetterman felt that he would do better.

Colonel Carrington, left at the fort, considered the main Indian threat to be from small bands of warriors mounting uncoordinated attacks numbering no more than 500 at worst case. He felt that his principal vulnerability was the need to protect wood parties and construct the fort. This tied up 50 men daily, not including civilian employees. The primary mission to secure the Trail for travellers appeared to play little part in this and frustrated his offensively minded and battle-hard subordinate commanders. Numerous skirmishes had already occurred, and Carrington's reports reflected a mixture of optimism constantly tinged with requests for reinforcements. Fetterman, who with Lieutenant Brown 'offered with 80 men to ride through the whole Sioux nation!'[3] disdained this viewpoint. He now had 81 men under command, one-third of the fort's effective combat strength and virtually all of its offensive power.

In reality Fetterman never anticipated that he would have to ride through the Sioux nation. Indians were incapable of massing anything like the strength that could threaten his technologically superior column. Yet from early autumn that year, and now into December, Red Cloud, the Oglala leader, and other hostile chiefs had been assembling braves along the headwaters of the Tongue River. The Sioux were prepared even to welcome their traditional tribal enemy the Crow. However, the 'confederation' was simply a loose association of Cheyenne, Arapaho, Sioux and Minneconjou transitorily held together by dint of Red Cloud's personality and a general desire to kill white men. Indians fought as individuals. There was no formal plan other than the intent to ensnare an army column. An ambush location would have to be agreed by all and the force would then come together. Individually their tactic would be to cut out weak elements from a column as in a buffalo hunt, and kill them. The requirement of the hunt necessitated co-operation to surround and trap the herd. Combat itself, or the kill, was the business of individual braves fighting loosely within war-bands. It is debatable whether Red Cloud was even present leading the assault about to take place. Black Shield led the Minneconjous and Crazy Horse the first war party of young Oglalas.[4]

The tactical significance in frontier terms of the elongated S-shaped ridgeline on the northern side of Lodge Tail Ridge was totally lost on the conventional Civil War-conditioned US Army mind. Army combat sensibilities had been shaped by estimations of the ranges of artillery and infantry volley fire and the time taken for lines of drilled infantry and cavalry to close or identify suitable ground to stand. There had been ambushes for Lieutenant Colonel Fetterman serving with the Union Army under Sherman while making 'Georgia Howl', but they tended to be in forested areas, covered depressions and valley bottoms, not high and elongated bare ridgelines.

For the Indian, the narrow high ground might be a place to panic a herd of buffalo into throwing themselves from the slopes, then harvest the result. They sought weak points, an opportunity to cut out part of the herd, then run it to ground. This is how the army column appeared to them. Cavalry up front were attempting to close with the decoys. These prevaricated, appearing to have difficulties with their ponies or suddenly and recklessly offering the approaching soldiers battle. Shots had been exchanged with skirmishers far forward. A second band of mounted infantry stretched some 300 yards behind, while the infantry, struggling and scrabbling across sheet mountain ice, sought to keep up 400 yards to the rear. Eighty men were strung out across nearly 1,000 yards. The seemingly innocent ridgeline was the focus of hundreds of pairs of eyes peering intently from behind cover, expectantly and with the growing tension that bespoke the certainty at last of a kill.

The narrow ridgeline is about 4,700 feet high, continuing north-west from its southern extremity. Across it ran the frozen ruts of the Bozeman wagon trail sketching out its elongated 'S' shape along the feature. Slopes fall steeply on either side, accentuated by the north-south course cut by Peno Creek on the west and a similar breach taking the drop of the ground off to the east. As the riders moved north they could see that both flanks of the ridgeline were inter-sected by ravines, previous watercourses cut into the sides by the flow of water from the top. Many of these were overgrown with brushwood. The course of the ridgeline presented nothing more than an impressive dazzling snow-white vista shining into the eyes of the column intent on running down its prey.

Many of the warriors had wrapped themselves in buffalo robes with the hair turned in, and had burrowed beneath the snow. Despite the cold, and thickly clothed with leggings of dark woollen cloth, high-topped buffalo fur moccasins and red Hudson Bay blankets, they stoically endured the temperatures and awaited their opportunity. As the column spread further along the ridge some began to edge expectantly forward up the slopes. Those near the apex, hidden beneath the stretched hides heaped with snow, attempted to control their breathing, hoping that the condensation clouds would merely be regarded as wind-blown mist. Cheyenne and Arapaho were on the west side of the ridgeline and Sioux to the east, many lying around the grassy flat areas. Further mounted braves waited patiently behind rocky ridges and also within the high grass of the northern Flats where the ridgeline descended steeply into Peno Creek. Every feature, bush or depression that offered cover from view was utilised for concealment. These men had disciplined themselves throughout their lives to endure and train for the hunt, the battle and the kill. They were able to lie perfectly still for long periods. The advancing column was enveloped by a classic horseshoe ambush, the opening at the head of the column tantalisingly baited by the decoys. Odds were a minimum of ten to one against the soldiers.

There was some flinching within the ambush position when the crash-boom of a mountain howitzer broke up the stillness of the frozen morning. The Indians who had engaged the wood convoy had withdrawn as Fetterman began to impose a threat ascending Lodge Tail Ridge and potentially menacing their rear. 'The gun that shoots twice' was a sinister weapon to the Indians and they were afraid of it.

The mountain howitzer had been fired on Carrington's orders when he saw this group of Indians from the fort, apparently coming up on Fetterman's rear. A spherical case shot arched through the air and exploded with a crash among the band, unseating one who tumbled from his pony. Thirty or so Indians were suddenly flushed from cover and rapidly fled north into the valley beyond Lodge Tail Ridge. Nobody appeared to remark on the significance of unexpectedly sighting even more Indians. This had been the pattern in many previous skirmishes. Carrington strolled off to his headquarters, concerned at the direction Fetterman was progressing but sure that he would not misinterpret his very clear command not to cross the ridgeline. This had been relayed during the preliminary orders, repeated again publicly as he left the fort and reiterated yet again to Grummond and his cavalry when they rode out shortly after to catch up with the departed foot column.

Captain Fetterman was hot on the chase. Despite a considerable fright two weeks before he had not revised his opinion of the inability of Indians to stand up to trained troops in battle. The near decoy disaster had convinced him that the troops needed remedial training to take on hostile warriors. Infantry firing practices despite ammunition shortages were ordered daily after Retreat, as also for the cavalry. Carrington clearly misunderstood the requirements of combat. Fetterman would kill at least some of these Indians and demonstrate the power of Army offence in capable hands. He pushed his command hard along the ridgeline.

Some of the more reckless Indian decoys were apparently hit by fire. The cavalry, in hot pursuit, began to move swiftly down the northern head of the ridgeline toward the patchy snow-covered grass flats below on the banks of the Piney Creek. Three hundred yards ahead, the Indian group subdivided and rode a figure '8' outline, the signal for the assault. It was midday.

With an ear-splitting tremulous whoop accompanied by echoing shrieks, scores of Indians, flinging aside snow-covered blankets and buffalo robes, boiled out of the small ravines and defiles along the ridgeline. Shots rang out, but only about a quarter of the Indians had firearms and these varied enormously in type and quality. Swarms of arrows arched through the air, hissing into the blue-coated ranks, who were thrown into immediate turmoil. An almost tangible reverberation of shock permeated the column. Hundreds of mounted Indians emerged from behind rock gullies and began forcing their ponies up the slope, yipping their war cries as they came.

Lieutenant Grummond immediately wheeled the leading cavalrymen about and began scrambling up the high ground back onto the Bozeman road. Blue great-coated figures porcupined with arrows began to tumble out of their saddles. Horses stumbled and rolled downhill as the cavalry sought to get back up on to the ridge and close the gap with the infantry, already too far away. Hope lay in one direction, back along the S-shaped ridge south toward the fort. Reinforcements would take at least an hour to arrive. Six or seven horsemen, including Wheatley and Fisher, dismounted and took cover among a group of substantial boulders half-way up and to the right of the line of retreat toward the fort. Both scouts, Civil War veterans, were familiar with the low-key skirmishing that characterised frontier warfare. To flee in the face of Indian attack was to die. Sometimes it was enough to simply present a determined defence. They therefore crouched among the rocks and began to pour a concentrated and damaging short-range fire into the charging Indians. Heavy-calibre rounds smashed bone and abruptly snatched warriors from their ponies. But unusually, despite momentarily faltering, the Indians pressed home their attack. There was only limited time in which to achieve the kill.

A few hundred yards beyond the crest was a lone tree, which intersected a natural shallow split in the ground, resembling a trench in the frozen-rock strewn grass. Fleeing cavalry troopers and inexperienced riding infantry, struggling to regain control of their horses amid the swish and impact of falling arrows, were more than aware of the difficulty of fighting on horseback. It was not what they were trained to do. Grummond, remaining on horseback, began to dismount his shaken and steadily dissipating force into some semblance of a skirmish line along the line of the shallow fissure. It was virtually impossible to shoot accurately and reload on horseback, particularly with mounts bucking and rearing at the noise and stinging pain of high-velocity arrow strikes. Thirty seconds was the average time it took a competent man to load the 1851 Colt pistol, involving a degree of fumbling dexterity with fingers to place the caps required to charge each of the six chambers. Veteran troopers would acquire more than one issue revolver during their time in service. One would be stuck in a boot, another in the belt or inside the top of a tunic jacket, anticipating the limited time there would be to reload. Feeding rounds inside the Spencer magazine tube could be equally awkward. Fear and the intense cold and the awful realisation of the likely outcome of this grossly unequal engagement began to paralyse minds. Taking cover among large boulders further along the ridge, the cavalry soldiers began to shoot into the shrieking masses to their front.

Lieutenant Grummond's achievement in withdrawing the few hundred yards while keeping most of his command together was considerable. Sergeant Augustus Lang of A Company assisted him in this. The pair were enveloped on the road by swarms of Indians

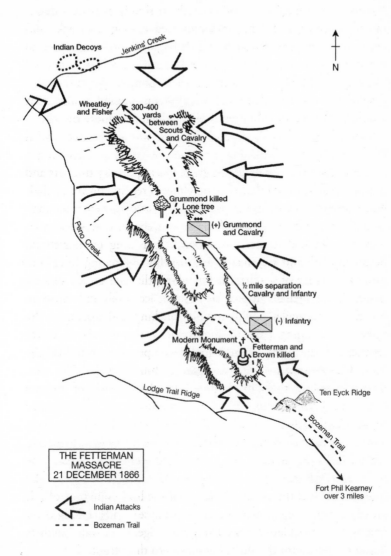

The Fetterman Massacre, 21 December 1866

Fetterman's column was so dispersed when overwhelmed by a concentric
Indian ambush that it was unable to amass sufficient firepower to prevent the
Indians from closing in.

mounted and on foot. According to Indian eyewitness accounts 'a soldier chief on a white horse' was seen hacking and slashing with his sabre. He neatly separated the head from the torso of an attacking mounted Indian warrior. However, both men, bristling with arrows, were dragged from their horses and hacked and clubbed to death with tomahawks and nail-spiked war clubs. Grummond's head was virtually severed from his body by hatchet strokes and his fingers, which had wielded the sabre so effectively, were cut off. He was stripped naked and shot full of arrows.

Lieutenant Brown had abandoned his borrowed pony near Grummond's skirmish line and fled along the ridgeline toward the infantry. Behind him the leaderless cavalry embedded themselves among a small group of boulders to the west of the track and, after a few fitful volleys, poured intermittent fire into the closing mass of Indians. Clouds of pungent-smelling blue-grey powder smoke floated momentarily across the ridge before being raggedly snatched away by the wind.

The infantry were taken aback by the violence and frenzied nature of an immediate close-in assault. It was prefaced by a lone mounted warrior who crashed into their rear with suicidal bravery before being cut down. Another fanatical warrior followed him on foot, equally berserk and intent on a glorious death before the total mass struck home into the unnerved soldiers. Despite wearing thick clothes and greatcoats, many were swiftly impaled by numerous metal-tipped arrowheads that struck home from 60 to 80 yards away propelled by an 80-pound pull load. They zipped into their ranks from the vertical and horizontal plane, striking heads and necks and arms and hands raised in protection or supplication. The Indians carried far more bows than firearms, and these could be fired with greater frequency and accuracy than the pistol over short ranges. It is claimed by some Indian accounts that as many as 40,000 arrows were fired during this battle, raining down on the column at the rate of 1,000 per minute.[5]

Infantry soldiers, demoralised and quaking with fear and cold, needed considerable presence of mind to reload their .58-calibre

Springfield Civil War muzzle-loaders. This step-by-step action of biting off the paper cartridge separating the round from the powder charge, dropping and pouring it down the barrel, ramrodding it into a compact mass and priming the cap to fire the weapon could take 30 seconds, or three rounds per minute for a practised firer. But there had been precious little practice. Fingers numbed by the cold, and dexterity fumbled through shock and fear, resulted in only one or two volleys before discipline under pressure from the assault began to break down. Commands could be barely discerned above the rolling waves of noise that assailed their senses. Lieutenant Brown, separated from the cavalry and with his pony shot from under him, joined Fetterman as the infantry group tenuously attempted to grope and fight their way to a higher segment of the ridgeline nearer the fort. Fetterman's command, separated from the leaderless cavalry remnants left behind on the boulder-strewn knoll, began to disintegrate before his eyes. Even the command to fix bayonets was drowned in the cacophony of noise that enveloped them all.

Wheatley and Fisher's small group of men sold their lives dearly. Piles of spent cartridges began to accumulate around the pile of rocks to the north of the ridge. Bodies of Indians lay surrounding the small breastwork of downed Indian ponies they had utilised for cover, but still the mass of braves fanatically pressed home their attack. The only way to deal with the rapid firepower of Henry Repeating rifles was to close in at best speed. As their ammunition ran out, the rocks were overrun and the small group, many already wounded, flailed with rifle butts and slashed with knives as, kicking, punching and biting, they were clubbed and hacked to death. Enraged at the ferocity and cost of this resistance, the Indians took fearful retribution on the bodies. Keen-edged knives cut into the skin around the hairline; clutching a fistful of hair, an abrupt tug would remove hair and skin gristle from the top of the scalp. This act of savagery, allegedly historically introduced by the white man, was accompanied by a primeval shriek of exultation, and the grisly talisman, proving individual prowess and victory in battle over the foe, raised exultantly to the sky. Wheatley's corpse was scalped and bristled with 105 arrows.[6]

Colonel Carrington recalled in the fort that 'at 12 o'clock firing was heard ... beyond Lodge Trail Ridge. A few shots were followed by constant shots not to be counted.' Others claim to have heard four volleys of fire. Margaret Carrington, the Commander's wife and present at the fort, claimed that 'every shot could be heard, and there was little doubt that a desperate fight was going on'. Captain Tenodor Ten Eyck was immediately dispatched, departing at 1215 with mounted and foot infantry and nearly 30 men from C Company, 2nd Cavalry, also on foot – Fetterman had already used up the fort's mounted offensive capacity. The remaining few horses had to be hitched to wagons, two of which, including an ambulance, were sent with the Surgeon and extra loads of ammunition. Virtually all the fort's remaining active strength had to be fielded for this rescue effort, only 119 men being left behind. Margaret Carrington, watching the flurry of activity accompanying the departure of the reserve force, remembered:

'All this time firing was increasing in intensity [across the Ridge], and in little more than 30 minutes – after one or two quick volleys ... a few scattering shots – a perfect silence ensued. There were then many anxious hearts, and waiting was perfectly terrible.'[7]

Ten Eyck, after fording the Piney Creek beyond the fort and initially turning north up the Bozeman Trail, switched to the higher ground to the right to aid the security of his approach. Carrington, seeking to effect the junction with Fetterman as soon as possible, mildly but damningly admonished Ten Eyck in a subsequent dispatch on the day. 'You could,' he wrote, 'have saved 2 miles toward the scene of action if you had taken Lodge Trail Ridge.'[8] It was something Ten Eyck would regret for the remainder of his short life.

On the ridgeline the dispersed column grouped themselves around the nearest defensible ground to the fort's approaches, their only and fast-diminishing hope. There was insufficient space atop the feature to form a conventional line of defence; it was a case of hastily formed semi-circles immediately assailed by break-ins by fanatically brave warriors. The infantry were neither armed, beyond the bayonet, nor equipped for hand-to-hand fighting, at which their assailants were supremely prepared and excelled. Only firepower could keep them at bay, and volley fire amid the noise, confusion and dispersion was no longer achievable. Ammunition among the cut-off survivors began quickly to run short. Indian scouts, monitoring the progress of the approaching Ten Eyck force, urged a quick kill. Care of the wounded was no longer possible in the fluid circumstances. Freezing conditions slowed the flow of blood and would simply make them more conscious of their approaching violent end. Frenzied final assaults across the area of the boulders resulted also in Indian lives lost to the vicious crossfire of swarms of arrows fired from opposite directions. Some infantry managed to flee to the higher ground where the cavalry remnants were still grimly hanging on. The rest were overrun and hacked and beaten, their remains slashed to pieces amid stinking clouds of abattoir steam rising from behind the rocks into the frozen air from eviscerated and grossly mutilated corpses. Fetterman and Brown fell together at the base of the ridge nearest the fort. Legend claims that a suicide pact eased their passing. 'Save the last bullet for yourself' was a byword of savage frontier skirmishing to avoid the inevitable and agonising torture that followed capture. Brown was badly hacked about and, despite his baldness, the tuft of hair at the back of his head was scalped. He was found, however, to have the telltale burn mark around a bullet hole to the left temple. Maybe he was finished off in the heat of battle, or Fetterman shot him. The latter's skull was caved in as he was brained by a war club and his throat cut. Arrows were then strummed point-blank into their twitching bodies.

There is no way of knowing if there were isolated last stands or if the column succumbed in the maelstrom together. The distribution of corpses suggests that the cavalry sheltering atop a

40-foot irregular rock shelf may have been the last to succumb on Massacre Hill. Whatever the end, it was brutal and quick. There was no time to torture or take captives. Army reinforcements might arrive at any time. German-born bugler Adolph Metzger, a veteran since 1855, fought until his Springfield ammunition ran out. Bleeding from several wounds, he fought over the bodies of his dead comrades with pistol and knife. He killed several Indians and was reduced to bludgeoning his bugle, used as a 'knuckle duster', into a shapeless mass, still keeping his savage opponents at bay until they finally cut him down. His body was the only one not muti-lated, and it was left near the present-day Fetterman monument, reverently covered by a buffalo robe. Although enraged by their losses, the Indians recognised outstanding courage.

Captain Ten Eyck reached the summit of the ridge at 1245, enabling him to overlook the scene: 'Just in time,' according to Surgeon Hines, 'to see the last man killed.'[9] As far as they could see, the ridgeline was covered by more Indians than they had ever seen in their lives. They were challenged to come down and taunted. Braves gesticulated and waved articles of blue uniform as they continued with the business of ritually scalping and mutilating the army dead.

On the frozen ridge the only creature from the column still living was a small dog that fearfully emerged from beneath a pile of white corpses being butchered and slashed by the victors. A Sioux warrior initially tried to capture the dog, but it was decided to dispatch it anyway with an arrow.

Casualties were heavy among the Indians, with perhaps almost 200 dead and wounded. The need to close and finish off the force before reinforcements could arrive required them to accept severe punishment. However, the cost to the Indians was not tangibly evident to the army, faced with the trauma of quite literally picking up the pieces. Colonel Carrington's official report, suppressed for 20 years, wrote of:

'Eyes torn out and laid on rocks; noses cut off, ears cut off, chins hewn off; teeth chopped out, joints of fingers, brains taken out and placed on rocks with other members of the body; entrails taken out and exposed, hands cut off; feet cut off; arms taken out of their sockets, private parts severed and indecently placed on the person...'[10]

Scenes like these were permanently etched on the psyche of soldiers obliged to serve on, instilling fear and loathing of the 'barbaric' Indian. John Guthrie, a hard-bitten cavalry veteran of the 2nd Cavalry, did not mince his words:

'We walked on top of their internals and did not know it in the high grass. Picked them up, that is their internals, did not know the soldier they belonged to, so you see the cavalryman got an infantryman's guts and an infantryman got a cavalry-man's guts.'[11]

There was a blizzard on the night of the massacre and snow drifted almost to the level of the man-high fort palisade. An urgent appeal for reinforcements was dispatched in the teeth of the merciless weather. Women and children were gathered in the fort's magazine and a powder trail laid to ensure that they would not be captured alive in an anticipated attack. Butchered bodies were recovered over two days. 'We brought in about fifty in wagons,' wrote Surgeon Hines as the first arrived, 'like you see hogs brought to market.'[12]

Lessons

Throughout the following spring and summer Indians continued to harass the garrisons at Forts C. F. Smith and Phil Kearney. Actions were sporadic, light on casualties and attacks rarely seriously pressed. During this relatively uneventful interregnum a shipment of 700 new M-1866 Springfield Allen .50-70-calibre breech-loading weapons was delivered to Fort Phil Kearney. This new weapon was actually a cheap modification of the .58-calibre

Springfield muzzle-loader, the standard shoulder arm of the Civil War and the infantry rifle during the Fetterman fight. It remained single-shot, but, utilising the Martin bar-anvil and centre-primed with an all-metallic cartridge, it could be loaded quickly, was accurate and reliable. 100,000 rounds of ammunition came with the rifles. Henry had offered his repeating rifle for Government patent but it was rejected in favour of the more politically expedient Springfield conversion: it would use less ammunition and therefore cost less money. Nevertheless, the weapon was a technological improvement and the Indians did not notice its arrival.

On 31 July 1867 Captain James Powell began his 30-day tour with C Company, 27th Infantry, to escort and guard civilian woodcutters serving the unquenchable timber needs of Fort Phil Kearney. A wagon-box laager was established 6 miles from the fort to provide storage and security for soldiers and civilian wood-cutters. Wagon beds – called boxes – were removed from the running gear and positioned in an oval shape. A trolley consisting of the wagon's axles and wheels was then available to more easily transport long logs from the wood to the fort. Each box measured 10 feet long by 4½ feet wide and offered a low 2½-feet-high firing parapet utilising the wagon sides. Fourteen such boxes created an oval defence area of 60 by 30 feet. Two other wagon boxes positioned outside the laager retained their hooped canvas covers to protect rations and stores from the weather.

Captain Powell had been Colonel Carrington's first choice to lead the hapless Fetterman group the previous December, having demonstrated maturity and judgement during the fast-moving decoying and skirmishing that had preceded the massacre. He was older and tactically more frontier-astute than the arrogant Fetterman. Twice wounded and brevetted for bravery during the Civil War, he appreciated and respected the worth of his Indian adversary fighting in his home environment. Powell assiduously trained his men to use the new Allen conversions and identified his best company marksmen. These, he directed, were to be served by less-capable shots as loaders.

The Indians attacked Powell's group on the morning of 2 August, having worked up their ardour as the result of a religious ceremony. The attack, preceded by numerous signal fires and suspicious activity, was not totally unexpected, except its size and ferocity. Woodcutting working parties quickly dispersed during the assault leaving a small group of 32 soldiers ensconced inside the wagon laager. Red Cloud, still coordinating the Indian confederated effort, sat with a group of chiefs spectating from a hilltop 3 miles away. Estimations of the size of the joint Indian force of Hunkpapas, Minneconjous, Oglalas, Brules and Sans Arcs with Cheyenne vary between several hundred to 3,000 braves – probably not as many as had gathered for the Fetterman Massacre.

So confident were the Indians of success that women and children accompanied their menfolk to assist in carrying off the plunder. After the woodcutters' camp was burned, livestock run off and scattered bands of white survivors had fled to the fort, the spectators settled down to witness the annihilation of the wagon-box laager.

This meanwhile was transformed into a hedgehog defence position. Loopholes were cut into the wooden sides of the boxes and reinforced with a lining of two-thick corn sacks placed on edge to provide protection against incoming fire. Blankets were spread over the tops of the boxes to obscure firing positions and lessen the impact of high-trajectory arrows. Gaps between the wagon boxes were filled with logs or stuffed with bales of blankets and clothing, corn sacks or any other available stores. There was a surplus of weapons and ample ammunition within the perimeter. Poor shots were earmarked as weapon loaders. Each man had two or three guns. A mule-driver, R. J. Smyth, recalled having two Spencer carbines and a pair of six-shot Army Colt pistols at his personal disposal.[13] Captain Powell, supported by his second-in-command Lieutenant Jenness, coolly stated the obvious to his men that they would be fighting for their lives. Nobody was to open fire until he gave the direct order.

The Indians, in no particular hurry, having burned the camp and removed the booty, now turned their attention to the remaining soldiers. A mounted force of 500 bore down in a tightly packed mass, intending simply to ride over this insignificant defence defying them on the plain. They broke into a gallop aiming to leap the boxes and create openings for the main body to pour inside and mop up the defenders.

As the mass of shrieking and waving warriors closed in on the tiny fortress it remained ominously silent. Inside the wagons the defenders had few illusions concerning survival should the Indians break in. Vivid memories remained of the brutal slaughter of the previous December. They waited in cramped conditions breathing in short nervous gasps. There was barely room to stretch out behind their loopholes. Powell ordered 'open fire' at 50 yards, with everyone's nerves taut at breaking point. Flame and smoke spat out of the squat fortress and scores of warriors and ponies went down. The charge continued, the Indians secure in the knowledge that after one or maybe two volleys they would close with the white men. However, instead of an accompanying silence a steady and persistent stream of heavy-calibre slugs flayed the Indian ranks. Pony after pony pitched into slurries of dust kicked up by dead and dying horses and men. So packed were the riders that one bone-smashing bullet would pass through a body and tear the limb or pitch another following warrior from his pony. Recoiling from the oval construction formed by the perimeter, the riders found themselves still close enough to fire inside the boxes from their mounted elevation.

Smyth, the civilian teamster, declared that 'during the first charge I emptied the carbines and the revolvers less two shots'. These he was reserving for hand-to-hand fighting and the last one for him. 'The balance of our men must have fired as many shots as I did.' Lieutenant Jenness's head exploded on contact with an Indian bullet as he raised his head above the 2½-foot wagon parapet

The Wagon Box fight, 2 August 1867
The Wagon Box fight demonstrated the impact of concentrated high-tech army firepower. The Indians realised that they must procure the white man's weapons if they were ever to fight on equal terms.

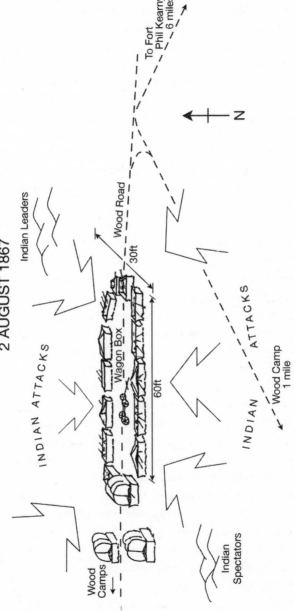

THE WAGON BOX FIGHT
2 AUGUST 1867

Indian Leaders

INDIAN ATTACKS

Wood Road

30ft

Wagon Box

60ft

INDIAN ATTACKS

To Fort
Phil Kearny
6 miles

N

Wood Camp
1 mile

Wood Camps

Indian
Spectators

to direct fire. Another soldier was cut down by the high-angle fire and two more were severely wounded. Meanwhile the mounted mass, thinned by persistent and accurate fire, broke and scattered, stumbling over the dead and dying warriors and ponies piling up around the boxes. 'In fact,' declared Smyth, 'shooting into such a mass of Indians as charged on us the first time, it would be nearly impossible for many bullets to go astray.'

It was a brutal repulse. Mercy was neither anticipated nor freely given. Soldiers firing through loopholes methodically picked off wounded Indians crawling around the laager. The wounded warriors, stoic in their suffering, used any opportunity to fight back and retaliate. 'We had to kill them for self protection,' Smyth claimed. In reality the defenders had other motives: it was also 'evening up the Fetterman deal', as Smyth admitted. However, it was not over yet. The soldiers would do whatever it took to survive. Smyth knew that 'the fight would not have lasted ten minutes after they got over the corral'.[14]

Having failed to ride over the opposition, several hundred Indians now stealthily attempted to approach the wagon-box defence on foot, utilising every advantage offered by broken ground and terrain. The intention was to reduce the defence through concentrated gun and arrow fire. Hundreds of heavy-calibre bullets began to shatter and gnaw at the wooden topside of the wagons. Overhead blankets, trapping the smoke and heat, began to sag with snagged arrows. Wood splinters showered dazed and thirsty defenders flinching at every impact with nerves assaulted by the cracking and whining report of impacts and ricochets. The grain bags prevented any further casualties. Silence was interpreted as success and hundreds of Indian braves rose to their feet and sprinted towards the boxes to mop up.

Once again a sheet of flame and smoke belched out from the squat defence, scything down groups of attackers. Unable to account for the continuous fire and assuming that there must therefore be more defenders than supposed, the Indians were convinced the fire must eventually slacken. They pressed home their attack until almost reaching the wagon beds. Spectators on the hill leaped to their feet with expectation, but were appalled at the slaughter of their menfolk before them. Six separate charges were broken by disciplined army firepower. Some gun barrels were rendered useless after becoming white hot. The Indians were to remember the struggle as 'the bad medicine fight of the white man'. They could not comprehend a technology that could 'make guns fire themselves without stopping'.[15]

A howitzer shell burst in among the Indian skirmishers as they attempted to recover their dead from around the laager. A relief force of over 100 men under Major Smith from Fort Phil Kearney advanced with trepidation. There was a mass of warriors before them and they were in the open. The Indians sullenly withdrew, still assailed by the deadly fire pouring from the small Wagon Box fort. Despite the vulnerability of the relief force, concentrated army firepower had already broken Indian resolve. Rising smoke from the howitzer strike merely signified the *coup de grâce*. It was over.

'This fight lasted about four hours,' declared Smyth, 'and was very hot from the start.' He and his comrades were amazed at the tenacity of the attacks: '[I] never saw the Indians make such a determined effort to clean us up before'. It was the largest force of Indians he had ever faced 'and the hardest fighting lot I ever encountered'. He and his men scalped any of the Indian bodies that remained. 'We thought we had killed and wounded some more than four hundred,' he claimed. Later optimistic estimates quoted as many as 1,137 or more. Captain Powell assessed 67 Indians killed and 120 wounded. There were 28 white survivors from the original force of 32. Captain Powell's wife recalls him indelibly affected by this nightmare experience for the rest of his life.[16]

As indeed was also Red Cloud, but from a different perspective. He had been treated to a lesson of the white man's technology that he would never forget. The Indians resolved that they must have just such weapons.

* * *

In a military age that paid scant attention to institutionalising lessons learned, more attention would be paid in the United States to subsequent wars of unification in Europe than to the outcomes of insignificant skirmishes with 'savages' on the Indian Frontier. More soldiers were lost in the 'battle of the hundred slain', as the Indians called the Fetterman Massacre, than any other army engagement on the US mainland since the Civil War. As Carrington's shocked gaze took in the scene of utter desolation across Massacre Ridge, he knew an Inquiry would follow. It was set for June the following year, but in a sense its findings would be glossed over as a result of the euphoria accompanying the more successful Wagon Box fight that occurred two months later, and the Beecher's Island battle the following year against the Cheyenne. Many lessons learned were glossed over as stemming essentially from Fetterman's reckless behaviour. Dead men could not argue with the outcome. Lessons from the Sioux War of 1866–68 were to be relearned ten years later on the Little Bighorn.

Indians did not conform to Hardy's Manual of 'Tactics' used by the Armies of the Civil War. Union victory in 1865 demonstrated the soundness of current doctrine, which on occasion did work against Indians. Fetterman was a 'hothead' who squandered his unit in action as a result of irrational decisions. Colonel Carrington was relieved after the debacle and ordered to Fort Caspar to command the 18th Infantry, being succeeded by Lieutenant Colonel H. W. Wessells. Two companies of the 2nd Cavalry and four of infantry were dispatched to Fort Phil Kearney. Reports accounting for the Fetterman Massacre were never seriously digested. It had no impact on army doctrine. In any case, there was no institutionalised method of capturing such experience.

Armies fight their campaigns on the basis of lessons learned from the previous one. Self-evident truisms often cloud tactical appreciation. The only sound generalisation of modern warfare might be that each engagement is unique, so differences are more likely to outweigh similarities in the next campaign. Indians did not 'learn lessons' in the formal classroom sense, but they appeared more astute, observant and flexible in developing tactics than their high-tech army counterparts. Indian tactics were unconventional, based more on the buffalo hunt than 'hammer and anvil' or 'fix and manoeuvre' Civil War practice. The use of decoys and splitting the herd to cut out weak or vulnerable elements for the kill was more relevant to frontier skirmishing than conventional lines of battle. Camouflage and concealment matched to a skilful and innovative individual use of ground was their forte as warriors. In particular, exploiting the tactical advantage of exposed ridgelines, which offered safe crossfire options and simplified the often complex coordination of closing in while avoiding friendly fire casualties were to be repeated in the subsequent Sioux War of 1876–77. The herd was thereby silhouetted and, if on the high end of a convex slope, would not detect a close-in approach. All escape options become obvious to the attacker, whatever the direction of advance. Simplicity has often been the byword for success in battle. Indian expertise drew on collective practical experience, which formed part of a laborious training process from boyhood to mature warrior. Little was missed. Army experience by contrast required formal teaching not assiduously practised at frontier locations, where its application against savages appeared irrelevant.

Both sides interpreted firepower lessons differently. Success during the Wagon Box engagement appeared to confirm the army's selection of the cheap but more efficient conversion of the existing Civil War Springfield muzzle-loader to the single-shot Allen converted rifle. Henry had offered Congress the repeating rifle that had performed so impressively during the Civil War, but political expediency, recoiling at the prospect of increased ammunition costs, guaranteed Henry's bankruptcy; Winchester subsequently took up the patent. There is a modern parallel in the British Government's decision, against much tactical advice, to adopt the SA 80 rifle in the 1980s, a more complex weapon than its predecessor; subsequent expensive teething problems placed a high price on the political expediency of buying British. Low-tech adversaries during the post-Cold War era preferred the simple and ubiquitous

Kalashnikov AK-47, an effective low-cost variant. Likewise the North American Indian saw the advantage of the repeating rifle. Wheatley and Fisher had amply demonstrated its deadly profi- ciency at short range during the Fetterman Massacre. The faster-firing Allen-converted rifles administered a further technological shock during the bloody Indian repulse at the Wagon Box fight. The Indians resolved to procure the white man's tech- nology. The acquisition of firearms, preferably rapid-firing, would be vital to meet the army on an equal tactical footing. Guns that did not need loading were 'bad medicine' if one was on the receiving end. Likewise the army was convinced by the outcome of the Wagon Box fight and the Beecher's Island battle the following year that disciplined firepower brought to bear at long distances was a battle winner on the frontier.

Two obvious lessons were missed by the US Army in 1868 and have been repeatedly relearned in many counter-insurgency actions and engagements against low-tech adversaries since. Sufficient troops and resources are still required to inflict decisive defeat on even low-tech enemies. Ominously the Plains Indians had also demonstrated, unlike in other Indian operational theatres in the south of the United States, that they were capable of massing in sufficient strength to overwhelm and defeat conventionally structured army formations. All this was missed in the recrimin- ations over Fetterman's reckless behaviour.

Although the US frontier army ostensibly won some victories, civilian passage along the Bozeman Trail remained untenable. The Oglala Sioux Chief Red Cloud, supported by other aspiring leaders such as Crazy Horse and Rain-in-the-Face, had formed a form- idable if loose Indian confederation. The army forts remained isolated. After eight months of dawdling and negotiations, Red Cloud and Man-Afraid-of-his-Horses, another Lakota Chief, finally agreed to a treaty signed at Fort Laramie on 4 November 1868. The Sioux War of 1866–68 had clearly established the dominance of the Oglala Sioux over US forces in northern Wyoming and southern Montana, east of the Bighorn mountains.

The Laramie Treaty between the Sioux nation and the United States recognised the right of the Sioux to roam and hunt in the 'Unceded Territory' between the Black Hills and the Bighorn mountains in Wyoming and Montana. No whites could enter it and it was to remain a hunting ground until the buffalo were gone. 'Unceded' meant that although the US did not recognise Sioux ownership of the land, it did not deny their hunting rights there. A reservation was established in Dakota Territory wherein:

'The United States now solemnly agrees that no persons except those herein designated and authorized to do so … shall ever be permitted to pass over, settle upon, or reside in the territory described in this article.'[17]

The Sioux were being granted perpetual ownership of this reservation, a progressive initiative, giving Indians territory they would administer. Few politicians or people objected to the terms and thereby sowed the seed of future conflict.

Red Cloud had demonstrated that he was as able and shrewd a politician as a warrior. He would be the only Indian to win a war against the United States and gain tangible concessions for his people. His successors may win battles but never a war. In the summer of 1871 Red Cloud was invited to Washington, experiencing the satisfaction of riding his old enemy, the 'Iron Horse'. Exposure to city life on the eastern seaboard of the United States was to change his outlook for ever. There is an anecdotal story of a handful of pebbles handed to one of the Indian delegates with guidance to drop one at every white village encountered to assess the strength of the white man. This rough count soon proved completely pointless. Omaha and Chicago passed en route made indelible impressions:

'The white man were as thick and numerous and aimless as grasshoppers, moving always in a hurry but never seeming to get to whatever place it was they were going.'[18]

Nearly all the Sioux demands were met in the 1868 Treaty. Especially sweet was the abandonment of the three disputed forts and closure of the Bozeman Trail. The Indians for their part agreed to move to the Great Sioux Reservation and take up farming. They promised not to attack settlers who would move into their former territory nor disturb Union Pacific Railway builders. Rail travel negated the usefulness of the Bozeman Trail in any case. There would be no further war against the whites and Indian buffalo ways would transition to 'civilisation'.

In August the last US Army units departed Forts Phil Kearney and C. F. Smith. The soldiers and troopers, with many shared and often painful memories of the effort required to establish them, gloomily observed the lazy columns of black smoke spiralling into the sky. The Indians triumphantly torched them before they were even out of sight.

Chapter 2

Clash of cultures

'Whose voice was first sounded on this land?'

Red Cloud, Sioux Indian Chief

The frontier army

Twenty-one days after the signing of the Laramie Treaty a regimental-size column of the 7th Cavalry was moving through deep snow among the sparsely timbered outskirts of the Washita valley. Winter winds had formed an icy crust that formed a fragile plate on the freshly fallen snow. Snaking its way through the winter-blackened trees, the column of some 720 cavalrymen made considerable noise breaking the surface as frozen snowballs coagulated around the horses hooves. Troopers were tightly wrapped in greatcoats and buffalo furs covered in a crystalline layer of ice. The smell of wood smoke permeated the air as advance elements of the force laboriously crawled to the edge of a bluff that overlooked the river valley below. 'I could not help thinking that we very much resembled a pack of wolves,' commented Captain Barnitz, a cavalry company commander.[1] A dog barked and the tinkle of a small bell could be heard. There was animated discussion of what might lie beneath, which was settled when a baby's cry was discerned wailing across the frozen air. It was a village.

The 7th Cavalry had been formed at Fort Riley, Kansas, five months before the Fetterman Massacre. Its commander, Civil War hero Lieutenant Colonel George Armstrong Custer, had been appointed second-in-command in 1867, but was the *de facto* commander in the absence of the regimental commander on detached duty. Custer had marched and counter-marched his unit throughout Kansas in 1867, chasing hostile Indians but achieving only two kills. Now there was a total Indian village at his mercy. He decided to split his regimental force into four battalions to surround the objective and strike simultaneously. This was the first time the command had operated as a complete regiment since its inception. Very rarely did one actually achieve surprise when fighting Indians.

This was not so unusual taking account of the size of the Northern Plains campaign area. It covered some 250,000 square miles, or two and a half times the area of the present United Kingdom. Indeed, the famed American explorer Clark had labelled it the 'Great American Desert'. Land of no particular value was hot and inhospitable and prone to floods with extremes of temperature in summer, and ice-cold in winter. There were more infantry regiments (ten) than the three and a half cavalry regiments to police the Northern Plains. In theory about 9,000 soldiers were obliged to cover 100 square miles. Captain Albert Barnitz's vivid diary and letter accounts of the 7th Cavalry in its early days describe the untenable strategic situation faced during the first year on the frontier:

'Our troops are scattered in parties too small to accomplish anything, through an area of about 10,000 [sic] square miles! By actual statistics 9,700 Indians, of various tribes, are known to be on the warpath.'[2]

The problems experienced by the small post-Civil War frontier army during the latter part of the 19th century are not dissimilar to those experienced by its 21st-century peace-keeping counterparts. These were primarily shortages of resources, personnel and the perennial problem of retaining and motivating soldiers burdened with wide-ranging mission tasks bearing little resemblance to their previous conventional Civil War experience. In contemporary terms, peace support expeditionary operations are totally unlike the massive conventional Cold War deployments and missions of the 1970s and 1980s. Barnitz opined in 1867 that 'it needs not less than 40,000 men to make a speedy end to this Indian business and we haven't a fourth of this number'. Twenty-first-century military commentators have frequently echoed his assessment that the Government was exercising 'a penny-wise and pound-foolish policy'.

Many officers serving with and commanding the frontier army would have been condemned to historical obscurity but for opportunities provided by the Civil War. Others benefited from the military nepotism that permeated its career management, and which arguably remains a feature of American military culture today. Superior officers tended to keep a paternal eye on favoured subordinates. Custer graduated last in his class at West Point, yet at the war's end he emerged a cavalry division commander and war hero. General Phillip N. Sheridan, his superior and Commander of the Department of the Missouri, was 34th in his class of 52 in 1853. General Sherman, the Army Commander, had resigned an earlier commission in 1853 and failed in banking and other business ventures. The war lifted him from failure and obscurity to fame. General and later US President Ulysses Grant had an unremarkable early military career, and on resigning was unsuccessful both as a farmer and real estate agent.

Custer's Civil War experience was to prove the most formative of his life. His meteoric rise to Major General in five years, and even to Lieutenant Colonel in the Regular Army, was a remarkable contemporary achievement, but he was not the youngest General to emerge from the Civil War.[3] As a consequence he was totally egocentric, with a character that has remained something of an enigma, probably due to his wife Elizabeth's insistence on scrupulously editing and preserving his image through the selective release of letters and papers after his death. Even during his lifetime Custer was a public relations media 'maestro'. He projected himself as 'Boy General' during the Civil War and successful 'Indian

Fighter' in newspaper articles and his subsequent book *My Life on the Plains.*

Egocentricity was a characteristic of senior command at a young age without the maturing benefit of a depth of experience that tends to accrue with graduated rank. He was an outstanding cavalry commander during the Civil War, quickly gaining a reputation for producing results. Apart from a minor thigh wound in 1863, his was a 'Glorious War', from which he emerged unscathed, sound in mind and limb at the end. Risk held few personal terrors for him and would influence his later conduct on operations. Even when surrounded by the carnage and totality of Civil War at its height in 1863, he felt moved to declare in a letter home:

> 'Oh, could you but have seen some of the charges that were made! While thinking of them I cannot but exclaim "Glorious War!"'[4]

'Custer Luck' and a feeling of invincibility permeated his actions and decisions throughout the subsequent Indian wars. He was slapped by spent musket balls in action and commented in wartime letters upon fearful losses about him, but these experiences appear to have had little more than a superficial effect. Utterly fearless, he was convinced 'that my destiny is in the hands of the Almighty'. 'This belief,' he confided to his wife, 'more than any other factor or reason, makes me brave and fearless as I am.'[5] Custer enjoyed war for its own sake and, although happily married, he was not distracted from his military career by the responsibilities of parenthood. After being the quintessential 'bad boy' West Point cadet, he was not matured by his wartime experiences, as demonstrated by his cavalier dress sense, which was to continue on the frontier. Barrack life was anathema. He lived for the fight and the great outdoors. The army would have been his hobby if not his career. He instilled extremes of emotion in commanders, peers and subordinates alike. James H. Kidd, who served as an officer with Custer's Michigan Brigade during the Civil War, venerated him as a tactician who instinctively sensed the exact moment to charge, retreat or hold, acting boldly on instinct without costly hesitation. 'Under *him* our men can achieve wonders,' he wrote in April 1864. 'His name is our battle cry.'[6] One of Custer's later company commanders on the frontier, Captain Albert Barnitz, had the opposite view of his new commanding officer in 1867, whom he described as 'bilious … very much on his dignity' and 'really quite obstreperous'. His wife Jennie echoed the sentiment when she joined her husband one year later, observing that 'you have no idea how generally unpopular he is, in civil life, since his last summer campaign.'[7]

Custer was a strong leader and conditioned by his Civil War experience to be an easy risk-taker, supremely confident in his personal ability to overcome any difficulty. Like many of his peers, he was frustrated by his reduction from brevet to regular rank. He was used to and revelled in greater responsibility. The US frontier army, acutely aware of its abruptly reduced status at the end of the Civil War, was unhappy with its under-resourced and as yet uninterpreted new role.

At the beginning of the Civil War the strength of the army was about 18,000, while at its conclusion more than a million citizen soldiers were demobilised during 1865–66. Congress authorised strengths of 54,000 in 1866, which decreased to 37,000 in 1870 and was cut again in 1874 to 25,000. Authorised strengths, moreover, did not necessarily reflect the true picture, as they rarely matched serving figures.[8] The primary mission of the much-reduced Regular Army was to occupy the defeated Confederacy, not deal with turbulence in the West. 'It was pretty dull soldiering down there in the South,' wrote new recruit Charles Windolph, a German immigrant. Arrivals from abroad were invariably sent to the frontier, not the southern states. Ten Military Districts were established, leaving only remnants left over for frontier duties, and several battalions of the 7th Cavalry were relocated from the West during 1871–73 to help police the southern states, where they assisted US Marshals arresting internal revenue law violators or combating night-riding Ku-Klux Klan insurgents. Such operations could be termed Peace Support Operations (PSO) in modern military parlance, and would result in a skills-fade of conventional war-fighting cavalry skills. Charles Windolph explained how his Regiment was broken up into companies and 'our job was to smash the Ku-Klux Klan, and run down illicit whisky distilleries' which 'wasn't much fun for energetic, spirited young men'.[9]

A further pressure on the new army was that Congress mandated half regular and half volunteer Civil War officers, a reward for wartime service, to man the new force. Major Frederick Benteen, one of Custer's company commanders who was brevetted Brigadier General following illustrious wartime service as a civilian volunteer, successfully applied for a regular Captain's commission. Former Confederate Army veterans were prohibited commissions, but could serve as 'Galvanized Yankee' NCOs, having substantial conventional combat experience; 22 Confederates were later to perish with the 7th Cavalry at the Battle of the Little Bighorn.[10] Promotion 'boom' in the Civil War army was to be followed by post-war 'bust', and the apparently fair distribution of officer ranks agreed by Congress was to sow latent tension within the command chain of the new army.

Division revolved primarily around the issue of so-called 'brevet' ranks. Regular rank was the actual rank held at staff or in the line, whereas a brevet rank was bestowed in recognition of notable service, often during combat. For example, many of Custer's company commanders held the brevet rank of Major and Lieutenant Colonel for combat achievements in the Civil War. Custer, a Lieutenant Colonel, was a brevet Major General. Officers might be addressed or identified by their regular rank and at other times by their brevet rank. Occasionally they wore brevet rank insignia, sometimes not, or both. It was a divisive and emotion-ridden topic. Charles 'Dutchy' Windolph, the newly enlisted German immigrant, recalled that it was the norm to refer to an officer by his brevet or honorary rank, but 'it was all a little confusing though'.[11] Some of Custer's Company Commanders had commanded formations larger than a regiment. They in turn were commanded by a gifted yet lucky Major General of only five years' standing who had achieved the actual rank of Lieutenant Colonel. Captain Albert Barnitz wrote about the emotional wedge that the seemingly unfair arrangement could drive between professional and social relationships within the claustrophobic confines of isolated posts, such as Fort Wallace in Kansas. A new officer was posted into the fort, Barnitz noted, and brevetted Lieutenant Colonel 'for *nothing!*'

'Captain Benteen only arrived here about a week ago, from Fort Hayes, direct, where he has been doing nothing ever since I left. And Captain West brevetted Colonel from the same date! – And I who have done far more than either of them, hundreds of times over in the volunteer service even – (and they have done nothing in the regular army) am not noticed!'[12]

A much smaller army meant that promotion would be measured in multiples of years, unlike the Civil War experience. Reductions in the number of commissions available meant that progress was literally 'dead man's shoes', unless recognition could be secured in combat. Successful Indian fighter George Crook, a brevet Major General at the end of the Civil War, was appointed in 1874 to the command of the Department of Arizona in his brevet two-star rank as a regular Lieutenant Colonel following a masterly campaign against Paiute Indians in the South. He subsequently jumped full Colonel to regular Brigadier General when President Grant broke the seniority tradition as a reward for his highly successful Tonto Basin campaign against the Apache Indians in 1873. Small wonder that Custer's career pulse quickened when he quietly surrounded a Cheyenne village on the Washita on 23 November 1868. 'How many military men have reaped laurels from their Indian campaigns?' he later wrote with some frustration the year before the Little Bighorn. 'Does he strive to win the approving smile of his countrymen?' he asked, but rhetorically concluded, 'That is indeed in this particular instance a difficult task.'[13] US society had had its fill of Civil War militarism.

Enlistments in the post-Civil War Army, of which the 7th Cavalry offers a typical cross-section, were former farmers, tradesmen, labourers, frontiersmen and previous Civil War soldiers. Many were would-be young adventurers, outcasts from society, fugitives from the law and newly arrived immigrants in the country. Jacob Adams, an 1873 enlistee in the 7th Cavalry, declared, 'I fairly ached to get into some action like that I heard veterans of the Civil War'.[14] German immigrant Charles Windolph avoided conscription in the Franco-Prussian War and emigrated to America. 'I was about the greenest thing that ever hit New York,' he said. They were picked up by recruiting Sergeants on arrival, cashing in on their vulnerability. 'I couldn't talk more than a dozen words of English,' Windolph admitted, 'and I had exactly $2.50 in money.' They at least got a new suit and shoes from the army. About half of the 7th Cavalry was foreign-born.

Militarism was not a dominant national characteristic following a bloody Civil War, and was conspicuously lacking as a motive for joining for a three- to five-year term that paid only $13 per day. Windolph pointed out that 'the Civil War had been over only five years, and there were lots of unemployed men those days, but they didn't seem to want to go in the army'. Like many 'hundreds of us German boys in that same fix' they joined 'because most of us couldn't get a job anywhere else'.[15] Unskilled labourers formed the largest group, with 50% coming from the ranks of the unemployed. Desertion was consequently rife during economic upturns, as also was the lure of an alternative life in the new western territories, once posted there. Eighty-five men deserted from the 7th Cavalry during one month in April 1867, and another 34 in July the following year.[16]

Training was rudimentary and consisted of three to four weeks at a recruit depot where emphasis was placed upon subordination and obedience to one's position in the army. Fatigues and fort construction work often took priority over military training. There was physical fitness training, and cavalry recruits received mounted and dismounted sabre-drill, horse-riding and bare-back equestrian skills. Marksmanship and weapons practice was rare; indeed, soldiers were rationed to only three practice rounds per year in 1866. They were expected to learn by association, and observing and emulating veterans, but might well be on active service within three months of enlistment. Little prepared them for the psychological shock of encountering Indian fighters who had honed their fighting skills since boyhood.

The small size of the Company group underpinned cohesiveness in the frontier army. It provided the main focus for soldier relationships, which formed around a 'bunky' or 'buddy-buddy' system of 'fours'. Two men commonly pooled blankets and slept together in the field. 'Fours' was also the lowest fighting unit in the cavalry. Columns marched in fours and, when dismounting to skirmish, a horse-handler would hold the reins of four horses while the other three fought on foot. Privates had little contact with officers beyond exchanging formal military courtesies, and NCOs were tough. There was generally a warmer and closer relationship between officers and NCOs, but the former rarely conversed with the men. Captain Barnitz's wife Jennie had some empathy for the rank and file at Fort Riley, Kansas, observing that:

'The officers assume a great deal here. The poor privates are perfect slaves. I do pity them from the bottom of my heart.'[17]

Life was harsh in the frontier army. Death was more likely from snakebite, grizzly bear or the forces of nature than the Indian. Transition to military life, whether one came from a city slum or a rural background, was extreme. Living conditions at forts were rudimentary. Elizabeth Custer described Fort Wallace in western Kansas as 'about as dreary as any spot on earth'. William T. Sherman, the Army Commander, saw soldiers at Fort Sedgwick in Colorado living in 'hovels in which a Negro would hardly go'.[18]

Rancid bacon and wormy bread became a staple of the men's diet, resulting in sickness and disease. Custer complained in 1867 that his soldiers were issued bread from boxes that had been marked baked in 1861.[19] Life was drudgery and encouraged rampant alcoholism, which afflicted all ranks. Captain Barnitz's diary observations of the 7th Cavalry often mentioned officer suicides. 'The fact is, Jennie,' he confided to his wife, 'there appears to be a premium offered for drunkenness in the army. Almost all the old officers drink a great deal.' Payday for the soldiers was 'a trying day for the officers,' his wife concurred, as 'the men are almost unmanageable as soon as they have a dollar'.[20]

'He must not think of enlisting in the regular army,' wrote an army officer to his mother, warning a relative not to make a serious mistake. 'He will regret such a move as long as he is in the ranks. I speak of what I know.'[21] Colonel Sturgis, the absent nominal commander of the 7th Cavalry, wrote to his son James, about to graduate from West Point in May 1867, warning of the perils of serving in the frontier army. 'In Artillery, you always have refined stations and access to books, and refined society, while the cavalry are thrown out to the frontiers.' He did not want his son exposed to 'temptations [that] increase a thousand fold, for drinking, gambling and all kinds of dissipation which destroys so many young officers'. Cavalry might be the romantic arm, but in Sturgis's view the cavalryman was little more than an Indian in uniform. 'You I hope will take a higher view of your future than all that.' James disregarded his father's advice and was to die at the Little Bighorn with Custer.[22]

The system was reliant upon harsh discipline, drill and hard Corporals to keep the young men under control, who were in turn taken aback at the drudgery and disorientated by desolate and grim conditions. In 1869 the desertion rate was about 30%. Paucity of resources ironically caused the Provost Marshal to attach more importance to recovering weapons and horses than absconded men. At one company post on the South Platte, the Captain commander discovered one morning that his First Sergeant and 40 out of 60 men from the garrison had decamped with their horses and equipment for the gold mines. Even the 7th Cavalry, reputedly a crack Indian fighting unit, had desertion problems from its very inception in May 1867, losing 1,200 men in the 14 months to July 1868. Custer blamed bad provisions, which caused bad health, 'inactivity led to restlessness and dissatisfaction' and scurvy and cholera became rife. 'For all these evils, desertion became the most popular antidote.' Half of his effective force was dissipated by absenteeism in one year alone. Custer had an equally bleak response to all this, which Captain Barnitz termed 'barbarous':

> 'He ordered certain men shot, for attempted desertion, and then hauled them through the hot sun for days, without allowing them medical attendance.'

Custer was court-martialled as a consequence and suspended from duty for a year. It should, however, be remembered that desertion during the Civil War – which had ended only two years before – was punishable by death. Even after Custer was temporarily cashiered, Barnitz declared:

> 'Oh, that I too could be similarly suspended! The fact is I am sick and tired of this treadmill life! I am weary, weary, weary, with never a moment to rest.'[23]

The frontier army was shaken by the ferocity of the Indian on the rare occasions they did meet in combat. 'Lo, the poor Indian,' the opening line of Alexander Pope's poem *An Essay on Man*, was soon subsumed to 'Lo', the soldier's preferred nickname for the Indian. 'Lo' instilled fear as a result of his uncompromising savagery and lack of mercy to captives or wounded. One lurid Kansas newspaper report in 1868 recounted that dazed white women captives, after witnessing the murder of their menfolk and enduring rape, did not move promptly enough to follow their Indian captors back to camp. As a consequence they were 'helplessly' dragged along with their plaited hair tied to horsetails.[24] Far removed from the frontier and with an idealistic view of the Indian, few Easterners appreciated the intense hatred, fear and loathing Westerners had for Indians. 'What should we do with the Red Man?' asked Senator James R. Dolittle of Wisconsin to a Denver audience in 1868. The response shook the stunned Senator when 'a shout almost loud enough to raise the roof of the Opera House' resounded 'Exterminate them! Exterminate them!'[25]

General Phillip N. Sheridan, the commander of the Department of the Missouri, wrote to his superior, General William T. Sherman, in 1869:

> 'Since 1862, at least 800 men, women and children have been murdered within the limits of my present command, in the most fiendish manner, the men usually scalped and mutilated, their privates cut off and placed in their mouths: women ravished sometimes fifty and sixty times in succession, then killed and scalped, sticks stuck up their persons before and after death. I have myself conversed with one women who, while some months gone in pregnancy, was ravished over thirty times successively by different Indians, becoming insensible two or three times during this fearful ordeal; and each time on recovering consciousness, mutely appealing for mercy, if not for herself, for her unborn child. Also another woman ravished with more fearful brutality, over forty times, and the last sticking the point of his sabre up the person of the woman. I could give the names of these women were it not for delicacy.'[26]

'Save the last bullet for yourself' was the stark maxim for soldiers serving on the frontier. Fear of the Indian at close quarters did have a debilitating effect on army fighting power. 'My courage had largely oozed out while I listened to the blood-curdling tales the old-timers recited,' admitted Private Alson Ostrander. 'A favourite method of torture was to "stake out" the victim,' revealed Colonel Richard Dodge:

> 'He was stripped of his clothing, laid on his back on the ground and his arms and legs stretched to the utmost, were fastened by thongs to pins driven into the ground. In this state he was not only helpless but almost motionless. All this time the Indians pleasantly talked to him. It was kind of a joke. Then the small fire was built near one of his feet. When that was so cooked as to have little sensation, another fire was built near the other foot; then the legs and arms and body until the whole person was crisped. Finally a small fire was built on the naked breast and kept up until life was extinct.'

The idealistic view of the battles on the frontier propagated by one-dime novels in the East belied the reality experienced by the frontier army in the west in the 1860s. Private Ostrander on operations conceded that it appeared that his unit and its scouts were applying all their experience and knowledge to avoid rather than seek contact with the enemy. 'Instead of looking for trouble and a chance to punish the ravaging Indians, the whole command was trying to get through without a fight,' he admitted.[27]

The frontier army, small and poorly resourced with only about 9,000 men spread across a vast area, was almost overwhelmed by its task. It relied upon civilian and Indian scouts to provide intelligence because its officers were untrained. Likewise, the previously sophisticated logistic systems of the Civil War armies had been dispersed and replaced by civilian contractors and sutlers. 'Civilianisation' or 'contracting out' logistic services has also been a feature of post-Cold War peace-keeping NATO forces. Tangible success as a consequence of large-scale regular operations was unusual on the frontier. Captain Barnitz's assessment was that 'the Indians must be thoroughly whipped before they will respect us, or keep any peace, and they haven't been whipped yet very much to speak of'.[28] The 7th Cavalry's reputation was largely based upon its

rare success in bringing its entire regimental resources to bear on a
Cheyenne Indian village in the Washita valley on 25 November
1868. Ironically this was two weeks after the Laramie Treaty had
been signed.

The Indians

About 50 lodges were discovered by Custer's force of 11 companies
of the 7th Cavalry during that early morning as frozen skies began
to lighten. Other forces, including three companies of the 3rd
Infantry, one company of the 5th and a further company from the
38th Infantry with 450 wagons, were supporting the expedition,
but the mounted element alone was conducting this foray. It was
decided that three cavalry companies would attack through the hills
to the north-east of the camp and two from the south. Two other
companies were to clatter down the shallow river line into the
village from the south-west. Custer aimed to assault with the main
effort of four companies, with a sharpshooter element under
Lieutenant Cooke, later his adjutant, covering from the west. Seven
hundred troopers were to mount this attack and they were armed
with Springfield repeaters, enabling a high rate of fire to be directed
from horseback without reloading.

Unbeknown to the attackers, reluctant to execute a further
reconnaissance in dark and uncertain terrain for fear of alerting the
village, there were other Indian settlements encamped next door to
Black Kettle's southern Cheyenne lodges. There may have been as
many as 6,000 other Indians camped nearby further down the
Washita River. They included other southern Cheyenne, Arapahos,
Kiowas, Comanche and Prairie Apache, either within gunfire
earshot or easily accessible by runners.

Black Kettle, the 67-year-old leader of this group of lodges, had
survived a massacre at Sand Creek four years before when his village
had been brutally sacked by two regiments of Colorado militia
under Colonel John Chivington. Women and children were killed
and atrocities and rape committed, as an act of revenge in kind

against earlier Indian depredations. Black Kettle's wife Medicine Woman barely managed to survive nine gunshot wounds during the outrage, perpetrated while the village was under the protection of the American flag. 'We were once friends with the whites, but you nudged us out of the way by your intrigues,' the old chief had declared. 'Why don't you talk, and go straight, and let us all be well?'[29] This was not to be.

'A single rifle shot rang sharp and clear on the far side of the village,' recalled Custer.[30] Bugles sounded the charge and, bizarrely accompanied by the strains of the regimental band playing 'Gary Owen', the attack signal, Custer's men swept virtually unopposed into the village. Half-naked men, women and children fled from their tepees into the frozen night, where they were gunned or ridden down by the troopers. Despite a spirited defence, the fighting petered out within 15 minutes. After the mopping-up operation, 103 Cheyenne lay dead in the mud and slush, including Black Kettle and his wife drifting in the shallow water of the river on the outskirts of the village.

Soldiers seized everything of material value in the village and burned it, a devastating blow to the fragile nature of the Indian community. The pony herd of some 875 horses and mules was slaughtered, shot when they became too troublesome to dispose of in any other way. Major Joel Elliot and an 18-man detachment disappeared to the east of the village to prevent Indians escaping through a gap in the encirclement. Elliot, who had allegedly shouted to Lieutenant Owen Hale, 'Here goes for a brevet or a coffin!', qualified for the latter. His non-appearance alerted the main cavalry element to the huge force of Indians that began sinisterly to congregate on the high ground around them. Custer postured in a feint that suggested he might be considering sacking another village in its turn. In reality it was custody of 53 Indian non-combatant captives, women and children, that likely saved his command. This illustrated the tactical value of securing hostages. Likewise, the capture of the pony herd was an unnoticed but tactically important part of his success in taking the village as it reduced the mobility of any counter-attack options. Custer withdrew to the north as increasing numbers of Indians from the numerous down-river camps increasingly made their presence felt. Elliot's detachment, cut off and literally dismembered by the Indian reinforcements, was not found until 11 December. Custer doubtless realised early on that he would not be able to assist him. Several other soldiers and officers were killed and wounded, including Major Barnitz, critically wounded in the abdomen.

The Washita engagement bared the Indian's 'Achilles' heel'. General Sheridan, Custer's short but aggressive commander, had applied similar 'Total War' tactics against the Confederacy when both had participated in devastating the Shenandoah Valley in 1864. The measure was equally applicable to the Indian at his most vulnerable, with poorly fed and immobilised pony herds in winter. General William T. Sherman, the Army Commander, equally pleased at the outcome, had similarly put Georgia to the torch during his celebrated Civil War march from Atlanta to the sea. Sheridan knew that he was preaching to the converted as he rationalised his actions in defence of his methods to his superior officer.

> 'I have to select that season when I can catch the fiends; and if a village is attacked and women and children are killed, the responsibility is not with the soldiers but with the people whose crimes necessitated the attack. During the [Civil] War, did anyone hesitate to attack a village or town occupied by the enemy because women and children were within its limits? Did we cease to throw shells into Vicksburg or Atlanta because women and children were there?'[31]

That this was a conflict of two totally opposing cultures was not lost on the Indian. Applying a 'Total War' philosophy to making war on families would yield quicker and more decisive results from the frontier army perspective. The Indian view was that the white soldiers had no souls: they attacked at night, killed ponies, and made war on women and children in winter. Red Cloud once declared, 'Whose voice was first sounded on this land? The voice of the red people who had but bows and arrows... When the white man comes in my country he leaves a trail of blood behind him.' Indian culture and ways were totally at variance with those of the white man. The Washita demonstrated that winter and distance did not impact upon the considerable reach of white soldiers – a salutary lesson. Najinyanupi, or 'Surrounded', encapsulated the misunderstood helplessness that was beginning to permeate the Indian psyche when he said:

'When the prairie is on fire you see animals surrounded by the fire; you see them run and try to hide themselves so that they will not burn. That is the way we are here.'[32]

Indians formed loose groupings rather than tribes, and there were about 75 such groups. These associations were fragile societies of extended families. They all lived marginally, constantly exposed to the excesses of nature, disease and conflict. It did not take much to decimate such vulnerable groups. About 200,000 Indians lived between the Canadian borders in the north and the southern border in Texas. Four elements, the Teton, Yankton, Yanktonnais and Santee, formed the primary Lakota Sioux groupings on the Great Plains. By the mid-19th century seven tribes made up the Teton Sioux, and these were the Oglala, Brule, Hunkpapa, Minneconjou, Blackfoot, Sans Arc and Two Kettle. Certain tribes on the Northern Plains were to become the allies of the United States, and these included the Crow, Eastern Shoshone and Pawnee; the Sioux and Crow were deadly enemies. Other non-involved tribes were the Northern Shoshone, Arapaho, Yanktonai, Gros Ventre and Assiniboin. The Cheyenne, Teton and Santee were occasional US enemies.

The term 'Sioux' derived from the Chippewa label 'Nadoweisiv', which meant 'Adder Snake'. Revisionist historians have often sentimentalised the 'noble' Indians as a vulnerable, innocent people who had their lands stolen from them by a rapacious and expansionist USA. The truth is they were perpetually at war with each other. The Sioux had displaced the Crow from their territories, encouraging them to offer their services to the frontier army as scouts. The Sioux had likewise pushed the Comanche south. These in turn had forced the 'Tinde' people into the sterile deserts of the South West where they were re-named the 'Apache', another merciless enemy to the whites. By 1875 the Lakota and their allies, the Cheyennes, had claimed lands that included the Black Hills of present-day South Dakota.

During the second half of the 18th century the Plains Indians tamed the horse, purloined following Indian revolts against Jesuit Missions and Spanish cruelty in the South West, setting herds free to roam. Originally called 'Elk-dogs' and eaten as game, they were initially employed as carriers, then adapted for riding and warfare. Plains Indians have earned the distinction of being included among the finest light cavalry in the world. Veteran cavalry commander G. A. Custer spoke of their 'marvellous abilities as horsemen' and 'one could not but admire the courage they displayed'. A 'warrior would fire and load and fire again as often as he was able to do'. They could hide on the opposite side of the pony at full gallop with only the foot clinging to its back and the Indian's face visible beneath the pony's neck. New army recruits firing on them were completely duped by the Indian's sudden disappearance, assuming he had been hit. Captain Barnitz's view of the mounted war-bands he saw was 'much resembling … squadrons of cavalry', invariably operating with 'admirable order'.[33]

Firearms were acquired from northern Europeans in Canada. Unlike the Spanish in the south, they were prepared to trade guns and ammunition to seemingly peaceful agricultural tribes. The northern tribes exchanged guns for horses with the southern tribes. In a relatively short time the Sioux, who outnumbered all the other tribal groups, came to dominate the Northern Plains, and thought nothing of removing other Indians from their traditional territories by force. Perhaps the irony of the developing situation on the frontier was not lost on Black Hawk, a Lakota warrior, when he said:

> 'These lands once belonged to the Kiowas and the Crows, but we whipped those nations out of them, and in this we did what the white man do when they want the lands of Indians.'[34]

At the centre of the cultural difference with whites was the Indian's naturalistic belief that saw little need to differentiate matter from spirit. Indian decision-making processes and their method of waging war reflected this basic tenet. They lived in an environment dominated by an all-pervading spirit. From early boyhood, aspiring Indian warriors were taught that seeing beyond into the spirit world offered personal power. This moral strength formed the backdrop to the later success of an Indian confederation loosely formed around Sitting Bull during the Sioux War of 1876–77. 'Visions' played an essential role in this, as well as a kinship with nature inexplicable to the white man. Materialism and a desire to dominate and exploit nature for that purpose drove white Calvinist theology, men who lived by the sweat of their brows. An Indian, by contrast, demonstrated the power of his personal spirit in war.

All the tribes were nomadic hunters and their primary staple meat diet was the buffalo, so settlers moving into these hunting grounds sounded the death knell of their nomadic way of life. At the vanguard of white expansion was the frontier army. 'Soldiers cut down my timber,' complained Kiowa chief Santana, 'they kill my buffalo; and when I see that, my heart feels like bursting; I feel sorry.' That the soldiers were profligate in killing buffalo is borne out by Captain Barnitz's tale of a competition among two teams of 7th Cavalry officers at a so-called 'Buffalo Hunters' supper, seeking to discover who could kill the most buffalo in a single day. 'Has the white man become a child that he should recklessly kill and not eat?' asked Santana. 'When the red men slay game they do so that they may live and not starve.' However, the Indian practice of driving herds over a cliff-top was also arguably excessive to their immediate needs. But they did not match the factory production disposal of great buffalo herds by railway construction gangs or white settlers; one particularly bizarre sport was to pot-shot at buffalo from moving trains. Before the coming of the white man it was estimated that 50 million buffalo roamed the North American continent; by 1888 they had been reduced to fewer than 1,000.[35] As warfare was a central part of this nomadic hunting culture, it is easy to understand why the Indian would not readily give up his way of life. Warfare was likewise a central theme of white culture, devastatingly demonstrated in the crucible of the Civil War experience and in the development of the early American states. A clash between these two opposing ways of life was inevitable. 'Kill the Indian, save the man' was a popular saying at the time.[36]

Indian warriors were physically and mentally prepared for war from early boyhood. This provided a depth of training and martial experience totally beyond the capability of white soldiers to oppose at close quarters. The latter were completely reliant upon the technological edge conferred by modern firepower. For Indians, training with the bow, lance and tomahawk – a form of fighting axe – began very early on, with practical hand-to-hand combat skills. Young men from about the age of ten were apprenticed by their fathers for seven years to a hunter-warrior society, or 'street gang' in modern contemporary urban parlance. At the age of 16 or so, when many of his white adversaries may have been farming or newly arrived immigrants, the fledgling Indian warrior would be 'tested' by his warrior society. Success in these rigorous tests of navigation, survival and 'field-craft' would result in admittance to the religious aspect of the group. Death might be preferable to the stigma of failure, as the alternative was to remain with the women, become an artisan, craftsman or, unusually, a medicine man. The significance of this process was that all males were given military training and would as a consequence be able to provide a reserve force should the village be attacked.

An Indian's status was dependent upon his performance in action in hunting and war. Hunting was not dissimilar to warfare and the skills required influenced and permeated Indian tactics, such as separating or cutting out weak elements for destruction from the main force or herd. Native American warfare practices of 'counting coup', which was to demonstrate bravery by merely touching the enemy with a coup stick or stealing his horse, were of more significance than the white soldier's concept of fire discipline, unit manoeuvre or capturing key terrain. Material gain, other than loot, was anathema to the Indian compared to the spiritual gain to be had from individual demonstrations of prowess in war. Bodies were painted and decorated so as to be clearly seen when committing these acts: Crazy Horse, a Sioux war-band leader, painted his body and face with images of lightning and hail, with a red-backed Hawk symbol on his head. There was no fixed Indian chain of command, nor was there any obligation or compunction to follow orders. Chiefs or headmen led by dint of personality.

As the Indian warrior's social position depended almost entirely on his individual warlike actions, he cultivated the trait of aggression. Savage behaviour was an attention-grabbing device, which, used in combination with cultural egocentricity and total insensitivity to persons and property outside the band, became a virtue in a warrior society that lauded and attached status to such power. Mutilating the enemy was not considered cruel, rather an accepted expression of the nomadic warrior culture to which the Lakota Sioux and Cheyenne belonged. Death was the precursor to entry into the spirit world, so incapacitating a foe both in this world and in preparation for the next was a prudent insurance measure. A photograph of Sergeant Frederick Wyllyams, scalped, stripped and mutilated after a skirmish outside Fort Wallace in June 1867, clearly shows extensive slash marks cut deeply into his thighs. The unfortunate 7th Cavalry NCO would have difficulty riding his horse should he seek vengeance in the spirit world. Despite seeming fanatically brave, the Indian would risk his life only when the advantage of numbers or terrain clearly lay with him. He would not necessarily fight a follow-on action nor engage in any activity that might compromise the security or safety of the village.

The village was the most important and vulnerable element of Indian society. The fragile nature of this society and the need to support its population by foraging around the surrounding area as well as the need for sanitation was a constraint on the village's size. Water supply invariably meant location on river lines, but health requirements obliged movement of the whole village every eight to ten days for a distance of about 14 miles, to procure fresh game and pastures for the pony herd. Primary living accommodation was within a tent, or 'tepee', a pyramid-shaped construction of poles covered in animal hides. Each tepee would house about four to ten people. A rough form of measure was to multiply the number of lodges or tepees by four to calculate the likely number of adult warriors. It was the head woman or squaw's job to erect the lodge, which could be set up in 20 minutes. Frequent nomadic practice meant that the village could be prepared for a move in less than one hour. The military significance of this was the difficulty of actually locating villages such as these constantly on the move. Likewise, the village's vital sociological significance as the main unit meant that conventional Civil War tactics of bringing the enemy to battle could work only if the village were threatened. This would also affect the aggressive nature of the Indian response if attacked.

General Sheridan, the commander of the Department of the Missouri, had already recognised the vulnerability of the Indian village in winter. 'Total War' had demonstrably produced strategic success in the Civil War and could now be applied to the Indian. The only problem in the vast area of operations that made up the frontier was where to find the village.

Chapter 3

The war for gold

'One does not sell the earth upon which the people walk.'

Crazy Horse, Sioux Indian Chief

Catch them by spring

The heavily wooded slopes of the Black Hills in the middle of the Great Sioux Reservation produced the distinctive black covering for which they were known. Ever since white expansion had made itself felt on the Northern Plains, the Black Hills were claimed as being the centre of the Sioux universe, a source of psychological strength and reassurance. They belonged to the Indians by treaty and were off limits to whites. Johnson Holy Rock, a contemporary elder in the present Lakota tribe, quoted Red Cloud's view of their significance. 'A man can be skin and bones when he enters the Hills, and when he comes out the next spring he is fat and slick like the buffalo. He says, that is my food source, that is where my people come from.'[1] Nevertheless, the Sioux and Cheyenne had dispossessed other tribes in setting up their new spiritual home.

Gold was discovered in the Black Hills during a rail survey in 1873. 'I get excited when I think about it even now,' admitted Sergeant Windolph of the 7th Cavalry, writing 72 years after the start of the 'Gold Rush'.

'It means fortune and adventure and all the things [you] never had. The gold fever is like taking dope. You're helpless when it strikes you.'[2]

'Yellow dirt' held no significance to the Indian. You cannot eat it or burn it to keep warm in the winter and it has no use as a medicine. Red Cloud had by this time retired to reservation life, resigned to the futility of attempting to take on white urban muscle and the 'ant-like' communities he had observed on the Eastern Seaboard of the United States. His dependants' cultural survival relied, he realised, upon coming to some form of accommodation with the white man. Different leaders from the non-treaty Indian community replaced him at the forefront to provide new inspiration. Sitting Bull began to provide the new focus for leadership. Although previously a warrior of considerable stature, by his early 40s he was a spiritual leader or 'medicine man'. His strict adherence to cultural and spiritual practices included a desire to isolate himself and his followers from white influence. Many Indians chose to depart the Agencies on the Great Sioux Reservation and return to the 'old ways'. Some traded and drew rations from the Agencies in the winter and become 'roamers', hunting with non-treaty bands, in the summer. Warlike Sioux and Cheyenne skirmished with each other, the Crow and Shoshone, and railway surveying expeditions with their army escorts.

In the spring of 1874 General Sheridan, the commander of the Military Division of the Missouri, directed Brigadier General Alfred H. Terry, his subordinate commanding the Department of the Dakota, to send a reconnaissance party into the Black Hills. The mission was to find a suitable location for an army garrison to monitor the Sioux. The Black Hills lay virtually in the centre of the Sioux nation, so even if the expedition was not intended as a show of force, it was certainly perceived as such by the Indians.

Custer led ten companies of the 7th Cavalry, supported by two of infantry and scouts and mineral surveyors, into the thickly forested hills. Nearly 1,000 men and 110 wagons departed Fort Abraham Lincoln on 2 July 1874. It was the first regimental-size deployment since the Washita battle and the second since the unit's inception. The reconnaissance travelled 1,205 miles, indulging in a form of military 'tourism', including hunting and fishing during which the geologists confirmed the presence of gold. 'It was something to stretch out before a big open fire and listen to the music' during evening concerts with an accompanying regimental band, declared Private Windolph. 'Soldiering wasn't half bad those times,' he ruefully reminisced.[3]

The Sioux were less sanguine. The territory belonged to them and the presence of such a substantially armed expedition represented a further example of broken Government promises. They called the expedition route the 'Thieves Trail' and Custer 'The Chief of all Thieves'. 'The white man is in the Black Hills just like maggots,' complained Baptiste Good, 'and I want you to get them out just as quick as you can.'[4] By early 1875 two major mining towns, Deadwood and Custer City, were thriving in hills populated by 15,000 miners; there were 11,000 in Custer alone. By the following year the number was up to 25,000, with Deadwood boasting the largest Chinese community in the United States.[5] No American Government, no matter how progressive, would have been able to stem the 'Gold Rush'. President Ulysses Grant faced a dilemma. He could not stop the civilian invasion of the Black Hills, but it was an illegal occupation. As cavalryman Charles Windolph expressed it:

'All the soldiers in the US couldn't hold back the tide then. You could sign all the Indian treaties you could pack on a mule, but they wouldn't do any good. Men would get through. They'd go after gold in spite of hell and high water.'[6]

Grant's administration was also under public pressure as a consequence of corruption allegations. The Indians were entitled to 'police' their territory and expel 'transgressors'. Inevitably the miners turned to the administration for protection. Government lawyers sought loopholes in the treaty in order to declare it null and void. One option might be to buy the Black Hills. An offer of $400,000 per annum was made for mineral rights or an outright payment of $6 million over 15 annual instalments. This was a derisory sum bearing in mind that a single Black Hills mine yielded more than $500 million in gold. But as one emerging war leader, Crazy Horse, declared, 'One does not sell the earth upon which the people walk.' Sitting Bull was even more uncompromising: 'We want no white men here,' he said. 'The Black Hills belong to me. If the whites try to take them, I will fight.'[7] There was no lease or sale. Rationalising an excuse for war with the Sioux seemed Grant's only course to resolve the matter.

Government lawyers eventually identified a potential loophole. Key to the case was the fact that many non-treaty Indians lived in the 'Unceded Territory'. They were allowed to hunt there, but the United States had utilised the 'unceded' expression in drawing up the original treaty to demonstrate they did not recognise Sioux *ownership*. Indians living in the contested territory were therefore considered as having broken the treaty. Government officials in any case were assuming that the Indians who signed the treaty were 'representative' of all. Actually, many did not feel bound to *any* treaty. Indian culture was the ultimate democracy. They did what they wanted as individuals.

Grant subtly chose not to declare war on the Sioux who remained on the reservations. The target was the 'roamers' on the pretext that they were committing atrocities on settlers beyond Indian borders. Once the Sioux were defeated in war, the Black Hills could be acquired as part of the spoils. Grant ordered the Bureau of Indian Affairs to issue an ultimatum to the Indians to return voluntarily to their reservation by 31 January 1876 or be obliged to by military action. Grant launched his war with neither the consent of nor consultation with Congress. Nobody argued. The seeds for future conflict sown in the Laramie Treaty were about to germinate.

Anticipation of war led the army to consider strengthening the units likely to participate in it. When recruit Nathan Short enlisted in the 7th Cavalry on 9 October 1875 at St Louis, Missouri, he was one of the 22% of troopers in the unit who, in 1876, had less than one year's service. At the age of 21, which was the minimum legal requirement, he was joining a young regiment with an average age of 23 for first and 32 for re-enlistments. Custer, the 'Boy General', was an 'old' man at 36. Short was a labourer on joining, but became the C Company carpenter on being assigned to Captain Tom Custer's command. He too may have been attracted to gold, joining to work his ticket West. He joined about 150 recruits at Jefferson Barracks, St Louis, who were to be transferred to the 7th Cavalry at Fort Abraham Lincoln on the Missouri River as the events leading up to the Sioux War unfolded. He shared the attitudes and concerns of other recruits around him. Private Peter Thompson, who enlisted at Pittsburgh the previous September, would join him in C Company. 'Let me say,' Thompson stated, 'that for a scientific exactness as to the amount of food to sustain life without starvation, Jefferson Barracks was the place.'[8] Recruit depots were notoriously unsupervised by the officers and NCOs in charge, and the quality of life for new entrants improved immeasurably when they arrived at their final company posts. This particular group of recruits was transferred eight months prior to the start of the campaign, spending only six months with the regiment before its departure in May 1876. They were generally poor horsemen and worse shots. No target practice was conducted before setting off on active service. Private William C. Slaper moved with the same group, being assigned to H Company commanded by Captain Thomas H. French. 'Any young man wearing the uniform of a US soldier was looked upon as an idler – too lazy to work,' he cryptically recalled on enlistment. During his six weeks at Jefferson Barracks 'we were instructed in the dismounted drill, and given some preliminary training at stables', but little else. Immediately prior to the forthcoming operation he felt 'only in the "shavetail class", having had no real experience in roughing it, much less of Indian fighting'.[9]

Grant's ultimatum was issued on 6 December 1875 for those still remaining in the Unceded Territory. During the previous month

Inspector E. C. Watkins of the US Indian Bureau completed his investigation of the Black Hills situation, blaming a rebellious faction of Hunkpapa Sioux, Oglala Sioux and Northern Cheyenne as being the nucleus of the problem. The Commissioner of Indian Affairs in Washington was told that this group, spurred on by famine and protesting Indian Agency corruption, had rejected the reservation and intended to live in their 'homelands'. Two categories of nomads ignored the ultimatum. The first were 'winter roamers', who spurned any white sustenance and preferred to live in the unceded area, while the second, the 'summer roamers', took the white man's dole in winter, but returned to their hunting grounds in warmer weather. The Indians were unimpressed with the Washington ultimatum, feeling relatively secure and beyond the reach of the authorities. It was an irrelevance to the winter roamers, who had no intention of committing cultural suicide within the repellent confines of the reservation in winter. In any case, atrocious winter conditions in 1875 meant that few non-Agency villages could physically attempt the laborious journey with families to return to their reservations by the deadline, which, although announced in the press, would not be read by Indians.

General Sheridan initially believed that he would only have to fight the winter migrants. The imperative, therefore, would be to conclude the campaign before the onset of spring and its influx of greater numbers of summer roamers. The future campaign was also based upon certain fundamental assumptions that the frontier army held about Indians: that they would not stand and fight against organised US forces; that, no matter the numbers, they would run; that they would offer battle only if soldiers threatened their villages; and that the time to strike the Indian was when he was at his weakest, in the winter, as their fragile societies were totally engrossed in the business of survival. Private Edward H. Pickard, one of the enlistees recruited the month before Nathan Short in September 1875, recalled 'stories about Indian fighting' while waiting at Fort Abraham Lincoln during the 'intensely cold winter' before the campaign:

'The old timers said that about all there was to it was to surprise an Indian village, charge through it, shooting the Indians as they ran, and then divide the buffalo robes and beaded moccasins before burning the lodges and destroying the supplies.'[10]

The army assessment was that this would be little more than 'policing', or in modern parlance a peace-keeping PSO operation. The problem lay in the execution. How, with such limited assets, was it to be achieved across the 10,000 square miles requiring coverage? Communications were rudimentary and G2 Intelligence (in modern military parlance) was dependent upon individual horse-riding civilian scouts. Their nomadic quarry would be difficult to find and 'fix' because they would seek to disperse before they could be surrounded.

In late 1873 the authorised strength of the US Army was 25,000 men. It was structured within 10 regiments of cavalry (8,450 men), 25 of infantry (12,085 men), 60 artillery batteries (2,600 men organised into five regiments), and logistic, engineer and other supporting elements (1,865 men). Regiments, however, were not up to established strength, leaving only about 20,000 men available for combat. General Sheridan's Division of the Missouri commanded the greater part of this army, consisting of 16,000 officers and men. He had eight of the cavalry and 20 of the infantry regiments and one battery of artillery. These troops were also partly committed to protecting the Canadian and Mexican borders as well as stationing troops in the former Confederacy to collect federal taxes. Two of the eight cavalry regiments were operationally deployed keeping the lid on the Southern Plains Indians, and two others in Texas, controlling Indians and the national border. A fifth was in Colorado, which left only three, with nine regiments of infantry, on the periphery of the Sioux reservation and the Unceded Territory. Sheridan's overall area of responsibility covered one million square miles, within which lived 175,000 Indians who might field 40,000 warriors.

When Sheridan received a copy of the Department of the Interior's order that Indians not residing within the bounds of the reservation would be deemed hostile after 31 January 1876, the three relevant of the five Departments were notified that action was pending. Brigadier Alfred H. Terry's Department of the Dakota, responsible for the northern region (now part of Montana and North and South Dakota), had his headquarters in St Paul, Minnesota. Under his command was one regiment of cavalry (the 7th under Custer), another four-company battalion of the 2nd Cavalry under Major James S. Brisbin, and five regiments of infantry. To the south was the Department of the Platte, commanded by Brigadier General George Crook and overseeing Wyoming and Nebraska, the other half of the potentially hostile region. His Omaha headquarters commanded the remainder of the 2nd Cavalry, 3rd Cavalry and four regiments of infantry. Further south was the Department of the Missouri, with three regiments of cavalry under Brigadier General John Pope, who could, if required, feed reserves to Crook.

It was envisaged that the Departments of the Dakota and Platte would field the main forces for this campaign. The former could deploy 13 companies of cavalry and 50 of infantry, amounting to 3,647 officers and men, while the latter had 20 cavalry companies and 40 infantry – 3,537 men. This force, however, was widely dispersed protecting settlements and Indian Agencies. Of the 33 cavalry companies available to the two Departments, 22 were stationed at five forts while the rest were penny-packaged across nine other posts, which might be shared with infantry and could include field guns. At the lower command level, five companies of the 7th Cavalry, for example, were stationed at Fort Abraham Lincoln, two at Fort Totten and two at Fort Rice. Three remaining companies seconded to the Department of the Gulf on duty in the former Confederacy were re-roled in time for the campaign.[11] The proposed force contingents had rarely trained or operated together.

Although the probability of war with the Sioux had been envisaged for some time, the army, over-tasked and constrained by resources, was unable to strategically re-deploy to meet likely camp-aign commitments. The force was not concentrated but widely dispersed and tied to garrison duties. There were insufficient large forts or posts near the envisaged area of operations. Any offensive action would have to be launched hundreds of miles beyond existing supply bases. Only 2,100 cavalry, the primary offensive arm, were available to search for their quarry in a wild and unmapped region of some 90,000 square miles with few roads and no rail transport. The nearest Union Pacific railhead was south of the Powder River Country and the Northern Pacific terminal was at Bismarck in Dakota, 250 miles from the likely area of operations in the Yellowstone region. What was to be attempted was the proverbial search for the needle in the haystack.

Intelligence on the Sioux was meagre. In 1875 there were about 50,000 Sioux Indians, of which non-reservation Indians numbered about 3,000, including 1,000 warriors. Summer roamer reinforcements might raise this total to 10,000. This haphazard nomadic wandering was unmonitored apart from the army's aware-ness of a spring migration, and neither could Interior Department agencies restrict any movement. There was consensus among army planners that the hostiles should be gathered up in the winter, when they were at their most vulnerable. A report by the Indian Bureau's Inspector E. C. Watkins dated 9 November 1875 illustrated just how easy the forthcoming operation was anticipated to be:

> 'These Indians [the hostiles] number, all told, but a few hundred men and these are never all together or under the control of one chief. In my judgement, one thousand men, under command of an experienced officer, sent into their country in winter ... would be amply sufficient.'[12]

Brigadier General Terry, believing that Sitting Bull was encamped near the mouth of the Little Missouri for the winter, felt that 'it will be possible in ordinary winter weather to reach their camp by a rapid march from Fort Abraham Lincoln'. Some skirmishing would doubtless result, but the army view was that this would essentially be a refugee-gathering operation. 'For such an operation,' Terry continued, 'there are available five well-mounted companies at Lincoln and two at Fort Rice, a force which I think would be sufficient.' Only temporary concentrations would be required to nip this campaign in the bud. The decision to mount an offensive in the winter was correct, but the dispersed nature of the forces available and supply issues would inevitably mean a late winter start, or at worst case in the spring. General Sheridan, in overall command, was fully aware of the worst-case outcome and was voicing some frustration and anxiety at the tardy pace of planning. 'I fully comprehend the difficulties of the country inhabited by these hostile bands,' he admitted to the Commissioner of Indian affairs on 4 February, 'and unless they are caught by spring, they cannot be caught at all.'[13]

First blow – debacle on the Powder River

Sheridan's dilemma was how to bring his dispersed forces to bear on an objective yet to be identified. The communicated intent to his Department commanders, Terry on the Dakota and Crook commanding the Platte, was simply to take advantage of the winter conditions and find and defeat the Indians. Little attention was devoted to developing a campaign plan. No overall commander was nominated between co-equal Department commanders, nor coordinating instructions issued. Sheridan's subsequent annual report reflected this apparent contempt for Sioux fighting capabilities. The coming operation was a generalised 'search and destroy' concept conducted loosely within a framework that granted freedom of action to commanders to operate virtually at will.

'General Terry was further informed that the operation of himself and General Crook would be made without concert, as the Indian villages are moveable and no objective point could be fixed upon, but that, if they should come to any understanding about concerted movements, there would be no objection at division headquarters.'[14]

The army was neither trained nor configured for the *gendarmerie* operation about to take place. It intended to 'police' the territories but employ standard conventional Civil War tactics to do so. Negotiation would not be sought with the 'hostiles' with opportunities to comply. Rather, offensive raids would intimidate the compliance sought.

Brigadier General George Crook had mastered the art of moving light mobile forces supported by pack trains against tribes in the South West, where he had established a proven Indian fighting track record; recent promotion to the Department of the Platte offered an opportunity to demonstrate similar capabilities against the Northern Plains tribes, and he did not seek to act in concert with the other Departments. After secretly gathering units from scattered Department outposts, he was the first to take the field. On 1 March 1876 he departed from Fort Fetterman near Douglas, Wyoming, with two infantry companies and ten companies of cavalry from the 2nd and 3rd Regiments. Sixty-two civilian packers drove his efficient pack train contingent of 400 mules, subdivided into 80-strong groups. Each group was assigned to five (two-company strong) cavalry battalions.

Colonel Joseph J. Reynolds was nominally in command of this column of 883 men as it moved through a crystal clear and bitterly cold winter landscape. Reynolds was aged 55 and could boast an earlier distinguished career. However, unlike the 46-year-old Crook, he was not a man of vigorous health and iron will. At his retirement board the following year he was to refer to himself as 'an old man'. Throughout the campaign he was obliged to wear a truss because of a rupture, and hydrocele (the adhesion of the testicles to the scrotum), seriously impeding his ability to ride comfortably. Moreover, he was toothless: 'My teeth are all artificial,' he complained, 'causing great inconvenience and suffering in the field.'[15] Crook retained practical control while Reynolds was virtually a supernumerary.

Trouble for the column began almost immediately. Indians dogged their progress and managed to stampede the livestock herd on the second day, depriving the troops of their only source of fresh meat. Three days later the Indians boldly raided the column's camp. Under the watchful eye of hostile Indians the expedition pressed on in the teeth of an even more persistent foe, the atrocious weather. Day after day snow fell and temperatures plummeted. Crook skilfully broke contact with the enemy shadow by counter-marching his infantry seemingly homeward towards the abandoned Fort Reno on 7 March. The cavalry alone resumed the northward march, stripped to a minimum subsistence supply level of 15 days. The ruse worked.

On 16 March Crook's chief of scouts, Frank Grouard, suggested changing the focus of the search from the Tongue River to the Powder River valley. To achieve this the ten companies were subdivided into a six-company strike element under Reynolds, with Crook retaining a reserve of four. The strike force was ordered to follow an Indian trail that Grouard suspected would take them to a village. Crook arranged to rendezvous with Reynolds at Lodgepole Creek the following day. Meanwhile, his chief scout, demonstrating remarkable tracking skills, guided Reynolds's command through the teeth of a blinding blizzard to the vicinity of a Cheyenne village. It appeared that Crook's column would indeed strike the first blow of the campaign.

Reynolds organised his force into three two-company cavalry battalions. They were E and M Companies of the 3rd Cavalry under Captain Anson Mills, I and K of the 2nd under Captain Henry E. Noyes, and E Company of the 2nd with F of the 3rd Cavalry commanded by Captain Alexander Moore. These units laboriously edged their way forward in column through driving snow towards the village. They had to wait motionless in the bitter cold at about 0230 hours, enduring temperatures of -30 degrees, while Grouard groped about trying to locate the village. Some 80 to 100 lodges were eventually discovered in a forested area west of a bend in the Powder River, sheltering between the high ground that bordered to the north and west. Reynolds issued less than precise orders for the attack. His concept broadly utilised Civil War 'hammer and anvil' tactics: the 'hammer' was a southern assault by Noyes's battalion, of which Egan's company would rush the village while the other, under the commander, was to stampede the pony herd. Moore's two companies would dismount and occupy the bluffs overlooking the west side of the village, forming the 'anvil' and providing supporting fire to shoot-in Egan's assault. Mills's battalion, the third element, received no mission other than to assist Moore on the high ground. Only one-third of Reynolds's fighting power was therefore actually committed to physically assaulting the village. As Egan initiated the attack at 0330, Moore was not in position on the bluffs.

There was panic in the camp. An 18-year-old Northern Cheyenne warrior, Wooden Leg, heard the shout 'The soldiers are right here! The soldiers are right here!' Egan's soldiers had already infiltrated between the pony herd and camp when the shooting began. 'Women screamed,' recalled Wooden Leg. 'Children cried for their mothers. Old people tottered and hobbled away to get out of the reach of the bullets singing among the lodges.'[16]

Forty-seven troopers with Egan's company, according to news reporter Robert Strahorn who was riding with them, 'bounded into the village with the speed and force of a hurricane'. At first the operation went well: 'With the savages swarming out of their tepees and scattering almost under our feet, we fired right and left at their retreating forms.'[17] As Moore was not in position, the Indians fled to the bluffs overlooking the action. He was too far away to interdict any retreating Indians and compounded his mistake by engaging some of their own troops in the village. Noyes had successfully driven off the pony herd, but then paused in the midst of the action to dismount and take coffee, before being recalled to the fight. Eventually Moore's and Mills's battalions belatedly and with no coordination entered the village. Egan's unsupported company was in danger of being cut off early in the assault. Lieutenant John Bourke, Crook's aide-de-camp accompanying Reynolds, observed that 'the Indians, seeing the paucity of our numbers, regained confidence and rushed forward to cut us off'.[18] They were held back by fire. Reynolds meanwhile became increasingly anxious about the safety and protection of his command, and instead of consolidating his position in the village, he peremptorily ordered its destruction, despite the need to salvage clothing and provisions vital to Crook's starved column. Some Indian property was destroyed, but the sudden withdrawal order left much overlooked. Reynolds's leadership was not held in high esteem by his discontented command: they had scant confidence in his tactical abilities and even less for his physical and moral courage. The attack was developing into a debacle. 'It seemed to one there must be a mistake,' Lieutenant John Bourke subsequently testified. 'There was no reason to fall back. It seemed to me the action had not commenced, and I was astonished.'[19]

The Indian population of the camp during the attack was about 450 people, including 150 to 225 warriors. Reynolds's force of 374 conducted a hasty evacuation under fire from the now increasingly confident and thoroughly antagonised Indians firing down from the bluffs. Dead cavalrymen, and allegedly some wounded, were left behind. Two enlisted men were with Private L. E. Ayers, disabled by a gunshot wound to the leg: 'We had to save ourselves,' one later said, when the Indians approached. Ayers was abandoned fully conscious. 'I think he said "For God's sake don't leave me!"' the trooper recalled. Looking back they saw a dozen Indians slowly encircling the fallen man.[20]

It got worse. During Reynolds's return march the Indians recaptured most of the pony herd. Beaten and ashamed, the humiliated strike force rejoined Crook at the mouth of Lodgepole Creek. Sixty-six troopers suffered various degrees of frostbite, having abandoned their greatcoats, cached prior to the assault. Twenty-six days after a departure marked with high expectations, Crook's entire force returned to Fort Fetterman, weary, defeated and dejected. Reynolds had snatched defeat from the jaws of victory at a cost of four killed and six wounded troopers. Bitter recriminations and three courts-martial followed. Custer, bogged down in Washington as a witness to a corruption scandal seriously embarrassing to President Grant, laconically observed, 'Crook's expedition is generally regarded as a failure.'[21]

Sheridan's original intention was for the various Departments to gather their scattered detachments, follow the Yellowstone River and converge. Geographical location would dictate that, despite separate operational plans, Crook would logically move north from Fort Fetterman in the south, while Terry would travel west from Fort Abraham Lincoln in the east. No pincer movement was, however, clarified in any set of orders at this stage. On 17 March Colonel John Gibbon's smaller Montana column set off westward from Fort Ellis following the line of the Yellowstone River. News of the Reynolds fiasco resulted in this small column being stalled on the defensive in mid-April, to await the arrival of the other Department contingents. The 31 January order had delayed the campaign launch until the worst of the winter weather had burst on the Northern Plains. Forward supply bases were not in place and commanders had misappreciated the *gendarmerie* nature of the operation placed upon them. The winter offensive had clearly failed.

Unbeknown to the army, the impact of the Powder River raid had a significant effect upon the Indian. Wooden Leg, the young Northern Cheyenne warrior, had witnessed the destruction of his village. 'Our tepees were burned,' he said, 'with everything in them except what the soldiers may have taken.' The outcome was nothing less than an unmitigated disaster for his fragile community. 'I had nothing left but the clothing I had on … everything else of mine were gone.'[22] If there had ever been any doubt that the Cheyenne should ally themselves with the Sioux, it was dispelled now. The Washington ultimatum and the attack on the village in mid-winter clearly indicated that the Indians were marked for extermination and their land destined for seizure. The dilemma for the Indians, used only to thinking and operating as individuals, was how to bring their strength and power together. They tended to act only when the threat was overwhelming, and this now appeared to be the case. Kate Bighead, another Northern Cheyenne, had already observed, ominously, prior to the ultimatum that:

'Word was sent to the hunting Indians that all Cheyennes and Sioux must stay on their reservations in Dakota. But all who stayed on the reservation had their guns and ponies taken from them, so the hunters quit going there.'

Self-preservation suggested an imperative to combine. Crazy Horse's Oglala Sioux village took in survivors from the Cheyenne Powder River camp after a distressing three-day struggle through snow. One of the refugees, Kate Bighead, said:

'The Oglalas gave us food and shelter. After a few days the two bands together went northward and found the Hunkpapa Sioux, where Sitting Bull was the chief. The chiefs of the three bands decided that all of us would travel together for the spring and summer hunting, as it was said that many soldiers would be coming to try to make us go back to the reservations.'[23]

Two hundred virtually naked braves encumbered by women and children and surprised in the dead of winter had driven off an attacking force of 375 soldiers. The determination of 'Lo' and his aroused passion to save his home and family was not matched by cavalry resolve to move in at close quarters and kill. Indeed, the cavalry had abandoned their dead and wounded in the sacked village. These warriors had not rated highly the army's fighting prowess, and had also recaptured their pony herd. Even the Crow, an acknowledged enemy of the Sioux, shared this sentiment. When White Mouth, a Crow leader, negotiated the employment of Indian army scouts with General Gibbon, he pointed out that 'you have already been down below ... and you turned back after a while without doing anything'. The Indians questioned Gibbon's resolve because he had paused following Reynolds's defeat. 'We are afraid that you will do it again,' accused White Mouth. Another Crow band-leader was similarly reluctant to expose his young men as army scouts, saying:

> 'If you go and find the Sioux and don't want to fight and tie the young men down, they would cry and break loose and go straight and get killed – and that would be bad. You had better go alone.'[24]

Sheridan had already observed the problem of catching hostiles in the spring and summer if they were missed in the winter. No lessons were learned from the debacle. Failure was personalised. Fetterman's command was massacred as a result of his recklessness; Reynolds and his commanders were castigated for incompetence. Nobody saw the obvious point that a rapid Indian recovery from surprise and their immediate aggressive response, despite the odds, was a factor of their fighting capability, especially if the village was under threat. The enemy was now thoroughly alerted and aroused. Ted Rising Sun of the present Cheyenne remembers:

> 'According to the stories that my Grandfather told, they say it was the time when "the People", meaning the Sioux, the Cheyenne, the Arapaho, all came together.'[25]

All Indians, despite their propensity to act as individuals, saw a need to combine in the face of the approaching threat. They were confident in their ability as warriors to contest the white soldiers. Unlike Red Cloud, who opted not to join, they had no conception of the industrial power base and population the white soldiers could call upon if required. They had finally realised, now it was too late, that it was 'win or lose' the employment of army Crow scouts. Conflict was inevitable.

They would fight.

Chapter 4
'Find and fix' – converging columns

'He was too hard on the men and horses.
He changed his mind too often. He was always
right. He never conferred enough with his officers.
When he got a notion, we had to go.'

7th Cavalry trooper's view of Custer

Where are the Indians?

Twenty-eight-year-old Corporal Thomas Eagon of E Company, 7th Cavalry, wrote to his sister 'that I will soon be on the move again' for the Bighorn country.

'The Indians are getting bad again. I think that we will have some hard times this summer. The old chief Sitting Bull says that he will not make peace with the whites as long as he has a man to fight.'

Eagon promised to write again as soon as he returned from the operation, 'that is if I do not get my hair lifted by some Indian'.[1] The letter was destined never to be written.

General Terry was meanwhile concentrating on planning for the forthcoming spring or summer campaign. Crook's failure at the Powder River facilitated the urgent reinforcement of the 7th Cavalry from its present nine companies to the 12 that Terry had requested, together with additional recruits. By April the entire regiment, with 28 officers and 700 men, was concentrated at Fort Abraham Lincoln. Corporal Windolph of H Company arrived from New Orleans and declared, 'You could hear more wild rumours than a dog has fleas.' It became apparent that they were to form part of a 'big expedition up the Yellowstone to round up the hostiles and drive them back to their reservations'. There were few illusions about what this would exactly mean. 'If they would not go peacefully,' Windolph explained, 'we would make good Indians out of them'[2] – 'good Indians' invariably meant dead ones. Anti-Indian sentiment was universal throughout the 7th and the frontier army. Private Peter Thompson of C Company felt that 'the Indians were more numerous than was consistent with their life and happiness'.[3] Another soldier, Private William Taylor, remembered an officer referring to the friendly Rees scouts accompanying the 7th Cavalry as looking like 'antiquated Negro washer women'.[4] 'Lo', the Indian, was a figure of awe and dread if met at close quarters, but regarded contemptuously if kept at a distance through the technical edge conferred by disciplined firepower. 'Never trust an Indian unless he was dead' was Thompson's maxim, decrying the Quaker image of the 'noble red man'. 'Those who have come into close contact with him' would know better and 'have found him to be a brute in human form'.[5]

Custer was absent on the eve of the 1876 campaign having had to testify during the winter to a Congressional investigation, the Belknap case. 'Of course that aroused a lot of talk and suspicion,' observed Corporal Windolph when he arrived at Fort Lincoln, alarmed that the commander was not there. Custer's indictment of Belknap, a friend of Grant and cabinet appointee, as being corrupt and dishonest was seriously embarrassing to the President. He regarded it as an attack upon himself by a subordinate. Grant virtually relieved Custer of his command, and intervention was required by Generals Sherman and Sheridan to secure him a place on the operation, but only as the commander of the 7th Cavalry. General Terry, who had also interceded for Custer's inclusion, was to command the Dakota column. Private Peter Thompson remarked that the news 'that General Custer was under arrest' was to cause 'a great commotion among the soldiers', and 'our company was made happy by the return of Custer to his command'. He threw himself into preparation for the coming operation. Windolph remembered that the reinstated 'Custer was as happy as a boy with a new red sled. He put a lot of zip into us.' He had one week to put his final stamp on the regiment before it would depart.[6]

Colonel John Gibbon's column from Fort Shaw was the next into the field, moving off into a winter wasteland at the end of March. It was an inauspicious start preceded by casualties from snow blindness and a number of desertions. Gibbon gathered his widely separated units at Fort Ellis and set off at the beginning of April with four companies of the 2nd Cavalry Regiment and five companies from the 7th Infantry Regiment. His column of 450 men and 36 wagons was infantry-strong (233 to 195 cavalry) and supported by two .50 Gatlings and one Napoleon artillery piece. The addition of Crow scouts and 25 other non-combatants raised his force to 475 officers and men.[7] He began marching east down the Yellowstone River.

Inclement weather considerably delayed the departure of General Terry's column into the field. At last, on 17 May, 12 companies of the 7th Cavalry under Custer and three and a half companies of infantry from the 6th and 17th Regiments left Fort Abraham Lincoln. There was a battery of three Gatling guns and 40 Arikara scouts in support. The enormous force train of 150 wagons was serviced by 200 civilian employees and included 250 pack mules. Fodder had to be carried for a total of nearly 1,700 animals. The total strength of the column has been calculated between 1,030 and 1,140 men, of whom 925 were soldiers, the rest scouts and civilian helpers.[8]

Two days prior to departure, Terry shared his estimate of Indian strength with Sheridan, derived from scouts as 'fifteen hundred lodges' and they 'are confident and intend to make a stand'.[9] As each lodge was assumed to support two to three warriors, this indicated that Terry anticipated encountering between 3,000 and

4,500 braves. Meanwhile, Crook, assembling his second expedition, wired Sheridan about his concern that considerable migrations of warriors were 'going north from the [Red Cloud] agency'. He voiced his frustration that nothing could be done to stop them and that 'indications are that we shall have the whole Sioux nation to contend with'. An Agency report on 7 June 'thought that from fifteen hundred to two thousand Indians have left the reservations since 10th May [and] a large proportion of those who have are warriors'.[10] These reports were even echoed by the popular press. The *Cheyenne Daily Leader* of 2 June reported that 'there are very few able-bodied warriors left at the Agencies'. Sitting Bull was reported 'somewhere near the mouth of the Powder River' and five days later to be amassing 'the great northern force to at least 2,000 young braves'.[11] Whatever the accuracy of the intelligence, it was clear that Terry and Crook knew that their adversary was numerous and likely to be belligerent. They remained relatively complacent, anticipating that the Indian burden of non-combatants and the lack of unified command would grant an unassailable advantage. Resource pressures and the availability of game and pasture should keep the enemy sufficiently dispersed to enable them to be gathered up or intimidated piece-meal into compliance.

General Terry ordered his column to parade around the fort in a demonstration of strength to allay family fears of heavy fighting in the weeks ahead. 'That morning it was foggy and dull,' recalled Corporal Windolph, 'and nobody was in a very good humor.'[12] The band struck up 'Gary Owen', the 7th Cavalry marching song, as the troops clattered and jangled by, company guidons flying, in column of fours, led by about 65 Indian scouts. 'The wives and children of the soldiers lined the road,' wrote Libby Custer, permitted to accompany her husband on the first day.

> 'Mothers, with streaming eyes, held their little ones out at arm's length for one last look at the departing fathers. The toddlers had made a mimic column of their own... They were

fortunately too young to realise why the mothers wailed out their farewells. Unfettered by conventional restrictions, and indifferent to the opinion of others, the grief of these women was audible.'[13]

Although the regiment anticipated a fight, it was confident; the general expectation for the campaign's duration was about six weeks. Apart from the wounded, no part of the 7th Cavalry was to appear for four months. Nevertheless, newly joined 'kid' soldier William C. Slaper in M Company believed that the 7th Cavalry 'was said to be the best equipped regiment as to horses, men and accoutrements, that Uncle Sam had ever turned out'.[14] No combined American expeditionary force approaching this size had embarked on operations since the Civil War. Casualties there may be, but success was certain. When the band struck up 'The Girl I Left Behind Me', pageantry and emotion came to the fore. The 'sad faced wives of the officers who had forced to their doors to try to wave a courageous farewell and smile bravely … now gave up the struggle at the sound of the music'.[15] They disappeared indoors to vent their grief privately. Corporal Charles Windolph felt his heart lift:

'You felt you were somebody when you were on a good horse, with a carbine dangling from its small leather ring socket … a Colt army revolver strapped on your hip; and a hundred rounds of ammunition in your web belt and in your saddle pockets. You were a cavalryman of the Seventh Regiment. You were part of a proud outfit that had a fighting reputation, and you were ready for a fight or a frolic.'[16]

'Spite our trying to seem pert and gay we was down hearted,' said Custer's orderly, John Burkman. 'I'd seen the General sayin' goodbye to the hounds early in mornin' and made me know things was serious 'cause usually he'd been takin' them with us on expeditions – into hostile country.'[17]

Libby Custer's description of the departure was filled with the same idealistic images that were to typify later John Ford epic western movies:

'As the sun broke through the mist a mirage appeared, which took up about half of the line of cavalry, and thenceforth for a little distance it marched, equally plain to the sight on the earth and in the sky.'[18]

No other witness appears to have observed this phenomenon, which may well have assumed its Olympian mantle with the benefit of painful hindsight. Burkman's grainy view of the final departure may also have been influenced by subsequent events:

'I reckon no living man of the Seventh can ever furgit how the leetle fort looked as we marched away from it, so lonesome and quiet, the mornin' sun shinin' over everything, the flag flutterin' high up on its pole, the women and children standin' thar, wavin' their handkerchiefs and cryin', squaws down in the Indian village wailin' and beatin' tomtoms.'[19]

Trumpeter Sergeant Henry Dose was later to write to his wife three weeks into the expedition with the universal family man's view of the coming fight. 'I wish for mine part,' he wrote, 'we would meet him [Sitting Bull] tomorrow.' 'Sergeant Botzer and me came to the conclusion, it is better anyhow to be home baking flapjacks. When we get home we will pay up for this and bake flapjacks all the time.'[20] Both were to be killed on the first day at the Little Bighorn.

Custer, by contrast, was not at all downcast. Mark Kellogg, the *Bismarck Tribune* correspondent with Terry's column, saw him 'prominent everywhere. Here, there, flitting to and fro, in his quick eager way, taking in everything connected with his command, as well as generally, with the keen, incisive manner for which he is so well known. The General is full of perfect readiness for a fray with the hostile red devils.'[21] As well he might. Nepotism in the form of Sherman and Sheridan's support had saved him from Grant's censorious displeasure, as also had intervention from Terry. After the debacle of the Powder River, his reputation for producing results was as important to them as it was to him to restore his career profile. He had been a Lieutenant Colonel for 11 long years since the end of the Civil War. At the age of 37, this might be his last chance for advancement.

As the Dakota column under General Terry wound its laborious 2-mile length through heavy mist and wet weather on 17 May, the paramount question was 'Where are the hostiles?' Recent information suggested that Sitting Bull's force of some 1,500 lodges supporting 3,000 warriors lay 150 miles' march to the west along the Little Missouri River. Hours before the column's departure, Lieutenant James Bradley, Gibbon's chief of scouts, more than 300 miles away, had already found them. 'It was two months to a day since we had left Fort Shaw for the purpose of cleaning out the Sioux nation,' the excited young officer was later to write. 'During all that time we had done nothing but march; march, and rest in camp; but now the enemy had been found and we were going over to whip them.'

At about 1600 the previous day his small reconnaissance group including Crow scouts had observed the telltale signs of a large village from the summit of a ridge overlooking a basin-like depression alongside the Tongue River. 'Up and down the stream the smoke was rising in different columns and uniting in a cloud which hung low over the valley.' The Crows estimated 'not less than two or three hundred lodges'. Bradley was convinced that 'we had struck a village of several hundred lodges', which 'afterward turned out ... contained about four hundred lodges, or from eight hundred to a thousand warriors'. Gibbon's column had located the strategic objective for the entire campaign as the remaining two columns under Terry and Crook were entering the field.

Gibbon's force had been hesitantly inching its way eastward along the Yellowstone River, displaying neither aggression nor resolve to close with the enemy. It was less than half the size of both the Crook and Terry contingents and clearly its commander, with an infantry-strong force, was looking for their support. Nevertheless, Gibbon decided to move on the village. Bradley, having created the opportunity, was enthused. 'The accumulated satisfaction of the sixty blessed days that had preceded, if combined in a single lump, could not have equalled that with which this order was received.' There were risks, however. It was a large enemy force and the Yellowstone, which would have to be crossed, was a torrent. But 'the great majority', according to Bradley, 'were hopeful, jubilant and full of the fire of battle'.

A debacle followed. Gibbon's night-time cavalry crossing of the Yellowstone in order to close with the village achieved little more than drown four horses. Only 40 horses were ferried across in four hours. The mishap 'proved to be the last straw that broke the back of our warlike enterprise,' Bradley ruefully admitted. Recriminations emerged within the force. Crow scouts branded the failed enterprise as cowardly. 'We failed to march against the foe,' Bradley observed, and 'there would ever be a difference of opinion as to the propriety of the course pursued,' but he stopped short of openly criticising his commander.[22] Gibbon had most likely assessed that his force of 450 men was not equal to the task. Inexplicably in the professional sense, but understandably in human terms, he failed to pass this vital strategic information to Sheridan.

On the morning of 18 May Custer said farewell to his wife Libby as Terry's column departed from Sweet Briar Creek. It was a poignant moment. 'Even now after all these years, it brings a lump to my throat, rememberin' how she clung to Custer at the last,' recalled John Burkman, his orderly, 'her arms tight 'round his neck, and she cried.' It was a delayed soldier's farewell.

'She want one to take on unusually but seemed like she jist couldn't go back and leave him that day. Thar was tears in his eyes too and he kept tellin' her she was a soldier's wife, she must be a brave little woman, soon he'd be back and then we'd all have good times at Fort Lincoln again.'

Mutual regard and affection between the Custers is a feature of all their correspondence. Although there were no children, they were clearly very much in love. The farewell represented the departure of a virtual Custer dynasty. Custer's younger brother Tom was a company commander, doubling as aide to the commander, while Boston, his even younger brother, was riding alongside as a civilian employee. Another company commander, Lieutenant James Calhoun, was married to Custer's sister, and Captain Myles Moylan had married Calhoun's sister. 'We stood watching [Libby Custer] ride across the praries, the General and me,' said Burkman. 'With her head bent and we knowed she was cryin'. We watched till she was jist a speck way off on the Plains.' Custer, white and sober, remarked to his orderly, 'A good soldier,' he said, low and quiet, 'has to serve two mistresses. Whilst he's loyal to one the other must suffer.'[23]

Converging columns

The largest and third column to take to the field was that of General Crook, which departed from Fort Fetterman 12 days later on 29 May. The force included 15 companies of the 2nd and 3rd Cavalry Regiments and five companies of infantry, and was later joined by 260 Crow and Shoshone scouts, additional teamsters and a contingent of miners, totalling eventually 1,350 effectives. Crook immediately struck north-west toward the Powder and Rosebud rivers. Like Custer, he was a man in a hurry. The debacle on the Powder River followed by humiliating courts martial had not been the most auspicious start to this enterprise. His reputation was at stake and would be restored.

General Sheridan's inability to profit from Gibbon's intelligence was indicative of the disjointed nature of the planning for the coming campaign. Sheridan had chosen not to establish a forward headquarters, unlike the previous experience of the Washita operation in 1868–69, when he had been at Fort Hays, Kansas. There was no such coordination in 1876. This was the Centennial Celebration year and Sheridan would remain either at St Paul or

Washington, and hopefully be able to capitalise on success in the midst of the national celebration. Despite the analysis available on Indian strengths, some of it potentially sinister, the outcome of this campaign was never in doubt. All the column commanders could boast distinguished Civil War records and were individually regarded as competent commanders in their own right. Sheridan pointed out to Sherman, his commander, that 'I have given no instructions to Generals Crook or Terry, preferring that they should do the best they can under the circumstances.' The concern was not the odds but that the Indians would scatter before they could be brought to battle. Combining columns before their discovery would be premature.

'As hostile Indians in any great numbers, cannot keep the field as a body for a week, or at most ten days, I therefore consider – and so do Terry and Crook – that each column should be able to take care of itself, and to chastise the Indians should it have the opportunity.'

Sheridan's assumptions were the only planning parameters.

'The following will occur: General Terry will drive the Indians towards the Big Horn Valley and General Crook will drive them towards Terry; Colonel Gibbon moving down on the north side of the Yellowstone, to intercept if possible such as may want to go north of the Missouri to Milk River.'[24]

This was a 'big hands small map' approach, relying on the threat of multiple-operating columns to 'force many of the hostile Indians back to the Agencies'. Strategy was based on the fundamental premise that Indians will run rather than fight. It was less a plan than rationalising the independence given to three exclusively acting columns separated by hundreds of miles. The forces were not only uncoordinated, but were also unbalanced in size. Gibbon's most northerly contingent, moving west to east, had already located the objective, but was less than half the size of the other two. It was implicitly demonstrating by its actions that it felt unequal to the task. Its sister and much stronger columns, under Terry approaching from east to west with 300 miles to go, and under Crook, moving north to south with 200 miles to go, were well over one week's march away and had no idea of the whereabouts of the enemy. Considerable physical effort was required even to get to the area of operations, never mind a strategy of combination on arrival. Where should they look on arrival, faced with a multiplicity of river lines covering the few maps as numerous as lines on an old face?

One issue to receive attention after the campaign was whether 'factions' within Custer's 7th Cavalry influenced the eventual outcome of events. There was nepotism and some favouritism. But the bonding that stems from mutually shared privations on campaign transcended emotional or personal differences, common in any army. No issue was important enough to detract from the coming mission. 'Lo', the fearsome Indian, concentrated the mind. He was the problem, not other commanders. Recriminations among the 3rd Cavalry in Crook's column after the painful events on the Powder River had a greater immediacy than any apparent factionalism in Custer's command.

There were, nevertheless, frictions within Custer's command, as in any military unit. Custer was never to instil the same motivation in his western troopers that had inspired his Civil War Michigan volunteers. The context and rewards were totally different. Few laurels had been won on any Indian campaigns. Custer was facing the prospect, after a court martial and blame in a political scandal, of no further advancement. In the West he was not generally liked by the men, who nicknamed him 'hard ass'. 'He was energetic, and it was mighty hard to wear him out,' Corporal Charles Windolph pointed out. Neither did he mix freely with the men. 'Custer struck me as being aloof and removed,' whereas other officers could be 'friendly and easy going with their troopers'.[25] Private Jacob Horner, with K Company, acknowledged that Custer 'was a dare devil, but most of the men didn't like him'.

'He was too hard on the men and horses. He changed his mind too often. He was always right. He never conferred enough with his officers. When he got a notion, we had to go.'[26]

This was the normal private soldier's gripe. 'In those years there was quite a gulf between the officers and the enlisted men,' said Windolph. Enlisted men did what they were told.

Custer's regiment was subdivided into two wings of six companies, under Major Marcus Alfred Reno, his second-in-command, and Captain Frederick William Benteen. Reno, by requesting command of the 7th during Custer's enforced absence at the Belknap case, had not endeared himself to his commanding officer. He was a brevet Brigadier General with a distinguished record during the Civil War – and since – but was unpopular. Although well known within the cavalry corps community, he lacked Custer's luminosity, especially after the premature death of his vivacious wife in 1874. As a consequence he withdrew into military routine and introspection and drank, but no worse than many of his brother officers. He was a proficient horseman and had some low-level Indian fighting experience, having served as a junior officer in the 1st Dragoons prior to the Civil War. Although 'a lot of the troopers didn't care much for Custer,' said Windolph, when it appeared that his second-in-command might take his place, 'most of us didn't know or care about Reno'. Private Thompson's C Company was commanded by Tom Custer, which was why he thought Reno's 'treatment of us was prompted by pure spite'. Whatever the speculation, C Company's verdict 'was that for the Custers, Major Reno had no love'.[27]

Captain Benteen was brevetted Colonel and had been promised brevet Brigadier General after distinguished service, but did not receive it before the war ended. More admired by frontier troopers than Custer, he was a colourful extrovert and an inspiring leader, but pitilessly frank with those he crossed. He was openly critical of Custer's alleged abandonment of Major Elliot's detachment, overrun during the Washita fight in 1868. 'There was a story,' according to Windolph, 'that Custer and Benteen had some hard words over that.' He would have found Custer's remarkable Civil War record uncomfortable. 'Custer's luck' was as legendary as his considerable skill, and Benteen felt that he also had a lot of the latter. Windolph's allegiance was with Benteen, his Company Commander, and the man who was eventually to promote him to Sergeant. 'My Captain, "Colonel Benteen", was one of those who didn't belong to the General's inner circle,' he said.[28]

Three of the 7th Cavalry's officers were related to Custer's family, and 61% of the officers had Civil War experience, including some Custer protégés. Corporal Windolph's assessment was, 'I suppose you could say about half the officers in the regiment were close to Custer, and the rest were not.' This would not be a remarkable statement about any contemporary American regiment commander. Many of the 7th's junior commanders and all seven of its primary staff officers had experienced greater responsibility commanding units of larger scale during the Civil War. All had served longer than five years. As a consequence they were well practised and competent dealing with these lesser western commands, but probably less committed against Indians. 'Lo' was considered a derisory foe compared to the former battle-hardened 'Johnny Reb'. Allegations of a fragmented command with decisions influenced by personal or emotional reasons came after the campaign, fuelled by a multiplicity of Inquiries and publications. Of more significance was the absence of 11 of 41 officers assigned to the 7th Cavalry.[29] When the column departed, one-quarter of its leadership was not available for duty. Sophisticated communications were only beginning to emerge as a key feature of 19th-century warfare. Leaders had to be seen, heard and felt on the frontier battlefield.

The rigours of campaigning were immediately more apparent to the soldiers than to the officers. Private Thompson with C Company had a jaundiced view of officers. 'Although US Army laws may refer to officers as "gentlemen",' he said, 'this was not universally true. You cannot make a gentleman out of a hog whether inside or outside of the United States Army.' Officers had roomy wall-tents and folding cot beds, whereas enlisted men had two-man 'pup' tents, which were shared by three. Private Ewart, who had accompanied the previous Black Hills expedition, described the effect on the men of frequent soakings caused by the early rainstorms:

> 'Even if an officer did get wet he could go into his tent and change for dry underclothing, but a poor unfortunate "Buck Private", unable to boast of such a thing as a dry change, would have to let the heat of his body evaporate in the rain.'

Eighty-five to 110 of the cavalry, notably recruits, had not received their mounts prior to the beginning of the march. They walked in riding boots, totally unsuited for a long march. Both they and the infantry 'poor fellows', as Thompson observed, 'had a hard time of it when the days were hot or when it rained'. The condition of their feet was to render them inoperable when they reached their objective.[30]

Custer may have been demanding, but he was a good cavalry soldier. 'He had a nose for scouting and finding the best trails, all right,' complimented Windolph. Terry, respecting his obvious experience, entrusted Custer with the task of picking out the campsites for the long 300-mile journey. 'He was a good plainsman, right enough,' confirmed Windolph. 'He had an eye for it.'[31] Custer had, after all, been one of the leading cavalry commanders during the Civil War. But ever the impatient, he resented the slow pace dictated by Terry, who was more compassionate to the physical demands on men and horses. He often stayed ahead with the scouts to avoid intimate contact with his commander, sensitive at losing the role of expedition leader. And these responsibilities were daunting. Private William Taylor of A Company recalled the difficulty of moving the supporting cumbersome and large wagon train 'over a trailless and unknown country', which 'was a slow and discouraging task', labouring across an obstacle-strewn terrain. 'Narrow streams had to be bridged, some of them very tortuous and in one case we made ten crossings in eight miles.'[32] Campsites needed to be cleared of rattlesnakes each night. Private Jim Severs of M Company, 7th Cavalry, was nicknamed 'Crazy Jim' for his propensity to prey on these for the cooking pot. Prickly pears and 'cockeburs' provided further irritation for troops and horses alike. Millions of tiny grasshoppers could occasionally rise up like dust from the feet of marching men and animals moving through the prairie grass, causing even more discomfort.

As the column laboriously marched west at an average 15 to 16 miles per day, homesickness and a feeling of isolation became increasingly prevalent. Dr De Wolf, one of the cavalry surgeons with the 7th, wrote 'a very easy march today' of about 10 miles on 26 May, with just two bridges to lay. 'The mosquitoes have bit my hands badly, my face they cannot get at for hair and dirt.' His fellow surgeon colleague Dr Porter offered 'a compliment on my cleanly looks but I suspect ... was fishing for one himself'. Three days later he continued, 'We have been two days coming 13 miles and built 11 or 12 bridges... You can imagine what hard times we are having.' General Terry described the condition of his fellow officers: 'as sun-scorched [a] set you never saw. Colonel Smith is ... red with a sub tint of black and then he has what painters call a "glazing" of dead skin which is flaking off his face in a highly picturesque manner.'[33]

It took 13 days to struggle the 166 miles to the Little Missouri, only to discover that there were no Indians. Terry had been convinced that the hostiles would be in their former favourite wintering ground in the Badlands near the river. Relations between Custer and Terry declined even further, not helped by the realisation that the campaign would last longer than expected. There was likely to be a long way to go. Custer insensitively pushed his independence. Terry's irritation was of a paternal nature. His reprimanded his subordinate for 'ranging' ahead and 'playing wagon-master,' complaining in his journal that Custer occasionally acted 'without any authority'. Custer was able to confirm after a 55-mile scout that no Indians had been around for six months. The decision was made to push further west, but progress was halted by the sudden appearance of snow at the beginning of June.

Gibbon, meanwhile, once again found what they were looking for. Two days before, and 140 miles further west, Lieutenant Bradley rediscovered the huge encampment originally reported on the Tongue River on 16 May. Smoke was picked out, this time in the area of the Rosebud River, 11 days later. Bradley focused his binoculars and 'found ourselves again in the vicinity of an immense Indian Camp'. Once again the ubiquitous Chief of Scouts had pinpointed the campaign objective.

'In numerous places up and down the valley the smoke was rising in columns and blending in a cloud over the camp; the break in the bluffs revealed the tops of several lodges – in a few instances, the entire lodge. The plain above the camp was dotted with hundreds of moving black specks that could only be horses.'

Bradley's first sighting on 16 May had been about 35 miles from Gibbon's command. Now he estimated that they had moved closer. They knew the whereabouts of Gibbon's column, yet had 'moved within easy striking distance'. This made him feel uneasy because it 'seemed to prove they held us in no awe'. Gibbon had received contradictory directions from Terry to join him to engage hostiles reported to be concentrating in large numbers at Glendive Creek. 'It is exceedingly unlikely that such a concentration is taking place,' concluded Bradley, because 'the village opposite us is apparently working the other way, having already crossed from Tongue River to the Rosebud'. These were obviously the same Indians.

Co-ordinating the campaign – General Sheridan's failure

General Sheridan, the campaign commander, loosely co-ordinated the movements of his three columns. This meant that the projected area of operations at the junction of the three commands might encompass several thousand square miles. Communications across this divide were achievable only through dispatch riders.

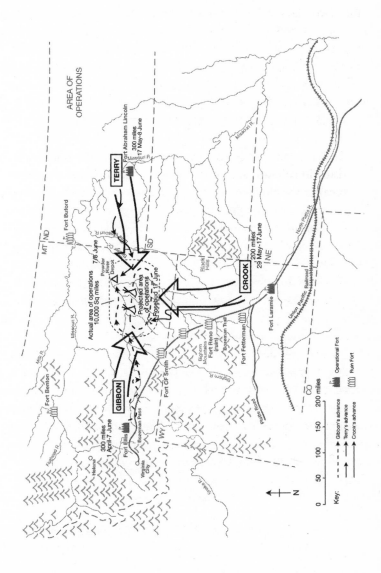

Subsequent reconnaissance was to confirm that the village contained about 400 lodges capable of sustaining a fighting force of between 800 and 1,000 warriors. 'Everybody wondered why we were not ordered over to attack the village,' Bradley wrote in his journal, but diplomatically accepted that 'the General probably had good reasons'. Gibbon's force of 450 would not have been able to muster a strike element exceeding 350. 'It was pretty big odds,' Bradley commented after the event, 'but I imagine the majority of our officers would not have hesitated to give them a trial.' Gibbon's explanation was the order to concentrate at Glendive Creek. No body of troops even the size of Gibbon's column had ever been defeated by Indians. Crook and Terry believed that they could operate with relative impunity and best any musterable hostile force. Gibbon was not a dashing cavalry officer like Custer. He had been Custer's artillery instructor at West Point and was past his prime. He kept his reservations and once again his information to himself. Gibbon's dispatch to Terry on 27 May only vaguely referred to sightings of hostile Indians, and buried Bradley's observations in a sceptical postscript.[34]

Terry's column was marooned in the so-called 'snow camp' on 1 June. Surgeon De Wolf wrote in his diary that the adverse conditions prevented him from reaching camp until 2am. 'It commenced raining at 6 and rained through the night, arose at 3 this morning found it snowing and the ground covered.' It snowed all day and men and livestock suffered intensely. 'The men in their dog tent have it the worse,' De Wolf continued. 'They have been standing around the fire most of the day.' 'Just think of it,' Terry wrote in his journal, 'six inches of snow on 1st June. Water froze in the tents last night.' As an officer he benefited from two tents pitched together.

> 'The front tent is our sitting room, the back tent our bed-room. In the sitting room is the Sibley stove, which just now is roaring away in the most jubilant manner and warming my back beautifully.'

Custer's orderly, Burkman, described a typical scene of glum and shivering troopers tramping around and cursing the snow, trying to keep warm:

'They was tired and wet and cold and hungry. Some of 'em was kneelin' on the ground shelterin' leetle flames with their hats, hopin' to cook bacon and coffee but it was no use. The snow pelted down constant, putin' out the fires. Some of them was munchin' hardtack whilst they cussed.'

Livestock suffered miserably 'hunched up agin' the storm, too plum discouraged to graze, jist standin' thar, heads down droopin'.'[35] Indian Arikara scouts were disturbed by the unseasonal nature of the storm, which appeared to portend some future misfortune.

In the absence of any information from Crook, Terry pushed further west on the basis of Gibbon's incomplete information. Temperatures rose sharply after 3 June, afflicting Terry with light sunstroke. Custer temporarily took command and mercilessly pushed the column 25 miles, double the normal day's march. Foot soldiers dreaded marching under Custer's command. De Wolf wrote that day in his diary: 'Hot as hell in the afternoon all headaches on our arriving in camp.'

Over the next few days the column, meandering like a blue snake, traversed the worst country to date, moving from luxurious grass valleys to arid sagebrush and cactus terrain prolific with rattle-snakes. 'Roads there were none,' Private Thompson complained, 'and where water was found it was very bad on account of the alkelie it contained.'[36] Horses churned up billowing clouds of alkaline dust powder, which stung as it congealed on sweat-covered sunburned faces, choking men and horses as the merciless sun beat down. Mules began to droop and collapse and die from exhaustion.

The further west they marched the more likely they were to be faced with unexpected hostile attacks. Custer's orderly, Burkman, observing the mountains and buttes and coulees around them, felt that 'they was still – too damned still'. They were convinced they were being watched 'whilst we rid along, quiet, no laughin' and shoutin' and singin' of songs'. The tension was palpable. 'We had a feelin' that somethin' more serious than usual was goin' to happen and we was wall anxious fur it to happen quick.'

On 7 June the pace was forced for 32 gruelling miles, bringing them to the final approach to the Powder River, exhausting men and beasts alike. 'Fightin' ain't so hard,' Burkman conjectured. 'You git all excited and kinda like it but jist endurin' this and that, day in day out, mile after mile, seein' horses droppin' in their tracks, petered out, shootin' em and goin' on, that what takes guts.' Many of the horses at the end of that day were too weak to carry their riders and were walked bare-back. One horse that broke its leg scrambling down a steep slope had to be shot. 'The fellow that owned him,' said Burkman, 'broke down and cried like a baby.'[37] General Terry proposed to rendezvous with the paddle-steamer *Far West* at Glendive Creek and liaise with Gibbon. There were cheers when the steamboat was sighted. The Dakota column had travelled 318 miles in 26 days at an average of 12.2 miles per day. But there could be no plan or strategy until the Indians were located – and there was no sign of Crook.

Crook, having overcome poor weather at the beginning of June, was pushing north-westwards along the Bozeman Trail and, unbeknown to the other two columns, was converging on the area of operations from the south. With a more efficiently configured pack train, Crook was moving fast, and deliberately so, because he intended to strike the first blow to avenge the winter's humiliation at the Powder River. However, disappointment awaited him when he arrived at the ruins of Fort Reno. Frank Grouard, his chief scout, had not mustered his Crow warrior scouts in time. Crook pressed on without his Indian contingents but, lacking Grouard's guidance, became lost. Mistaking the headwaters of Prairie Dog Creek for Little Goose Creek, Crook led the column to a campsite 6 miles from where his advance party awaited him. Eventually the column encamped at the confluence of Prairie Dog Creek and the Tongue River and remained there for four days. During this period he was reinforced by a contingent of Black Hills prospectors. On 9 June the Tongue River encampment was raided by Sioux or Cheyenne warriors. These were quickly repulsed by four companies of Crook's cavalry, but gave warning that the Indians were nearby and prepared to fight.

On 11 June Crook led his column 11 miles back up Prairie Dog Creek, then a further 7 miles to the forks of Goose Creek (the present-day Sheridan, Wyoming). A permanent camp was established and three days later Grouard arrived with 261 Shoshone and Crow allies, a welcome and important addition to the expedition. Crook was now ready for offensive operations with a force totalling 1,300, but had yet to identify the location of the Indian village. On 2 June the *Cheyenne Daily Leader* newspaper was claiming under the banner headline 'Its Royal Red-Skinned Highness [Sitting Bull] challenges General Crook' that 'a bold stand will be made by the Sioux, and their whole savage force will be concentrated in the Big Horn Country'. This and its following statement had a ring of disturbing authenticity. 'Should the two northern columns under Generals Terry and Gibbon not arrive at the scene very soon, this command will have its hands very full.'[38] The two columns were within sight of each other, but Crook was 100 miles distant from them.

The columns were hardly converging, but the potential search area had reduced to something like 5,000 square miles, marginally better than the original 'needle in a haystack' configuration. On 16 June Crook was about 22–30 miles from the Sioux camp, Gibbon perhaps 65 to 75 miles distant, and Terry with Custer converging 120 miles away.

Crook was supremely confident and suspected that the Indian village was close by. He would strike first.

Chapter 5
Check on the Rosebud

'Like swarms of blackbirds, there were
so many of them and in such rapid motion.'

Eyewitness account of the Indian assault on
Crook's column at the Rosebud River

'Blind man's buff'

The Indian camp had moved west from the Powder River at the
end of April to the Tongue River at the beginning of May. From
here it had slowly meandered southward. Gibbon's Chief of Scouts
had made two sightings, one on 16 May at the Tongue River and
the other on 27 May, when the Indians were observed to have
changed direction and entered the Rosebud Valley (see the
accompanying map). Thereafter they moved south-west beyond
Green Leaf Creek to a point 8 miles below the mouth of Lame Deer
Creek by early June. This was the site chosen for the annual Sun
Dance, a profoundly religious Sioux ceremony. At a time of
supreme threat it was the moment to reaffirm faith and rejuvenate
strength of purpose. Sitting Bull, a courageous and admired warrior
in his younger years, was recognised and revered as the spiritual
leader or medicine man. In supplication to their great god
Wakontonka, Sitting Bull cut one hundred pieces of flesh from his
arms, and fasted and danced while gazing at the sun. In this trance-
like state he saw a vision of soldiers on horses bearing down on an
Indian village. They rode upside down with their feet high in the
sky and their heads to the earth so that their hats fell off. Clearly

they were dead. A resurgence of hope, spirit and resolve permeated the Sioux and Cheyenne people. This was a gloriously provident sign of coming victory. Their culture would survive. Those present were thrilled by the vision and prophesy. Spiritualism was an all-pervasive part of their lives. Not only should they fight – they would win.

On 15 June Crook ordered his entire force into action, and they reduced scales for a forced march. Each man was allowed one blanket, 100 rounds of ammunition and four days' rations. 'As little as possible' was to be taken, reflected Frank Grouard, Crook's chief scout, which meant 'much less than we needed'. The wagon train would remain behind and the infantry would ride on pack mules. It is not clear what prompted this sudden decision, apart from likely information gathered by Grouard and his Crow scouting activities.

General George Crook's reticence to tell anyone what was going on bordered on rudeness, and was legendary. 'He has a faculty for silence that is absolutely astonishing,' wrote Second Lieutenant E. H. Foster of the 3rd Cavalry. Aides and subordinates found him infuriatingly uncommunicative. 'There is one thing very certain,' Foster emphasised. 'None of the General's plans will ever be discussed until after they are executed.' One could only guess at his plans and expectations for the coming operation. Some would question if he indeed had any. Local press accompanying the expedition described the 'Gray Fox' as 'physically a man of iron'.

'He endures heat or cold riding or walking with Indian stolidity. If he feels discomfort he never expresses the feeling. While apparently frank with all who approach him, he is never communicative, except occasionally to his aids. To all others he is a Sphinx.'[1]

Crook's reputation stemmed from his subjugation of the Apache and other south-western Indian bands. Success had been won by stripping his heavy wagon trains to produce light mobile columns supported by pack mules. He achieved the same tactical dexterity as his nimble foe and promoted the use of Indian auxiliaries as allies against their own kind. He was mercilessly persistent in running his quarry to ground. Harassing groups were employed around water holes in the desert areas of the south-west, simplifying the process of fixing an elusive enemy whose winter vulnerability was also identified and exploited. These local successes, however, were achieved against bands numbering scores. The hundreds that nature could sustain on the Great Plains were an entirely different proposition. Crook's winter experience on the Powder River had been a salutary lesson and he was entering the field with the largest of the three columns converging on the area of operations. Incompetence by junior commanders and the absence of his personal direction was rationalised as the cause of the setback, rather than Indian capabilities. Errors would not be repeated.

Crook's infantry was given 24 hours to transition to mule-borne cavalry at Goose Creek, inexplicably glossing over four days idling at Prairie Dog Creek awaiting the arrival of Indian reinforcements. John Finerty, a press correspondent, commented that the 'unhappy' infantrymen's approach to their task was anything but awe-inspiring. Frank Grouard allowed himself a chuckle at their expense. 'I never saw so much fun in my life. The valley, for a mile in every direction, was filled with bucking mules, frightened infantrymen, broken saddles, and applauding spectators ... the entire command took a half-holiday to enjoy the sport.'

Captain Chambers's infantry officers reluctantly persevered to the obvious delight of onlookers. Finerty gleefully recorded that 'mules would buck right where they stood, and then a soldier might be seen shooting up in the air like a rocket, and his very dull thud would soon after be heard as his body struck mother earth in his fall from among the clouds'. It was an inauspicious start for the unfortunate foot soldiers. Saddles were adapted load carriers to which baggage had previously been tied. They represented the equivalent of sitting across a narrow bench, and even with a blanket were excruciatingly uncomfortable to ride. Chambers's men were being re-roled to engage some of the finest light cavalry in the world. By noon, Finerty observed that most of the infantry 'had acquired sufficient mastery over their mounts to enable them to keep their saddles with a doubtful degree of adhesiveness'.[2]

Unperturbed, the single-minded Crook led his force of more than 1,300 soldiers, Indians and civilians out of the Goose Creek encampment at 0600 hours on 16 June. If he knew the precise whereabouts of the village, he was not admitting it yet. Information was stale. Lieutenant Foster recorded in his journal a report of 'a Sioux village of 700 lodges ... which means 2,500 warriors, is on the Rosebud, about 45 miles from here'.[3] Crook crossed the Tongue River 6 miles to the north, then turned west, traversing the ridgeline that brought the column to the headwaters of the Rosebud Creek, where it bivouacked for the night.

Six days before, General Terry, unaware of Crook's activities and also armed with stale intelligence, had issued new orders. The Dakota column was encamped 25 miles above the mouth of the Powder River, while Gibbon's was further north near the confluence of the Yellowstone River. Information suggested significant Indian activity further west in the region of the Rosebud or Bighorn valleys. Major Marcus A. Reno, Custer's second-in-command, was directed to take his cavalry right wing of six companies (B, C, E, F, I and L) on a reconnaissance of the Powder River to the south, then west to the Mizpah Creek and Tongue River. A detachment of Arikara scouts under an experienced guide, Mitch Bouyer, was given to him, with 100 pack mules and a Gatling gun pulled by four condemned cavalry horses. Under no circumstances was Reno to venture west of the Tongue should he alarm any Indians that may be on the Rosebud Creek. The reconnaissance was to finish at the mouth of the Tongue to the north, where he would rejoin Custer with the rest of the 7th regiment. Terry envisaged a southward advance of two parallel columns, with Custer's cavalry on the Tongue and Gibbon's mainly infantry force west of him on the Rosebud. Once the Indians were located, Custer was to turn west and converge with Gibbon. Both would combine for the final blow as they descended the Rosebud Creek.

All this was, of course, conjecture, and Reno's orders do not clearly indicate whether his mission was 'search and destroy' or conventional reconnaissance. Lieutenant Bradley had found the village for Gibbon with a small group of 26 men. Reno was dispatched with in excess of 300 men (half a regiment) in a different direction with no clear orders of what to do if he found something. Custer was exasperated that he was not leading the mission, which meant further delays. Any main body move or convergence of forces must await the confirmed objective. Thirteen days had elapsed since the Indian village had been discovered, and not a single coordinated measure had been implemented across the three columns.

Terry may have given Reno the mission to 'spare the rod' on Custer's right wing, but the reconnaissance was conducted at a punishing pace. Reno covered 156 miles in the first seven days – half the distance again that the Dakota column had taken 26 days to travel. Reno failed to scout all the Mizpah Creek but essentially followed Terry's orders until 15 June. The going was often rough. Privates Nathan Short and Peter Thompson rode with C Company during this gruelling ride. Thompson remarked that 'the trail was so narrow that the horses were jostling and jamming one another all the time'[4]. A further impediment was the need to unhitch the Gatling gun horses in order to manhandle the gun carriage across obstacles and ravines. Reno, riding with Mitch Bouyer, learned about Bradley's sighting of a village on the Tongue River in May and realised that if he continued down the Mizpah as ordered they would miss it. After descending the Tongue River for only 8 miles, the command deviated west to investigate the suspect sight. On the day that Crook's column began its march on the Rosebud, Reno's troops reached the month-old campsite. All the signs suggested that it had contained about 400 lodges and that they had continued west toward the Rosebud Creek. This posed a dilemma. Having violated Terry's orders to scout the Mizpah and Tongue, Reno's scout Bouyer was urging him to follow the trail even further west. Both Crook and Reno – unbeknown to Terry – were irresistibly attracted to the Rosebud. Reno elected to disobey his commander's direct instructions and proceeded up the Rosebud. Another two vacated encampments were passed, connected by an enormously wide travois trail caused by the scouring from lodge tent poles ploughing up the ground as they were dragged with their possessions along the valley by the migrating Indian village.

That night Reno camped on yet another abandoned Indian village. Crook's column was meanwhile about 50 miles away, over a day's march, and drawing near. In effect, Sheridan's three disparate commands were conducting a form of 'blind man's buff', rummaging about in an area of shrinking convergence. Reno's reinterpretation of Terry's orders had already nullified the point of pushing southward with parallel columns. That same day the Indians turned away from the Rosebud, moving 12 miles to the west across the Wolf Mountains ridgeline to Ash (later renamed Reno) Creek, just short of the valley of the Little Bighorn. They were no longer in the area originally encompassed by Terry's pincer movement. But it was no longer 'blind man's buff'. The Indians had seen Crook.

Crook's column was about a mile long and shrouded by a pall of dust. It was easily detectible by Indian observers straddling the ridgelines they were obliged to cross. They were wary, and aware that they were the intended targets. Crook's progress had been monitored from Fort Fetterman onwards and his encampment on the Tongue River raided by Sioux or Cheyenne warriors on the night of 9 June. This was a 'phoney war' period for many in Sitting Bull's village, as his nephew Lazy White Bull, a 26-year-old Minneconjou Lakota recalls:

'During May and June, Sitting Bull's great camp was hunting on the Rosebud and the Little Bighorn, and all this time Sitting Bull kept scouts out. But for a long time they had nothing to report.'

Shortly after the encampment moved to Ash Creek, White Bull

remembered that 'Cheyenne scouts came in and reported the valley of the Rosebud black with soldiers.'

Little Hawk, a 28-year-old Northern Cheyenne warrior, spotted the column. 'It seemed as if the whole earth were black with soldiers,' he reported. Sightings were by chance and not part of an Indian early warning screen. They did not plan or gather intelligence in Army G2 terms; instead there was a spontaneous and aggressive response to events. It was a question of proximity to the village. The earlier raid conducted against Crook had not been part of a general surveillance and reporting scheme, but soldiers being so close caused some consternation, prompting alarm and urgency. 'When they got near the camp,' Little Hawk explained, the scouts 'began to howl like wolves to notify them that something had been seen.' Soon the whole camp was aroused and 'all the men began to catch their horses and to get ready'. Debates were exhaustively conducted around the Council Lodges until about 2300 hours, when it was decided that action must be taken. Animated chatter followed, punctuated by wild rides around the camp perimeter, shooting off weapons as the braves worked themselves up into frenzy. 'All painted themselves,' said Little Hawk, 'put on their war bonnets, paraded about the camp two-by-two, and then struck out for the soldiers going straight through the hills.' Young Two Moons, a Northern Cheyenne warrior, realising that the soldiers 'may come right down the Rosebud', decided to act. The village was threatened. 'As soon as they could get ready, all the young men set out.'[5]

This was not a disciplined night march. War-bands sped off into the night after their individual leaders as soon as they were ready. On the flanks of these hordes riding south were the 'Akecita', or camp police, a group responsibility taken in turns by the tribes. They sought to prevent hot bloods racing too far ahead and compromising surprise. Individual chiefs held their loose groups together as they galloped through the night. The braves travelled light with only a blanket astride the pony and weapons. Rations were a bag of 'trail mix', consisting of dried meat (pemmican) and berries or roots, which could be eaten on the march. The Ash Creek encampment was probably about 500 lodges, which might muster 1,000 warriors. Leaving some behind as security, while others may have been out hunting or raiding, meant that the mass of warriors streaming through the night could not have exceeded 750 to 800 men.[6]

The warriors were relatively well provided with guns. Whereas about 15–20% of the Indians at the time of the Fetterman Massacre had a mixed technological array of muskets, pistols and rifles, now about one-third or more of the hostiles owned modern weapons, including repeating rifles.[7] The Lakota warrior White Bull rode with only a blanket and a cartridge belt of 100 rounds for his 17-shot repeating rifle, which 'he had purchased from an Indian Agency at Fort Bennett'. Custer himself had presciently written the previous year about 'the wonderful liberality of our Government' in equipping its soldiers with 'the latest improved style of breech-loaders' to defend themselves and 'is equally able and willing to give the same pattern of arms to their common foe'.[8]

The Indian host took different routes to cover the approximately 30 miles south, following tributary stream-lines into the Rosebud Valley, arriving some 11 miles north of its great bend. Smaller bands converged into a mass as a twilight dawn appeared in the sky. Warriors had only recently come from the Agencies and were eager to fight soldiers and gain honours, count coup and capture horses and weapons. Warfare played an essential part of their development into manhood. There had been scant opportunity to gain laurels apart from intermittent internecine strife since Red Cloud's war had ended eight years before. For many it was their first battle and new generations had to be blooded. Some were afraid but were driven by a fierce pride to outdo their fellows and achieve the tribal recognition for which they craved and fought. The Indians briefly assembled below a ridge on the high ground approaching the Rosebud, pausing to enable the stragglers to close in. There were essential ceremonies to perform and ornaments to attach to their bodies before the fight. John Stands in Timber's grandparents witnessed these events and pointed out the importance of such preliminaries: 'A man without power of some kind did not go in close that way. He did not dare,' he said. As the bands intermingled, the chiefs gave the order to make the final preparations. 'The warriors howled like wolves' in answer, said Stands in Timber, 'and scattered here and there to begin picking out their shields and war bonnets and other things they used'.[9] There was no plan or any orders. Having ridden through the night they were to launch their attack off the line of march. Up ahead were the hotheads, desperately vying for the honour of striking the first blow.

'Like swarms of blackbirds'

Crook's troops had marched 35 miles the previous day and were roused at 0300 hours on 17 June to continue marching north along the south fork of the Rosebud Creek. It was soon evident from whence it had got its name. 'Wild roses by the thousand laid their delicate beauties at our feet,' recalled Crook's orderly, Lieutenant John Bourke, and 'a species of phlox, dainty blue in tint, was there also in great profusion.'[10] Any holiday atmosphere prevailing after the grandiose arrival of the Indian scouts and the fun of the infantry 'rodeo' had long since dissipated. Crow and Shoshone scouts were markedly apprehensive. Although there had been no sightings of hostiles, they sensed their presence. The soldiers were distracted by fatigue and the early start, and the mule-riding infantry were suffering considerably. At 0800 hours Crook called a halt on the line of march. No disposition apart from security pickets was made for defence, despite being deep within hostile territory. Cavalry dismounted and loosened saddle girths and men relaxed along the mile-long column, spread along the gently sloping and in some parts boggy bottomland of the Rosebud stream. They were resting in a form of amphitheatre, enclosed by ridgelines on three sides. Troops started to boil coffee and gnaw hardtack biscuits for breakfast. John Finerty, the war correspondent with the column, recalled 'the sun became intensely hot in that close valley, so I threw myself on the ground, resting my head upon my saddle'.

Two dozen Crow scouts and a lone Shoshone warrior pushed
northwards up one of the re-entrant valleys to seek a more
appetising breakfast of buffalo. The battalions of Captains Anson
Mills and Henry E. Noyes were with the vanguard north of the
Rosebud stream. Behind them was Captain Van Vliet's two-
company battalion to the west. Alexander Chambers's battalion of
mule-borne foot soldiers was next in line, with the remainder of the
Indian allies. Bringing up the rear was Captain Guy Henry's cavalry
battalion and the *ad hoc* company of civilian miners and packers.
Crook sat with his personal staff and began to play cards.

'At about 8.30 o'clock, without any warning,' Finerty said, 'we
heard a few shots from behind the bluffs to the north.' This was in
the area of the Crow scouts. Complaints followed from officers
frustrated by their apparent inability to maintain fire discipline in
an obviously sensitive area. More shots followed. Sinister implications caused raised eyebrows when Finerty realised that 'the
alternate rise and fall of the reports' indicated 'that the shots were
not all fired in one direction'. Lieutenant J. Bourke recalled that the
firing 'down the valley to the north' was 'followed by the ululation
proclaiming from the hill-tops that the enemy was in force and that
we were in for a fight'. 'Saddle up, there – saddle up, quick!'
shouted Finerty's Company Commander, Captain Mills. Indian
scouts were riding back down the valley slopes 'with incredible
speed'. 'Shot after shot followed on the left,' observed Bourke, 'and
by the time that two of the Crows reached us, one of them [was]
severely wounded and both crying, "Sioux! Sioux!"' These three or
four minutes' warning provided by the Crow scouts probably saved
Crook's command from total annihilation.[11]

The Battle of the Rosebud, 17 June 1876: the situation at 0800–0830 hours

The unexpected Indian attack caught Crook's long column
completely by surprise. Only a last-minute warning by Indian scouts
prevented the command from being overwhelmed in the first rush.

Red Sabbath

From the top of the high ground overlooking the 'amphitheatre' the Indians could see a vista of pine-covered ridges and deep ravines. It would take several minutes to ride from top to bottom, and as the vanguard of the Sioux and Cheyenne crossed the ridgeline, they inadvertently bumped into the screen of Crow scouts who had ridden up from the valley below. These were the hot bloods and fire was immediately exchanged.

The approaching main body of hostiles saw the column resting below and spontaneously launched their assault with the minimum of appreciation. It was difficult to control the enthusiasm to get into the fight as the bands crossed the bluffs that overlooked the Rosebud Valley. 'Almost a thousand warriors had assembled,' said Lazy White Bull, 'Cheyenne, Oglala, Minneconjou, Sans Arc, Brule [and] Hunkpapa.' At the first shots:

> 'The whole war-party whipped up their horses and charged for the hill. There they found a Sioux wounded, and a horse killed. They rode over the hill and saw five Government scouts dashing down the hill to the troops. They charged these five men shooting all the time, and wounded one of them. Still they pressed on, following the five scouts, close to the soldiers.'[12]

They sped down four or five stream approaches that ran down between the ridgelines leading to the widely dispersed and obviously relaxing soldiers lying along the valley floor. As they galloped among the bush lines of the watercourses they passed the 'Buffalo Jump' cliffs on their left. Romantic notions of buffalo hunting portrayed in Fremington's famous paintings did not always accord with reality. Indians would slaughter their buffalo *en masse* if given the opportunity to drive a herd over a cliff-top; overkill was not just the prerogative of white hunters. There was an element of parody as they galloped by these cliffs seeking to stampede the white soldiers below to panic-stricken destruction. After being compromised, it was the attackers' only remaining course of action.

Crook's column only narrowly escaped this fate, a factor over-looked by patriotic newspaper accounts of the action. Bourke claims that 'the battle of the Rosebud was a trap', and that in any case 'there was a strong line of pickets out on the hills on that flank'. In reality it was the warning and rapid counter-measures taken by the Crow and Shoshone auxiliaries that blunted the surprise Sioux attack. John Finerty remembers that 'Flying Crow and Snake [Shoshone] scouts, utterly panic stricken' rode into the column 'shouting at the tops of their voices, "Heap Sioux! Heap Sioux!" gesticulating wildly in the direction of the bluffs, which they abandoned in such haste. All looked in that direction, and there, sure enough, were the Sioux.'

Private Phineas Towne in Captain Henry's 3rd Cavalry battalion recalled that 'while we were putting our horses to graze the whole range of hills in our front became literally alive with Indians'. Despite probably outnumbering the attackers, the soldiers were shocked and intimidated by what they saw. One observer described them 'like swarms of blackbirds, there were so many of them and in such rapid motion'. Major H. S. Byron claimed that 'all the Indians in the world seemed gathered right there in front of our troops'. The attack was totally unexpected. The column had anticipated surrounding and attacking an Indian village. Nobody expected the reverse. The imperative had been to catch the Indians before they scattered. But now, as Byron lamented, 'I saw enough Indians to last me the rest of my life.' Another witness claimed that 'there were at least a thousand of them in plain sight' and 'how many others there might be, no one could tell'. Crook's aide John Bourke judged that 'it was plain that something out of the common was to be expected'. But the wily Crook was not confused. He could not imagine that these Indians would travel so far to attack him. Terry's scout was right – there must be an Indian village on the Rosebud.[13]

Crook sought to regain the initiative, glossing over the embarrass-ment that his command had been saved by his Indian allies. 'While our Indians were making their charge upon the Sioux,' observed

Private Towne, 'General Crook gave orders to saddle up.'[14] By 0830 hours Crook's Indian allies were hotly engaging the Sioux and Cheyenne on the high ground north of the dispersed column. Heavily outnumbered, they conducted a fighting withdrawal back to the main body. Volley fire began to crash out from the battalion groups, causing the Indian torrent to begin changing direction into riverlets, flowing around or gushing off islands of resistance in their path. Horses were re-saddled during the brief respite and discipline maintained. Crook swung into action and asserted his experienced judgement. His Civil War experience drove him to lash out aggressively, rather than remaining *in situ* to calmly break up the Indian attacks through superior and disciplined firepower. Such a mass Indian attack was a rare and inviting target. The precedence of the 1867 Wagon Box fight and Beecher's Island the following year was that real damage could be meted out by standing ground. Crook, however, was convinced of the need to secure the high ground around the amphitheatre basin, where he had been caught napping.

Captain Van Vliet with C and G Companies, 3rd Cavalry, was ordered to anchor the column's rear on the high ground to the south. These high bluffs were providently scaled in time to drive off a small Sioux band approaching from the east. Captain Mills, commanding six companies of the 3rd Cavalry (A, B, E, I, L and M), was ordered to clear the hostiles from the high ground to the north-east, while Lieutenant Colonel Royall pursued Indians attacking the rear of Crook's camp and out to the left flank toward the north-west. This was a conventional and classic Civil War response. Cavalry was securing the flanks and rear while Major Chambers's five companies of infantry, and three companies from Captain Noyes's 2nd Cavalry formed a dismounted skirmish line and advanced up the high ground in the centre, pushing the Indians out of the amphitheatre.

The ground over which this battle was fought was broken with boulders and dry watercourses in between, causing heavy going for both sides. The Indians, however, with their superior mobility, always appeared more fluid. Mills's battalion 'went like a storm and the Indians waited for us until we were within 50 paces,' recounted Finerty. The mounted cavalrymen were going too fast to use their carbines 'but several of the men fired their revolvers'. The Sioux broke and fled and, according to Finerty, 'were compelled to fall back in confusion all along the line'.[15] This was a misinterpretation of the Indian tactics. Unlike their previous Civil War adversaries, hostile braves refused to be 'fixed' or drawn to ground. Key ground was anathema to them. They elected to withdraw to higher ground and seek further opportunities to inflict damage. White Bull, a Lakota warrior, described it as 'back and forth that day. All day long the Indians of both sides charged back and forth on horseback and not a few were killed on both sides.'[16]

Mills's cavalry charge forced the Indians to withdraw north-west along the ridgeline to the next crest (today called Crook's Ridge). Three of Mills's mounted companies (A, E and M) then conducted a further charge, driving the Indians again north-west to a conical hill feature. Chambers and Noyes pushed forward up the high ground in the centre in support, and by about 0930 hours had joined Mills. Crook's ridge was now occupied by the bulk of his force, including his headquarters and the packers and miners. Lieutenant Colonel William Royall, Crook's second-in-command, was advancing rapidly to the north-west on a parallel ridgeline about a mile away to the west, where he chased the Indians as far as the head of Kollmar Creek. One hour into the battle, the whole command seeking high ground had dispersed itself over a frontage of almost 3 miles. Crook could still see all his disparate commands, but they were engaged in three separate fights. There was infantry skirmishing in the centre, Mills's cavalry engaged on the right, and an ebb-and-flow battle on the left as it became more apparent that Royall's force may have over-extended itself beyond the main force.

It was a battle of ever-rising crest lines. 'After we had taken the first line of heights,' said Finerty, accompanying Mills's Company, 'the Indians rallied on the second and beckoned us to come on.' Even as each line was attained, there was no advantage. The Indians refused to be fixed and carried on retreating beyond enticing false crest lines. 'Under Crook's order we charged and when we got there another crest rose on the other side of the valley. There were the savages again,' observed Finerty.[17] Crook became exasperated. The battle was not going well. Despite occupying key terrain, little damage was being inflicted on the hostiles, who invariably returned after being momentarily dispersed to snipe at the soldiers from long range. The packers and miners in the centre conducted a firefight at extreme range with the Indians ensconced on Conical Hill, to no apparent effect. Single warriors or small groups of Indians demonstrated their valour by charging forward and exchanging close-range fire with the troopers. If pressed they immediately retreated.

One such drama was enacted in an area of petrified forest remains in the Gap, part of a re-entrant next to Crook's hilltop headquarters. The fossilised setting was a reminder of the extinct forests that now provide much of the coal deposits near present-day Sheridan. During one such 'bravery run', designed to entice soldiers to over-commit themselves, Comes-in-Sight, a Cheyenne warrior, had his horse shot from under him. Crashing into a flurry of swirling dust amid cheers from the successful long-range shooting infantry, it became evident that he was still alive. A deadly game of 'cat and mouse' ensued. Little Hawk, another Cheyenne warrior, remembered that the horse's hind leg was broken and the accompanying Cheyenne group retreated to the high ground. Comes-in-Sight was left on foot. 'He was walking away and all the soldiers were shooting at him as hard as they could.' Capture for an

The Battle of the Rosebud, 17 June 1876: the situation at 0850–1230 hours

Crook, like Custer, divided his command to counter anticipated Indian mobility, but unexpected Indian aggression and firepower resulted in his column being fought to a standstill. So high was the ammunition expenditure that Crook felt obliged to retire, but this key information was not passed on to Terry's column, on day's ride away,

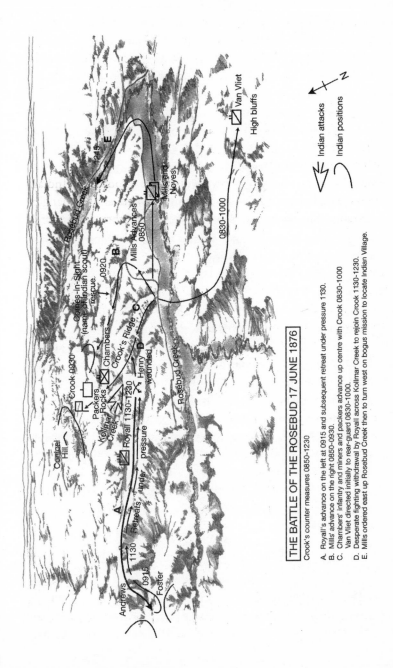

THE BATTLE OF THE ROSEBUD 17 JUNE 1876

Crook's counter measures 0850-1230

A. Royall's advance on the left at 0915 and subsequent retreat under pressure 1130.

B. Mills' advance on the right 0850-0930.

C. Chambers' infantry and miners and packers advance up centre with Crook 0830-1000

D. Van Vliet directed initially to rear-guard 0830-1000.

Desperate fighting withdrawal by Royall across Kollmar Creek to rejoin Crook 1130-1230.

E. Mills ordered east up Rosebud Creek then to turn west on bogus mission to locate Indian Village.

Indian was the ultimate disgrace. Unusually, the previous night a woman had ridden unnoticed with the Indian bands. This was Buffalo Calf Road Woman, the downed warrior's sister. Indians were generally suspicious of squaws on the battlefield, fearing that they may haunt the spirit of the braves. Despite the intense fire, Little Hawk related how 'she looked down and saw her brother there and rushed down to meet her brother and he jumped behind her and she brought him off. Neither was hit.'[18] It was the practice of the United States Army to name battles on the American continent after the name of the nearest watercourse; an exception was Gettysburg, as a consequence of Lincoln's Address. This engagement was to become known as the Battle of the Rosebud. Indians named battles for significant events, and this became 'the battle where the sister saved her brother'.

A hard fight

Crook was facing the nightmare scenario of maybe repeating the Powder River The Battfiasco. There appeared to be no way of tying down his elusive opponent. Moreover, he was being increasingly drawn to the high ground to the north-west, which was not where he wanted to go. His objective was the village, which, as indicated by this fierce attack, had to be nearby on the Rosebud Creek. At 1030 hours Crook ordered Mills and Noyes to withdraw eight cavalry companies of 475 men, one-third of his available combat strength, from their present positions. Their mission was to follow the Rosebud stream north and find the village. Van Vliet's battalion was taken from its anchor point south of the Rosebud to reinforce their departure.

Mills's force departed unnoticed by the Indians, who, in milling around looking for opportunities, were beginning to focus on potential prey to the west. Royall's situation on the left flank had continued to deteriorate. I Company had rejoined Crook by crossing the adjoining Kollmar Creek valley bottom. The company had run such a gauntlet of fire that Royall decided to withdraw the remaining four companies south-east along the ridgeline that had been the axis of advance that morning. A crisis was adverted when Van Vliet's battalion arrived just in time to check an Indian charge along Kollmar Creek that almost reached the Rosebud and would have left Royall completely cut off. The reckless and now over-extended hostile force was charged in the flank by Crook's Crows and Shoshones and scattered. Royall fell back further south-eastwards and assumed a second defensive position. Crook, now concerned, ordered him to cross Kollmar Creek and rejoin the main command, but he was increasingly assailed on three sides by Sioux and Cheyenne attacks, growing increasingly bold and tenacious at the prospect of potential success. Crook, by dispatching Mills on a search-and-destroy mission to an unspecified location, had dispersed his command even further and committed its only reserve.

Royall's exposed ridgeline position bore sinister parallels to Fetterman Ridge. Such terrain was particularly suited to the Indian tactical penchant of identifying then cutting out the weak link from within a herd. Royall was the lame calf. No overall leader was coordinating the Indian effort; chiefs such as Crazy Horse were present, but braves followed those revered and chosen by them-selves, and indeed in the ultimate democratic sense decided themselves where they should go. Almost spontaneously the whirling and milling mass of warriors circling the battlefield sensed the distress being exhibited by the actions of Royall's over-extended command. Breaking off contact at a myriad of points, they converged on Royall's second position. 'They came near to killing a whole company,' the Northern Cheyenne Little Hawk recalled.[19]

By 1130 hours it was becoming apparent to Crook, observing the ridge on the other side of the valley, that Royall's command was fighting for its very existence beneath the gunpowder smoke and dust-tinged melee of activity. He dispatched orders to Mills to break off his village quest and turn west to strike the rear of the Indians surrounding Royall.

'It was impossible to hold our present position against such overwhelming odds,' declared an anxious Private Phineas Towne, engaged with F Company on the ridge. 'I must say that I never saw so great a body of Indians in one place as I saw at that time.' Royall slowly edged his command back down the ridgeline. Failure on Fetterman Ridge in 1867 was the consequence of a breakdown of fire discipline; panic can be infectious, and it was up to officers supported by NCOs to maintain unit cohesion. Towne was scared. 'It seemed that if one Indian was shot, five were there to take his place.' The dismounted troopers adopted a 'U' formation with horse-holders reassuring the mounts in the centre. All the time the Indians pressed in at the sides seeking to break the core. One *Chicago Tribune* correspondent described how crossfire coming 'from their left and rear' unsettled a rapidly thrown together segment of the line formed from 'a few men who had become separated from their proper commands'. Leadership held them together under a fire so intense that it

> '…induced a small number of men to break away, saying that they could stand a fire from the front, but, when it enfiladed them and came from the rear, it was rather rough. The officer in charge appealed to them to go back, saying, "Men, we must hold the hill." "All right, sir," replied one of them doggedly; "If you say so we'll hold it till hell freezes over."'[20]

As Royall gradually retreated the length of the ridgeline he sacrificed the advantage of steadily decreasing height. Disciplined fire controlled by officers and NCOs kept the enemy at bay. By 1230 Royall decided he could wait no longer and began to withdraw his troopers into the Kollmar ravine preparatory to mounting their horses. This was a risky process. Even in the age of armoured personnel carriers, it is not an option normally considered when under fire. The word was passed to mount up in order to move across the valley floor to Crook. With 5 yards of space required for each horse and 130 men in the four companies, this was a tricky dispersion to be managed across a ridgeline already swept by fire. The command was in an especially vulnerable position. 'The Indians,' according to an accompanying correspondent's description, 'seeing the soldiers retreating, imagined they were being beaten and, being encouraged by the thought, displayed a dash and courage not before seen on that day.' Royall's men were required to dash through a hail of fire in order to reach Crook's main position. Crow and Shoshone scouts counter-attacked the pursuing enemy at the same time as two companies of infantry were pushed forward to provide long-range covering fire from the north side of the ravine.

Private Towne, with Henry's battalion, believed that 'if we had remained in our first position we would all have been killed', and in his opinion 'I consider we retreated in the right time'. At that moment Captain Guy Henry's face exploded under the impact of a heavy-calibre projectile. Henry, a 3rd Cavalry battalion commander, reeled in the saddle as the bullet pierced both cheekbones, emerging from his left eye socket and tearing out much of the left side of his face. 'He was spitting blood by the handful,' described one witness. He then toppled from the saddle. The retreat had begun and a desperate fight ensued for the fallen officer. An old Shoshone chief, Washakie, defended him and managed to lift the still-breathing Henry back into the saddle. He was a popular officer and his apparently ugly demise was a palpable shock to his command.[21]

Royall's command suffered grievous casualties during this retreat. It provided an object lesson of how much damage a low-tech opponent can inflict (as in the case of the Fetterman Massacre) if allowed to close within the comfort zone established by high-tech firepower. Correspondent Reuben Davenport related how 'death had just begun his work among them'. The nine killed and 15 wounded during Royall's desperate retreat represented nearly 80% of the total army dead and wounded in this battle as a murderous enfilading fire swept many troopers from their saddles.

'I dismounted at several points during our retreat and fired with the skirmishers... The tide of retreat now grew more excited and turbulent and I was pressed back... A swarm of

Sioux were within 1,000 yards of me in front and I heard their shots in the rear as they murdered the poor soldiers of the rearguard of the retreat.'

This was not conventional war. Surrender was not an option. 'A recruit surrendered his carbine to a painted warrior,' recalled Davenport, 'who flung it to the ground, and cleft his head with a stroke of the tomahawk.' Crook, watching this unfolding catastrophe from the high ground, spent some anxious moments as the pursuing warriors tore in and out of the retreating cavalrymen. 'The Sioux rode so close to their victims,' said Davenport, 'that they shot them in the face with revolvers.'[22] The unfortunate Private Towne was caught on foot trying to save a wounded Sergeant. A lariat was thrown over his head by a party of about 20 warriors, who beat him about the head, shot him, then dragged him along the ground. 'The intention of the Indians [was] either to drag me to death at the heels of the pony or after getting me away to torture me in some other manner.' After being dragged across rocky scrub for some distance he was saved by a cavalry counter-attack. 'They captured one other comrade of mine by the name of Bennet, of L Troop, Third Cavalry,' he lamented, 'and completely cut him in pieces. His remains were buried in a grain sack.'[23]

Mills meanwhile, having driven off a small group of Sioux near the bend in the Rosebud, felt that he was almost on top of the village he had been ordered to strike. His column halted just short of a very narrow canyon opening into the Rosebud Valley, his scouts being extremely reluctant to proceed, believing an ambush and disaster awaited them within its narrow confines. The dilemma of what to do next was ended by the arrival of Crook's messenger with new orders. He was to return at once. Mills's eight companies climbed laboriously out of the canyon and began to ride west towards Conical Hill.

When the relief column appeared on the Indian's flank, the Sioux and Cheyenne broke off contact and retreated. Captain Mills did not arrive in time, however, to assist Royall's withdrawal. Crook still refused to believe that he had missed the village. Another foray was launched up the Rosebud after gathering his mounted units, but the scouts again refused to enter the narrow canyon at its end. The battle was over.

'It was a hard fight,' recalled White Bull. The Indians regarded it as a victory. They had chosen to break contact. 'It lasted all day,' but so far as White Bull was concerned there was little doubt about the outcome. 'When it was over "Three Stars" [Crook] took his troops and hit the trail back to his base.' The Indians rode home 'leaving scouts behind to watch "Three Stars"' movements.' Young Two Moons of the Northern Cheyenne saw the arrival of Mills's relieving column and claimed that 'the soldiers were still coming but there were so many Indians they stood them off. Here the fight stopped.' There was no headlong retreat. It was decided they had done enough. 'The Cheyennes and Sioux stayed there a little while and then went away and left the soldiers. Many men were wounded and many horses killed and wounded so that many Indians were on foot.' They went home.[24]

Crook's column was in a state of shock. They had been fought to a standstill. Nobody had seen so many Indians before. Lieutenant John Bourke, Crook's aide, pointed out that:

'General Crook's horse was shot from under him, and there were few, if any, officers or soldiers, facing the strength of the Sioux and Cheyennes at the Rosebud who did not have some incident of a personal nature by which to impress the affair upon their memories for the rest of their lives.'[25]

By the standards of Indian warfare it had been an extremely long and bloody engagement. Estimates of Indian casualties run as high as 102 killed and wounded, but only 13 scalps were taken. High numbers were perhaps based on press reports of 150 dead horses and ponies found on the battlefield. The Indians invariably took their dead with them. Army losses were declared as 21 wounded and 10 killed. Lieutenant Bourke initially described it as 57 killed or wounded, some of the latter only slightly. Standards of army marksmanship had been demonstrably appalling – 25,000 rounds had been fired, requiring at best case 245 rounds (or two and a half times each man's ammunition allocation) to hit one Indian. The Indians may have fared better.

Crook could have pursued the Indians, but having expended 60% of his total ammunition (barely sufficient to keep the hostiles at bay), was persuaded to withdraw. Lieutenant Bourke claimed that 'as we had nothing but the clothing each wore and the remains of the four days' rations with which we started, we had no resource but to make our way back to the wagon trains with the wounded'.[26] If the column had been more offensively inclined, rations and ammunition could have been redistributed from infantry to cavalry and contact maintained. This is what the Crook of South West fame would have done. Alternatively he might have consolidated his present position and used the infantry mules for re-supply. The truth was that Crook's command were feeling vulnerable. They had intended to attack the village, not the other way round.

Inexplicably, Crook declined to communicate with the other columns. There was a moral obligation to inform Terry that the Indians were not running, the basic Intelligence assumption underpinning the whole campaign. Moreover, they were reasonably well armed with firearms, as testified by the mauling that Royall's command had received at close quarters. Common also to a number of recent setbacks was the Indians' propensity to isolate their adversary on ridgelines. This tactic enabled crossfire from below, while the defender had to expose himself to engage from the high ground. Had Terry known all this he would have reconsidered his plans.

Concerned for his wounded, short on supplies and taken aback at the ferocity of the Indian assault, Crook returned to his camp on Goose Creek to await once again the arrival of reinforcements. He was to remain there for seven weeks. Plains Indians were more lethal opponents than the scattered bands Crook had encountered in the South West. This second tarnishing of his reputation as a famed 'Indian Fighter' after the Powder River debacle doubtless contributed to his reticence to inform Terry. No force his size had ever been fought to a standstill in any Indian campaign to date.

The biggest of the three columns fielded thus far was to play no further part in the events about to unfold on the Little Bighorn.

Chapter 6
Where is the village?

'Things were getting a little exciting.
We'd have some real fighting soon.'

7th Cavalry Corporal

'Where the Indians are not'

Twenty-five miles away and barely one day's march from Crook,
Reno's column was on the move further up the Rosebud. Having
already disobeyed Terry's orders, Reno's dilemma was whether to
turn north for the junction with the Yellowstone or follow the
Indian trail south, the direction the hostiles appeared to be moving.
He rode a further 7½ miles toward Crook, halting at his nearest
point to the battle raging on 17 June. Scouts were sent ahead and
they located another village site, indicating that the Indians were
migrating in a south-westerly direction. There was tension.

'We began to speculate as to what Major Reno would do,'
recalled Private Thompson. Moving toward the Indians increased
their own chance of being discovered, but had to be balanced
against the immensely important information they were gathering.
'Orders were given that no bugles were to be blown,' said
Thompson, riding with C Company, 'no loud noises was to be
made, and double pickets were to be placed around our camp.'[1]
Mitch Bouyer, his chief scout, accurately assessed that if they
continued they would probably overtake the Indians within a day's
march. The senior Arakan scout, Forked Horn, was asked his
opinion. 'If the Dakotas see us, the sun will not move very far

before we are all killed,' was his sinister pronouncement. 'But you are the leader and we will go on if you say so.'² Reno changed direction, departing the abandoned campsite at 1600 hours and marching 15 miles down the Rosebud Creek. On 18 June the column reached the Yellowstone and turned east, where, moving along the south bank, he came across Gibbon's command camped on the other side of the river. Gibbon was initially confused, anticipating that Reno would appear at the confluence of the Tongue, as he had been ordered. After an exchange of dispatches across the river, Gibbon grasped the significance of Reno's discovery. 'The only remaining chance of finding the Indians now is in the direction of the headwaters of the Rosebud or Little Bighorn,' he wrote to Terry. He provocatively added, appreciating that Terry's plan to trap the Indians on the Rosebud was null and void, that he 'shall be glad to meet you to hear of your future plans'. Despite the implications that clues and Lieutenant Bradley's outright discoveries had already provided, 'blind man's buff' between the three columns seemed set to continue. No single command had definitively placed the location of the Indian village.

Men and animals within Reno's column had suffered drastically during the punishing march. Surgeon Dr James De Wolf described the terrain as 'dreadful badlands, nearly impossible to traverse'. Reno informed Terry in a brief note that 'my animals are very weary and need shoeing. We have marched near to 250 miles.' Terry, scanning this note, realised that Reno had been on the Rosebud and had exceeded his orders. Frustratingly, all he was telling him was that 'I can tell you where the Indians are not'. Incensed,

'Blind man's buff': the search for the Indian village, 10–25 June 1876
The three relatively sightless columns blundered about in a search area at a junction point covering thousands of square miles, and information was not readily passed between them. Despite Bradley, from Gibbon's column, locating the village on 17 and 27 May, it took Custer until 25 June to launch an attack on an identified location.

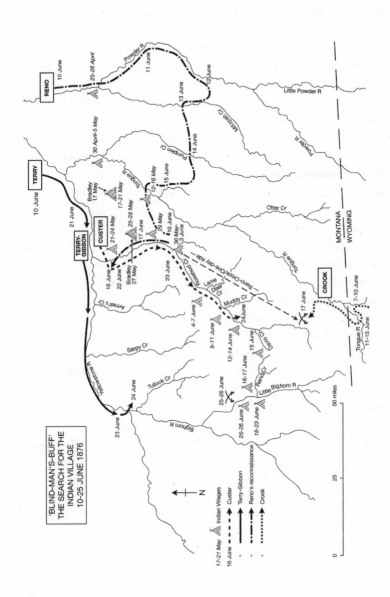

'BLIND-MAN'S-BUFF'
THE SEARCH FOR THE
INDIAN VILLAGE
10–25 JUNE 1876

General Terry gave Reno a major dressing down on arrival. 'He had
flagrantly disobeyed my orders,' he subsequently wrote to his
sisters.

> 'He had been on the Rosebud, in the belief that there were
> Indians on that stream and that he could make a successful
> attack on them which would cover up his disobedience.'

This chastising was unfair, because Reno had saved him the
embarrassment of launching a major pincer operation that would
only nip thin air. 'Of course,' the irritated General continued, 'this
performance made a change of my plans necessary.'[3] Custer joined
in the condemnation, confiding to his wife that Reno's 'failure to
follow up the trails has imperilled our plans by giving the village an
intimation of our presence. Think of the valuable time lost.' The
effect this had upon Reno's self-confidence would become apparent
later. He was already under emotional pressure, having lost his wife,
and was burdened by the practical difficulties of raising an only son
while living an isolated soldier's life. This public rebuke simply
added to his introspection. 'General Custer upbraided him very
bitterly,' Private Thompson of C Company observed, 'for not
finding out the exact number and the direction the Indians were
taking instead of supposing and guessing.' Thompson commented
on the soldiers' view of the outcome of the mission, which was
different. 'The scouting trip under Reno had proven somewhat of
a success,' they agreed, despite the physical rigours. 'There had
been some sharp questions and short answers,' Thompson
observed. Reno came out of it badly. Meanwhile, the rest of the 7th
Cavalry were abuzz with excitement. 'There were rumours that
Reno and his six troops had found hot Indian trails,' Corporal
Windolph remarked, 'and that there were plenty of Indians on to
the south and east, eighty or ninety miles away.'[4]

Terry reconfigured a second pincer movement similar to the
first. Following a conference on the steamboat *Far West*, Custer was
directed to ascend the Rosebud and follow the trail of the Indians.

If the trail diverged west from the Rosebud he was to continue along the same line to ensure that the Indians would not escape to the south. Once near the headwaters of the Rosebud Creek, Custer was to cross the ridge into the Little Bighorn drainage. Gibbon's force would concurrently move up the Yellowstone River, then turn south up the Bighorn and wait at the mouth of the Little Bighorn so as to close the loop. Terry's written orders provided total flexibility for Custer, should he see fit, to diverge from them.

'The Department Commander places too much confidence in your zeal, energy and ability to wish to impose upon you precise orders which might hamper your action when nearly in contact with the enemy.'[5]

Paradoxically, the orders also enumerate a specific set of instructions that Custer should follow and provide the genesis for a subsequent controversy as to whether Custer later disobeyed orders or not. The directives were actually more about attacking Indians than a village. No conference notes were taken at the meeting on the *Far West* between Terry, Custer, Major James Brisbin, commanding the 2nd Cavalry, and Gibbon. All were clear at the time what Terry wanted; problems only developed later with hindsight. Significantly Reno – Custer's second-in-command and the only senior officer with up-to-date knowledge of the trail – was not included. Gibbon did not receive a written order, either because he was to accompany Terry in any case, or because the latter felt the need to 'cover' himself. Custer was unlike the absent commander of the 7th, Colonel Samuel Sturgis, who was known to be mature and wise. Custer could be impetuous. Sheridan, the supreme commander, had overcome considerable political difficulties to ensure that a man such as Custer was leading the cavalry field force. He wanted results, and his bruising subordinate was likely to provide them.

It was still not clear where or when the final blow was to be struck over an operational area spanning 100 square miles. Predictive plotting during the conference assessed that Custer would cover

30 miles per day and Gibbon, with his infantry, perhaps 20. The balance of probability appeared to favour the upper Little Bighorn, but the target village had by this time established itself on the lower reaches. This constituted a two-day probability error even before the start. Although Terry seemed to be aiming for a synchronised approach, no pre-battle records hint at a simultaneous attack at any time. Gibbon's force had no further movement instructions beyond establishing a blocking position.

Custer was now given all 12 of his companies as distinct from the nine previously on offer in the first plan. He was also offered the remaining four 2nd Cavalry companies and the Gatling guns, but declined. He was given 15 days' rations, whereas Gibbon's pincer arm of four cavalry and five infantry companies were given six days' worth. It was obvious that Custer's was seen as the main strike force. He was also given the majority of the scouts and the pick of Gibbon's. This affirmation of Custer's ascendancy was received without a murmur by the rest of the force. 'We have little hope of being in at the death,' wrote Lieutenant Bradley, 'as Custer will undoubtedly exert himself to the utmost to get there first and win all the laurels for himself and his regiment.' The 7th knew it too. 'Things are getting a little exciting now,' commented Corporal Windolph. 'We'd have some real fighting soon.'

Custer had established the 7th Cavalry's consolidated bivouac alongside the south bank of the wide and fast-flowing Yellowstone River. 'It was good to see our old pals again,' said Windolph, 'when the whole regiment got together there on the Yellowstone.'[6] Gibbon's command was on the opposite bank. It was a large encampment encompassing 40 acres of picketed and grazing horses and tents. Half the 7th had benefited from a few days' break during Reno's scouting expedition. Private Peter Thompson had noticed that 'our horses had become quite jaded' after the additional 240 miles, 'for our grain had all been consumed and the grazing had been poor'. Custer's orderly Burkman remarked on the poor state of Reno's pack mules: 'Jist back from the scoutin' trip [they] was right petered out.'[7]

Campaign wear and tear was having a cumulative impact upon the strength of the 7th Cavalry on the eve of going to battle. Ninety of its assigned strength of 791 enlisted men had been left behind at the very start for duties, sickness or confinement for disciplinary reasons. A further 120 fell out at the Yellowstone, including 30 fresh and 10 recent recruits, leaving 575 to 580 men available for combat. The absentees included 80 'veterans' and the majority of the troopers who had crippled themselves walking the 300 miles from Fort Abraham Lincoln in riding boots. Such are the Clausewitz 'Frictions of War', the normal attrition attendant on any campaign. 'Already we was tired from our long march,' Burkman admitted, 'horses, men and mules.' The regiment knew what was coming. 'We now began to brace up for a rough trip,' said Private Thompson, 'for all the men knew that General Custer, if left to his own devices, would soon end the campaign one way or another.' A further 120 troopers were lost for lack of mounts, even after purloining those of the regimental band. Serious damage had already been inflicted on Custer's command. The regiment totalled just over 600, and authorised company strengths of 70 had shrunk to about 40 combat effectives, of which some 15% were recruits.[8]

'Numbers of us felt that when Custer took active charge of the expedition there would be no more funny work,' said Private Thompson. 'He meant business.' The 7th was aware that it had been annotated as the strike force in the coming operation. Custer ordered the pack mules to be prepared in the morning with 15 days' rations of hardtack, coffee and sugar and 12 days' rations of bacon. Twelve mules were assigned to each company. There would be no wagons – like Crook, they were to travel light. A further 12 of the strongest pack animals were earmarked to carry 24,000 rounds of reserve ammunition. Each trooper would carry 12 pounds of oats for his horse, which would be slung across its neck. Thompson pointed out:

'The load that a cavalry horse has to carry is not light. Besides his rider and saddle, he has to carry an overcoat [which many left behind], extra blanket, one half of a dog tent, one hundred rounds of ammunition, gun, pistol [and] several days' rations.'[9]

Custer was characteristically uncompromising during his initial brief at Officer's Call. According to Lieutenant Godfrey, he said:

'We will follow the trail for 15 days unless we catch them before that time expires, no matter how far it takes us from our base of supplies... You had better carry along an extra supply of salt; we may have to live on horse meat before we get through.'[10]

'There was plenty of excitement around the camp that night,' said Corporal Windolph. Sutlers and merchants brought up with the *Far West* plied their wares along the south bank of the river. A number of officers, including Reno and soldiers – among them Private Nathan Short – purchased straw hats for 25 cents each. These were lighter and cooler in the hot sun compared to the regulation wide-brimmed felt hat. Short marked his with a number '7' and crossed sabres on the outside, and his company number '50' inside. They were a good buy, cheaper than what the sutlers were asking for them. Short was to lose his in intriguing circumstances on the trail the next night.[11]

That last night made an indelible impression on many in the 7th. Burkman relates:

'I'll never forgit that night, Bud, as long as I live... Fur awhile, across the river, in the cabin of the *Far West* they was a light twinklin'. They was probably playin' poker down thar and maybe drinkin' some.'

A high-stakes poker game was indeed being played out on the *Far West*. Captain Tom Custer, Lieutenant James Calhoun and others played against Captain William Crowell of the 6th Infantry Regiment. There was reckless betting from those reconciling themselves to the perils of the uncertain looming ahead. It was a game between the living and those soon to die. Captain Crowell emerged the richer by some several thousand dollars.[12]

Custer abstained from drink and like many others was hunched over a flickering lamp writing last letters. When it became obvious that the regiment was to be committed to combat, Lieutenant Godfrey remembered that 'nearly everyone took time to write letters home, but I doubt very much if there were many of a cheerful nature'. Some made wills or arrangements to dispose of personal property as if 'they seemed to have a presentiment of their fate'.[13] Not all the letters were downbeat. Success was anticipated and mail reflected this as well as normal domestic concerns. Custer wrote a brief final letter to his wife. 'Do not be anxious about me,' he wrote.

'You would be surprised how closely I obey your instructions about keeping with the column. I hope to have a good report to send you by next mail.'

He clearly foresaw victory. 'A success will start us all toward [Fort] Lincoln' and home. Boston Custer, writing to his mother that night, likewise had no doubts about the outcome of the coming operation:

'I am feeling first rate. Armstrong [Custer] takes the whole command, and starts up the Sweet Briar on an Indian trail with the full hope and belief of overhauling them – which I think he probably will, with a little hard riding. They will be much entertained.'

He was undaunted by odds. 'Be the number great or small,' he wrote, 'I hope I can truthfully say when I get back, that one or more were sent to the happy hunting-grounds.'

Trumpeter Henry Dose in G Company, like all family men, offered a more domestic perspective. He 'was a great deal troubled,' writing to his wife, 'that I didn't get no letter from you. I am all right if I only know that you and them children are all well.' He too appeared confident about the outcome of the campaign. 'General Tarry [sic] said if we get Sitting Bull and his tribe soon, then we are going home, but if we don't, we will stay three months and hunt for him.' They were to find him within days and perish. 'Don't forget your Husband and wigth [sic] to me when ever you get a change [sic] for I am lonely her [sic] to hear from you.' He was like many troopers, counting the days to get home.[14]

Activity in camp that night was typical of any on the eve of battle, which was forced gaiety tempered by the realisation of hard days ahead. 'Thar'd been a lot o' drinkin' goin' on that day amongst the troopers,' recorded Burkman, 'and some officers, they bein' human and liquor tastin' good to their innards arter so much alkeli water.' Providing a sober backcloth to the forced frivolity was the steady and monotonous beat of Rees and Crow scout tom-toms. They were 'dancin' their death dances,' said Burkman, 'and havin' their death pow-wows. The Indians is like dogs,' he remarked. 'They can smell death a long ways off.'

On the morning of 22 June Custer's orderly found him hunched over his cot, pen in hand, having removed only his coat and boots. He was fatigued even before the start. 'I hated to rouse him,' said Burkman, 'he looked so peaked and tired.' 'Strangely enough,' said Windolph, 'a sense of depression seemed to pervade the camp and not a few of the letters voiced this feeling.' Sentimental later accounts of the final departure of the 7th play on the tragic consequences that were to follow. 'It was as if a premonition of coming catastrophe was in the men's hearts which they could not shake off,' he said. However, Windolph honestly relates that 'dejected spirits' may well also have been the consequence of 'a more substantial cause than premonition of coming evil'. Some of the officers had lost considerable sums of money at poker on the *Far West*. 'One of the stiffest ever played on the rivers,' admitted its Captain, Grant Marsh, well attuned to the norms. Many soldiers were also suffering after a night of hard drinking. Mule-packers were strapping on loads 'with more haste than care', according to Burkman, 'doubtless due to late night hangovers'. Careless stowage was to cause difficulties during the march. 'I can't say as any o' the Seventh felt specially glum that mornin',' concluded Burkman, 'except maybe some that'd lost in poker the night before.' There were of course doubts and premonitions of what might lie ahead, but in general soldiers are robust about such matters. 'I don't believe many of the troopers were very worried,' agreed Windolph. 'We knew there'd be some hard fighting, but a soldier always feels that it's the other fellow who's going to get it. Never himself.' Burkman echoed this positive sentiment:

'The feelin' in general was that we was proud as hell 'cause it was the seventh bein' sent out to git the Indians 'stead o' Gibbon's men or Terry's.'[15]

That day Custer, ostentatiously dressed in a yellow buckskin fringed suit, departed the Yellowstone with his regiment of 12 companies comprising 598 soldiers and numbering about 652 men in all including scouts and other attachments. At 1200 hours his mounted companies trotted by in column of fours before a reviewing party consisting of General Terry, Colonel Gibbon and Major Brisbin and their orderlies. Terry had a pleasant word for each company commander as they passed in review order, with Custer alongside radiating pride in his regiment. They were the vanguard and everyone knew it. Victory was assured. As Lieutenant Bradley, with Colonel Gibbon, expressed it:

'Should we come to blows it will be one of the biggest Indian battles fought on this continent, and the most decisive in its results, for such a force as we shall have united will be invincible, and the utter destruction of the Indian village, and overthrow of Sioux power will be the certain result. There is not much glory in Indian wars, but it will be worth while to have been present at such an affair as this.'[16]

Gibbon would block, but only after Custer's first strike. As
Custer turned his horse after a cheerful goodbye and best wishes for
a successful pursuit and victory, Gibbon called out to him, 'Now
Custer, don't be greedy, but wait for us!' Custer gaily waved back.
'No I will not,' he responded ingenuously and galloped after his
command.

Shortly after, Terry and Gibbon led the remaining force of four
cavalry and five infantry companies numbering 723 men westwards
along the Yellowstone River towards the mouth of the Little
Bighorn. Terry had split his force in half, not realising that, four
days earlier, the same force that Custer was going to attack, with
less than half the potential, had almost overwhelmed Crook's
greater column.

Approach march

Custer reached his first camp after a 12-mile march conducted at
about 3 miles per hour. This brisk pace was designed to shake out
the column and test equipment and pack-mule stowage. The troops
wound their way among the tree-lined twists and turns of the
Rosebud River, covered in the bushes from which it derived its
name. 'At this season of the year the air was laden with the odour
of the roses,' recalled Private Thompson with C Company. 'But for
the fact we were on business, our march in its vicinity would have
been pleasant.' Cavalry horses bore exceedingly heavy loads even
before the rider set foot in the stirrup. Troopers themselves averaged
between 130 and 150 pounds in weight, so the horses would be
ridden for an hour then walked for 30 minutes to avoid over-
exhaustion. Temperatures were in the 80s and 90s on this, the
longest day of the year, and it was very dry. As the sun's rays began
to pick out the horizontal strata on the rocks, the column
approached its first halt. To the right was the dark blue mass of the
Wolf Mountains. As the soldiers set about their evening routine,
the metallic whirring of crickets seemed to accentuate the almost
tangible dryness in the air.[17]

At Officer's Call that night Custer uncharacteristically discussed his future expectations and plans. He explained why he had declined further support from Terry, acknowledging that they may encounter at least 1,000 hostiles judging from the number of lodge fires counted by Reno's scouting expedition. There would be some hard marching, he pointed out, about 25 to 30 miles per day. His officers were taken aback by his manner; normally brusque and aggressive, he never discussed anything. Today he appeared unusually conciliatory and subdued. Lieutenant Wallace of G Company became gloomy, confiding to his friend Lieutenant Godfrey commanding K Company that 'I believe General Custer is going to be killed'. Godfrey asked why he should think so, and Wallace responded, 'I have never heard Custer talk in that way before.' Custer was weighing his options and found them sobering. Mitch Bouyer, his chief scout, transferred from Gibbon, assessed that they may be up against 1,000 to 1,500 Sioux, and concluded, 'I can tell you we are going to have a damned big fight.'[18]

Custer was applying generalisations to 'Lo', the Indian foe common to any frontier army contemporaries. The village was seen as the tribe's economic and political epicentre and source of strength. Sensibly it became the target. Indians were obliged to move to seek game, their main food source, and they would need to locate the village near water. Movement was therefore predicated on the direction of streams and rivers. These also provided the natural thoroughfares across rugged terrain. Sanitation dictated regular moves. As a consequence of all these joint needs, no village could be of overwhelming strength; a gathering of more than 1,000 was unlikely. Despite the individual bravery of Indians, which conferred some military effectiveness, they formed loose associations around a charismatic leader. Co-operation between such groups was impromptu and only between small bands. Such a disjointed approach to fighting could never match co-operative and disciplined cavalry tactics. Custer anticipated a fight before joining Terry, but his target was seen as a village that would scatter at the first contact. He would therefore need to divide his force to contain the dispersal. This had been the accepted tactic on the Washita in 1868, and Reynolds's plan at the Powder River that winter.

Custer's perspective would have made sense to any cavalry commander in the 7th, 3rd or 2nd Cavalry Regiments on the 1876 expedition. It is useful to measure the appropriateness of such a response against a modern-day military appreciation of the same. 'Fighting power', according to British military doctrine, can be crudely broken down into three interrelated aspects: the 'Physical', 'Moral' and 'Conceptual'. The physical part is concerned with comparing numbers, manpower and resources (such as weapons) needed to execute the mission; the moral is the 'hearts' aspect, requiring willpower and determination to conduct it; while the conceptual is the 'minds' or intellectual input. This is the plan or strategy required to achieve the objective.

From the physical perspective, the 7th Cavalry was likely to be outnumbered by odds varying from two, three, or even four to one, greater if the army force was subdivided. A village strike would increase the odds even further because the old, young and other 'non-combatants' would join in the conflict. These might include warriors who had failed entry to a warrior society but had been comprehensively trained to fight. Custer's troopers were being increasingly worn down by the rigours of campaigning, while the Indians and their ponies would be fresh. Cavalry horses were reliant on insufficient forage and so were 'jaded', as one trooper described them. Many had travelled 1,000 miles, and half the regiment had arrived back exhausted from Reno's scout only two days before departing. Indian ponies were able to live off the land now it was spring and were lighter and faster. Substantial numbers of Custer's officers and NCOs had been absent even before the expedition set off, and companies were now down to 60–70% of their effective fighting strengths. Unknown to Custer was the extent of Indian firepower: perhaps as many as 30% of the braves were equipped with modern firearms. Indians were, however, burdened by their non-combatants and constrained by natural resources, but their village had expanded to a size rarely seen in living memory. The

Indians clearly had the advantage from the physical component perspective.

Comparing 'hearts' from the moral component perspective offers a similar conclusion. The 7th would be like the 3rd and 2nd Cavalry, who had already demonstrated at the Rosebud and Powder rivers that their combat determination was not as great as the Indian. Whereas they were engaged on punitive military raids, the Indians were fighting for their families and their very existence. The importance of Sitting Bull's mystical vision at the Sun Dance should not be underestimated. He, like Red Cloud before, had become an accepted moral rallying point. His dream had only partly been fulfilled by Crook's repulse at the Rosebud. The Sioux were convinced that the soldiers would die if they came back to the camp. They were full of confidence, having demonstrated tactical superiority in worsting Crook's column. Cavalry ranks had been previously thinned by desertion and weakened by the physical rigours of the march to the Yellowstone River. Despite feelings of racial superiority, 'Lo' was feared as a savage ogre at close quarters. There was a gulf between the officers and enlisted men, whereas the Indians were experiencing a degree of unprecedented spiritual unity. In the moral sense it could be argued the Indian was also in the ascendant.

Conceptually the cavalry, being the organised force, ought to be superior so long as it was able to bring disciplined firepower to bear. Indians avoided pitched battles, preferring hit-and-run guerrilla tactics, which is precisely the type of combat the 7th Cavalry was anticipating. They would scatter on contact. There was no coordinated planning, discipline or centralised structure on the Indian side. They fought, as they would hunt, using opportunist tactics to cut out weak links and destroy them. They were devastating opponents at close quarters. Although conceptually ahead, Custer's cavalry were trained for ceremony, not war. Their background operational experience consisted primarily of the 33 separate skirmishes and engagements conducted against Indians since the formation of the regiment in 1867.[19] This represented an average of only three incidents per year. Fatigues with reduced company strengths tended to take priority over ceremonial drills, the only joint mounted manoeuvres ever conducted. Fire discipline was of limited consequence if marksmanship training did not take place. As it rarely did, most riflemen were insufficiently accomplished to make use of the optimum longer range of the Springfield carbines. Officer supervision was vital for range estimation and fire control, but many in the 7th were absent. Cavalry were insufficiently armed for close-in combat, retaining only a pistol. Sabres were useless against the Indian, and the regiment had left theirs behind at the Yellowstone depot. There was no bayonet or fighting knife equivalent, apart from personal purchase, to match the lance, stone club, tomahawk or bow and arrow. In conclusion it could be argued that despite a theoretical army conceptual superiority, it bore little substance in the face of alternative Indian realities.

An objective and scientific examination utilising modern military criteria suggests that Custer was heading for defeat. This was, however, at variance with a more prejudiced view of Indian potential held by Custer and his contemporaries. Defeat at the hands of a group of savages was unimaginable. Nevertheless Custer was sobered by his thoughts and had passed on some of this disquiet at the first Officer's Call during the march. He would rely upon the legendary 'Custer luck'. But the 7th Cavalry were not the veterans he had previously relied upon during repeated intense engagements in the Civil War. However, this should not be too much of a problem as all the other contemporary cavalry commanders accepted that Indians were incapable of massing more than 800 warriors for long. Artillery and Gatling guns were not taken along because mobility was the key to counter the anticipated scattering of the target on contact. They were not to know that they would encounter more than twice this number and that Crook's experience had shown that they would attack and not disperse.

'We hit the trail at 5 o'clock sharp that second morning,' recalled Corporal Windolph, and it was to be a long march of some 32 to 35 miles. Within 8 miles the column re-acquired the trail that Reno had previously left. It was an intimidating sight: the ground was badly scoured by lodge tent poles over an immensely wide area. In modern terms it would have been like following a regiment of tanks. Indian braves owned two to three ponies each, compared to one horse, now worn out, being ridden by each cavalry trooper. So polluted and heavily grazed was the ground that Custer had to cross over to the other side of the Rosebud to enable his own animals to feed. 'We were in Indian country right enough,' declared Windolph. 'There were all kinds of signs that hundreds of Indians had been here.' Three abandoned village sites were passed one after the other. For the soldiers, each one meant that battle was approaching and every mile covered was one towards home. Temperatures remained at 30-plus degrees, and it was very dry; dust perpetually shrouded the main body of the column. Soldiers observing the immensity of the spoor stretching ahead drew their own baleful conclusions. 'The trail was wide and so torn up by teepee poles that we found it a difficult matter to secure a good camping place for the night,' said Private Thompson with C Company. 'This was especially so around watering places, which were so necessary to us.' Each campsite passed represented eight to ten days of Indian residency, so in one day Custer was catching up several weeks. Welcome though this was, it also gave cause for sober reflection. 'There was no foolishness,' remembered Corporal Windolph. It was hard riding.[20]

Fatigue was beginning to have an insidious effect upon the column. The regiment's 300-mile approach to the Yellowstone, coupled with Reno's 250-mile march for six companies, was clearly having an impact upon men and horses. Leather equipments were starting to wear out. Horses, like vehicles, require servicing. They are subject to various illnesses – colic, constipation and lameness – all adding to general dilapidation. Thompson had noticed on a number of occasions 'how poor and gaunt they were becoming'.

'This was not to be wondered at when we take into account the long marches they had made without any grain to sustain their strength; nothing but dead grass or perhaps a little green grass which was very short at this season of the year.'[21]

Soldiers themselves were beginning to suffer intestinal problems, mainly constipation caused by long periods on the trail without sufficient liquids. Prairie dysentery came from poor water and increased the need for fluid intake even more. Hardtack biscuits were no antidotes; they were the equivalent of modern 'energy bars', offering carbohydrates but little else. So-called 'trail mix' supplements of extras, or 'goodies' in soldier parlance, purchased at the fort, had long since been exhausted at the initial stage of the campaign. Trumpeter Henry C. Dose in G Company complained to his wife as early as the Powder River that 'the rations are running out very near'. There were no greens or roughage. Soldiers supple-mented rations by buying from the Indian scouts. 'Myself and Hageman and Weis got some antelopes meat from them,' wrote Dose, 'but had to pay $2 for a quarter of it.' Perennial teeth problems meant that they could not easily bite or chew the hardtack, which was issued three times per day. They were good for a week but offered little protection against the inevitable onset of scurvy. 'I spended [sic] already $8 for eating,' complained Dose.[22] Paradoxically, the Indian scouts loved hardtack.

Forensic studies of cavalry trooper bodies uncovered during recent archaeological research at the Little Bighorn reveal how distressing and uncomfortable these long forced marches might have been. One survey concludes:

> 'For a group of men so young, an undue number had back problems, arthritis and other pathologies and injuries that are infrequent among the young today. By present standards the incidence of injury and back problems is very high, and the dental health is atrocious.'

When the weight of equipment was combined with heavy carbine and hard saddle, 'butt-jarring' rides across rugged and unforgiving terrain must have resulted in excruciating pain. This was the consequence of the compression of inter-vertebral disks, which could cause chronic back pain. The same study concludes that 'nearly all the riders must have suffered and some men must have been nearly incapacitated'.[23] As the horses became thinner, both suffered. Saddles were hardly off and sores became increasingly prevalent.

Even if the troopers did not lack resolve, men and horses were exhausting their energy banks. Captain Frederick Benteen, one of Custer's wing commanders, recalled the parlous state of Dr Lord, one of the cavalry surgeons, at the end of the second day's march. He arrived in camp hours after everyone else, totally spent, 'telling me that he had halted alone some miles back, being completely tired out, broken down, so much so that he had given up all hopes of getting to camp'. Lord was at the end of his tether and provides an indication of the punishing pace of the pursuit. 'He declined tea, and wanted nothing to eat or drink.' All he wanted to do was sleep.[24]

John Finerty's newspaper description of Crook's command on the campaign could just as easily be applied to Custer's men:

'A more unromantic looking set of heroes the eye never rested upon than ours. Dust, rain, sun and sweat have made havoc of the never very graceful uniforms. The rear portions of the men's pantaloons are, for the most part, worn out. The boots are coffee-coloured. Such a thing as a regulation cap is not to be seen... Every face is parched – nearly every beard unshorn, and the eye is wearied by the unending display of light blue pants and dark blue shirts, all in a more or less dilapidated condition.'[25]

Custer's command were wearing out. Drooping with fatigue, they would not have taken in the dramatic scenery they passed, conical hills with strata layered in all shades of red, brown and moss green. Above them stretched the 'big sky' of Montana. At the

conclusion of a long day's march the cavalry troopers' responsibilities were considerably greater than their infantry counterparts,
who had only to lay their heads down on a bedroll. Two to three
hours' work was needed to brush down, water and feed the 630
horses and 140 mules in the column. Two hundred acres of grazing
required a substantial guard perimeter. Every man in the regiment
would be on sentry duty for two hours during the night, further
adding to sleep deprivation. 'Custer seemed tireless himself,'
observed Thompson, 'and seemed to think his men were made of
the same stuff.' Physical attrition was taking its toll on everyone.

> 'It was a hard sight to see men, who have been roused out of
> their sleep at half past three in the morning; not only once but
> day after day, sleeping in their saddles; and lucky indeed was
> the man who had a quiet and steady horse that allowed the
> luxury of a sleep while traveling.'[26]

In the past Indians had harassed sentries at night, but strangely
enough the column had thus far escaped detection.

The bivouac on the second night was within sight of the strata-
coloured cliffs that had dominated the Indian Sun Dance site,
where Sitting Bull had seen his vision of soldiers falling into camp.
All the signs indicated that the Indians were full of confidence after
defeating Crook. If the soldiers came back they would surely die.
Troopers were insensitive to the significance of the apparent signs
and remembered it only from the grisly mementoes of light-
coloured scalps hanging from a ridgepole. Speculation varied as to
how they got there. Windolph's company 'figured it was that of a
man who had been with Gibbon's Montana Column'. Thompson's
concluded 'from the appearance of the hair one belonged to a man
and [the] other to a woman'. The Indian scouts were considerably
awed and unsettled. Thompson observed 'as these signs increased in
numbers' that Bloody Knife, one of Custer's favourite scouts,
'became greatly excited, and his followers partook of his spirit and
became excited also'. Red Star, one of the Rees scouts, later claimed

that the Arikara scouts interpreted the signs as 'the Dakota medicine was too strong for them and that they would be defeated by the Dakotas [Sioux]'. All the scouts were in agreement. 'The Dakotas were sure of winning.'[27]

The column continued on in a cloud of swirling dust, steadily eating up the miles and decreasing the distance between themselves and the foe. Twelve miles on the first day was followed by a hard 30 to 35 on the second. On 23 June another 28 miles were covered. The pace was relentless. They were unaware that there was only 30 miles to go. Custer ordered the men to march in parallel columns as a security measure to reduce the dust. They remained undetected, unlike Crook, who had been picked up from the start. The Indians were not looking; the concept of a joint and coordinated multiple-column offensive was incomprehensible to warriors who thought and fought tactically as individuals. A merciless sun bore down upon blue-bleached shoulders covered in a fine mantle of dust. Lips were chapped and the smell of horses, dung and sweat permeated this dust-layered gritty-tasting air. Gnats and flies tormented man and beast alike. Company pennants hung lank in the hot still air. Saddle sores on the salt encrusted backs and flanks of horses itched and stung. Tongues investigated sore lips unalleviated by swigs of alkali-tainted water from lukewarm water canteens. The column moved steadily on. 'The march during the day was tedious,' recorded Lieutenant Godfrey with K Company. 'The weather was dry and had been for some time.'[28]

As they nodded listlessly along on horseback with heads down, or plodded on foot to give the horses a break, the men in the column were lost in their own thoughts. Custer was single-minded and pushed a punishing pace. This might be the last decisive Indian battle to be fought on the American continent. Promotion might be achievable if success could be delivered, like an ancient Roman Triumph, on the eve of the Centennial celebration. Custer was a fighter. That was why he was spearheading the strike force. Opportunities for promotion were rare and, at 36 years, he was the oldest soldier in the column.

Dialogue in the ranks may have been incomprehensible to many. There were 379 immigrants from 25 different countries. Trumpeter John Martin from H Company spoke in a barely comprehensible and heavily accented Italian English; he had been a 14-year-old drummer-boy in the Italian War of Unification against Austria. Language difficulties among newly arrived immigrants may have affected communications and perhaps regimental cohesion. The irony was that more immigrants arrived each year than there were Indians on the Great Plains. Red Cloud, during his visit to the eastern seaboard of the United States, had long ago recognised that the white men were 'as thick and numerous … as grasshoppers', wisely distancing himself from a war he knew there was no hope of winning.

Officers kept their individual thoughts and emotions to themselves. Major Reno, following several career-bruising encounters with Custer and Terry, would no longer question orders, although Captain Benteen may have had a certain empathy with Reno's difficulties, raising an only son after his wife's death, as he himself had lost his youngest that winter. 'I lost four children in following that brazen trumpet around,' he recalled sorrowfully later.[29] Newly arrived Second Lieutenant James 'Jack' Sturgis was fresh-faced and was the 'darling' of the ladies at Fort Rice. 'One of the most lovable boys who ever came out of the United States Military Academy,' wrote Katherine Gibson, an officer's wife. His father, brevet General Sam Sturgis, the absent commander of the 7th Cavalry, had discouraged his son from joining. Sturgis had disregarded this advice and relished the prospect of recognition in the coming battle. His father reconciled himself to the inevitable but had enjoined newly recruited Private William Slaper with M Company 'to take good care of him' while at Jefferson Barracks, St Louis, 'which we gladly promised to do,' Slaper said. The young Sturgis was further congratulating himself at his good fortune to be transferred to Fort Lincoln – regimental headquarters – in place of Lieutenant Francis Gibson, and was now serving with E Company, away from Slaper's M Company. Gibson's wife Katherine had dissuaded her husband from serving directly under Custer's command, pleading with him to remain with Benteen's company at Fort Rice. All this was based on little more than a Cassandra-like premonition of disaster. Gibson followed his wife's advice, despite the career implications, and would survive the coming battle.[30] Sturgis did not.

Lieutenant Donald McIntosh was plagued with the problem of social acceptance by brother officers, because of his half Indian and half Canadian parentage. Colonel Sturgis's view at Fort Leavenworth appears to bear this out, commenting, 'If he were an enlisted man he would pass as a malingerer.'[31] Others nursed previous physical injuries. Second Lieutenant John Crittenden had lost an eye in an accident nine months before joining the 7th the previous month, filling one of the numerous vacancies created by news of the expedition's imminent departure. His father, Colonel Thomas Crittenden, the commander of the 17th Infantry Regiment, successfully petitioned Custer to take his only son along with him. The 22-year-old officer, like Sturgis, relished the prospect of action, with his father's advice fresh in his ears: to do his duty and never retreat. 'If he does not come back,' his father was alleged to have remarked, 'I never again can look his mother in the face.'[32] John Crittenden may have begun to feel vulnerable at the prospect of closing with Indians with only one eye, and would have been more reliant on his comrades than most. He was not to return.

Mark Henry Kellogg, the newspaper reporter with the *New York Herald* (as well as correspondent for the *Bismarck Tribune*), saw himself on the verge of scooping the greatest story of his life. He was accompanying the famed General Custer on the likely final great battle of the Indian wars. 'The hope is now strong and I believe well founded,' he wrote in his final dispatch to the editor, 'that this band of ugly customers known as Sitting Bull's band will be "gobbled" and dealt with as they deserve.' Custer was excellent 'copy' – 'a brave, faithful, gallant soldier, who has warm friends and bitter enemies, the hardest rider, the greatest pusher, with the most untiring vigilance.' Kellogg warred with adjectives. 'The pen picture is true to life, and is drawn not only from actual observation,' he stressed, 'but from an experience that cannot mislead me.' Kellogg basked in the self-satisfaction of realising that when he got back he would file the story of the Centennial and his journalistic career would be assured. It needed to be. He was a widower, who had lost his wife, aged 28, nine years before and he was supporting two daughters aged 13 and 14. His scoop was to prove posthumous.[33]

The soldiers were from all walks of life. Private Nathan Short with C Company had been a labourer, and was now the company carpenter. Soldiering might offer him an opening to settle in the West. German-born Private Durslew in A Company was reputed to have been a Lieutenant during the Franco-Prussian War of 1870. There was some irony in his situation, as was also the case with Private James Henry Russell in C Company, whose father had been a Major in the Confederate Army, and here he was fighting his opponent's battles. Sergeant Finlay in the same company dwelt on the health of his pregnant wife back at Fort Abraham Lincoln. Many of the soldiers had relished this expeditionary operation, a 'lark' compared to the drudgery of life at the fort. These feelings had by now been overtaken by the rigours of the march. Any study of the service records of the 7th Cavalry reveals a large incidence of misdemeanours: drunkenness, desertion and scrapes with women and authority. These were not the issues that concerned them now. They were men of flesh and blood, intimately familiar with each other as a consequence of the isolated lives they led. Most saw the battle approaching as an indicator that soon they would be on their way home. 'But Sis,' wrote Private Thomas Meador with H Company, 'I can go on this one for it will be my last one.'

> 'I will come home next fall if nothin' hapins Sis tell Jerry that the best place is at home and not for him to leave home for it does not make any difference how humble it is there is no place Like home.'[34]

Meador was destined never to see his sister at home.

Second Lieutenant George Wallace with G Company still nursed his previous sense of foreboding as the column rode onward. A blanket of dust seemed to hang over the marching soldiers like a funeral shroud. At the halt by the 'Sun Dance' lodge he had observed the General's headquarters flag blown over by a stiff southerly breeze. It remained pointing in the direction they had come. Lieutenant Godfrey picked it up and stuck it in the ground but it toppled over again. This time he more determinedly bore the staff into the ground where it stayed upright, tenuously supported by a sage bush. Godfrey turned and thought nothing of it. Wallace, however, remained troubled. 'He regarded the fact of its falling to the rear as a bad omen,' he later remarked to Godfrey, 'and felt we would suffer a defeat.'[35]

Chapter 7
Fatal decisions

'He was not a reckless commander
or one who would plunge into battle
with his eyes shut.'

Union cavalry officer's view of Custer

'Worms wriggling in the grass'

'The trail was growing fresher every mile,' Private William Taylor
with A Company observed. 'The whole valley was scratched up by
trailing lodge-poles.' Custer and his scouts and soldiers saw
increasing signs of the Sioux village throughout the day on 24 June.
Trampled meadows were speckled with dry pony droppings. 'Our
interest grew in proportion as the trail freshened,' Taylor revealed,
'and there was much speculation in the ranks as to how soon we
should overtake the apparently fleeing enemy.'[1]

Custer was troubled. Tracks were leading both in and out of the
rutted path to his front. Lieutenant Godfrey with K Company saw
that 'the valley was heavily marked with lodge-pole trails and pony
tracks, showing that immense herds of ponies had been driven over
it.'[2] Custer's niggling fear was that elements of the Indian village
might already be dispersing. The truth was that tracks were converging, with even more Indians joining the main body. Summer
roamers were turning up and adding considerable numbers to the
assembly that had already caused Crook's retreat.

It has been estimated, reconstructing the available data, that the
total population from the Sioux and Cheyenne tribes participating in

the war of 1876 numbered some 21,870. About 8,000, or 37%, were absent from Government Indian Agencies during the conflict. John S. Gray has assessed that the period following the battle of the Rosebud witnessed the greatest influx of summer roamers to Sitting Bull's big village. From 18 to 23 June it swelled from the 400 lodges of winter roamers twice spotted by Lieutenant Bradley in May, to 960 in June. This 140% increase of summer wanderers, which had not been the US Army's intention to engage, coincided with the surge of morale that followed Crook's check and retreat. It also represented a massive US Army intelligence failure, because Custer's force was given no inkling of the aggressive spiritual and numerical surge within the Indian force that accompanied it. A village of nearly 1,000 lodges would include about 7,120 persons able to field 1,780 adult males, which alongside fledgling warriors might muster a force of 2,000 braves.[3] These men were bred to fight, and grossly outnumbered Custer's approaching force of fewer than 600 volunteers with their varying degrees of experience and service. By any objective analysis, Custer was hurrying to likely defeat – and possibly disaster – should he further increase the odds by adopting the accepted tactic of dividing his force to apprehend a scattering target.

At 1945 hours on 24 June 1876 Custer's command bivouacked at the Busby Bend of the Rosebud Creek, in the shadow of the Wolf Mountains. Men and horses could not drink properly as the water at this site was badly tainted by alkali. It remained unclear whether the Indians had continued up the Rosebud or turned west toward the Little Bighorn River. Four of Custer's scouts resolved the conundrum at 2100 when they revealed that the trail lead westwards. Custer now faced a dilemma. Terry's orders were to turn west only after reaching the headwaters of the Rosebud so as to synchronise with the projected arrival of Gibbon's column. There were risks associated with Terry's direction. They might blunder into Indian scouts if they continued, lose contact with the Indian village, or leave Gibbon to face them alone.

Custer's first major decision point was his choice to maintain contact and follow Sioux tracks westwards across the ridgeline or 'divide' between the Rosebud and Little Bighorn rivers. He was technically disobeying orders, and ironically had castigated Reno for doing the same. This was not a difficult decision for an aggressive cavalry commander. Terry had expressed his reluctance, reflected in his instructions, 'to wish to impose ... precise orders which might hamper your action when nearly in contact with the enemy'. Custer took him at his word. Terry was well acquainted with the personality of his 'pushy' subordinate. He was appointed leader of the strike force to exploit this very propensity, likely to produce results. There would be time to formulate a more precise plan and include Gibbon's column once contact with the Indians had been established. The imperative remained to find and close with the enemy. Custer was totally focused on the need to catch up with the village, and sensed that his prey was within sight.

Custer's Crow scouts were familiar with this area, which had been their tribal lands before the Sioux had pushed them off. They advised Custer that there was a lookout point not far away in the Wolf Mountains that would enable him to look into the valley of the Little Bighorn. At 2120 Lieutenant Charles Varnum, the Chief of Scouts, was dispatched to this natural observation point, called the 'Crow's Nest', to see if he might pinpoint the location of the Sioux village. Custer began to formulate the genesis of a plan. It would be sensible to move under cover of darkness to the dividing ridgeline between the Rosebud and Little Bighorn. He could afford to lay up there during daylight on 25 June, having achieved a covered approach, hidden in the small depression at the base of the Crow's Nest feature. This would permit time for a detailed reconnaissance of the village approaches to set up a dawn attack for 26 June. Gibbon should by then have reached his blocking position.

The Crow's Nest comprised a series of ridges enclosing its bowl feature and was often used to conceal stolen horses after Crow raids on the Sioux or Cheyenne. It was in effect a 'nest', from which it likely derived its name. Lieutenant Varnum arrived during the pre-dawn hours of 25 June accompanied by Charley Reynolds, Mitch Bouyer and a dozen Crow and Rees scouts. A steep climb through the tree line led to the top of a promontory facing west towards the Little Bighorn Valley, 15 miles away. At about 0430 hours the first rays of the sun began to glow atop the surrounding high ground enabling the keen-eyed scouts to pick out campfire smoke and what appeared to be elements of a vast pony herd, grazing on low hills bordering the far side of the valley. Despite concentrating hard, Varnum was unable to detect anything of substance.

'The Crows tried to make me see a smoke from the village behind the bluff on the Little Bighorn and gave me a cheap spyglass, but I could see nothing. They said there was an immense pony herd out grazing…'

He was urged to look out for 'worms crawling in the grass', the ripple effect of thousands of ponies moving around at great distance. Varnum confessed that 'my eyes were somewhat inflamed from loss of sleep and hard riding in dust and hot sun and were not in the best of condition'.[4] Nevertheless, he did not dispute the unanimous verdict of his scouts. The month's long search since leaving Fort Abraham Lincoln was yielding a climax. The village had at last been found and was on the Little Bighorn. Varnum sent a dispatch to Custer at 0500 hours recommending that he come and conduct a leader's reconnaissance.

Meanwhile, the main column, after being force-marched for three days to reach the Busby Bend of the Rosebud, was less than enthusiastic to receive news that their anticipated night's sleep was to be denied. Twenty-eight miles that day were to be followed by an additional night march of indeterminate distance. 'We'd finished our supper and were just starting to rest when we got warned that we'd start again,' said Corporal Windolph. They were tired of rations. 'It hadn't been much of a supper' and the water at the Bend was tainted. They reluctantly prepared for the night march. 'We were all fairly tired, men and horses alike,' recalled Windolph, 'but we weren't anywhere's near being worn out.' Captain Frederick Benteen, one of Custer's wing commanders, resigned himself to the preparations with something like equanimity. 'We move at 11 o' clock pm sharp tonight,' he heard. 'All right, then, there's no sleep for your humble again tonight.' Soldiers had averaged five or so hours' sleep over the past three days. Picket duties, administering animals and the propensity of rank and file to talk when they should be sleeping had taken its toll. There had been no urgency to get to sleep on arrival at Busby, and the unexpected news made it too late. 'Second night's loss of sleep,' Benteen laconically logged in his account.[5]

At half past midnight on 25 June Custer led his soldiers out of the Busby Bend camp towards the divide. 'It was dark as pitch when we started out again,' complained Windolph. 'You couldn't see twenty feet ahead of you.' A night approach march towards the enemy is a difficult phase of war. Physically demanding, the adrenalin-induced mental pressure of chance discovery further saps strength. It took nearly three hours to march the first leg of 7 miles across rugged and rolling countryside, the column winding its way between knolls and the first craggy outcrops of the Wolf Mountains. They gradually climbed in elevation from 2,340 to 4,000 feet, negotiating occasional wood copses. 'The best we could do was to follow along behind the troop ahead,' said Windolph, 'letting the rattle of the tin cups and carbines on the saddles guide you.' The column was immersed in volumes of suffocating dust, which according to Lieutenant Godfrey with K Company made it 'impossible to see any distance and the rattle of equipments and clattering of the horse's feet made it difficult to hear distinctly beyond our immediate surroundings'. Should Indians be concealed nearby, the soldiers would never detect them. Captain Benteen relied on the 'ding-donging of the tin cup, frying pan – or something' for direction, 'the pounding of that on the saddle of the horse on the left of the troop preceding mine, being all I had to go by.' Godfrey recalled that 'we could not see the trail and we could only follow it by keeping in the dust cloud'. There were difficulties maintaining bearings, and energy-sapping halts and starts. Occasionally 'we were obliged to halt to catch a sound from those in advance, sometimes whistling or hallooing, and getting a response we could start forward again'. The night march was another endurance-sapping ordeal for animals and soldiers short of sleep, rest and water.[6]

Private William Taylor with A Company described how:

'You see something like a black shadow moving in advance. You are conscious that men and animals are moving within a few paces, and yet you cannot define any particular object, not even your horse's head. But you hear the steady, perpetual "tramp-tramp-tramp" of the iron hoofed cavalry, broken by an occasional stumble and the half smothered imprecation of an irate trooper, the jingle of carbines and sling-belts, and the snorting of the horses as they grope their way through the eternal dust, which the rider can feel in his throat.'[7]

A halt was called at 0315 hours at Davis Creek, to cook breakfast about an hour before sunrise. Eating was not the soldier's first priority. 'None of us had had much sleep for several days,' recalled Windolph, 'so we were glad to lie down and grab a little rest.' Their lot was not improving. Some soldiers attempted to make coffee 'but the water was so alkaline we almost gagged on it'. Custer as ever could not sleep. He was 'hyper' with anticipation of what lay ahead. He moved between groups of soldiers chatting. Troopers lay down, but being on call to move at any time, got no rest. 'No orders for anything [were] received,' recorded an irate Benteen. 'So, the Packs remained on mules; saddles and bridles on horses.'[8] The frequency of bad water was denying the men and horses vital fluids, exacerbating the condition of those plagued with Prairie dysentery. At about 0730 hours Custer received Varnum's message from the Crow's Nest. Inside half an hour he was on his way to observe for himself.

He arrived at about 0900 accompanied by his scouts, Frank Gerard and Bloody Knife. By then the sun was higher and the horizon hazier than it had been in the cool light of dawn. Custer had his expectations but, like Varnum, was unable to detect the pony herd, campfire smoke or any indication that his objective was in sight. Once more the insistence of the scouts and obvious evidence of fresh trail spoors during his approach convinced him that there was indeed a large hostile gathering in the valley of the Little Bighorn.

He began to formulate a plan as he surveyed the terrain to the west. A line of light-coloured bluffs blocked his view into the valley. He discerned the zigzag line of Ash (later Reno) Creek reaching out towards the bluffs where it disappeared by their left edge, probably draining into the Little Bighorn River. Only the northern end of the village may have been visible where the signature of early-morning cooking fires had been seen. There was an area of green noticeable beyond the bluffs, later known as the 'Bench', which were the slopes upon which the giant pony herd – 'worms wriggling in the grass' – was grazing. Although Custer could not pick them out, he accepted the judgment of his scouts. Custer's interrogation of these men, due to the repetitive and probably frustrating interpreter process, must have taken time and patience. Detail would have been lost in the process of telling. If the pony herds were still visible, Indians had to be there. This was the obvious and exciting conclusion for Custer – but had his approach been detected?

The scouts reported seeing two Indians moving south to north and another group on a knoll to the north, travelling west to east. There was lengthy discussion over whether the column may have been spotted.

As Custer moved to the rear of his lookout point a plan was coalescing in his mind. His men were tired and needed a hot meal. The horses were approaching the end of their reserves and needed attention. The Crow's Nest feature offered the opportunity to lie up and rest during the day while the vital reconnaissance of the objective was made. Custer himself had been without sleep for 29 hours. Fatigue had been kept at bay by his excited state at the prospect of meeting the enemy. His scouts suggested that a stealthy approach was now impractical, pointing to the main cavalry column now moving to the foot of the Crow's Nest. Custer was incensed, an irritation fuelled by tiredness. Who had given the regiment permission to close without first confirming a secure route?

Fifteen miles distant, in the valley of the Little Bighorn, the village was gradually waking up as the sun climbed into the sky. Women carrying buffalo-bone hoes were moving into the surrounding hills to dig for wild turnips. Others were working preparing skins or engaged in domestic skills such as quillwork or beading. Boys and some men were out fishing. It was a peaceful lazy day. Dancing had kept warriors up the night before, celebrating and boasting about the victory over 'Three Stars' (Crook), and many were sleeping in. Streams of summer roamers continued to arrive, adding to a certain carnival atmosphere. Few people expected trouble. The white soldiers had gone and Sitting Bull had told them they would all die should they return. They were spiritually and physically reassured by the large numbers massing in the camp.

Estimates of the size of this village vary widely. It was probably some 1½ miles long by 300 yards wide, perhaps covering an area of a quarter of a square mile. According to Indian sources it stretched from the westernmost loop of the Little Bighorn River near Shoulder Blade Creek in the south to the mouth of Medicine Tail Coulee (or ravine) to the north. This was theoretically within Custer's capacity to attack and defeat, not dissimilar in size to the village on the Washita in 1868. His Indian scouts claimed from their Crow's Nest observations that it was the biggest village they had ever seen. Indians were not, however, renowned for exactitude. 'One-two-many' was an arithmetical process that could not deal in large quantities. 'More than honest men need know' was often the Indian response to dealing with large numbers.[9] Custer was not intimidated. Size was not a factor when dealing with a target-rich environment.

There was no security or lookouts apart from a rudimentary 'crier' early warning system. G2 Intelligence was an alien concept to the Indian, as there was no centralised method of information-gathering or organised scout programme. Neither was there a centralised Indian command, defence plan or scheme of manoeuvre if attacked. The chain of command was war-bands within which there were spiritual and combat leaders. Tactics were reactive and security rudimentary. Young boys had the responsibility of guarding the pony herd. Nobody was aware of the approach of Custer's column because Indians were not familiar with any grandiose concept that would encompass joint actions between three separate yet interdependent US Army contingents. The soldiers had been driven away and nobody was looking for them any more.

During Custer's absence, Major Reno had moved the column forward to a position just north of the Crow's Nest. Custer, now obsessed with security, gave Reno another dressing down for possibly compromising the command. He also received further bad news. One of the inexpertly packed mules had lost a 50lb hardtack box during the night march. A detail was dispatched to retrieve it, and discovered several hostile Indians rummaging through its contents. Shots were fired and the Indians scattered. This latest breach of security forced an over-tired and possibly over-wrought Custer to disregard his previous plan for a stealthy approach. Unknown to him, the group of Indians apprehended by Sergeant Curtis, the detachment commander, was on its way back to the Government reservation, not the village. As there was no centralised Indian security plan, Custer's presence would not be reported by these hostiles until after the battle.

Custer had no way of knowing that. He now made his second momentous decision, which was to prove irreversible, and decided that instead of concealing his command during daylight on 25 June, he would immediately approach and attack the village. This intent was contrary to the rudimentary synchronisation previously agreed on the *Far West* to coincide with Gibbon's arrival at the blocking position. Another rational option could have been to monitor the village, accepting the risk of dispersal, and wait until Terry's combined forces could be brought to bear. Custer's decisions at this stage were influenced by lack of rest and the mental pressure his ruthless pursuit of success was applying. He had received less sleep than any other man in his command. He had to compose and issue orders, ride to the Crow's Nest, and the other additional mileage anticipated of any cavalry commander. Hard though Custer was, fatigue may have had an insidious effect. Captain Benteen was uncomplimentary about the quality of direction he was receiving at this time. After the halt at Davis Creek 'the column moved forward no orders however, for some were gotten, but my troop and I followed the procession: [toward the Crow's Nest] then came almost as sudden a halt: no orders for that'. Reno, who received the blame for the undirected move to the divide, could have been forgiven for engaging in constructive concurrent activity, but evasively claimed after the event:

'I discovered the column was moving. I was not consulted about any of those things. The organisation into battalions and wings had been annulled before we left the Yellowstone River. I never received any orders direct myself. I exercised the functions of what I imagined to be those of a Lieutenant Colonel.'

When excited, it was claimed by some that Custer appeared to speak faster than he thought. He could be harsh and rude to his subordinates. Lieutenant Godfrey had spoken of his 'rasping manner'.[10] Reno was currently feeling his ire, doubtless exacerbated by his tiredness and a catalogue of seeming bad luck.

Surveys conducted by the British Army of the Rhine during the 'Cold War' in the 1970s identified the impact lack of sleep can have upon decision-making and routine military procedures. Mistakes tend to occur within 24 hours of no sleep and become grossly magnified at the 36 to 72 hour point. Custer had reached the bottom end of this scale, with the impact worsened by intense physical (hard-riding) activity as well as mental pressures. During the Gulf War of 1991 the 1st UK Armoured Division commander directed on the third day of operations with virtually no sleep that key orders were to be faxed electronically rather than given orally.

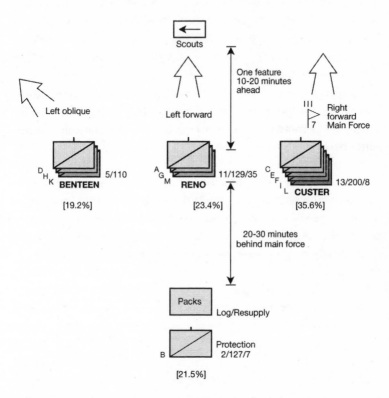

ADVANCE TO CONTACT
Custer splits his force shortly after crossing
the Divide after midday 25 June 1876

Scouts

One feature
10-20 minutes
ahead

Left oblique

Left forward

Right
forward
Main Force

D H K **BENTEEN** 5/110

A G M **RENO** 11/129/35

C E F I L **CUSTER** 13/200/8

[19.2%]

[23.4%]

[35.6%]

20-30 minutes
behind main force

Packs Log/Resupply

B Protection
2/127/7

[21.5%]

Notes:
% Figures approximate of whole regimental forces. (Scouts variable numbers).
Numbers: Officers/Men/Civilian (includes Scouts) e.g. 2/127/7

Advance to contact

Custer advanced on the village with 60% of his strength, attacking initially with
only 23.4% of his combat power. At no stage during the battle did the
regiment fight together.

This was to avoid errors that continuous operations were inflicting on standard decision-making and orders procedures.[11] Custer's command was on its fourth day of successive operations with minimum sleep, poor diet and insufficient water. All of them were beginning to make mistakes. Reno, in claiming to exercise his functions as a senior officer during the move forward to the divide, said, ' I was at different positions in the column, sometimes on the flanks and sometimes in the rear.' Was he in control or beginning to feel the pace also? He was not directing this move. 'The column moved out,' he said, 'and I followed it.'

At 1050 hours Custer gathered his leader group for an Officer's Call and announced that there was to be no rest. His soldiers had been force-marched across 90 miles of rugged territory with minimum sleep, poor rations and tainted water. 'We were tired and dirty and hungry,' said Corporal Windolph. 'Our horses hadn't had a drink of good water since the day before and we weren't much better off.'[12] Custer informed them that he intended to move immediately on the village. Much of the approach route was visible to them from where they stood on the divide ridgeline. The village lay behind the pronounced line of bluffs before them to the west.

There was to be a battle that day.

Advance to contact

Custer divided his regiment into four manoeuvre elements. Captain Benteen with a three-company battalion of 115 men from D, H and K Companies was to perform a 'left oblique' move of 45 degrees to the line of march and scout the hilly terrain to the south-west of the village. This was a containment mission to pick off any Indians fleeing in that direction and to secure the flank of the advance. Major Reno was given another three-company battalion of 140 men from A, G and M Companies and the majority (35) of the Indian scouts to move left forward towards the village on the south bank of Reno Creek. Custer, leading the main effort of five companies numbering 213 men and eight scouts, would move right forward on the north bank of the same creek toward the Little Bighorn. The fourth element, the pack train under Lieutenant McDougall with B Company numbering 136 men, was to follow a tactical bound, or about 20 minutes behind the main force. Up ahead would be the scouts, who would remain in visual distance one terrain feature ahead.

Custer had an average of only two to three officers with his companies (excluding the headquarters staffs), while Reno's battalion had three to four and Benteen one or two each. The ratio of officers and NCOs with the manoeuvre elements is significant, because the operational tempo had changed. Custer was now required to fight his command as a cavalry regiment. Up to this point they had simply marched. Now they would be required to manoeuvre and fight as interdependent units. The 7th had operated as a regiment on only two occasions during its history: at the Washita nine years before, and during the Black Hills Expedition in 1874. Its experience was mainly tactical. There had been on average one or two skirmishes involving isolated companies during each year of the regiment's service. Field manoeuvres were not generally practised. Range firings were a rarity and the only coordinated drills mastered had been those on the parade ground.

The American Civil War had demonstrated the impossibility of fighting cavalry as a manoeuvre arm in the teeth of high-intensity fire. Appalling casualties inflicted by more accurate weapons had negated conventional Napoleonic mass cavalry charges, which was why Civil War mobile tactics had transitioned to a mounted infantry concept of cavalry warfare. Both Custer and Sheridan had participated in these cavalry developments. On the frontier it was different. Elusive Indian hit-and-run tactics restored the previous efficacy of cavalry as a fluid flexible arm where mobility was paramount. Indians rarely offered battle and scattered on impact. Cavalry tactics developed a compromise solution. Civil War tactics tended to be applied, but were often inappropriate. Crook's battle experience on the Rosebud one week before exemplified this confusion: it began with a series of wheeling and manoeuvring cavalry charges and volleys and ended as a dismounted infantry action. Royall's force was tactically outmanoeuvred by the finest light cavalry on the Plains and had to resort to disciplined dismounted firepower to hold its own. Indian firepower had increased, but not to Civil War proportions. Crook, being reasonably rested, was astute enough to adapt his tactics accordingly. He too had divided his force as Custer was proposing to do, but kept them in sight. Custer had yet to scout the terrain over which he would fight but had already adapted his command to the conventionally held frontier army wisdom that one divided the force to attack an Indian village to prevent their escape. His manoeuvre units would not be in visual contact with each other.

Custer's plan on leaving the Crow's Nest had been to lie up for the day and scout the village approaches in some detail. In his fatigued state he felt impelled to attack immediately, convinced that operational security had been breached. It is likely that Custer had managed little more than a catnap during the previous 36 hours. His manner at the Officer's Call on the divide was strange and irascible. Reno was rebuked for conducting a sensible concurrent move forward, but with the fatigued state of all the officers and men the command appears to have simply drifted forward to join him as a 'good idea' at the foot of the Crow's Nest.

Benteen may have been slighted at his 'left oblique' mission, which meant that he would not spearhead what might be the final push resulting in the demise of the Plains Indian. 'Hadn't we better keep the regiment together, General?' Windolph heard Benteen ask Custer. He was logically questioning the wisdom of subdividing the force on the basis of a 15-mile-distant observation of the objective, but was put in his place. 'You have your orders,' Custer responded.[13] Being preoccupied with his reluctant decision to attack now, Custer was not the sort of personality to consider any better ideas to the contrary. 'Custer luck' had delivered in the past, or an aggressive and energetic response. Nobody doubted Custer's competency as a cavalry commander, but he was tired.

Top: Red Cloud: his war gained land ceded to the Sioux, but when he saw the size of the cities along the United States eastern seaboard he realised that they would never keep it.

Bottom: Fetterman: cited for gallantry and brevetted Lieutenant Colonel during the Civil War, Captain William Fetterman offered 'to ride through the whole Sioux nation' with 80 men – but failed.

Above: The present-day silhouette of a trooper stands atop Pilot Knob. Fort Phil Kearney is in the valley below and the ridgeline that Colonel Carrington ordered was not to be crossed is beyond.

Above: Massacre Ridge has a distinctive 'S'-shape. The ground over which the Indians attacked falls away steeply on either side.

Above : A lone tree marks the spot where Grummond and the majority of Fetterman's cavalry were overcome at the northern edge of the ridge. Wheatley's group was out of sight below the end of the ridge ahead.

Above: A stone marker marks the spot where Captain Fetterman and Lieutenant Brown were killed. The infantry perished further along the trail beyond.

Below: An example of one of the wagon boxes detached from its running gear at the site of the Wagon Box fight. A primitive 'fort' was formed by these boxes and a handful of men armed with new breech-loading M-1866 Springfield Allen rifles kept the Indians at bay, exacting a fearsome toll.

Above: The line of Reno Creek is marked by the tree line as seen from Custer's battalion perspective. The advance moved from left to right, with Reno's three companies on the other side of the creek.

Above: The site of the Lone Tepee where Custer decided to move on, leftwards, at best speed to attack the Indian village, knowing that he could be seen.

Above: The 'Flats' viewed from Reno's side of the creek. Custer, observing Indians silhouetted on the ridgeline to the left of the rocky outcrop (Weir Point in the distance), assumed that he was looking at the village entrance. When he attacked, right flanking, he found to his consternation that a sheer drop prevented him from supporting Reno engaged on the valley floor below.

Left: Private Peter Thompson served with Private Nathan Short in C Company. Left behind with a 'blown' horse when Custer ascended the bluffs above the village, he later rejoined Reno's command. The abandonment saved his life.

Above: Custer's Arikara scout Bloody Knife was sent by Custer to accompany Reno and was killed.

Below: Reno's skirmish line formed up in the area of the red-roofed buildings 300 yards from the edge of the Indian encampment, which stretched off to the left, observed from the area of the Indian pony herd. Reno's disorganised retreat took him up to the high bluffs via the re-entrant to Reno Hill in the far distance.

Above: One of Custer's camps, photographed during the 1874 Black Hills expedition, depicting the likely scene during one of the halts during the laborious 300-mile trek of Terry's Montana column. *(South Dakota State Historical Society)*

Below: The 'sphinx-like' Crook on campaign rarely discussed his thoughts or plans with subordinates. Fought to a standstill at the Rosebud one week before Little Bighorn, he studiously neglected to report to Sheridan or Terry that the Indians were attacking and not running.

Right: A typical (3rd) Cavalry bivouac in Texas, unworn by campaign rigours.

Below: Crook's Indian scouts would have had this view of the initial Indian charge at the Rosebud. To the right is the 'Buffalo Jump' cliff feature. The Indians attacked downhill through the re-entrant gap.

Left: Details from Amos Bad Heart Bull's pictographs showing Custer's men under considerable pressure in the retreat ...

... Reno's command fleeing amid the carnage inflicted en route to the river ...

... and Reno's men butchered as they attempt to cross the river.

Above: A panorama of the direction of attack from the Indian perspective as they charged down into the 'amphitheatre'-shaped valley area where Crook's column was caught at rest at the outset of the Battle of the Rosebud. The 'Buffalo Jump' is to the left as also the high ground where Captain Mills's first counter-charge would later occur. Crook's infantry was to assault up the slope toward the camera in the centre. On the right is the wooded high ground secured by Captain Van Vliet's rearguard.

Right: The McClellen army-issue saddle, giving some indication of the back-breaking fatigue experienced by cavalrymen riding hundreds of miles on campaign.

Below: The area between the hills is the petrified forest area where Cheyenne warrior Comes-in-Sight was rescued by Buffalo Calf Road Woman. As a consequence, the Indians named the Rosebud 'the battle where the sister saved her brother'.

Above: The present-day Busby Bend, Custer's final bivouac prior to the Little Bighorn battle. Water was so badly tainted by alkali that it was undrinkable.

Below: The bowl feature that forms the 'Crow's Nest' where Custer intended to hide his command overnight. Entry is past the vehicle, bottom right. The 7th Cavalry column moved from right to left in the middle ground beyond, riding from Busby Bend.

Top: Custer's view from the Crow's Nest. The Indian pony herd could be discerned as 'worms crawling in the grass' among undulations above the ridgeline hiding the village in the far distance. The line of Reno Creek is the dark zigzag, centre right. Individual Indian groups were seen crossing the middle ground, causing Custer to assume that after the skirmish over the hardtack box, his column was compromised. He chose to attack immediately.

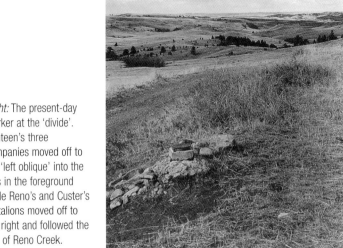

Right: The present-day marker at the 'divide'. Benteen's three companies moved off to the 'left oblique' into the hills in the foreground while Reno's and Custer's battalions moved off to the right and followed the line of Reno Creek.

Right: Private William Taylor, riding with A Company, scooped water from the Little Bighorn as they traversed to attack the village with Reno and 'drank the last drop of water I was to have for over 24 long hours'.

Above: Sgt Edward Botzer from G Company was killed in the river, and his remains were finally recovered in 1989.

Reno's line of retreat viewed from the top of Reno Hill. The fleeing soldiers emerged from the timbered area in the foreground and plunged into the Little Bighorn River, crossing at the foot of the re-entrant to the right. They next frantically climbed the steep ravine sides towards the camera.

Above: Minneconjou ford viewed from the Indian side, showing the shelved nature of the cavalry approach to the Little Bighorn.

Above: Captain Yates's feint attack emerged from Medicine Tail Coulee and encountered heavy fire when it reached the Minneconjou ford shown here. Across the river is the site of the massive Indian encampment; the pony herds were grazing just short of the high ground beyond.

Above: A gathering of Sioux warrior Indian veterans of the battle three years later. Elizabeth Custer wrote that 'none of them do any manual labour to produce muscle and their bones are decidedly conspicuous'. A Plains Indian man would never walk if he could ride. However, they were superior to Custer's soldiers at hand-to-hand fighting.

Above: Breech-loading the cavalry Springfield carbine.

Left: First Lieutenant James Calhoun commanded the initially effective L Company rearguard covering the junction of Yates's and Custer's companies before the final phase of the battle.

Dividing the force was his only option to achieve surprise against a more mobile enemy. Influenced by his experience on the Washita in 1868, he was following the recognised tactic of attacking the village from different directions in order to surround it. Virtually all US Army actions against Indian villages in the past, including Crook at the Powder River in March, had done the same. Capturing some non-combatants was a minimum objective, which had secured the safety of the 7th against counter-attacks at the Washita. Custer wanted a more decisive result than securing hostages: he was seeking to defeat the Indians. To do this he would have to fight his command as a regiment, but had already dispatched just under 20% of his fighting strength under Benteen on a separate, albeit related, mission. Reno, on the other side of what was later known as Reno Creek, had nearly one-quarter of his combat potential, and a further half lay with the five companies retained under his own command on his side of the stream. His real 'Achilles' heel', however, was the packs. They were guarded by a force equal to both Reno's and Benteen's respective commands, or just over 20% of his strength, dragging behind like a ball and chain and impeding the mobility of the whole regiment.

The 7th Cavalry mule train was a far less capable organisation than Crook's efficiently handled operation managed by professional civilian teamsters. On the morning of 15 June, when Custer had departed the Powder River, only 18 of 97 assigned mules were regular pack mules; the remainder were probably wagon mules. No pack mule train had ever been put together in the past in the Department of the Dakota. Lieutenant Godfrey pointed out that 'neither officers, men or mules had had any experience with this method of transportation' and 'there were very few "packers" [civilian employees] to give instructions'. Thirteen had broken down completely following Reno's 240-mile scout, and several more broke down soon after the start toward the Rosebud. Delays dogged the pack train throughout the march. Efficient packing was crucial to avoid debilitating the mules. Four to six weeks was the acknowledged time needed to train and prepare an efficient pack train. The gait is important and the walk or trot is part of the instruction to reduce excessive load movements. Private Thompson with C Company described what could happen:

'One of our mules named Barnum stumbled and fell. He went rolling down the hill with two boxes of ammunition on his back. As we watched his rolling we made calculations as to how much mule would be left in case the ammunition exploded. But contrary to all expectations, when he reached the bottom of the hill, he scrambled to his feet again with both boxes undisturbed and made his way up the hill again and took his place in the line as soberly and quietly as if nothing had happened.'

Captain Benteen, detailed to secure the pack train during the march on 23 June, recalled that 'it took one and a half hours to get the pack train across Rosebud Creek, so by that time Custer's column was all of six miles ahead of my train – and out of sight'. These delays resulted in many troopers arriving late at the bivouacs, far behind the main column, thereby adding further to fatigue. Many of the mules had festering sores on their backs due to inexpert loading by troopers. Cargoes came loose, and required frequent repacking. Just such an incident compromised the security of the entire force.

The packs were vital because they carried the regiment's 24,000-round ammunition reserve. Normally, a mule carrying 250lb might be able to travel 20 to 25 miles per day at 4 to 5 miles per hour. This would reduce to 15 miles when crossing rugged terrain with a lesser load of 200lb. The 7th's pack train rarely achieved these speeds. Because of this slow and cumbersome performance on the march, Custer felt obliged to provide additional security. Corporal Windolph pointed out that Captain McDougall had been earmarked with B Company to protect them, and also Lieutenant Mathey with six men and a corporal from each of the 12 companies. 'That meant that along with the civilian packers, there was more than 130 armed men in the pack train.'[14] The logistic train was an essential part of the fighting regiment and needed to be in sight and able to re-supply on demand. Custer, ever impatient to catch the Indians before they might scatter, was prepared to risk putting distance between his manoeuvre elements and his 'satellite' pack train. Crook was grateful for the efficient management of his train at the Rosebud, and fired off the majority of his reserve ammunition. If Custer manoeuvred offensively as light cavalry he would require less ammunition in the pursuit. To function effectively as mounted infantry would require correspondingly more ammunition than Custer countenanced using. His wing commanders, particularly Benteen, were to be influenced by the slow pace of the pack train. They did not share Custer's dash, and would wish to keep the reserve ammunition in sight, impressed as they were by the intimidating size of the scarred lodge-pole track stretching ahead.

Custer had made his third irreversible decision: to subdivide his command. Benteen had his doubts and had expressed them, and then carried on. He was to be vociferously critical about this after the event. 'Now isn't that the whole and sole reason that we were so badly beaten?' he later asked. 'That is the regiment being broken up into four columns, and none of the four within supporting distance of either of the others... True?' Reno, after all the previous scolding, was asking no questions. He was following orders.[15]

'Nobody was doing any talking when the word was passed to mount,' said Corporal Windolph. Whatever the conferences going on between the officers, 'we knew right enough that this was *the day*. This was IT. This was what we had been training for and working for all these years.' Benteen's three companies swung to the left oblique of the axis of advance, raising a diverging cloud of dust. They began to snake out into the hilly ridges stretching ahead, little realising as they glanced back at their fellows that they would not see many again. Major Reno's three companies began their advance to the left of Reno Creek, Custer's five companies to the right. The pack train struggled along in the rear. Windolph recalled how Benteen used to say, 'The Government pays you to get shot at.' Now, as even more dust began to refract the rays of the sun, marking the progress of the various columns, he added, 'and I suppose the dumbest, greenest trooper in the Regiment figured that this day he'd get shot at plenty.' The advance to contact had begun.[16]

Reno's and Custer's forces rode four abreast in column of march, with 50 or 60 feet between companies. Reno's column stretched back about 400 yards on the left bank of the stream and Custer's larger force of about 500 on the right. The significance of the cavalry 'fours' was key to tactical organisation in the coming battle. Each man, beginning at the head of a company, would call out his number – one, two, three, four – until the company column was numbered into sets of fours. The structure was designed for the mounted infantry role, with troops required to dismount after an advance, charge or manoeuvre, designed to hold ground. 'Number four remains on his horse,' explained Private Thompson and 'numbers one, two, and three dismount and hand their bridle reins to number four who holds the horses.' The others would then 'deploy as skirmishers or as otherwise directed'.[17] This would be set up prior to the advance to contact now under way. Any encounter with an unexpected enemy would develop into a 'meeting engagement'. Tension was high. The troopers had no idea that they still had about 16 miles to go.

Lieutenant Godfrey described the route being followed by the two spearhead columns as 'very tortuous, and sometimes dangerous, followed down the bed and valley of the south branch of this creek, which at that time was dry for the greater part of its length'. Thompson, riding at the head of Custer's column, saw that the going for Reno was easier, for on the left 'the country was flat, on the right it was very rough and broken'. The undulating ground broadly followed the line of the creek. Up ahead, the crest line formed by the line of bluffs cloaking the village dominated the approach. They had still not apparently been seen. Godfrey pointed out that 'the high bluffs which screened the village' meant that 'it was not possible in following the trail to discover more'. They were totally blind and reliant on the scouts occupying the next feature forward for early warning. 'Nor was there a point of observation near the trail,' Godfrey remarked, 'from which further discoveries could be made until the battle was at hand.'[18] These dips and folds that the strike force was negotiating had not been visible from the Crow's Nest. Visibility was restricted to a few hundred yards ahead. Benteen's unit was now completely out of sight, swallowed up by the undulating ground to their left. Only dust clouds offered visual contact and still the Indians had not seen their approach.

At 1400 hours, Custer, pushing a fast pace, crossed a saturated area known as the 'morass'. This was an area of stagnant seepage that formed a bog containing the spring and winter rain run-off from the Wolf Mountains. It was starting to dry and crack at the edges in the heat. Despite the temptation to water his very thirsty horses, Custer, impelled by the tension of his as yet undiscovered approach, pushed on. This caused acute frustration in the ranks. Private Theodore Goldin with D Company claimed that 'there were not twenty canteens of water in either Reno's or Benteen's squadrons'. Only alkali-tainted water had been available on 24 June. 'Following this came the gruelling night march,' said Goldin, 'with not a sign of water until we halted, before daybreak of the 25th' at the divide. Some water was found but it was undrinkable, even when boiled with coffee. 'Even the horses, thirsty as they must have been, turned away from the water.' Men and horses were to go into battle in the intense afternoon heat considerably dehydrated. 'Our advance,' Goldin declared, 'at least that of Reno's squadron', and Custer's across the dried up bed of Reno Creek, 'had no opportunity of either filling our canteens or watering our horses, [even] had water been available.'[19]

Captain Benteen began his reconnaissance enthusiastically enough on the left but, after crossing a series of ridgelines without finding Indians, he began to suspect that perhaps Custer was deliberately excluding him from the fight. It was logical to dispatch a senior officer such as Benteen to cover the flank and close potential escape routes. He was an experienced officer whom Custer knew well, and had performed competently at the Washita in 1868. 'It was rough, rolling country we were going over,' declared Windolph, accompanying him, 'and it was hard on the horses.' Benteen's sense of urgency began to dissipate in the face of the heat and heavy going. 'Indians have too much sense to travel over such country as you have been going unless they are terribly pushed,' he reasoned, so he decided, 'you'd better get back to that [Custer] trail.' 'Even to the troopers in the ranks,' agreed Windolph, 'it looked as if we were on a wild-goose chase.' Benteen gave the order to 'right oblique' and proceeded to rejoin Custer.[20]

Custer and Reno had meanwhile advanced down Reno Creek until they united at approximately 1400 hours on the right bank at the site of a solitary tepee. This had been the location of the village during the Rosebud fight. On raised poles was the body of Old She Bear, mortally wounded during the engagement. He had died a slow lingering death after an army bullet had shattered both hips. A few kinsmen had stayed on to the end even after the main village had relocated 4 miles downstream in the valley of the Little Bighorn. Custer's arrival caused considerable excitement. A number of hostile Indians were at the site looking for firewood or paying their respects at the funeral platform. Custer's scouts, instead of maintaining observation of the route ahead, had broken into the burial lodge and were eating the dead man's funeral feast and counting coup on the body. Custer's interpreter, Frank Gerard, having climbed a small knoll nearby, caught a glimpse of the massive pony herd beyond the bluffs, and hallooed to Custer, pointing out the Indians now running for their lives. 'Here are your Indians, running like devils!' he shouted. The scene precisely fitted Custer's expectations. The Indians will run – and here they were, doing just that. Thus emboldened, and despite the confirmation that the column had been spotted, Custer picked up the pace, leaving the Lone Tepee at 1415 hours at a rapid trot. Security had been blown. Larger groups of Indians could be seen observing their approach from the ridgeline that appeared to overlook the village.

Both columns advanced a further 3 miles on either side of the stream to a flat area between Reno Creek and its north fork, known as 'the Flats'. A column of smoke briefly surged into the sky as the Lone Tepee was torched behind them. More Sioux came in sight. Custer now ordered Reno to follow Reno Creek to the Little Bighorn, to 'move forward at as rapid a gait as he thought prudent, and charge the village afterward'. His adjutant, Lieutenant Cook, delivered the message, saying, 'the village was only two miles above, and running away'. Reno was assured that 'the whole outfit would support him'. In effect Reno was to charge the village in order to establish a block or 'anvil'. Custer's main force would strike from a different direction with the main force or 'hammer'.[21]

Reno tried to control his column preparatory to spreading out into an assault line as they crossed the river. Here there were problems. The Little Bighorn was 50 to 70 feet wide, with 2 to 4 feet of clear icy cold water. This was a compelling attraction to men and horses following the alkali-tainted water they had been reluctantly sipping for days. 'Into it our horses plunged without any urging,' said Private William Taylor with A Company. Horses and riders were thirsty. The pace slackened and the column bunched as horses refused to be urged onward. They stood and drank heavily. 'While waiting for them to drink I took off my hat,' said Taylor, 'and shaping the brim into a scoop, leaned over, filled it and drank the last drop of water I was to have for over 24 long hours.'[22] Ten minutes later they were beginning to by-pass the bare rock at the end of the line of bluffs and swung into the valley. Saddle girths were tightened for the coming charge. The horses' bellies were swollen with water, not the best condition to begin a charge and pursuit. But the halt had been irresistible.

After Reno's departure, Custer briefly followed him until about 1500 hours, when he reached the north fork of Reno Creek. Custer was further formulating his tactical plan, but it was too late. He had already launched Benteen, who represented 19.2% of his fighting strength, and now Reno, a further 23.4% of his combat potential. Thus nearly 43% of the force was irreversibly committed without having yet seen the enemy. They had been dispatched on blocking manoeuvres to prevent the very stampede he was witnessing with his own eyes as cut-off Indian refugees desperately sought the safety of the village. Custer was attracted to the high ground to the left of Luce Ridge in the vicinity of a promontory later to be called Weir Point. Groups of Indians were watching him from the ridgeline above the village. They appeared to mark a possible entry point to the village, a conduit through which the 'hammer blow' to support Reno might swing.

Custer was taking a number of seemingly illogical and un-characteristic decisions. Clarity of thought may have been clouded by tiredness. This was not the Custer of the Civil War. James H. Kidd, who had served with him at that time as a subordinate officer, was to later argue:

'He was not a reckless commander or one who would plunge into battle with his eyes shut. He was cautious and wary, accustomed to reconnoitre carefully and measure the strength of an enemy as accurately as possible before attacking. More than once the Michigan Brigade was saved from disaster by Custer's caution.'

Where had this caution manifested itself? Custer may have lost some of his edge. The fading of skills after nearly ten years' absence from high-intensity operations could have left its mark. This was the unpromoted Custer, court-martialled and suspended for a year and bruised by a political 'sleaze' scandal brush with the President of the United States. His personal confidence, departing for the expedition only one week after his arrival from that encounter in Washington, may not have been at its height. And now he felt

Custer's crucial decision points
There are six reversible decision points that Custer could have taken that may have altered the eventual catastrophic outcome of the battle.

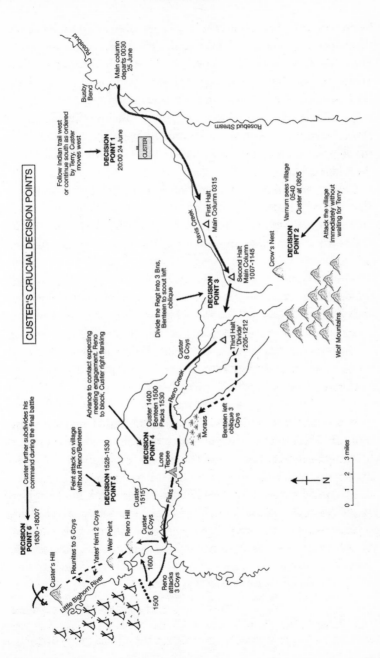

CUSTER'S CRUCIAL DECISION POINTS

Follow Indian trail west or continue south as ordered by Terry. Custer moves west

DECISION POINT 1
20:00 24 June

CUSTER

Main column departs 0030 25 June

Busby Bend

Rosebud

Rosebud Stream

First Halt
Main Column 0315

Davis Creek

Second Halt
Main Column 1007-1145

Crow's Nest

Varnum sees village 0540
Custer at 0805

Attack the village immediately without waiting for Terry

DECISION POINT 2

Wolf Mountains

Divide the Regt into 3 Bns, Benteen to scout left oblique

DECISION POINT 3

Third Halt "Divide" 1205-1212

Custer 8 Coys

Benteen left oblique 3 Coys

Morass

Reno Creek

Advance to contact expecting meeting engagement. Reno to block, Custer right flanking

Custer 1400
Benteen 1500
Packs 1530

DECISION POINT 4

Lone Tepee

Feint attack on village without Reno/Benteen

DECISION POINT 5
1528-1530

Custer 1515

Flats

Custer 5 Coys

Reno Hill

Weir Point

1600

Reno attacks 3 Coys

1500

Little Bighorn River

Yates' feint 2 Coys

Reunites to 5 Coys

Custer's Hill

Custer further subdivides his command during the final battle

DECISION POINT 6
1630 -1800?

N

0   1   2   3 miles

impelled to follow a course into an operation, and in the Centennial year he could not afford to fail. Private Thompson recalled C Company enjoying a comment prior to the Yellowstone River departure when one wag suggested that this campaign would 'end just as soon as we could catch old Sitting Bull'. Amid the general mirth came the remark that 'Custer will take us with him to the Centennial'. 'Of course,' continued the wit, 'we will take Sitting Bull with us.'[23] Victory was personally important to Custer and would have implications for his future career.

Custer was committing his main force on the basis of 15-mile-distant observations. He had yet to detect the main Indian force and had still not actually seen the village. Caught up in the excitement of the chase and aggressively seeking to maintain tempo as he watched scattered groups of Indians running before him, Custer released his scouts. It was not their business to fight a battle. What Custer had not detected, and it was too late for his scouts to advise, was that the Indians signalling an apparent entry point were standing on the gently sloping lee side of the ridgeline. Behind them was the weather side, with a vertical incline – often the case in this region – varying from about 200 to 300 feet. It was not negotiable on horseback except opposite certain river ford crossings. Reno was out of sight and Custer had released the scouts that might have discerned this vital information. Had he been more intuitive he might have remained with Reno, because there was now a physical barrier hindering the support that Reno anticipated receiving – a sheer bluff line.

Having decided to divide his force, Custer took his fourth and arguably most significant fatal decision. He sounded the charge without seeing the enemy. The limitations of 19th-century military communications meant that only the bugle or a dispatch rider could sound the recall. Once a cavalry charge was launched, there was no calling it back. Custer was committed.

Chapter 8

First blood

'I did not believe it. I thought it was a
false alarm. I did not think it possible
that any white men would attack us,
so strong as we were.'

Low Dog, Indian warrior

The vision fulfilled

Late melting snow had caused the Little Bighorn River beside the
camp to run wider and deeper than normal this year. It was 40
yards wide in places with pebbly natural fords where water swirled
over shallows. Children were swimming and fishing. At other
points it was deep enough to swim a horse. The camp was
established 15 miles or so from the mouth of the river on a level
grassy flat area above the undulating prairie. It was an ideal site
tucked in behind bluffs that rose 300 feet above the river. Because
of the drop in the valley floor, where most of the village was located,
it was visible only at the last moment from a south-east approach.

Each tribe camped according to the order in which it travelled,
custom governing the placement of camp circles. At the south end
of the village and nearest to Reno's line of advance were the
Hunkpapa Sioux with 260 lodges, including 25 of Yanktonnais and
Santee Sioux. They were the largest element and the last to arrive,
providing in effect a rearguard. Next to them was the Oglala Sioux
circle of 240 lodges, and further along the Minneconjou Sioux with

150 lodges. The Sans Arc, with 110 lodges, were alongside the combined Blackfoot, Brule and Two Kettle Sioux circles. At the northern end and head of the village was the Northern Cheyenne circle of 120 lodges. In all there were about 1,000 lodges containing 7,000 people who could muster up to 2,000 fighting men including older boys.[1] Many leading war chiefs were in the camp. Dirty Moccasins and Old Bear from the Cheyenne, and Crazy Head, Lame White Man, Old Man Coyote and Last Bull. Big Road and He-Dog represented the Oglala Sioux, but another revered yet unelected leader, Crazy Horse, was also there. Spotted Eagle and Fast Bear led the Sans Arcs, Lame Deer the powerful Minneconjous and Hump, Fast Bull and High Backbone. Hunkpapa war chiefs included Gall, Crow King, Black Moon and the overall Indian coalition leader, Sitting Bull.[2] Kill Eagle, a Sioux war-band leader, described the Indian village as huge 'and the Indians there as thick as maggots on a carcass, so numerous were they'.[3]

Many of the villagers were still sleeping late after the all-night scalp dance the evening before, celebrating the week-old victory over 'Three Stars'. 'Young men went from one circle to another to dance with the girls until daybreak,' recalled Cheyenne warrior Wooden Leg. Following a late breakfast he was asleep in the shade of the cottonwoods by the river, relaxing after a swim with his brother. There were temporary brush shelters on the outskirts of tepee circles catering for new summer roamer arrivals. Fresh-killed animal hides were out drying in the sun. 'The day was hot,' recalled Red Horse, a Sioux warrior.[4] Hobbled horses grazed here and there while dogs lurked in every part of the village. To the south of the camp on the higher ground, or 'Bench', massive pony herds were feeding. Women were about busying themselves with administrative tasks and looking for roots and turnips to supplement cooking already under way. Kate Bighead, a Northern Cheyenne woman visiting the Minneconjou circle, was bathing with friends in the river. Everyone was having a good time, she recalled, and no one was thinking of battle. Red Horse, a 46-year-old Minneconjou chief, was accompanying some of the women a short distance from the camp digging for wild turnips. 'Suddenly one of the women attracted my attention to a cloud of dust rising a short distance from the camp,' he said. An ominous cloud of dust was moving along the valley floor, coming closer and closer to the village. One Sioux man, on his way back to the Government Red Cloud Agency, changed his mind when he saw it, convinced that 'a herd of buffalo was coming near the village'. People reluctantly began to comprehend what this might mean – 'Three Stars' had come back.[5]

The massive size of the camp had engendered complacency. 'I did not believe it,' claimed one warrior named Low Dog. 'I thought it was a false alarm. I did not think it possible that any white men would attack us, so strong as we were.' After Crook's setback nobody seriously believed that the soldiers would attack a village of this size. 'I have seen my people prepare for battle many times,' declared Pretty White Buffalo, a Hunkpapa squaw. 'This I know: that the Sioux that morning had no thought of fighting.' Reno's battalion assault was coming into sight, a sinister cloud of dust rolling down the valley, and it was to achieve complete surprise. Two Moons, a Cheyenne warrior, thought the phenomenon 'looked like a whirlwind'. Chaos ensued. 'Soon Sioux horsemen came rushing into camp shouting "Soldiers come! Plenty white soldiers!"'[6]

Shortly after 1500 hours Reno's columns of four moved smoothly into line of assault on entering the head of the valley, utilising abundant manoeuvre space. Shortly after, the cavalry charge was drumming out a cacophony of horse's hooves coming down the valley in two waves. A and M Companies were in the first line, with Lieutenant Varnum and the Indian scouts to the left and G company in the second line as reserve. With 5 yards between horses, the 175-man force fanned out to a 130-yard-wide attack line, hardly filling the valley's width, which varied from 800 yards to a mile in places. This was an exhilarating moment for the troopers, closing with their elusive objective at long last. However, the 'charge' was to stretch across 2½ miles, a 15-minute ride. Beginning at the fast walk, the attack lines broke into a trot as they bore remorselessly down upon the village. However, excessive drinking allowed at the ford soon took its toll on the horses. 'As the charge went on,' recalled Soldier, one of Reno's Arikara scouts, 'the poor horses trailed out far behind.' Initial whooping and yelling with the exuberance of the attack was quickly dampened by Reno. 'I was so completely exhausted,' claimed Lieutenant Varnum, 'that I could hardly sit in the saddle.' Custer and the other scouts must have been similarly tired. Varnum pointed out:

> 'Nothing but the excitement of going into action kept me in the saddle at all. I had travelled about twenty miles further than the troops [as had Custer with less sleep], and I can assure you there was a vast difference between going along on the trail and scouting all over the hills.'[7]

He rode with eight to ten Indian scouts alongside Lieutenant Hare to the left of the line. Their task was to draw off parts of the Indian pony herd, but they were too few to marshal such a massive gathering. 'Boys,' Custer had said to Young Hawk, one of the Arikara scouts, 'I want you to take the horses away from the Sioux camp.' Little Sioux, a companion, was enjoined 'to run off all the horses you can'.[8] This mission, effectively permission for the scouts to loot, might provide a distraction from the charge.

Raising considerable dust, the two lines of horsemen broke into a rapid trot. To their right the irregular bluff line, criss-crossed by innumerable watercourse lines, was starkly silhouetted against a clear blue sky. 'On our right was the heavily wooded and very irregular course of the river,' recalled Private Taylor, riding in the front line with A Company, 'flanked by high bluffs.' They had maintained a steady pace for 8 to 9 minutes but could not see the village ahead. Taylor noticed 'low foothills' to the left, then gained his first sight of the huge pony herd. Presently he distinguished Indian 'mounted men riding in every direction, some in circles, others passing back and forth'. Lieutenant Varnum noticed that 'there was so much dust in the air that it was impossible to judge anywhere near as to the number of Indians there'. Suddenly the village extremity came into view. 'We observed a number of Indian tepees,' Varnum said, 'and as we worked out toward the left, we could see yet more.' Indians frantically circled around the southern end of the village seeking to obscure its outline with dust. It came into sight only at the last moment because the main concentration of tepees was positioned on a shelf below the level of the plain. 'Then as little puffs of smoke were seen and the "Ping" of bullets spoke out plainly,' said Taylor, 'we were ordered to charge.' Reno, having initially ordered a quiet approach, now let the battalion loose. 'Charge! Charrrge!' was the command Taylor heard. Glancing along the line he saw 'a lot of set, determined faces, some of them a little pale perhaps, but not altogether with fear'. Reno was about to draw the first blood.[9]

A young Sans Arc youth called Deeds was probably the first fatality at the Battle of the Little Bighorn, gunned down by one of Reno's Crow scouts as he sprinted through the brush alongside the river, shouting the alarm of approaching white soldiers. Varnum's scouts also killed six fleeing women and four children in the small timber grove on the southern outskirts of the village. They were dispatched with that typical emotionless aggression Indians reserved for those not of their tribal community. The soldiers would be blamed. Chief Gall, whose Hunkpapa circle was the nearest to the onrushing advance, lamented, 'My two squaws and three children were killed there by the pale-faced warriors, and it made my heart bad.' The murder of these non-combatants at the start gave a clear indication of what this assault portended, immediately raising the emotional tempo for revenge. 'After that,' said Gall, 'I killed my enemies with the hatchet.'[10] The desire was not just to kill, but mutilate. Gall had lost virtually his entire family.

Surprise was complete. Wooden Leg, the Cheyenne warrior, was abruptly woken from his pleasant nap on the riverbank 'by sounds of shooting that came from the upper end of the camp, where the Hunkpapas were located: they heard shouts that soldiers were upon them'. Women and children began to flee to the high ground or splashed frantically across the river. Iron Thunder, a 33-year-old Sioux warrior, did not know anything about an attack until Reno's men 'were so close that the bullets went through the camp, and everything was in confusion'. The attackers were already in among the pony herd. 'The horses were so frightened,' Iron Thunder said, 'we could not catch them.' Horse herd boys tried to drive the ponies into the camp, 'and the less able warriors and the women caught horses and got them ready,' recalled Sioux warrior Low Dog.[11]

As the charge progressed, Reno scanned the ground ahead searching for the village. 'It was almost impossible,' declared Varnum, 'unless one was well out on the plain, to see much of the village in coming from the direction that we came.' Even if this village was as large as that attacked on the Washita in 1868, few soldiers had ever seen one as large. Varnum, like Reno, could not estimate the strength of the opposition except to say 'there were certainly more Indians than I ever saw together before'. As the command approached, the hostiles boiled out of the village to offer combat. 'It was a very large village – I could see that very plainly,' Varnum eventually concluded. Reno ordered his bugler to sound 'form a skirmish line'. It was about 1518 hours. 'Dismount and prepare to fight on foot,' heard Sergeant O'Neal with A Company. Three troopers from four dismounted and handed their reins to the fourth, who moved back 6 or 7 yards to the rear of the line forming up. This was conducted under fire. 'Bullets began to whistle about us,' declared Private William Slaper with M Company. 'I remember that I ducked my head and tried to dodge bullets which I could hear whizzing through the air.'[12]

It is not easy to halt a cavalry charge and form a skirmish line. Although an accepted mounted infantry tactic, it caused some surprise among the less experienced soldiers, who anticipated crashing into the village and putting the hostiles to flight. An abrupt halt required discipline and horse control. Slaper recognised that 'our horses were scenting danger before we dismounted', and to the horror of onlookers in the line 'several at this point became unmanageable and started straight for the open among the Indians, carrying their helpless riders with them'. As these men, desperately wrestling with their mounts, entered the village, they were pulled from their horses and hacked and beaten to death by young boys and squaws. 'One of the boys, a young fellow named Smith of Boston,' Slaper recalled, 'we never saw again, either dead or alive.' Sergeant John Ryan, the M Company first Sergeant, saw Private James Turley blunder into the village. Indians waving blankets surrounded him, dust was thrown up into his and his horse's face, and amid flailing tomahawks he was clubbed to the ground. His body was later discovered with his own hunting knife driven up to the hilt in his right eye.[13]

With every fourth man acting as horse-holder, the fire of 95 carbines was directed at the village, but at 300 yards they were at the limit of effective fire. The resonant heavy boom of carbines contrasted with the lighter reports from Indian repeater rifles and other weapons. Reno's fire was more alarming than effective. 'When the skirmish line was formed,' said Lieutenant Varnum, 'I saw a good many excited men shooting right up in the air.' An ominous aspect was that 'there was very heavy firing going on both sides'. Large numbers of Indians were shooting back and with more firearms than expected. Cavalry fire went high, a factor of inexperience and because the tepees were shielded by being on a lower ground shelf. Dust obscured the target. Officers and NCOs did not exploit the 'splash' impact that can be derived by directing fire low, which can bounce ricochets into advancing Indians while confirming the fall of shot. One Hunkpapa Lakota squaw, She Walks With Her Shawl, recalled 'a terrific volley of carbines' but 'the bullets shattered the tipi poles' overhead. However, not all escaped this profusion of fire.

'I saw a warrior adjusting his quiver and grasping his tomahawk. He started running towards his horse when he suddenly recoiled and dropped dead. He was killed near his tipi.'

Most rounds whistled harmlessly over the top, encouraging the Indian rally. More warriors joined the fight. Reno's line, reduced from 140 to 95 men at 5 yards apiece, shrank in length to 400 yards, and shorter as men sought the security of their comrades and to concentrate fire. Individual marksmanship was poor. Barely 15 practice rounds had been fired per man in the regiment the year before. Civil War area volley fire was applied, not individually aimed shots. Targets dodged about and few were seen to fall. 'There were a good many of them at long range,' Varnum observed. 'They would pass around us and keep out of range, circling around.' The heaviest fire was towards the right of the line and nearest the village. Reno began to feel the pressure. Indians moved out and infiltrated through the pony herds on the left, not dispersed by the army scouts. As they encircled the left of the skirmish line the rear became vulnerable. 'By this time the Indians were coming in closer,' observed a concerned Private Slaper, 'and in increasing numbers, circling about and raising such a dust that a great many of them had a chance to get into our rear under cover of it.' Slaper saw Sergeant Miles O'Hara 'the first one of my own company comrades fall'. The fight was not going as anticipated. It was to have been a charge followed by a pursuit. Instead, they were engaged in a firefight and taking casualties. Troopers were violently flung out of the line as heavy-calibre bullets struck them. 'Then I observed another' man go down, declared Slaper regretfully, 'and yet another.'[14]

Meanwhile, elements of Custer's battalion had been spotted silhouetted on the line of bluffs nearly 2 miles from Reno's skirmish line when it was established at 1515 hours. Custer was seen waving his hat. Although momentarily reassuring to the troopers, Reno was aghast. After establishing a block, he was expecting Custer to arrive on his flank at any moment 'directly supporting him', to deliver the 'hammer blow' upon the village. Custer had now shown himself to be at least 40 minutes away. 'I saw the gray horse [E] company of the battalion [with Custer] moving along the line of bluffs,' observed Varnum. They 'were probably about three-quarters of a mile from where we were'. Actually it was further, and there was no way that Custer's strike force could descend the 200-foot weathered escarpment. Varnum gave it no further thought. 'I just looked up there, but as we had plenty to do down below, I didn't attach any importance to it.' Custer was not moving towards them – he was briskly trotting further along the bluff line.[15]

Reno's battalion had resorted to 'terror tactics', riding up to the edge of the village. Some had shot into the air, believing their unexpected advance would preface a rout or virtual stampede. It did not happen. They were attacked even as they approached. Fire from the skirmish line had not been effective. Troopers, squeezing rounds off at the rapid rate of 12 to 13 per minute, would exhaust their 100 rounds after only 8 to 9 minutes of concentrated fire. A further complication was that 50 rounds of carbine and 24 rounds of pistol were on the man, but the remaining 50 rounds of carbine ammunition remained in their saddlebags. This reserve was held by horse-handlers preoccupied with controlling their charges. Fire on the line slackened as men moved back to replenish. Varnum calculated that they were up against 400 to 500 Indians, suggesting odds at about four or five to one. 'There may have been a great many more,' he said. The biggest surprise, however, was the intensity of incoming fire. 'It was so rapid that there were bullets in the air all the time.' As more Indians rode up, it increased. 'As a rule,' Varnum continued, 'the Indians fired from their ponies; they were just scampering around us and pumping those Winchester rifles into us as fast as they could.' Private Slaper, with M Company, shared his concern, complaining that the Indians were 'pouring such a hot fire into our small command, that it was getting to be a decidedly unhealthy neighbourhood'.

Reno's battalion began to feel over-extended. 'There certainly was a feeling of uneasiness in the command regarding Custer while we were fighting in the river bottom,' said Varnum. 'I was thinking "Has he got in the same fix we are in?"'[16] Nineteenth-century military communications did not permit the 'what if?' options for cavalry commanders conferred by modern-day radio receivers. Reno's men had anticipated an advance through the village, but a single bugle call had changed that to a static dismounted infantry action. This was not unprecedented, but nobody knew what was going to happen next. Within 15 minutes of arrival, Reno was under pressure and considering moving into a wooded copse to the right of his firing line. If he did not act he might be outflanked or, at worst case, surrounded. There was no agreed regimental plan and little sign that Custer could respond to his urgent plight. His officers and NCOs knew of no fall-back option. Battle drills were reliant upon a shouted command or bugle call. Leadership and direction was unclear. Although Reno's companies were not as deficient in officers and NCOs as Custer's battalion, two officers, four sergeants and one corporal had been absent from the outset of the campaign. Soldiers needed tangible direction, and those on the skirmish line were starting to realise that their situation was becoming critical. They were pressed to even hold the line.

There were no such misgivings from the Indian perspective. Although there was not a plan, there was an immediate and accepted response, as illustrated by Minneconjou chief Red Horse:

'We came out of the council lodge and talked in all directions. The Sioux mount horses, take guns, and go fight the soldiers. Women and children mount horses and go, meaning to get out of the way.'

In battle they acted as individuals, yet thought alike. Their instinctive initial reaction was to get the soldiers out of the camp and away from their families. The second was to kill them. One Hunkpapa Lakota squaw had already lost her brother. 'My heart was bad,' declared She Walks With Her Shawl. 'Revenge! Revenge! For my brother's death… I was a woman but I was not afraid.'[17] These soldiers had already died in Indian eyes. Their appearance at the camp had fulfilled Sitting Bull's vision. Renowned war-band leaders such as Crazy Horse of the Oglala Sioux began to ride up with their followers. They provided inspiration to the direction that was clear to all – drive out and kill the white soldiers.

Custer, viewing from the bluffs, saw the battle from an entirely different and distant perspective. 'What has become of him? Has he been thrown off?' thought the hard-pressed Lieutenant Varnum. 'Custer had promised to support Major Reno, but he was not there.'[18] The commander of the 7th had experienced his first defeat in this battle by being overcome by terrain. He was still actively seeking a passage down to the village, wrongly assuming that the Indians on the bluff signified an entry point. As he looked down on the battle below, a further assumption was proved false. The Indians were fighting, not running.

Custer's five-company strike force of about 220 soldiers and scouts had formed into columns of fours for the ascent up the bluffs after leaving Reno. This was in effect a right flanking move. 'At this time,' reported Private Peter Thompson with C Company, 'our horses were in a trot.' At the top of the high ground 'we came in sight of the Indian village and it was truly an imposing sight to anyone who had not seen anything like it before'. Most had not. The village appeared enormous to the inexperienced soldiers. Tepees stretched out to about 1½ miles, 'the white canvas [hides] gleaming in the sunlight,' said Thompson. 'Beyond the village was a black mass of ponies grazing on the short green grass.' The companies became excited as this vista unfolded before them. 'They gave the regular charging yell,' said Thompson, 'and urged their horses into a gallop.' Sergeant Kanipe remembered:

> 'Well, sir, when the men of those four troops saw the Indian camp down in the valley they began to holler and yell. We galloped along to the far end of the bluffs, where we could swoop down on the camp.'

But there was no route down.

Private Thompson at this point realised the nightmare of every trooper on the march. His horse was blown. 'I was gradually left behind in spite of all I could do to keep up with my company,' he said. Horses are not like mules, which are intelligent enough to slow down when fatigued, as witnessed by constant delays with the pack train. The more generous-hearted horse gives his all, but not in terms of brainpower. He will abruptly collapse after his physical reserves are expended. As with Reno's 2½-mile 'charge', Custer's punishing pace littered the trail behind him with exhausted mounts. Sergeant Kanipe passed Sergeant Finkle riding just behind Captain Tom Custer commanding C Company. 'Finkle hollered at me that he couldn't make it, his horse was giving out.' Kanipe rode by and shouted, 'Come on, Finkle, if you can,' but he began to drop back. 'All urging on my part was useless,' declared Thompson. This was not cowardice. Falling out of the line of march meant exposing oneself to marauding hostiles, more dangerous than fighting it out on the line. 'There were others in the same fix,' said Thompson. 'Hearing an oath behind me, I looked back and saw my comrade Watson trying to get his horse on its feet.' It appeared hopeless. 'The poor brute had fallen and was struggling to gain an upright position.' Watson's horse 'finally gained his feet with a groan' and the stragglers attempted to catch up with their companies. Progress was painfully and now vulnerably slow. 'I mounted my horse again,' said Thompson, 'but found that a staggering walk was all I could get out of him.' A mixture of fear and spent horses suggests that a larger number of soldiers than originally thought may have given up and fallen out of the line of march on Custer's route. More stragglers eventually ended up with the pack train or Reno's command than were ordered by Custer. Twenty-six soldiers beyond the original 84 originally earmarked, which had been one NCO and six soldiers from each company, appeared with the pack train, further depleting Custer's strike potential.[19]

Custer, vexed at his inability to close with the Indians due to the vertical incline on the weather side of the bluffs, was also sobered at the number of Indian warriors and their aggressive response to Reno's attack. Observing from the promontory later called Reno's Hill, he realised that he must have Benteen's support and immediate access to the pack train's ammunition reserve. Sergeant Daniel

Kanipe was taken from C Company and dispatched to Benteen with the message to move the pack train hurriedly cross-country. 'Tell McDougall,' he was ordered, 'to bring the pack train straight across to high ground.' It was an urgent command, based on the growing appreciation there would be a firefight. 'If the packs get loose, don't stop to fix them, cut them off. Come quick. Big Indian camp,' he ordered. Kanipe exchanged glances with Private Nathan Short. They were in the same company and Kanipe was to remember it as his salvation point. 'If Sergeant Finkle had not dropped back a few minutes before he would have got the orders – and I would not be telling this story.'[20]

As he rode off, Custer looked back along the route for telltale columns of dust that would signify the progress of Benteen's battalion and the pack train. There was no dust. Benteen's command had by now rejoined Custer's route, but the battalion had paused to water its horses at the 'morass' area. When Benteen departed at approximately 1500 hours the packs arrived with Lieutenant McDougall and they stampeded into the muddy pool to drink. It was virtually impossible to prevent the animals from doing otherwise. This may well have coincided with Custer looking for dust signatures to see if they were on their way. Kanipe, riding back, was to orientate himself on their dust cloud.

Custer's plan was unravelling. Complete surprise had been achieved by the initial attack, but only 23.4% of the regiment had conducted it. Only 95 carbines engaged a village of 7,000 inhabitants with 1,800 to 2,000 warriors. Another 19% of his command had been dispatched under Benteen on a 'left oblique' manoeuvre to sweep up possible hostile escapees, and were now an hour away. A further 21.5% of his force was 1½ hours away, guarding the logistic train carrying his vital ammunition reserves. Custer's strike force, with the remaining 35%, had been due to crash into the village flank synchronised with Reno's blocking action, but was stuck up on the bluffs 200 feet above the battle unable to get down. Custer had subdivided his tactical forces, his second defeat. He was not fighting his command as a regiment.

Dilemma in the valley bottom

Custer was failing to execute operations in his normal competent manner. His conduct at Gettysburg in 1863 during the Civil War, for example, was renowned more for aggression and persistence in the attack, and a willingness to accept casualties, than for masterly tactical handling. He achieved positive results. One veteran Union campaigner, commenting on his performance during the Gettysburg battle, declared that 'he is a glorious fellow, full of energy, quick to plan and bold to execute and with us he has never failed in any attempt he has yet made'.[21] Praise, but not tactical flair. Even by Civil War standards, Custer's handling of his regiment was demonstrating shortfalls. Objective analysis of the 7th Cavalry's competence would suggest that it was not as good as its reputation and arguably not the premier regiment it aspired to be, in comparison with the more Indian-battle-experienced 9th Cavalry Regiment.

Custer's third defeat following that of terrain and the subdivision of his regimental command was a tactical misappreciation. He launched a pursuit operation by fragmenting his force to envelop hostile escapees before he had even conducted the charge and won the firefight. Custer fought Civil War conventional tactics against a foe that refused to be fixed. Such a regimental attack would have seen Reno execute an approach and block as happened, followed by the remainder of the force. Custer's five companies, combined with Benteen's three, could have attacked, left flanking, through the Indian pony herd. Utilising the generous manoeuvre space, the regiment could have smashed into the village with eight companies driving through at its narrowest point, probably splitting it in two – to use 19th-century Prussian military parlance, 'punching' the resistance core instead of 'prodding' it, as he had done with three companies. In the confusion the Indians would have been denied the mobility of the pony herd. Non-combatant hostages could have been taken stampeding through the village, deterring Indian counter-attacks, as happened on the Washita in 1868. Using Reno's approach the entire regiment could have followed, securing the route for the packs. These, despite their sluggish pace, could have safely occupied the high ground vacated by the pony herd. McDougall's security contingent would then have been available to provide a fire bastion in the event of an Indian counter-attack. Readily available detachments, already detached to McDougall, could then have moved forward with their additional ammunition to support their parent companies. A synchronised regimental assault employing the very Civil War tactics Custer had previously mastered would have had the weight to dismay the startled Indians into retreat. Sufficient ammunition to fight a prolonged volley fire defence, the very stratagem that saved Crook at the Rosebud battle, would have been available. There was sufficient space in the valley of the Little Bighorn for mobile infantry or cavalry operations. All Custer's units would have been in sight and the command could have maintained a reserve. Custer's fatigued state may have precluded such thinking, but it was an identifiable option.

Reno had been shaken by a series of surprises. Not only was the village larger than anyone had ever seen – its true size hidden until the last moment – but instead of running, the Indians had boiled out of its interior buzzing like a horde of enraged hornets. Sergeant John Ryan in M Company thought that 'there was probably 500 of them coming from the direction of their village'. It was an unanticipated and aggressive response. One of the Arikara scouts, Young Hawk, described how 'one Dakota charged the soldiers very closely and was shot about sixteen feet from the line'.[22] Reno was further taken aback by the intensity of fire being directed at the skirmish line.

Having fought the skirmish line for about 15 minutes, at 1530 hours Reno was thinking of withdrawing his command to the wooded area flanked by the river to the right. The Indians 'overlapped our skirmish line to the left,' observed Sergeant Ryan, 'and were closing in on the rear to complete the circle'. They sensed that the soldiers' resolve was weakening. 'When we were nearing the fringe of the woods,' said She Walks With Her Shawl, an order was given by Hawkman to charge. 'Ho-ka-he! Ho-ka-he! Charge! Charge!' Surging forward, the braves attempted to cut the line. 'We fired volleys into them,' remembered Sergeant Ryan, 'repulsing their charge and emptying a number of their saddles.' Private William Slaper, also with M Company, recalled the change of position: 'We got back there about as quickly as we knew how,' he said. This manoeuvre was fraught with difficulties. It took time for the unanticipated message to travel the line and soldiers are always reluctant to move under fire. Once formed lines buckle it is difficult to reform. 'In this excitement,' Slaper continued, 'some of the horse-holders released their animals before the riders arrived. Feeling vulnerable, 'they were "placed afoot", which made it exceedingly critical for them'. Instinctively the Indians realised that Reno's men were on the verge of collapse. Soldier Wolf, a 17-year-old Northern Cheyenne warrior, described the dispersal of the skirmish line:

> 'The troops retreated and the Indians all rushed in among them. They were all mixed up. The soldiers seemed to be drunk [probably they were panic-stricken]; they could not shoot at all. The soldiers retreated to the timber and fought behind cover.'[23]

Once in the 'timber' Reno found that the proximity of trees and underbrush required a tighter defence density. This was not appro-priate to the large expanse his small command had now to deny. His men were running low on ammunition. Saddlebag reserves were often inaccessible because some horses were running to and fro out of control. Heavy-calibre bullets smacked into trees, splintering and bringing down small branches with whining explosions. Having almost enveloped Reno, the Indians began to set fire to the woods. Fingers of flame licked through the undergrowth, obscuring the fighting with smoke. The situation was critical. Reno rode to Captain French, the M Company commander, and shouted 'Well, Tom, what do you think of this?' French responded with alacrity, 'I think we had better get out of here.'

It was difficult to move around inside the wooded area on horseback; troopers were hemmed in by narrow intricate paths. The Indians could not see what was going on inside the trees, and preferred to entice the soldiers out and destroy them by close combat in the open. Reno attempted to reassert control in a small clearing in the middle of the timber area. Private Thomas O'Neill with G Company recalled that 'at this time the fighting was terrific, the Indians charging up very close'. Describing their tactics, he said, 'They would deliver their fire, wheel their ponies and scamper to the rear to reload.'

Reno bellowed 'Mount!' But many of the troopers, engrossed with survival and amidst intermittent smoke and dust clouds, missed the order. 'I did not hear it,' said Slaper, 'neither did I hear any bugle calls or other orders or commands of any sort.' Private Henry Koltzbucher, belonging to his company, was suddenly shot through the stomach 'just as he was in the act,' Slaper observed, 'of mounting his horse'. He toppled to the ground. Slaper and Private Francis Neely dismounted to help him. They dragged him, writhing in agony, beneath a clump of heavy underbrush, concluding that 'he was probably mortally wounded, so we left him a canteen of water'. Nothing more could be done, and hiding him might enable his body to escape mutilation. They remounted and left him behind. Horses were screaming as incoming volleys of fire struck them. 'Just at that moment,' said Sergeant Ryan, 'Private George Lorentz of my company ... was shot, the bullet striking him in the back of his neck and coming out of his mouth.' He fell forward, splashing and gurgling blood on to his saddle, and slid to the ground. The vulnerability of the troopers became more pronounced as they began to form up and wait. Bloody Knife, Custer's personal scout, was hit standing next to Reno. His head exploded on impact with a heavy-calibre round, splattering Reno's face with blood and gore. Totally shocked, the Major ordered 'Dismount!', then, still apparently dazed, countermanded with an order to 'Remount!' Confusion reigned. 'I dismounted twice and mounted again, all in a few minutes,' said Private Taylor with A

Company. 'But why, I do not know, unless it was because I saw the others do it and thought they had orders to.' Holders attempted to control bucking horses as soldiers rushed around. 'I could hear nothing but the continual roar of Indian rifles and the sharp resonant bang-bang of cavalry carbines,' said Slaper, 'mingled with the whoops of the savages and the shouts of my comrades.'

Lieutenant Varnum was to the right of the line with the interpreter Frank Gerard and scout Charley Reynolds. They were out of earshot. 'I heard cries of "Charge, Charge, we are going to Charge!"' He was nonplussed. 'There was quite a bit of confusion and I jumped up and said, "What's that?"' There are contradictory accounts of what happened during the melee in the timber. Sergeant Ryan, realising the gravity of the situation, shouted to his company commander Captain French that 'the best thing that we can do is to cut right through them'. Private Taylor heard someone say, 'We must get out of here, quick!' Major Reno had by now lost his hat and his hair was tied with a red handkerchief. An Arikara scout, Red Bear, watched him begin the retreat at the head of his men, 'his mouth and beard white with foam, which dripped down, and his eyes were wild and rolling'. Reno was traumatised. Ryan saw him ride up to the mounted elements with M Company and say, 'Any of you men who wish to make your escape, follow me.'[24]

Custer had no time to wait for Benteen and the pack train, and continued to move north-west. Exposed and vulnerable at the edge of the bluff line, he descended into Cedar Coulee, a ravine pointing north. He remained offensively minded, intending to take on the village, but to achieve this he had to gain access to the river and shield his approach from Indian view. Leaving the column safely out of sight in a bend in the coulee, Custer rode to the crest of the highest promontory available (later called Weir Point), accompanied by several scouts including Mitch Bouyer and Curly, a Crow scout. Custer got there just before 1530 hours and watched Reno's skirmish line heavily engaged below. The full extent of the village was now visible with no intervening ground in the way. It was a sobering sight. Sounds of battle carried up from the valley bottom;

there was heavy firing and some movement within Reno's dismounted skirmish line. If Reno could hold his ground – and he had been battling already for 30 minutes – Custer's command might be able to engage and support from the flank. From his new observation platform Custer could make out an approach from the dead ground in the coulee where his strike force was waiting. Cedar Coulee joined another ravine (Medicine Tail Coulee) branching westwards leading to what appeared to be a ford (Minneconjou ford) across the river. This re-entrant, covered with grass and sagebrush, opened into a gentle flat approach to the village. The immediate need was to support Reno, but Custer still intended to defeat the Indians. Glancing northwards, he saw the ground appeared featureless in the hazy heat of the afternoon sun. He needed manoeuvre room, and the area in this direction appeared to offer space for a wide cavalry sweep that would enable him to charge into the rear of the village. The mid-afternoon angle of the sun made the ground appear dun-coloured and indistinct, a deceptively flat landscape. He was not to know that as the sun set further in the afternoon, contoured ridgelines would appear. Custer, in his tired state, was in any case more concerned with trying to find a route down to the camp to support Reno.

Impressed by the sheer size of the village, Custer was reminded of the need for Benteen's support and the pack ammunition. He glanced southwards in the direction from which they had come. It was difficult to pick out any following dust clouds; the variable indivisibility of the meandering bluff line precluded this. There was dust but not distinct clouds. Benteen and the packs were following one another in line with the angle from which he was viewing. Custer had seen enough to formulate the next stage of his evolving tactical plan, but Indian responses were breaching decision points before the intent could be achieved. He was losing the initiative but had not accepted this.

Trumpeter John Martin, Custer's orderly bugler that day, recalled Custer saying as the village came into view that they had 'got them this time'. Reno, fighting below, had totally mesmerised

Indian attention, leaving the main strike force undetected. Martin, looking down into the village, recalled:

> 'There were no bucks to be seen; all we could see was some squaws and children playing and a few dogs and ponies. The General seemed both surprised and glad, and said the Indians must be in their tents asleep.'

Leaving Curly and Bouyer on Weir Point to watch Reno's fight in the valley bottom, Custer rejoined his command. 'Hurrah, boys!' exclaimed the confident Custer, according to Martin, 'We've got them! We'll finish them up and then go home to our station.'

Custer ordered Martin to take a message to 'Colonel' Benteen. 'Ride as fast as you can,' he was told, 'and tell him to hurry.' He swiftly gabbled the message, which Lieutenant William Cooke, his Adjutant, wrote down, suspecting that the Italian immigrant may not have grasped it. Tearing a lined page from his memorandum book, Cooke swiftly scrawled the gist of the message. This ghostly document exists today, soiled and torn at the intersection point where it was folded in four. 'Benteen. Come on. Big Village. Be Quick. Bring Packs. PS Bring Pack. W. W. Cooke.' So indistinct is the rough handwriting that Benteen's copper-ink-coloured neat translation is written above it. This was to be a vital document after the event. 'My horse was pretty tired,' Martin said, 'but I started back as fast as I could go.'[25] Looking back over his shoulder, he saw the command for the last time, galloping down the ravine and into history.

Boston Custer, impatient to join his brothers for the fight and frustrated at the slow progress of the packs, had ridden on ahead alone. At about 1430 hours Lieutenant Winfield Scott Edgerly saw him with Benteen's battalion, having just rejoined the Custer trail. Moving at the trot, 'he gave me a cheery salutation as he passed,' recalled Edgerly, 'and then with a smile on his face, rode to his death'. Boston Custer was not to know that within a further half mile, Benteen would delay at the 'morass' to enable his horses to drink, which would place him between 60 and 90 minutes behind Custer. Shortly after Bugler Martin left Custer, he too met the latter's brother coming the other way. 'Where's the General?' Boston asked, and Martin replied, 'Right behind that next ridge you'll find him,' and he sped on, his horse 'riding at a run'. This was the last live sighting of Boston Custer. It is assessed that he probably overtook Custer's column by about 1549 hours.[26]

Custer was heartened by his brother's news. Benteen was not far behind and he had been given a confirmed location of Lieutenant McDougall and the packs. A time and distance appreciation would suggest that they would not have too far to go. But they were unaware that Benteen and McDougall would delay, watering their horses, placing them 1 hour's and 1½ hours' march away respectively. Custer therefore felt that he could delay in order to gain the ammunition and fighting reinforcements he needed. Nevertheless, immediate action was required to take the pressure off Reno. He proposed to launch two companies under Captain George Yates at the village in a feint, while he would remain on high ground he had detected just to the north on Nye-Cartwright Ridge. Once reinforcements arrived a more deliberate assault could follow.

Custer's column moved in dead ground from Cedar Coulee and entered Medicine Tail Coulee, preparatory to a strike on the village. Curly and Bouyer were up on Weir Point watching the progress of the Reno fight in the valley bottom. As they observed they became aware of a sudden commotion and the movement of the line into the woods. Fires were breaking out and ever-darkening masses of braves were bearing down on the shrinking perimeter. Reno was in serious trouble and probably defeated. Realising the importance of this development for Custer's proposed plan, the two scouts descended Weir Point and galloped after his column.

Once again the aggressive Indian response had breached Custer's decision cycle.

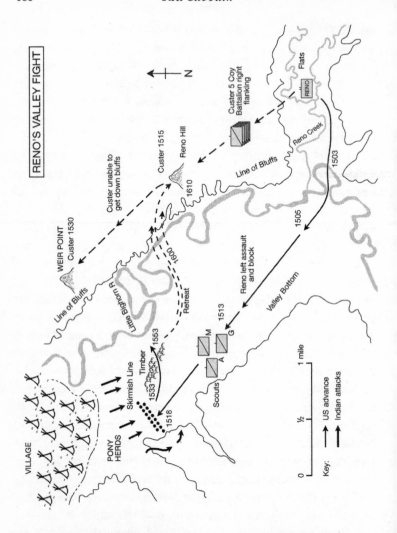

Reno's valley fight, 25 June, 1500–1600 hours

Reno assaulted on the left with three companies and blocked, opening the battle with a skirmish line in front of the village, while Custer marched in a right flanking move with five companies. Despite promising to 'support' Reno, Custer found that he was unable to find a passage down from the unreconnoitred high bluffs into the village. The isolated Reno was panicked into a disorderly retreat that decimated the combat power of his battalion.

Chapter 9

Divide to conquer

'A sight to strike terror in the hearts of the bravest of men.'

7th Cavalry Corporal

The column of death

Down in the valley bottom, at about 1553 hours, Reno's troopers suddenly burst out of the wooded area, some two to a horse. In the confusion of passing on the unexpected order, Private Thomas O'Neill in G Company noticed that 'the fire from the troopers slackened very materially – in fact, it practically ceased'. The Indians realised that something was going to happen, and the reduction in fire 'gave [them] greater confidence than ever,' continued O'Neill, 'and they pressed in on us in greatly increasing numbers'. The troopers felt on the point of being overwhelmed. 'Their forces were greatly augmented by hundreds of others arriving every minute from the lower end of the village.'[1] A Northern Cheyenne warrior, Soldier Wolf, watched this reinforcement. 'When the people in the lower villages heard the shooting up above, they all rushed toward it, everybody went.' 'Let's all charge at once!' cried One Bull, a Minneconjou Lakota to a group of warriors, determined to finish off the whites. Raising his tomahawk, he prayed, 'Wakontonka help me so I do not sin [with cowardice] but fight my battle. I started to charge,' he said.[2]

Reno subsequently called this operation a 'charge', although many of its participants remember it as a panic-stricken rout. The plan was that as the soldiers emerged from the thicket in twos, each side would fire outwards. 'Every man of our small command seemed to realise fully the desperate situation we were in,' said O'Neill, 'and what was expected of him – which was to keep up a constant fire and make every shot tell.' It was not a coordinated movement. 'I have no idea how the order to charge or fall back was communicated to the troops,' said Varnum. 'All I heard was some men yelling that they were "going to charge", or something like that.'[3]

'If they had remained in the timber,' claimed Soldier Wolf, 'the Indians could not have killed them; but all at once – perhaps they got frightened – they rushed out.' Reno's scout, Frank Gerard, was equally bemused. 'I was surprised at this change of position,' he said, 'as we had excellent cover and could hold off the Indians indefinitely, but the orders were to mount and charge.'[4] So surprised were the Indians initially at this sudden breakout that some beat a hasty retreat, but before long it was realised they were not attacking but running away. 'The soldiers are running!' became the cry. Private Slaper was circumspect about the military precision of this retreat, admitting that the move did not have 'a very military appearance, but I can say that I saw nothing disorderly about it'. This would depend very much upon an individual's place in the column, as they emerged into the open in fits and starts. 'So many had gone on ahead of me and were so far in advance that what they did,' confessed Slaper, 'or in what order they retreated, I cannot say with positive certainty.' What began with some semblance of order at the head of the column, capitalising on the initial surprise of the Indians, turned into a debacle for those desperately trying to keep up in the rear.

'As we emerged from the thicket the war whoop burst forth from a thousand throats,' recounted a terrified Private O'Neill. 'It was a race for life.' Once the Indians realised what was really happening, they pressed in closely on both sides, firing at point-blank range into the column. There was no direction from the head. Major Reno, comprehending that the mass of Indians surrounding his command would not permit a withdrawal to the original river crossing point, led the flight toward the high ground where he had last seen Custer. Somebody might still be there to support. Totally stressed, his face splashed with the gore from Bloody Knife's mortal head wound, he rode pell-mell for the river. No attempt was made to drop off a rearguard or conduct a phased withdrawal. 'I don't know that any point was designated where the command could rally or retreat on,' said Lieutenant Varnum. He found himself saying, 'This won't do, this won't do – we have got to get into shape.' No officer was directing operations from the front. It was every man for himself in a 'column of death'.

About 17 officers and men, including scouts, were left behind in the burning thickets. Either they had lost their horses or had not heard the word to retreat. 'There was such a cloud of dust' obscuring the back end of the column, that scout George B. Herendeen said, 'No one could see where he was going.' Suddenly his horse fell and he had to run back to the 'timber' to take his chances in the thickets. Private O'Neill was equally hard pressed.

'It was hand-to-hand conflict, both Indians and troopers striving to pull each other from their horses, after emptying their weapons, and both succeeding in a great many instances. I saw six or seven of our men in the act of falling from their horses after being shot. One poor fellow close to me was shot in the body, and as he was falling to the ground, was shot again through the head. I heard the shots as they struck him.'

To fall was to die. After running the gauntlet for a short distance, O'Neill's horse was struck by a bullet and crumpled in a slurry of flying clods and dust. This was every white man's nightmare, alive and at the mercy of pursuing Indians. 'I was paralysed with fear, and did not know what to do,' he admitted. As well he might. Runs the Enemy, a Two Kettle brave, saw the black interpreter Isaiah Dorman, married to a Hunkpapa woman, pause to shoot an Indian from his pony. As he did so his own horse was peppered by bullets from other pursuers and went down. It collapsed and rolled over on to the desperate black man, pinning him down sufficiently long for a group of Indians to close in. Private Roman Rutten from M Company dodged by him at the gallop and heard him cry out, 'Goodbye, Rutten.' Dorman was later found pinned to the ground with an iron picket thrust through his testicles. Indians clubbed and tortured him, repeatedly shooting him in the legs and partially skinning him alive. O'Neill had no illusions as to what fate awaited him if he fell alive into Indian hands. 'So I faced about and legged it,' he said, in the direction of the thicket, 'expecting every moment would be my last on earth.' He had 200 yards to go.[5]

American Horse, an Oglala Lakota, said that the retreat 'was like chasing buffalo, a grand chase'. 'The Indians kept killing them right along,' claimed Tall Bull, a Northern Cheyenne. Thundering hooves were mixed with the shriek of eagle bone whistles and howling and screaming braves. Dust enveloped everything, reducing the outline of charging troopers and Indians to bizarre shadowy figures. This galloping movement is captured by Indian 'pictographs', tapestries of figures painted on animal hides. Wooden Leg drew a picture of a trooper being yanked off the back of his saddle by a brave pulling at the soldier's slung carbine. Hats and droplets of blood fly into the air from the smashing concussion of stone clubs into faces and heads. Troopers pitch from saddles, shot in the backside because they are cowering low down on their horses, blood gushing from noses and mouths. Eyes are wide with terror. One man, turning to fire his pistol at his pursuers, has been transfixed in the mouth by an arrow. Another soldier has pitched from his horse with three arrows protruding from his spinal column. His head has been hacked from his torso.[6] Some braves derisively counted coup on troopers, striking them with the flat of their bows before restringing and dispatching them from the saddle with repeated arrow strikes. Most of the fleeing column were more concerned with riding for their lives than fighting back. Private William Taylor had already ripped off his right stirrup when emerging from the underbrush and was having difficulty maintaining balance on his horse. He was riding for survival. 'Out of the clouds of dust, anxious to be in at the death, came hundreds of others, shouting and racing toward the soldiers, most of whom, and I was one, had never fired a shot from a horse's back.'

'It was a wild rush for the river with the Indians on all sides, yelling like devils, shooting into our ranks, and even trying to drag men from their horses,' said James Darcy, fleeing with the remnants of M Company.

'One big Sioux rode alongside of me as we went along full gallop, and tried to pull me from the saddle. He had been shot in the shoulder, and every jerk he made at me the blood gushed from the wound and stained my shirt and trousers. He was a determined devil and hung on to me until we almost reached the river.'[7]

Wooden Leg, a Cheyenne warrior, saw one Lakota brave shoot arrows into a soldier's head and back, and watched the trooper tumble from his horse. Riderless horses became more numerous in the column as still more soldiers were felled by clubbing or stabs from war lances. 'You are only boys. You ought not to be fighting,' the warriors jeered derisively. Varnum gave some reason for the taunting. If the Indians 'saw that a man was not using his pistol they would ride close to him and fire'. The baiting continued throughout the retreat. The soldiers were at the mercy of the Indians, who knew it and would not grant it. 'We whipped you on the Rosebud. You should have brought more Crows or Shoshones with you to do your fighting.'[8]

'I followed the soldiers,' said One Bull, Sitting Bull's Minneconjou adopted son, riding amongst the stampede. 'They were running for the river. I killed two with my tomahawk.' Reno's tired horses were gradually being overhauled by the fresh Indian ponies, exposing even greater elements of the column, now strung out like a wild horse race, to greater punishment from the gauntlet of converging Indians. 'There were a good many Indians scampering along with their rifles across the saddle, working the levers of their Winchesters on the column,' said Varnum. The cavalry race was being driven towards an unreconnoitred point at the Little Bighorn. There was a fording place but it was narrow and deep, causing the fearful troopers to cluster. 'The Greasy Grass river [as it was called by the Indians] was very deep,' recalled She Walks With Her Shawl. Vigorously pressing home their attack, the Indians inflicted heavy casualties on panic-stricken soldiers who had to jump their horses into the water from the high banks. 'Their horses had to swim to get across,' said the Hunkpapa Lakota squaw:

> 'Some of the warriors rode into the water and tomahawked the soldiers. In the charge the Indians rode among the troopers and with tomahawks unhorsed several of them. The soldiers were very excited. Some of them shot into the air.'[9]

Many of the troopers hesitated at the water's edge – rarely do individuals simply plunge into an unknown body of water. Horses were urged stiff-legged into the river, unnerved at the prospect of leaping into the unknown. Desperate late arrivals had no compunction. Private James Darcy saw a trooper shot down in front of him, then Reno's Adjutant, Lieutenant Benjamin Hodgeson, was hit by a bullet. 'My horse stumbled over Hodgeson and went over the bluff into the stream' with a resounding splash. He 'got to his feet again and carried me across'. The high banks made it difficult to enter or leave the water. The Indians took full advantage of this physical check and a hand-to-hand melee developed in the water. Horses and men plunged in amidst huge clouds of spray or tumbled out of their saddles and splashed into the river. Private William Taylor 'saw a struggling mass of men and horses' when he arrived at the riverbank, 'from whom little streams of blood was colouring the water near them'. Gunpowder smoke and dust punctuated by the flash and resonant boom of firearms fired point-blank in the river bottom, mingled with the shrieks and groans of the wounded and dying. Troopers frantically struggling out of the churned mud on the far bank were set upon by groups of stabbing hacking Indians. Private Solomon 'Snopsy' Myers's horse had become unmanageable during the retreat and had suddenly bolted into the surrounding Indian lines. Miraculously he shot his way out of his predicament with his six-gun, only to have his horse killed under him careering down the bank. He plunged into the water on foot, managing to apprehend the stray horse that a wounded Lieutenant Hodgeson was trying to grab. Hodgeson hung on to the stirrup while Myers dragged him across. When he stumbled to his feet on the far side, an Indian sniper felled him. Red Feather, an Oglala Sioux warrior, saw a trooper slide from his saddle and become ensnared by his foot in the stirrup. He was dragged all the way into the river.

The crossing point is graphically illustrated in Amos Bad Heart Bull's vivid pictograph. Riderless horses can be seen emerging from the far bank, some dragging troopers. Soldiers with upraised arms are in the stream, seemingly in supplication as more horses career into the water at a gallop. Riders with arrows protruding from their backs are about to jump in. A bugler, arm outstretched, is impaled on the end of a lance at the moment of entering the water. The whole image exudes movement, confusion and suppressed sound. Two Moons, a Northern Cheyenne, described how 'they began to drive the soldiers all mixed up – Sioux, then soldiers, then more Sioux, and all shooting'. The mob hit the riverbank. 'I saw the soldiers fall back into the riverbed like buffalo fleeing,' he said. It was total chaos. 'They had no time to look for a crossing.' Water erupted on the surface from a series of splashes from incoming rounds. 'Quite a lively shower' was caused by the bullets, said Lieutenant Varnum. 'Whether ... from the bluffs above or from the river bottom, I don't know.' Many soldiers were overcome in the churned-up shallows. Spotted Horn Bull's squaw recalled, 'I saw boys pull men from their horses and kill them on the ground.'[10]

Archaeological research has provided a glimpse of the nightmare at the river crossing, supplementing Amos Bad Heart Bull's and Wooden Leg's pictographs. Sergeant Edward Botzer of G Company perished at the ford, and his bones were finally uncovered by erosion on the riverbank in 1989. Other remains had been long washed away, leaving a skull and a left humerus and right clavicle. Forensic examination, backed by photographic research to discover his true identity, suggests that he was struck across the mouth by a lance or gun barrel. Sufficient force was applied to fracture the bone and the crowns of three teeth, all of which would certainly have unseated him if he had been on horseback trying to reach the river. As he fell he might have struck his face on a log, rock or other object. Nobody knows how he was finally finished off because no other injuries are evident on the remaining bones. The evidence provides an archaeological 'snapshot' of the frenzied melee by the river.[11]

Most of the troopers were killed at the approaches to the river, in the maelstrom between the two banks and during the steep climb on the other side. Private Slaper got across unscathed. Later he claimed:

'I believe one reason why so many of the men escaped was because of the intense dust which was raised by the horses and ponies of the combatants. It hung in dense clouds, and it was almost impossible to see fifty feet ahead in any direction.'

In short, Slaper's view was that it was a miracle *anyone* had survived the disaster. 'After getting across the river' there was the next hurdle – 'I had the steep bluffs to climb.' These were so steep in places, 'so very abrupt that many of the already wearied horses were unable to carry their riders to the top'.[12] Soldiers stumbled upwards, leading their exhausted horses, under intermittent fire from below. Reno, plodding up the slope, was so stressed by his nightmare experience that he had no thought of throwing together a skirmish line to cover the retreat. The broken nature of the terrain precluded such an option, but no one had the presence of mind to order it. Fleeing troops were broadly channelled by even higher ground at the sides into a re-entrant that funnelled its way to the top. They individually staggered or rode together in ragged clusters, constantly striving to reach a crest that tantalisingly suggested safety. They had been tired and verging on exhaustion even before the 2½-mile charge down the valley. Now, with eyes glazed with fear and fatigue, they had endured the most harrowing experience of their lives, and it was not over yet.

Lieutenant Varnum was labouring up the ravine. 'Ahead of me I could see Dr De Wolf and his orderly.' He was disorientated and toiling up a re-entrant branching away to the left beyond the mainstream of retreating troopers. A few soldiers saw approaching danger. Indians were picking their way laterally across the slope to apprehend survivors. 'Some of the men were yelling at me,' said Varnum, 'but I could not hear what they said, except that they kept pointing ahead and beckoning me to come where they were.' De Wolf was a medical surgeon, not a soldier. He came with fewer practical survival instincts and was vulnerable. They shouted to De Wolf. 'Suddenly some shots rang out and I saw both the doctor and his orderly pitch forward dead.' De Wolf was hit in the abdomen. His isolated group was quickly overrun by the approaching warriors, who clubbed and shot him in the head and face. Varnum was shaken. 'That would have been my own fate,' he realised, 'if those men had not yelled and warned me to come where they were.'[13]

The troopers struggled upwards over rugged ground with irregular re-entrants running left and right. 'I know the horses were pretty well tuckered out,' said Varnum, 'panting and climbing that awful grade.' Private William Taylor's horse was blown by the pace of the retreat. It had got him across the river but was defeated by the ascent on the other side. 'He stood trembling with fatigue,' he said, 'and refused to go any further.' Ungratefully giving it a parting kick in disgust, he started up the slope after his comrades. Little encouragement was required because 'little puffs of dust' began 'rising from the ground all around as the bullets buried themselves into the dry dusty hillside'. Soldiers were dehydrated and many in shock. Continuous folds in the ground were covered by scrub, coated with long grass now glowing in the afternoon sun and dotted with sun-dried silvery trees. Diverging re-entrants broke up the retreat. Separated troopers hardly observed a soul as they stumbled and scrambled their way upwards. This encouraged a belief that they had suffered catastrophic losses. False crest lines accentuated fatigue, further depressing soldiers convinced that they might be one of few survivors. Beneath them was flaming and smoking timber. They could hear echoing shots, high-pitched screams and a fearful and all-pervasive buzzing, the Indian signature, punctuated by occasional war whoops. Extraneous equipment was discarded but nearly all retained their weapons, using carbine butts as crutches to lever themselves up the ever-steepening gradient. As they stumbled across the dry rustling grass, their clothing snagged on low cactus thorns, scratching and tearing at exposed limbs.

'There was quite a number of the men firing,' said Lieutenant Varnum as they gained the relative safety of high ground, but still no organised resistance or delay.[14] There was not a natural line upon which to regroup. Indians were in among them on the flanks, while others shot at soldiers from below. Taylor briefly joined with a comrade from his old M Company and ran 'quite close together for a few feet when with but the single exclamation of "Oh", Myers pitched forward face down to the ground'. Taylor was shocked. 'I bent over him but he was dead, shot between the left ear and eye.' His stomach churned. Taylor fearfully began 'zig-zagging as it were but ever going up'. With rasping breath and heaving chests, the troopers suddenly found themselves at the top. Able to orientate and look around, they were reassured at the sight of other companions, some seen for the first time. Stragglers emerged from the broken ground into uninterrupted bright sunshine at the top. There was surprise that others had made it. Relief was palpable. 'I have wondered how a man felt, when he believed that almost inevitable, sudden death was upon him,' Taylor reflected. 'I knew it now.' It had been a close-run flight. 'Our escape was little less than miraculous,' he concluded, 'when one considers the overwhelming number of Indians and the pitifully disorganised condition in which we made our death-encircled ride in the valley and up the bluffs, pursued by a howling mass of red warriors.'

Major Reno attempted to reorganise his men at the top of the bluffs and form a rudimentary skirmish line. This was not easy. 'Most of the men had thrown themselves on the ground to rest for they were well nigh exhausted,' said Taylor. Reno had lost his hat during the valley-bottom fighting and had bound a red handkerchief about his head, 'which gave him a rather peculiar and unmilitary appearance,' claimed Taylor. 'A few minutes later a column of troops was in sight coming downstream toward us,' observed a much-relieved Lieutenant Varnum.[15] It was about 1620 hours. Benteen had arrived.

This had been the worst day of Reno's life. He had ridden into battle with 140 soldiers and 35 scouts. The command had suffered a catastrophe. Thirteen wounded soldiers had scaled the bluffs and 57 men were missing. Reno had lost 40% of his command. His troops were confused, dazed and looking for their friends. One assumption among modern western military norms is that a unit is considered combat ineffective when losses exceed 20%. Forty of Reno's battalion lay dead on the battlefield, including three officers.

It has been assessed that the Indians suffered 12 fatalities in addition to the 10 non-combatants killed at the start of the attack. This might indicate about 36 Indian wounded if one accepts an established norm of one dead to three wounded. Indians, however, were alleged to have had a remarkable tenacity for life. One assessment of Indian casualties during the Custer fight comments that 'unless he was shot through the brains, heart or back, there was no certainty at all about his dying'. Casualties could be expected to make speedy recoveries. Lieutenant P. Clark, acting as an Indian Agent at Fort Robinson in 1876, claims to have seen many Indians shot through the body in different places enjoying excellent health one year later. Six of the 12 warriors killed in the valley bottom appear to have died at the hands of the Army Rees scouts, further emphasising army deficiencies in close combat and particularly marksmanship. Cavalry losses appear to have been in the ratio of five to one in favour of the Indians.[16] Small wonder the Indians taunted the cavalry during their pell-mell retreat. Spotted Horn

Bull's squaw, a cousin of Sitting Bull, was scathing in her commentary on the combat performance of Reno's battalion.

> 'The man who led those troops must have been drunk or crazy. He had the camp at his mercy, and could have killed us all or driven us away naked on the prairie. I don't believe there was a shot fired when his men commenced to retreat.'

Her husband corrected her statement, saying 'not much firing by the Indians'. Even so, she continued, 'when they began to run away they ran very fast, and dropped their guns and ammunition'. Perhaps this was more a statement about the lack of combined combat power levelled against the village by the army. Sioux warrior Crow King stated 'that if Reno had held out until Custer came and then fought as Custer did, that they would have whipped the Indians'.[17] For the first time in living memory a properly formed US Cavalry battalion had been routed by Indians in battle. The Indians were left buoyantly confident at their achievement.

'Scalp him!' the 13-year-old youth Black Elk was ordered. He stood in the open flat area before the riverbank, stripping clothes, guns and ammunition from the trail of dead and wounded soldiers strewn about in a haphazard line stretching back to the 'timber' area. A wounded trooper lay writhing on the ground near the water's edge. 'Boy, get off and scalp him,' the warrior repeated. Black Elk slipped from the back of his pony, unsheathing his knife. The 'Wasichu' [white man] twitched and ground his teeth in pain as the young boy cut and pulled at the scalp lock. It was not easy. Tiring of the struggle he placed his revolver at the white soldier's forehead and fired at point-blank range. That morning he had been an adolescent herding horses. Raising his grisly trophy in the air proclaimed him a warrior. He rode back to the village to show it to his mother.[18]

Down in the valley bottom the defeated were left facing the consequences of their unexpected reverse. To be left wounded was to die. The one-third generalisation of fatalities to wounded did not apply in Indian warfare. In the brush area Indian boys were setting fire to a section where a crazed cavalryman was stumbling about, seeking to escape. Two warriors, Eagle Elk and High Horse, watched as they constantly shot arrows into him, but still he thrashed around.[19] About 17 troopers and scouts were left behind in the 'timber' area. They looked on fearfully as squaws with young boys combed the battlefield, dispatching the wounded. 'The dead bodies of our men they stripped of their clothing,' a pensive Private O'Neill observed, 'and cut and mutilated them in every conceivable way with the knives they carried.' Lieutenant Charles de Rudio, stranded with O'Neill, was terrified. 'I cannot find words sufficiently expressive to describe my many thoughts during those hours of suspense,' he later wrote. Fire appeared to be constantly seeking them out. As the flames ran through the valley they consumed the body of Lieutenant Donald McIntosh, sprawled at the foot of the bluffs he had failed to ascend; kept at a reserved social distance by his brother officers because of mixed parentage in life, he was to be embraced by the fraternity of the 7th in death.

Lieutenant de Rudio was hiding in dark thick undergrowth at the bottom of a dried-up stream. He was startled by a number of pistol shots in his vicinity followed by 'the silvery, but to me diabolical voices of several squaws'. They were finishing off and stripping the dead. 'I found the women at the revolting work of scalping a soldier who was perhaps not yet dead.' He described how two of them cut away while two others performed an apparent macabre ritualistic dance around the scene. 'I will not attempt to describe to you my feelings at witnessing the disgusting perform-ance.' 'Some of their actions we could plainly see,' commented the despairing O'Neill, hiding in the same area. 'It made me faint and sick, not knowing how soon they might be disfiguring my own body in a similar manner, and I determined to sell my life dearly.'

Sergeant John Ryan with M Company had survived the ascent of the bluffs and now gazed at a scene of utter desolation in the valley bottom below. 'The prairie was all afire,' he said. Somehow they would need to rally the men, but their position appeared hopeless. They monitored the activity on the flat ground they had traversed 'where the Indians were' with morbid fascination, 'and could see them stripping and scalping our men, and mutilating their bodies in a horrible manner'.[20]

The crash of volley fire reverberated to the north. It was distant firing. Almost immediately the plain before the bluffs began to empty of Indians. American Horse, an Oglala Lakota, looking up at the bluffs from below, saw another column of troops moving towards the remnants of Reno's command still reorganising on the high ground. They continued to pick through the cavalry dead. 'While they were doing this,' he said, 'they heard the shooting and the calling down the river.' Other braves were already leaving the plunder and spurring back towards the village. American Horse tried to discern what was going on. There was 'a man calling out that troops were attacking the lower end of the village'.[21] Custer was at last in the fight.

Buying time

Captain George W. Yates had been detached from Custer's battalion with E and F Companies, two depleted units of 38 and 29 men totalling 67 (as 54 were detached elsewhere). Custer kept approximately 150 men on Nye-Cartwright Ridge while Yates's small force was directed to engage the edge of the Indian village by Minneconjou ford. As they moved down the initially narrow Medicine Tail Coulee (or re-entrant) it expanded to a wider, flat approach to the river. Custer had subdivided his force again, separating 44.6% of his fighting power for this feint to draw off pressure on Reno. This was the second blow administered to the village, but hardly punitive. Reno's first assault had prodded the village into a violent and aggressive reaction with only 95 carbines. Its failure raised Indian confidence and appeared to fulfil Sitting Bull's prophecy that any assault on the village would prove catastrophic for the soldiers. Yates's feint, initially unexpected, was to have the same negligible impact, with only 50 carbines directing fire, or 67 without horse-holders. Custer at no stage in this battle applied the full regimental combat power of command of over 600 men in a single blow. It was to prove his undoing.

Custer was using standard Civil War cavalry tactics, probing for weakness. If Yates detected a vulnerability, Custer could follow up with a larger second wave. Conversely, Custer may have been buying time, awaiting the imminent arrival of Benteen's battalion and more ammunition. He was still on the offensive. Even if Scout Mitch Bouyer and Curly, having seen Reno's likely reverse, could convince him that the situation was becoming fraught, it appears that Custer, in his fatigued condition, could not countenance that a battalion of his regiment could be defeated – checked, perhaps, but no cavalry battalion had ever been routed on the field by Indians.

The hostiles, unused to multi-faceted and coordinated cavalry operations, were shocked and surprised by the appearance of Yates and the Custer strike force. Two Moons, a Northern Cheyenne warrior sitting astride his pony by the river in the village, said, 'I saw flags coming over the hill to the east.' Runs the Enemy, a Two Kettle war-band leader, having already engaged Reno, was aghast at what he saw. 'As I looked along the line of the ridge they seemed to fill the whole hill,' he exclaimed. There would be another fight and perhaps on different terms. 'It looked as if there were thousands of them, and I thought we would be surely beaten.' Short Bull, the Oglala nephew of the great Red Cloud of the first Sioux war, was equally dismayed. 'I thought there was a million of them,' he said. Iron Hawk, a 14-year-old Hunkpapa, who had already fought on the Rosebud, was undecided what he should do next. An Indian named Little Bear resolved his dilemma. 'Take courage, boy,' he said. 'The earth is all that lasts.'[22] He followed his companion in the direction of the new threat.

There were only about a dozen Indian warriors in the vicinity of Minneconjou ford able to offer resistance at this village entry point. It appeared to the approaching cavalry they had achieved complete surprise and might even enter the village with impunity. It was deserted. Most of the fighting men had been engaging Reno at the southern end of the village and the non-combatants had fled or were seeking ponies from the herd on the west side.

Custer's command on Nye-Cartwright Ridge was not in direct support of Yates's feint. The river crossing point was 1¼ miles distant and obscured by intervening ridgelines. By the time they reached the water's edge, E and F Companies were out of sight from those on the ridge. There was no need to cross the ford to dominate it. F Company supported from terraced steps going down to the ford and the high bluffs bordering either side of the entrance to the swirling gravelly crossing. Custer's limited line of sight on the ridge confirms the likelihood that this was more a feint than a forceful probe into the village. An E Company detachment approached the water's edge, supported by their own skirmishers and those from F Company on the higher ground.

There is controversy as to whether soldiers entered the ford and were shot in the river. It was a classic 'meeting' engagement. Both sides were surprised. Initially the cavalry may have been encouraged to enter a seemingly deserted and vulnerable part of the camp. A forceful assault with the entire Custer battalion may arguably have created one of those 'moments' for which Custer was renowned for exploiting in the past. He remained, however, on Nye-Cartwright Ridge, preferring to rebuild his further divided and, as a consequence, depleted combat potential. Yates's sally was a feint to draw off the Indians from Reno's shocked command and it succeeded. The Indians were totally taken aback by this new attack from a completely different direction.

Utilising a small ridge on the other side of the ford, a small Indian group offered courageous resistance. There was initial dismay at this fresh incursion, but Cheyenne warrior Bobtail Horse declared, 'Only the Earth and Heavens last long. If we four can stop the soldiers from capturing our camp, our lives will be well spent.' The 500 or more warriors that had been fighting Reno at the other side of the camp were now streaming back through the village heading towards the threat identified at the ford. 'All the men rushed down the creek again, to where the women were,' said

Soldier Wolf, a Northern Cheyenne brave. More and more Indians galloped up at the ford. 'All rushed back on the west side of the camp, down to a small dry run that comes in from the east,' said Tall Bull, another Cheyenne warrior.

> 'There, down close to the river, were the soldiers. The Indians all crossed and they fought there. For quite a long time the troops stood their ground right there; then they began to back off, fighting all the time, for quite a distance, working up the hill.'[23]

Yates, appreciating the growing strength of the resistance already beginning to spill across the river in his direction, began to direct an orderly withdrawal. Skirmish lines were drawn up and soldiers moved back on foot and mounted as repeated volleys crashed out. The sound of these ordered exchanges of fire offered some comfort to Reno fugitives seeking shelter in the 'timber', awaiting an opportunity to rejoin the main force up on the bluffs. They could see that the Indians were clearly thinning out, moving in the direction of the firing.

Custer, up on the high ground on Nye-Cartwright Ridge, was also engaging and brushing off Indian groups with volley fire. Archaeological research has illuminated this lesser-known aspect of the battle. Some 480 .45/55-calibre cases and cartridges have been unearthed along the route taken by Custer between Luce and Nye-Cartwright ridges as he moved broadly north-west, shadowing Yates's action to the south. Smaller clusters of finds to the south of this trail indicate lesser but connected actions.[24] It is not clear in which direction Custer's three companies were directing their fire, but it confirms that there was a number of volleys, possibly also audible to Reno's men reorganising at the top of the bluffs. These rolling volleys were not a signal to mark his location, simply Custer dispersing smaller groups of Indian resistance. They do suggest that, having spotted the new cavalry column, Indians were already surging up the adjoining valleys and re-entrants leading up from the village. The aim was probably to engage and surround this newly identified force. Custer was buying time awaiting reinforcements.

Meanwhile, Captain Frederick Benteen's independent frame of mind was squandering time. Unlike Custer, advancing rapidly to contact, Benteen allowed his command to water its horses at the 'morass' once he had rejoined Custer's route. Lieutenant McDougall's thirsty pack train required no bidding, following Benteen's example and stampeding into the mud. It was logical to consider the horses. The Custer column was paying the penalty of discarded exhausted horses throughout subsequent battle manoeuvres. Benteen was a veteran soldier applying professional judgement in maintaining the battle efficiency of his command. Horses would need water now to maintain operational tempo later. There was no agreed regimental battle plan at this stage apart from the instructions Custer had issued prior to subdividing his battalions. Direction had been given for a cavalry pursuit and mop-up operation, not a major dismounted infantry action. Benteen was now an hour behind Custer, and the reserve ammunition 30 minutes behind him. At this point Benteen had no perception of the serious nature of the threat ahead, a surprise already to Reno and Custer alike. If he had known, he would have pushed the command harder. All were aware of the potential size of their adversary – the immense churned-up track leading the way to the village was proof of that. It made sense therefore to look to the security of the pack train with its precious reserve of ammunition.

Sergeant Kanipe, dispatched by Custer, reached the packs first. 'I gave Captain McDougall the orders sent him,' he said, 'and went on toward Captain Benteen as I had been told to take them to him, also.'

As Trumpeter John Martin passed the Reno fight, heading toward the rear, he glanced down and saw the skirmish line, still belching fire but falling back. He was shot at several times by Indians, one round striking his horse in the hip, but he broke through. 'It was a very warm day and my horse was hot,' he remembered, 'and I kept on as fast as I could go.' He had no idea where Benteen's command was 'but I knew I had to find him'. Dust clouds provided the first indication and presently a column of cavalry came into sight. 'As soon as I saw them coming I waved my hat to them,' said Martin, 'and I spurred my horse, but he couldn't go any faster.' Benteen and Lieutenant Weir were 200-300 yards ahead of their troops, who were riding 'at a fast trot'. This was a purposeful advance, but not exuding urgency.

Martin's report did not immediately change the tempo. 'Where's the General now?' Benteen asked, having been informed 'it was a big village and to hurry'. Martin's response probably reassured him because he stated that 'the Indians we [Custer] saw were running, and I supposed that by this time he had charged through the village'. Benteen glanced at the message indicating that his support was urgently needed, but it appeared that the battle was going to plan. Martin was one of many foreign immigrants serving in the 7th Cavalry. Communicating with these individuals may not have been easy, and Benteen wanted to get moving. Martin was only a bugler and, as he admits, 'I didn't speak English so good then.' Benteen realised that Martin's horse was wounded and arranged for him to receive a replacement. The pack train in any case 'was in sight, maybe a mile away,' Martin observed, 'and the mules were coming along, some of them walking, some trotting, and others running.' Benteen pushed on 'faster than the packs could go,' said Martin, who rejoined his troop in the column. 'Soon they were out of sight, except that we could see their dust.'[25] Benteen's complacency would soon be shattered. From now on his independent judgement was to be under serious pressure as, like Reno and Custer before him, he was to be subjected to many surprises.

'We could hear heavy firing now,' said Corporal Windolph with H Company in Benteen's command. Sergeant Kanipe, having delivered his message to Lieutenant McDougall and the packs, was chasing Benteen, and passed some of Reno's scouts going in the opposite direction. Some were driving captured Indian ponies. 'They had come from Major Reno's command,' he realised, being initially alarmed that they may be hostiles. 'They were that scared that they did not stop until they reached the Powder River.' Corporal Windolph began to realise as they approached the Little Bighorn Valley 'that somewhere in this neighbourhood there was hard fighting going on'. Tension heightened within the column. 'Benteen ordered us to draw pistols and we charged up the bluffs at a gallop,' recalled Windolph, 'expecting at any moment to run into hostiles.' Suddenly the valley came into view on their left, revealing 'a sight to strike terror in the hearts of the bravest men'. Down in the valley, 'maybe 150 feet or more below us, and somewhere around half a mile away, there were figures galloping on horseback, and much shooting'. All this was reviewed in short 'snapshots' as they rode furiously along the top of the bluffs. Further along the river 'there were great masses of mounted men we suspicioned were Indians'. Sergeant Kanipe, following on behind, was aghast when he realised that he was witnessing Reno's command being cut to pieces.

> 'The Indians were following close at their heels, shooting and yelling, and men were dropping here and there. They, the Indians, would hop on them and scalp them before we could rescue them.'[26]

Benteen had no idea what was going on. He did not know where Custer was. For one horrifying moment he may have thought that he was witnessing the disintegration of the main body. Defeat of even a single cavalry battalion by Indians was unprecedented. 'I'll never forget that first glimpse I had of the hill top,' said Windolph. 'Here were a little group of men in blue, forming a skirmish line, while their beaten comrades, disorganised and terror-stricken, were making their way on foot and on horseback up the narrow coulee that led from the river, 150 feet below.' They recognised Major Reno and Lieutenant Varnum. Trumpeter Martin saw the excited Major dismounted and, with a handkerchief around his forehead, raise his hand and call, 'For God's sake, Benteen, halt your command and help me. I've lost half my men.'

Benteen accepted the need to halt. This shambles would have to be sorted out before he could join Custer. 'It's no use pretending that the men here on the hill, from Reno down, were not disorganised,' said Windolph, 'and downright frightened.' Reno's command was vulnerable and would need protection while they reformed and resupplied from the pack train that was still an hour distant. Windolph's view was that 'they'd had a lot of men killed, and it had only been by the grace of God, and the bad aim of the Indians, that had let them escape across the river with their lives'. 'Where's Custer?' was the rhetorical question. They gazed northwards. 'We could hear the sound of distant firing echoing down through the hills and valleys from that direction,' Windolph recalled. 'Custer must be down there.'[27]

Benteen faced a dilemma. His horses were 'played out' at this point, having galloped up to the bluffs to rescue Reno. Custer had to be at least an hour away and the frustratingly slow packs a further hour behind. Benteen was an 'up and at them' soldier, a quality he was to demonstrate in the fighting to come, and a competent defender. But he was no intellectual and neither was he a dashing mobile cavalry commander adept at 'seizing the moment' like Custer. His commander was clearly in trouble, as evidenced by the severe mauling Reno's command had experienced. Benteen was to be troubled by his conscience in later years, but instinctively felt reluctant to abandon Reno. He was being directed to commit his force to the vagaries of supporting Custer forward on the basis of a short and scrappy note. He felt he had a moral obligation to remain with Reno until his command had recovered.

Libby Custer would never forgive him for this.

Chapter 10
So near yet so far

'The first stand was probably made by Lieutenants Calhoun and Crittenden on the hill marked D [Calhoun Hill on a map presented to the Inquiry] to protect the troops passing along the ravine at its foot. The men and their empty cartridge shells were found in a semi-circle around the crest. Calhoun and Crittenden were killed here.'

Lieutenant Maguire at the Reno Court of Inquiry

'I saw Lieutenant Calhoun's company were killed in regular position of skirmishers. I counted 28 cartridge shells around one man, and between the intervals there were shells scattered.'

Lieutenant Moylan at the Reno Court of Inquiry[1]

Sifting evidence

Trumpeter John Martin was probably the last white man to see Custer's command alive. He recalled, on departing to deliver his message to Benteen:

'The last I saw of the command they were going down into the ravine [to attack the Indian camp]. The gray horse troop [E Company] was in the centre and they were galloping.'[2]

What happened to Custer's five companies after this point is conjecture. Source material is limited to eyewitness accounts of body finds, existing battlefield markers – allegedly where corpses were hastily interred – Indian accounts of fighting and archaeological material unearthed after the 1983 prairie fire.

Assessments based on the positions of bodies later found were used during the Reno Court of Inquiry to rationalise the catastrophe. Witnesses were influenced by a self-interested need to preserve reputations. Benteen later described the spread of corpses as 'scattered corn', suggesting a rout – knowing full well that his failure to reinforce Custer on time was under scrutiny.

Bodies were buried where they fell and the site marked with a stake. Subsequent recoveries and movement of remains followed, but maintained the cohesion of the original information. Recent archaeological investigations have suggested that although there are more markers than bodies, inferring that 40 to 70 may be incorrectly sited, they do provide a broadly accurate picture of body locations.[3]

Indian testimony of the final moments of Custer's command is contained in recorded oral accounts and pictographs, but frustration over inconsistencies marred their initial acceptance. Poor translations, a desire to please interrogators, or interviewers promoting individual theories all tended to pervert the accuracy of the final result. Pictographs, like medieval tapestries of significant events, celebrate brave or impressive deeds in a form of early pseudo-propaganda. Some Indian pictographs are sufficiently grainy to indicate a degree of authenticity. A parallel example is the famous portrayal of Harold Godwinson in the Bayeux Tapestry at the Battle of Hastings in 1066, with a Norman arrow in his eye. Although this pictorial representation is not forensically provable, it does offer a credible view. If the figure portrayed is not Harold, others around him probably suffered similar injuries from high-trajectory arrows. Indian pictographs offer similar eyewitness interpretations. Minneconjou Lakota Red Horse drew pictures of the dismemberment of Custer's dead troopers after the battle and showed dead

Indian warriors. This is an attempt to relate a scene as they saw it, rather than lauding heroic deeds.[4] Recent finds suggest that greater credence could be applied to these oral and pictorial Indian testimonies.

Archaeological evidence and forensic studies derived from a site picked over in some detail by tourists since the 1890s must by definition be flawed. How much so is difficult to assess, perhaps an accuracy of about 40%. Only a small proportion of skeletal remains have been subjected to modern scientific scrutiny. The Custer battlefield has yielded about 375 human bones, and 141 of these (34.3% of the whole) came from one individual; altogether they represent the remains of perhaps 34 persons.[5] Only a fraction of more than 4,000 available artefacts can be 'forensically' or clinically assessed. They have, however, considerably added to our knowledge of the battle and debunked a number of heroic myths that emerged in intervening histories.

The Little Bighorn battlefield is probably the first example of a site where finds have been systematically plotted on to a computerised grid to illustrate the progress of a historical engagement. Precise locations have been recorded for every relic found and modern ballistics technology applied to a combat field. These archaeological insights have opened certain windows since the prairie fire of 1983. They confirm the accuracy of body find reports. Huge numbers of non-army cartridge cases have been found, demonstrating that Indian firepower was considerably greater than originally assumed. Plotting and computerising this data has revealed snapshots of the likely conduct of a fight previously cloaked in historical obscurity. Ejected cartridges from army Springfield carbines and impacted Indian bullets offer indications of where cavalry troopers probably fought. Likewise, impacted army bullets and other calibre cases point to Indian positions. Each cartridge struck by a firing pin makes a unique impression, as do extraction marks. Forensic research backed by computer plotting has enabled the movement of individual Indian and army guns to be tracked around the battlefield. Explanations can therefore be offered on deployments and concentrations of fighting power. But the evidence is 'unclean' in a courtroom sense, having been picked over by countless amateurs before the present scientific filters could be applied.

Taken in total, evidence relating to body finds, broadly confirmed by archaeological checks on existing markers and crude forensic surveys conducted on cartridge cases and impacted bullets, all add credence to previously questioned Indian testimony. The last moments of Custer's battalion should be considered in the light of this evidence and its validity set against other factors: time, terrain, military judgement and human nature on the battlefield.

Indian evidence implies that the final battle was short-lived, 'as long as it takes a hungry man to eat his dinner'. Indian inexactitude is matched by a white army readiness to rationalise the disaster in the best possible light. Like the British Second World War defeats at Dunkirk in 1940 and Arnhem in 1944, this invariably results in portraying the unfortunate outcome in 'heroic' terms. Imprecise conclusions can result. Nineteenth-century technology had yet to produce a synchronised timepiece. Clocks were of variable quality and told different times. Military planning therefore resorted to general-isations such as dawn, dusk, days, numbers of hours, prearranged signals or bugle calls. There was nothing precise enough to produce the modern equivalent of 'H' hour.

J. S. Gray's excellent time and motion surveys of the Battle of the Little Bighorn offer exhaustive breakdowns of timelines based on performance times.[6] They provide invaluable insights by plotting events up to the separation of Custer's battalion from the rest of the regiment. Gray, however, was not a soldier. Time is also required to appreciate a military situation, come to a decision point, then relay orders to often disparate commands spread about the field of combat. Custer, while attempting to retain momentum during his advance to contact on the village, is likely to have followed a logical prearranged scheme in his mind. This might have altered as things went wrong. Gray's clinical time-keeping is not able to portray indecision. As Custer's plan began to unravel, the time taken for decisions probably increased commensurate with attempts to stay on track or alter direction. This occurred on a number of occasions, such as when the height of the unscouted bluffs prevented a synchronised initial attack on the village, and Reno's reinforcement. Despite his reputation for decisiveness and prompt decision-making, Custer may have prevaricated when it became apparent that he could lose a battle for the first time in his life. There was stress from the career stakes and the shock impact of multiple reverses. All this may well have strung out Custer's decision-making process. Even atop Nye-Cartwright Ridge he was fully engaged in firing off volleys in an unconfirmed direction. He had to be defending his command at the time because Yates was too distant to be the recipient of this support. Indian sources suggest that the command was surrounded by the time it came together again. Indecision as to whether to proceed with or without Benteen could have considerably strung out the movement times, clinically calculated by Gray, to a previously uncalculated degree. Through fatigue and dismay at reverses, Custer was in uncharted territory in terms of previous experience. He may well have dithered to an irrecoverable degree. Perhaps he was wounded. No one can tell.

Yates's sally forward with E and F Companies, numbering only 67 men, achieved its objective. Reno's command, having been chased up to its hilltop position at the eastern end of the village, was no longer under pressure. Indians were now streaming down the length of the village to deal with the newly discovered Custer command, which was bearing down on the centre of the village along Medicine Tail Coulee from the north-east. Three companies remained menacingly atop Nye-Cartwright Ridge. The crash-boom of heavy-calibre cavalry volleys from the ridgeline contrasted with the rising and falling 'pick-pock' of different Indian weapon types. Survivors from Reno's command and in the valley bottom claim to have heard this gunfire, doubtfully audible at 2 to 3 miles distance. Recent acoustic tests have not provided definitive conclusions, as they cannot replicate the numbers of weapons fired. Atmospheric conditions would play a role, as also the variable hearing abilities of witnesses. Some officers giving evidence to later Courts of Inquiry may have had dubious hearing, a consequence of damage meted out by high-intensity Civil War volley fire and artillery duels.

By many accounts, Yates conducted a well-fought and orderly withdrawal from Minneconjou ford. 'The troops formed in line of battle,' said Oglala American Horse, 'and there they fought for some little time.'[7] He very likely retreated in a northerly direction up a steeply sloping open valley – Deep Coulee – while Custer moved westwards across the Nye-Cartwright ridgeline, sufficiently intimidated by mounting opposition to desire a junction with Yates as rapidly as possible. There were casualties. Soldier Wolf, a 17-year-old Northern Cheyenne warrior, commented on the stiff resistance put up by Yates's retreating command.

They began fighting, and for quite a time, fought in the bottom, neither party giving back. There they killed quite a good many horses, and the ground was covered with the horses of Cheyennes, Sioux and of white men, and two soldiers were killed and left here.'

Trumpeter Henry Dose, one of Custer's orderly buglers, was later found 600 yards from Minneconjou ford. He and his friend Sergeant Botzer would never return to 'bake flapjacks' as they had reminisced in final letters home. Botzer's body was tentatively identified at the Reno river crossing site in 1989. 'Soon the Indians overpowered the soldiers,' said Soldier Wolf, 'and they began to give way, retreating slowly, face to the front.' 'They fell back up the hill' covered in prairie grass and mottled with sagebrush bushes, obscuring folds in the ground.[8] The first white gravesite markers are visible today on climbing Calhoun Hill. They appear in ghostly snow-white pairs and groups, reflecting sunlight, about half-way up.

The junction between Custer, skirmishing his way toward Yates, and Yates himself, partly obscured coming up from the low ground, could not have been easy. 'The troops fought on horseback all the way up the hill,' said American Horse. 'They were on their horses as

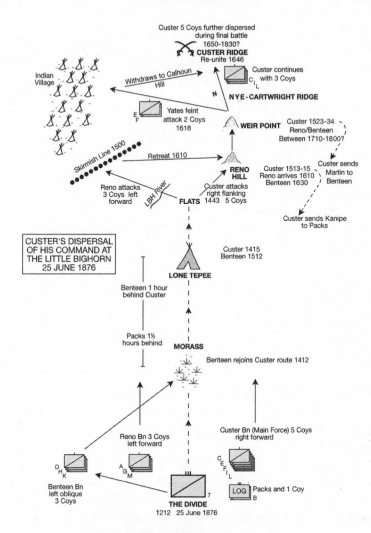

Custer 5 Coys further dispersed
during final battle
1650-1830?
CUSTER RIDGE
Re-unite 1646

Custer continues
with 3 Coys

C I L

Indian
Village

Withdraws to Calhoun Hill

N

NYE-CARTWRIGHT RIDGE

Yates feint
attack 2 Coys
1618

E
F

WEIR POINT

Custer 1523-34
Reno/Benteen
Between 1710-1800?

Skirmish Line 1500

Retreat 1610

RENO HILL

Custer 1513-15
Reno arrives 1610
Benteen 1630

Custer sends
Martin to
Benteen

Reno attacks
3 Coys left
forward

LBH River

Custer attacks
right flanking
1443 5 Coys

FLATS

Custer sends Kanipe
to Packs

**CUSTER'S DISPERSAL
OF HIS COMMAND AT
THE LITTLE BIGHORN
25 JUNE 1876**

Custer 1415
Benteen 1512

LONE TEPEE

Benteen 1 hour
behind Custer

Packs 1½
hours behind

MORASS

Benteen rejoins Custer route 1412

Reno Bn 3 Coys
left forward

Custer Bn (Main Force) 5 Coys
right forward

A
G
M

C E F I L

D H K

LOG Packs and 1 Coy
B

Benteen Bn
left oblique
3 Coys

THE DIVIDE
1212 25 June 1876

Custer's dispersal of his command at the
Battle of the Little Bighorn

Custer fragmented his regiment at every juncture of the Battle of the Little
Bighorn, convinced that he needed to do this to prevent the Indians scattering
on contact. Crook's experience at the Rosebud, if shared, would have convinced
him to fight his regiment as an integrated group. Although Crook did divide his
command, he at least managed – unlike Custer – to keep most of it in sight.

long as horses lasted, but by this time the Indians had got all around them and they were completely surrounded.'[9] Firing from horseback is less accurate than from a skirmish line on the ground. Indians were closing in under this desultory fire and gaining confidence as they did so. Custer's men needed to avoid 'friendly fire' accidents as the company groups converged, moving and firing in different directions while attempting to control their horses. Junior leaders, of which there was a deficit, would have been severely tested. Custer decided to establish a rearguard of dismounted troopers to break clean and seek to regain the initiative. Calhoun's company may indeed have been ordered to dismount and deploy initially to cover the junction of forces. Fighting around Custer's three-company contingent had thus far been sporadic and at long distance. Once fusion was achieved with Yates's E and F Companies, the whole command was in the thick of the fight.

Mitch Bouyer, Custer's chief scout, was becoming pessimistic. He had observed the extent of Indian infiltration by stealth reinforced now by masses of warriors surging up the valleys and re-entrants from the village. He turned to his young Crow companion Curly and told him, 'You better leave us here.' Curly was instructed to ride to a higher ridgeline to the east. 'Watch awhile,' he was directed by Bouyer. 'See if the Sioux are besting us and you make your way back to Terry and tell him we are all killed.' Curly was later to relate that Custer dispatched a further message even at this late stage, 'handed to a young man – on a sorrel roan horse – who galloped away'.[10] Private Nathan Short of C Company was riding just such a horse and his body was later allegedly found 80 miles away near the Yellowstone River. There is no confirmation who was dispatched, and whether it was a message for Benteen or Terry. The messenger appears to have set off northwards – towards Terry.

Calhoun Hill

Custer established his rearguard with Calhoun's 46-strong L Company on a hill to later bear the latter's name. It is not certain how long Custer's column had dallied waiting for Benteen, but sufficient time, it appears, for the Indians to begin establishing a loose ring around his command. Sitting Bull later described how 'at first' the Indians directly assaulted the force they had located across the river, 'but afterwards they found it better to try and get around him'. It was the classic example of a buffalo hunt – split the herd, then take out the weaker elements. Sitting Bull said that 'they formed themselves on all sides of him except just at his back'. Custer's command was invited to place its neck in a loosely formed noose. When asked how long it took to surround the column, Sitting Bull answered 'as long as it takes the sun to travel from here to here', referring to the shadow of a tent pole. His interpreter assessed this measurement as 'probably meaning half an hour'.[11] Custer felt under pressure to break clean, and Calhoun was dropped off to achieve this. For the first time the battle was teetering between offence and the need to survive. Offence was required to break out. The development of the next phase would determine whether Calhoun's role was sacrificial or rearguard.

Archaeological evidence relating to Indian firepower unearthed by the prairie fire in 1983 was as unexpected to historians then as it was to Custer more than 100 years before. Finds relate to 371 individual firearms used on the battlefield, of which 209 are probably Indian. An archaeological team[12] concluded that 43.6% of the individually identified guns belonged to the army. Henry and Winchester 1866 and 1873 model repeating weapons amounted to 31.2% of all the firearms evidence, and 55% of the Indian total. According to the statistical models applied, the 209 non-army firearms probably represented 30 to 35% of the battlefield archaeological record. If one includes the weapons not found, and accepting the statistical methods applied, the Indians might potentially have mustered 597 to 697 individual firearms. It is assessed that between 354 and 414 of these might have been used against Custer's five companies alone. If so, his strike force was outgunned by about two to one.

Of particular significance are the numbers of Henry and Winchester repeating rifles; it is projected that the Indians had between 198 and 232 (with more later employed against the Reno-Benteen defence site). If each magazine was full at the outset of the battle, 3,792 rounds would have been available to be fired at the rapid rate. 'Our young men rained lead across the river,' claimed Sitting Bull, 'and drove the white braves back.' More than 18 bullets were available to fire at each man who eventually died in Custer's contingent – and this does not include the myriad of other firearms making up the other 45% of the Indian total. Custer was seriously outgunned and, like historians for the succeeding hundred years, did not know it.[13]

Corporal Windolph with Benteen's command later stated:

'It has been generally accepted that all the red warriors were armed with the latest model repeating rifles and that they had a plentiful supply of ammunition. For my part, I believe that fully half the warriors carried only bows and arrows and lances, and that possibly half the remainder carried odds and ends of old muzzle-loaders and single-shot rifles of various vintages. Probably not more than 25% or 30% of the warriors carried modern repeating rifles.'

There were between 1,500 and 2,000 warriors in the village. Taking the lower estimate would suggest that 375 Indians were armed with muzzle-loaders and single-shot rifles. If 25% were carrying repeating rifles, then the 375 warriors matched rapid-firing repeaters against 210 army single-shot carbines. In all, 116 repeating firearms have been positively identified on the battlefield, giving a statistical projection of probably 340 to 403 (based on a 30 to 35% sample) actually employed. These figures do not greatly differ from Windolph's eyewitness projections.[14]

An examination of Indian pictographs further confirms these assumptions. Red Horse drew five pictographs, now in the US National Anthropological Archive, illustrating 61 dead warriors after the battle. Virtually all (some 53) are shown to be carrying a rifle, and 41 of these can be identified as repeaters. Nineteen years after the battle White Bird, a Cheyenne warrior, drew a panorama now hanging in the West Point collection, depicting the Custer and Reno-Benteen fights. Six of nine warriors engaging Reno Hill clearly have rifles, and about 40% of the warriors overrunning Custer. Flying By, a Minneconjou Lakota, claimed that he 'had considerable ammunition' on entering the Custer fight. 'I had a Winchester rifle with 14 shots [and] many Indians had pump guns.'[15]

In the aftermath of the fight many white interviewers could not comprehend that a low-tech opponent could defeat their army deploying modern weapons. It was also a telling statement of Indian logistic capacity that they could individually reconstitute ammunition after exhausting their previous stocks against Crook on the Rosebud only one week before. Crook fired off most of his ammunition reserve to keep the same Indian force at bay and retired from the battlefield ostensibly to reinforce and restock. Indian summer roamers from the Agencies had meanwhile reconstituted their supply. Indian oral and pictorial evidence has been consistent about their capabilities, but misinterpreted by white historians. History can repeat itself. US Special Forces and Rangers engaged against Somali irregulars in Mogadishu in 1993 could not comprehend how a sophisticated weapons platform like a Black Hawk helicopter could be shot down by a low-tech foe using a rudimentary RPG-7 anti-tank rocket-launcher. Like Custer's baptism of modern repeater fire, once tactically surprised by a technological misappreciation, high casualties can result, especially when the fight is fought on the enemy's terms and in his own backyard. The Indians were allowed to close.

Calhoun's company was only 46 men strong because 11 others were with the packs, six had been left behind on the Yellowstone, and three were detached elsewhere. Strung out in extended line with 7 yards instead of the accepted 5 between men meant that Calhoun could barely cover a frontage of 300 yards. His company was to play a pivotal role in the fight, but his allocated frontage was too broad.

The advent of breech-loading rifles had reduced the number of men per front compared to the accepted Civil War norm, and brutal casualties suffered during that conflict encouraged greater dispersion – each man's occupied space increased by 25%. Between 1815 and 1866 the number of troops deployed per mile dropped from 20,000 to 12,000. Once troops could individually take cover, junior command burdens progressively increased. As one historian described it, 'Entire armies turned into clouds of uncontrolled skirmishers, especially when on the attack.' The resulting junior command and control dilemma was not to be settled until the advent of the radio.[16]

Calhoun was defending, not attacking, but this remained a mobile and volatile battle. The role of the junior commander was essential in an era when command was dependent upon the shouted word, messengers or bugle calls, and flags and pennants denoted the location of headquarters. Custer's five companies were short of junior leaders and Calhoun's especially so. Custer's battalion was short of seven officers, eight sergeants and three corporals in total. Calhoun's situation was tenuous – the company was under strength. Three of four officers, including the commander, were on detached duty – Lieutenant Calhoun was acting commander in the absence of Captain Sheridan. His only other officer was Lieutenant John Crittenden, partially disabled with one eye, who had joined the company barely one month before the start of the campaign. He was also deficient by two sergeants and one corporal.[17] It would be difficult for Calhoun to react to tactical surprises.

After dropping off Calhoun, Custer continued north-west along a razor-backed ridge to a conical hill, where he positioned his headquarters. Ahead of him lay E and F Companies, while C and I Companies were on the northern side of the ridgeline in dead ground to the village to the south. Custer continued to follow an essentially cavalry concept of operations – he remained mobile. Some historians have paid attention to Emory Upton's *Cavalry Tactics* published in 1874 as influencing the tactics of this battle. Upton was one of Custer's West Point classmates, but the treatise was already ten years out of date when it was released, and based on infantry tactics. Civil War cavalry had already evolved to dismounted infantry tactics, and Custer's commanders applied their Civil War experience. Field training was rarely conducted at western outposts in any case; basic military routine and fatigues, apart from parades, fully taxed the reduced manpower. Two years would not be sufficient for Upton's *Tactics* to be seriously considered in the West where conceptual teaching would take a poor second place to the practical exigencies and shortages of the moment.

Having achieved a junction of forces, Custer proceeded to subdivide his command for the last time. E and F Companies were dispatched south towards the river and village, where they came under pressure from the Indian advance and began to deploy in a form of salient about 300 to 400 yards from Custer's headquarters' conical hill position. I and C Companies were still drawn up in column between Custer and Calhoun's L Company. Custer's five companies were spread in a 'V' formation, one prong stretching 1,300 yards to the north-west and another 400 to 500 yards radiating south-west from the conical hill. Indian probes were becoming increasingly aggressive from all directions. Forays were being mounted from a war-band led by Crazy Horse from the north side of Custer's column, having ridden up a deep re-entrant (the present-day Cemetery Gully) that meandered in a northerly direction from the western extremity of the Indian village.

Calhoun Hill represented a further tactical opportunity overlooked by Custer. When he first observed the terrain over which he would fight from Weir Point it appeared featureless, due to the sun's angle, and probably suited for mobile cavalry operations. Now his command was increasingly threatened, Custer sought ground offering tactical advantage. The 'V' formation he adopted suggests that he was drawn forward seeking ground for offence, not defence. Calhoun Hill could have provided a satisfactory regimental defensive position, because of its palisade-shaped raised slopes to the south and east. Closing up his regiment in defence instead of being drawn north-westward in cavalry column formation might conceivably have resulted in a more lasting opposition, at least until a junction with Reno and Benteen was achieved. There was sufficient flat ground astride the plateau at the top to establish a perimeter with about 150 men. The conical hill that Custer's headquarters had occupied and the razor-backed ridge connecting it to Calhoun Hill offered no such advantages. The ridgeline was not even wide enough to drive a wagon along. A regimental bastion established atop Calhoun's position, despite no water and 100 rounds per man, would have posed a serious check to the Indian advance; Indians were reluctant to assault prepared positions. Even with his reduced force, Calhoun was to deflect the Indian approach and inflict more casualties on it than any other army position on the battlefield. The Oglala Red Hawk claimed that 'at this place the soldiers stood in line and made a very good fight'.[18]

Calhoun's defensive semi-circle was soon hotly engaged, its outline discernible from grey-blue powder smoke and flashes spitting out from the skirmish lines. Indians began to move on foot, utilising the ridgelines and folds in the ground, blanketed by the long grass, to close in on the troopers. 'The warriors all dismounted before they began to fight,' said Cheyenne warrior Wooden Leg, 'leaving their ponies in gullies, safe against the firing.' They sought a more advantageous range for their repeating rifles, analogous to the range and rate of fire of bows, arrows and revolvers. They infiltrated forward in waves, sending out flankers to surround the position. 'Fighting at long range continued for about an hour and half,' continued Wooden Leg, 'during which time the warriors crept steadily closer to the soldiers, who could not see them though they could see the soldiers all the time.'[19]

Archaeological research has identified the broad parameters of this advance. Calhoun's men had unwittingly deployed in the midst of an Indian crossfire of about 76 identified weapons. About 100 yards south-east of Calhoun Hill is a small ridgeline where at least 23 Henry and six Winchester repeating rifle signatures have been located, according to cartridge case evidence. Three revolvers and seven .50/70-calibre guns were also fired from here. This position was labelled 'Henryville' by the archaeological team due to the density of these repeater rifle positions. Additional heavy Indian fire was directed from south and west of Calhoun's position from the lower levels of the Greasy Grass Ridge. This included 22 .44 lever-action weapons, 13 .50/70-calibre guns, two Spencers, a further .50, and a Winchester repeater – these are minimum numbers. If one postulates the statistical model portrayed across the battlefield, that finds represent 30 to 35% of the total, by any measurement Calhoun's company was subjected to a devastating crossfire: 46 single-shot long-range army rifles were up against 60 or so shorter-range repeating weapons and more than 100 Indian firearms altogether.

The cacophony of sound reverberating from this intense Indian rifle fire sounded the death knell for Custer's chosen concept of operations to fight this battle. It was a tactical and technological surprise from which he would not recover. His companies were committed to a 1,300-yard-long elongated 'V' deployment on ground not of his own choosing. The terrain was criss-crossed by gullies and re-entrants that offered limited fields of fire, breaking up the coherence of disciplined army formations. But it was well suited for Indian infiltration-approach tactics. Most of Custer's overstretched companies were in various stages of mount and dismount, and from this moment on he surrendered the initiative. No longer could he direct regimental actions. His cavalry column was surrounded on the line of march. Company commanders were on their own.

Kill Eagle, a Sioux warrior, described the firing as 'terrific' at this point, and, according to his translator, he 'illustrated its force by clapping his hands together with great rapidity and regularity'. Cheyenne chief Two Moons said that 'the shooting was quick, quick. Pop-pop-pop, very fast'.[20] The Indians below Calhoun Hill at 'Henryville' were looking up at a tufted crest line. It was a convex slope framed by long wispy grass and mottled sagebrush bushes. Cavalry troopers were starkly exposed targets as they raised themselves up to shoot down. Commanders were primary aiming points, not to break up army cohesion but because there was more honour in killing chiefs. Using folds in the ground, the Indians crept closer to the soldiers. Arrows, which could be fired safely from cover in steep trajectories, rained down on the heads of the troopers. The aim was to separate the soldiers from their horses. 'We tried to kill the holders,' said Hunkpapa chief Gall, 'and then by waving blankets and shouting we scared the horses down the coulee'[21] where Cheyenne women caught them.

A group of 15 to 20 riders from C Company came galloping down to reinforce Calhoun's right flank in the Greasy Grass Ridge area. It is not clear who sent them, perhaps Custer or their commander, his brother Tom. Custer's predicament was becoming dire. He may by this time have experienced a post-adrenalin low point, impacting on his leadership resolve. So many reverses had happened that the possibility of defeat, and at the least disgrace, was dawning. More characteristically, Custer would have aggressively resolved to fight on and break out. Perhaps he was already wounded. Whatever his circumstances, he was no longer in control of events. Calhoun's headquarters was about 900 yards from the conical hill, and he could just discern Custer's headquarters through the smoke of battle. Captain Keogh's company, sheltering in the dead ground behind the razor-backed ridgeline, could see Custer's headquarters but not Calhoun's, forward on the crest of the hill he was holding. E and F Companies to the south could probably only see Custer's hill, about 300 yards away. The companies were not mutually support-ing, and few of them could even see each other. They strained their eyes to discern company pennants amid dust clouds punctuated here and there by explosions of powder smoke. Individuals could not be identified, only resistance clusters.

Custer's soldiers fought alongside the ghosts of Fetterman and Royall on the same type of exposed ridgelines where catastrophe had previously resulted. Indians preferred to trap and expose their prey on such narrow high ground, which served to break up the sym-metry of defence, having isolated smaller units from the main body. Once again, it was the tactics of the buffalo hunt. As on Fetterman

Ridge, and Royall's position at the Rosebud, the cavalry were silhouetted and had to expose themselves to engage the Indians below. Firing upwards meant that the Indians were safe from their own surrounding or flanking crossfire. Picking off isolated companies one by one maximised Indian numerical superiority at a given point. Odds at individual locations could be as high as 30 to 1, combined with greater firepower. With some 1,500 warriors in the battle, Indian odds were limited only by their ability to pack more braves into the gullies and covered approaches leading to the soldiers isolated on the ridgelines.

Calhoun was completely engrossed in his desperate rearguard action, having already deflected numerous incursions. Reinforcements from C Company extended his frontage to more than 400 yards, but had only a transitory impact. C Company was weakened from stragglers falling out from the line of march and numbered barely two platoons. Included among them was a fearful and apprehensive Private Nathan Short. The 41-year-old Minneconjou chief Red Horse observed:

'One band of soldiers was in the rear of the Sioux. When this band of soldiers charged, the Sioux fell back, and the Sioux and the soldiers stood facing each other. Then all the Sioux became brave and charged the soldiers.'

The fighting was hotly contested. 'The soldiers were shooting a lot, so the Indians were thrown back,' said Eagle Elk, an Oglala warrior. A company pennant was snatched from a soldier, but 'the Cheyenne was shot through the heels and his horse stumbled and broke his legs'. Calhoun's brother-in-law, Lieutenant Myles Moylan, examining the scene after the engagement, claimed that he saw signs of cohesive defence. 'Lieutenant Calhoun's company were killed in regular position of skirmishers,' he stated. Firing was intense. 'I counted 28 cartridge shells around one man,' he said, 'and between intervals there were shells scattered.' Moylan and Second Lieutenant Wallace, serving with G Company, observed shell case mounds varying from 25 to 30 and 40 rounds. The noise from weapon reports was deafening, while battlefield haze began to swallow up the lines of resistance. 'Bullets were just raining,' said Minneconjou Standing Bear. Concerted long-range fire lashed around the Indian advance. Some elements were beaten back, but the bulk of the force approached nearer. 'At that moment I saw a horse shot through the head near the ear,' said Eagle Elk. 'He did not drop, but went around and around.'

The Hunkpapa Gall, burning with resentment at the massacre of his family, conceded that Calhoun put up a fierce fight. Eleven Indians allegedly fell on the southern slope of the hill. Cheyenne warrior Wooden Leg crept and dashed forward in short bursts alongside hundreds of others, reaching out for the soldiers on the crest of Calhoun Hill. Wounded warriors groped their way down past him.

'I saw one Sioux walking slowly toward the gulch, going away from where were the soldiers. He wobbled dizzily as he moved along. He fell down, got up, fell down again, got up again. As he passed near to where I was, I saw that his whole lower jaw was shot away. The sight of him made me sick. I had to vomit.'

Eagle Elk passed a similarly bizarre casualty. A warrior lay prostrate on the ground. 'He wore a bird on his head, and the bullet went through the bird and his head.'[22]

Calhoun's reinforced company resolutely stood its ground. 'I never before nor since saw men so brave and fearless as those white warriors,' commented Sioux warrior Low Dog. They were brave but inexperienced. 'They did very poor shooting,' observed Low Dog. 'They held their horse reins on one arm while they were shooting, but their horses were so frightened that they pulled the men all around, and a great many of their shots went up in the air and did us no harm.' Target acquisition by the troopers was difficult and rudimentary. Engaging bobbing and fleeting Indians dodging and rushing from cover to cover was beyond their experience and training. Fieldcraft was not an army forte: Civil War practice required them to stand their ground and direct area volley fire and accept casualties. Disdaining cover, they were inexorably picked off by the murderous crossfire that enveloped them. Repeater rifles flailing the line close in had more impact than single aimed shots in response. A recently conducted battlefield firearms test suggests that 13 repeater rounds can be deliberately fired in 30 seconds compared to four cavalry Springfield rounds. A repeater magazine can be loaded in seconds. Sitting Bull referred to the disparity in rates of fire. 'They could not fire fast enough,' he claimed of the army in an interview. 'But from our side it was so,' he said, and demonstrated. 'He clapped his hands rapidly twice a second,' described his interpreter, to express the repeating Henry and Winchester rates of fire. 'They could not stand up under such a fire,' he concluded.[23]

Standing in this hapless line to the right of L Company on Calhoun Hill was Private Nathan Short. His personal experience encapsulated those all about him. Like his fellow troopers in a C Company weakened by losses from blown horses, he was tired. The sights and sounds of this battlefield with its deafening noise, unpleasant smells and the gritty taste of powder and dust in his mouth would have disorientated him. Short had been force-marched for three days before the battle had even begun. There had been scant sleep and food over the previous 33 hours, hardly any water – and much of that spoiled – and few oats for the animals. Sixty miles had been covered the previous day and he had just ridden a further seven at operational tempo. This had involved extended trots and gallops interspersed with wild dashes involving charges or rapid escapes. The long-anticipated assault on the village had deteriorated into a number of feints, sallies and volley-firing from horseback on Nye-Cartwright Ridge. At no stage had a serious regimental attack against the village occurred. E and F Companies had been sent off and now they were back. L Company had then halted and dismounted, presumably as rearguard, but Short had little idea what was going on. Not relishing L Company's apparent fate, C Company was then suddenly ordered to 'pitch in' alongside them. His heart probably sank as he rode toward the lower southern slope of Calhoun Hill. Conversely he may have felt like Private Peter Thompson, a straggler from his own company, who declared that 'we were becoming so tired that the presence of the Indians was no longer a terror to us'. 'When they rode up', said Sitting Bull,

> '… their horses were tired and they were tired. When they got off from their horses they could not stand firmly on their feet. They swayed to and fro – so my young men have told me – like the limbs of cypresses in a great wind. Some of them staggered under the weight of their guns. But they began to fight at once.'[24]

On arrival the 15 or so troopers were strung out in a rudimentary skirmish line that soon became ragged under the impact of an increasingly lethal crossfire. Short was scared. There were few officers and NCOs to stabilise the line. Thoughts were mixed. Some looked anxiously to the rear, realising that they were to be sacrificed. Others, no longer fearful of the present, resolved to hold their ground, accepting that they may well die and purposefully returning fire at the fleeting targets to their front. Standing defiantly in the open with no attempt to take cover, they began to fall.

Considerable recoil and muzzle blast emanated from the 1873 Springfield carbine with its 55 grains of powder per cartridge. Short's shoulder became progressively sore, possibly influencing his aim as he engaged targets to his front at the rapid rate of 12 to 13 rounds per minute. Each round that spat out from the skirmish line spurted grey-blue powder smoke, obscuring its outline.

Occasionally there would be an extraction failure. 1873 Springfield .45 carbine cases were made of copper, which, unlike later brass shells, did not contract as cooling began. Should a soldier permit his cartridges to become dirty through exposure to dirt and dust, there might be an extraction failure on lifting the breech cover. This could only be cleared by prising out the expended case with a thumbnail or knife. This happened to Private Thompson during the battle. When opening his breech lock while under pressure 'to throw the shell out', he found that 'it was stuck fast'. An inexperienced trooper could be reduced to panic in these circumstances. 'I worked at it in a desperate manner,' said Thompson, 'and finally got it out far enough to use my thumbnail, which proved effective.' One Little Bighorn myth, suggesting that too many extraction failures contributed to the disaster, has been effectively answered to the contrary by archaeological findings. Only 2% of the total number of recovered specimens exhibit signs of extraction difficulties. Sixty-nine guns on the Custer battlefield show a 4.3% failure rate, as also 5.6% of 62 different guns later used on Reno Hill. Indian repeater rifles show 8% to 9% ejection failures and other stoppages, often caused by firing the wrong calibre round for the chamber. An overall 5% army failure rate according to statistical surveys of 131 guns – or 22% of those used – indicates that about 30 carbines might have been affected during the battle. Both sides experienced such failures, with the Indians not unexpectedly faring marginally worse. This did not have a significant impact upon the outcome of the battle.[25] Nathan Short was in no doubt what the problem was. His ragged skirmish line was being overwhelmed by sheer weight of numbers and firepower, and army shooting was not too accurate.

As the braves closed in, firing became even more intense. Arrows and 19th-century soft lead bullets caused fearful wounds. Short, who had been in the army for less than a year, would have been shocked and sobered by the sights around him. Victims would sag to the ground in agony on being struck by an arrow, or flung out of the line by the impact of a soft lead bullet. Most arrowheads were cut from sheet or strap iron. They invariably bent over on striking bone and became 'pinched' in place – extraction was physically difficult and painful. Loosely bound heads tended to break off in the wound, further complicating withdrawal. Deep penetrating trunk wounds were commonly fatal. A draw-pull weight of 80lb released at 60 to 80 yards from the target might cause the shaft to go completely through the body. Arrows could be fired off in close combat as rapidly as six-chamber revolver fire. To be struck by an arrow or incapacitated in any way during this battle meant death to the troopers once the Indians closed in. An archaeological sample of 34 troopers on the battlefield reveals that knives, arrows and hatchets were used on 21% to finish them off, while blunt force trauma from clubbing accounted for 41%.

Most of Short's comrades were initially struck by long-range gunfire. Impacts were traumatic and horrible to witness. As the missile strikes, a small entry wound is produced, which blasts out tissue in a conical shape. The accompanying shock wave carves a considerably larger exit wound. Lead 'splatter' occurs when bone is struck, or the soft lead may embed itself in the bone shaft. Bone and other damage produced a mangled appearance of flesh and tissue. In essence, a miniature explosion might occur on the body part hit. The vast majority of bullets buzzed by like swarms of angry bees. Others might whine through the long grass or tumble by as a ricochet after a violent dust splash on the ground. William Morris in M Company described the fate of a comrade shot in the abdomen during the valley-bottom fight. 'I dismounted to help him mount behind me,' he said, 'but he was in such agony that he shrieked, "Leave me alone, for God's sake".' He would not stand. All Morris could do was drag him to a tree and prop him up against the trunk.[26]

Calhoun's position collapsed in a welter of braves. Custer lost his brother-in-law, just behind the crest of the hill, the first member of his family to die. Lieutenant Crittenden, vulnerable in the final hand-to-hand melee with only one eye, fell nearby with his men. His body bristled with arrows, one protruding from the socket that had housed his glass eye. His father, who had petitioned Custer at the last moment to take him, thus realised his worst fear, and would never now be able to look his mother in the eye.

So near yet so far

On this same day General Sheridan, the supreme commander, sitting at his Chicago headquarters, was viewing the battle from an entirely different and distant perspective. Dispatches had informed him that his three field columns would shortly converge. Having launched the campaign, he could offer no further assistance. He abrogated his responsibility as overall commander at the operational level to coordinate and synergise the combat power of his three columns. There was little need in his view to formulate anything so grandiose as a campaign plan to round up bands of 'savages'. He was focused in any case on the forthcoming Centennial celebration. The Exposition Fair had already opened on 10 May, seven days prior to Custer's departure from Fort Abraham Lincoln. President Grant accompanied by the Emperor of Brazil had ceremoniously pulled the switch on the gigantic Corliss engine that powered the machinery of the exposition. Nearly 500 acres of mechanical exhibits were displayed, varying from a mowing machine to a typewriter, even a 'roll your own' cigarette device. Alexander Bell's improved telephone was also on display. The Pacific Railroad was revelling in a much-publicised crossing of the continent by the 'Lightning Express' from New York City via Chicago, Omaha and Reno. It took only 84 hours, 12 hours less than scheduled. The outcome of a campaign against a few tribes of Plains Indians would be more predictable.

Philadelphia was gripped by the elation of a World Fair that was to be unrivalled for years to come. There was avid public interest in westward expansion. All eyes were on the Pacific Railroad's replica *Hunter's Camp* in the Colorado Rockies; *Scouts of the Prairie* featuring 'Buffalo Bill' Cody had been a smash hit in April. Whites were fascinated and appalled by blood-curdling tales of Indian barbarity – fiction or fact. Mark Twain's best-selling classic *Tom Sawyer* featured a mixed-blood Indian as its primary villain. There was a morbid fear of and interest in any artefacts connected with the West. A Sharpes breech-loading rifle or Winchester magazine-loading '73' repeater could be purchased for as little as $10 in eastern cities, while Colt's six-shot revolvers sold at $5 and lesser brands for $3.50.[27]

President Grant, facing November elections, had few clear-cut issues to campaign for, other than countering widespread dissatisfaction with his administration. A hostile Democratic House of Representatives, angered by Grant's seemingly humane policy toward the Indians, among other things, was energetically directing ire against the possibility of a Republican third term in office. Grant continued to reel from the implications of the 'Belknap's Anaconda' article published in *The Herald* on 31 March, which implicated his brother Orville in War Department scandals. Custer had suffered from the Presidential fall-out of public gaze directed at the illicit sale of army supplies destined for military outposts and Indian reservations; it had even resulted in his temporary arrest on orders from Grant.

Sheridan's mind was more on the impact of an announcement of the campaign's impending success and the timing of its delivery rather than on coordinating its execution from his Chicago headquarters. After 100 years the Union was intact and he and many of his top political and military contemporaries had been instrumental in preserving it during its sternest test, the Civil War. He had just launched the largest US Army Field Force ever seen on the frontier. An announcement of the settling of the Plains Indian problem would provide political icing on a declaration rich in the symbolism of continental westward expansion, an aspiration the Centennial seemed to exemplify. Sheridan looked forward to its climax at Washington in the confident assumption that his three highly experienced and Civil War-distinguished column commanders would deliver success. Each column was judged sufficiently strong to do the job itself, requiring little further coordination from him. It was only a matter of time. Victory would arouse sentimental and patriotic emotion. Anyone associated with it could anticipate credit and advancement.

* * *

Smoke from the conflagration still licking around the inert forms of Reno's dead in and around the 'timber' rose despondently into the sky. It was spotted by the leading scouts of Terry's column struggling valiantly through harsh terrain to reach him. 'I learned that some of the Crows who had gone up Tullock's Fork in the morning,' reported Lieutenant James Bradley, 'had discovered a smoke in the direction of the Little Bighorn.' This was significant, and 'was thought to indicate the presence of the Sioux village'. They needed to close quickly.

'The cavalry and Gatling battery, accompanied by General Terry,' Bradley noted in his log, 'were pushing on with a view of getting as near it as possible tonight.' Terry's column was lost and struggling. The infantry had already marched 23 miles. Terry was paying the price for detaching most of the scouts to Custer. 'The men had emptied their canteens of the wretched alkali water they started with,' Bradley said, 'and were parched with thirst as well as greatly fatigued with clambering over such ground.' They were making haphazard progress and already behind the synchronised timelines agreed with Custer on the *Far West*. At this rate there would be no joint effort at the kill. Observing the lazily rising smoke emphasised their inadequate progress. 'A worse route could not have been chosen,' admitted Bradley, 'but destitute of a guide as we are, it is not to be wondered that we entangled ourselves in such a mesh of physical obstacles.' The 25th of June was developing into a thoroughly unsatisfactory day. It began to dawn on Terry that he was falling behind schedule. 'Every now and then a long halt was required,' declared a clearly exasperated Bradley, 'as an avenue of escape was sought from some topographical net in which we had become involved.' Successive showers of rain fell after darkness, at first refreshing but reducing visibility as the column continued to push grimly on up the Bighorn River. Exhaustion dissipated their sense of urgency. 'About midnight we halted,' noted Bradley, 'unsaddled, and threw our weary forms down on the ground for a little rest, the cavalry having marched about 35 miles and my detachment, in consequence of its diversions from the main column, about 55.'[28] Without realising it, Terry's column was two days' march from the area of operations.

While Terry sought to negotiate difficult terrain to gain entry into the area of operations, General Crook's column continued to sit at its edge. During Custer's approach march to the Little Bighorn on 22 June, correspondent John F. Finerty reported that 'hunting and fishing are the main recreation'. Despite being a similar distance away to the south of the Indian village – perhaps two to three days' march – he was in no way poised to contribute further to the campaign. Crook's force languished on the banks of Goose Creek (present-day Sheridan). 'We revelled in the crystal water,' said Finerty, 'and slept beneath the grateful shade of the trees that fringed the emerald banks of those beautiful tributaries of Tongue River.' Crook had the strongest command in the field, but was biding time awaiting reinforcements. 'My notebooks about this time seem to be almost the chronicle of a sporting club,' declared Lieutenant John Bourke, General Crook's aide-de-camp, 'so filled are they with the numbers of trout brought by different fishermen.' Fish were biting voraciously under the influence of the warm weather in the creek. 'The first afternoon 95 were caught and brought into camp,' declared Bourke. All thoughts of the campaign were banished. 'I do not pretend to have preserved accurate figures, much being left unrecorded,' said Bourke. Sport fishing became the primary occupation, with Captain Mills of the 3rd Cavalry establishing 'a record of over 100 caught by himself and two soldiers in one short afternoon'. On the opening day of the Battle of the Little Bighorn Finerty could remark on 'the monotony of camp'. Even sport fishing became tiresome. 'Officers who normally were of good disposition became irritable and exercised their authority.' Unwelcomed by the soldiers, it resulted in 'friction and occasional sulking'.[29]

During the afternoon Captain Anson Mills, with the 3rd Cavalry, riding a reconnaissance in the foothills near the camp, 'reported a dense smoke toward the north-east at great distance'. This was the fiery aftermath of Reno's retreat from the 'timber'. Anson 'called the attention of several to it, and all agreed that it must be a prairie fire or something of the kind'. Crook's scout Frank Grouard observed similar signatures, and pondered the likely sinister implication. They were 'Indian signals down on the divide between the Rosebud and Little Bighorn'. Passing on the information to officers in Crook's camp, he deduced that 'these signals were to the effect that the Indians and troops were fighting and the Indians had the best of it'. Crook did not react. According to the diary of Oliver Penny Hanna, writing on 25 June, he 'was up on the mountain fishing with General Crook'. One of the columns was in contact with the Indians, but this elicited no reaction. Crook neither changed his alert status nor even sent scouts to investigate. He would have realised that whatever unit was engaged, it would be under pressure, having experienced the same himself. The General was in a defensive frame of mind, awaiting reinforcements. If Terry scored a victory, he would be seriously embarrassed. 'Monotony of camp despite the beautiful surroundings becomes more intolerable,' wrote Finerty two days later. Lieutenant John Bourke continued to log the results of the fishing competition. 'Mills and party has another fishing record with over 146,' he laconically reported on 28 June.[30] Custer could expect no assistance from this, the strongest army unit in the field.

The only other sub-unit of any military consequence to the 7th Cavalry that day was the paddle-steamer *Far West*. She was tied up 30 miles north on the Bighorn River. It was a fortified bastion of no consequence apart from its communications and logistic support function. Captain Grant Marsh's pilothouse was lined with thick curved iron boilerplate and its lower deck was protected by grain sacks supplemented by 4 feet of cordwood stacked on the end and around the gunwales. Lieutenant James E. Wilson of the Army Corps of Engineers continued a daily routine of checking and recording temperature ranges on the Yellowstone and Bighorn rivers. It was hot. Beneath a thin layer of cloud he recorded a variation that day of a 63-degree low to a high of 91 degrees.[31] On the high dry ridges of the Little Bighorn the temperatures were considerably greater. The heat together with the proximity of supporting forces was not propitious. Only one force was in a position to assist Custer by the late afternoon of 25 June.

Benteen had arrived at Reno's position at 1620 hours with 115 men from three companies (D, H and K). Reno's demoralised companies (A, G and M) totalled a similar number, but had lost 40% of their original strength. By about 1730 hours the packs arrived with B Company numbering a further 136 men, swelling the 7th Cavalry force to about 366 soldiers. This represented 40.7% of the regiment's uncommitted strength and more than 59% of the whole, including Reno's battered men. At no stage in the battle thus far had more than three companies (averaging between 19% and 23% of the regiment) been committed in a combination against the village. At 1730 hours, therefore, 59% of the regiment was about an hour's ride from Custer, as Calhoun's hill position was in the throes of final collapse. Yet no 'shock action' was instituted to relieve Custer's remaining four companies. Another foray into the village by a force this size might have been sufficient to alleviate the pressure on Custer, as he himself had done for Reno earlier. But this force was displaying no visible signs of aggression. It had been intimidated by what it had witnessed in the valley bottom. Indeed, the Indian response to its approach was almost derisory. It would be next.

Lieutenant Winfield Scott Edgerly set off after his company commander, Captain Thomas Weir, at 1645 hours, with a 47-strong D Company. They halted at Weir Point 15 minutes later and observed the dying moments of Custer's battalion in the distance. They were there for two hours. Later Edgerly remarked:

'I also most firmly and positively believe that we should have gone "to the sound of firing" after Reno and Benteen united, and further I believe that if we had tried to join Custer at that time we would have shared his fate.'[32]

Weir was equally desperate to 'pitch in' and help Custer, but subsequently had to admit to Reno that 'there were enough Indians there to eat up his company a hundred times over'.

Custer would have to fight his battle alone.

Chapter 11
Red Sabbath

'It was a rout, a panic,
till the last man was killed.'

Captain Benteen, Reno Court of Inquiry

'There were bodies lying around so far as we could see in every direction in irregular positions.'

Question: 'Did they give evidence of company organisations?'

Answer: 'No sir…'

Question: 'State what to your mind were the evidences of the struggle, whether that of a desperate struggle or of a panic or a rout without much resistance?'

Answer: 'Knowing the men as I did I have no doubt they fought desperately for a few minutes.'

Question: 'Did you notice the knolls over the field, whether they were rallying points for officers and men?'

Answer: 'I did not go all over the field. There were evidences of rallying points about General Custer, and about Captain Keogh and Lieutenant Calhoun were evidences of fighting, but not of being rallying points.'

Lieutenant Edgerly, D Company, at the
Reno Court of Inquiry, Chicago 1879

Weir Point, 1700–1745 hours

This was the worst day of Reno's life. His battalion had lost 60 officers, men and scouts, wounded or missing. This included the majority of the Arikara scouts, many of whom melted away during the initial attack on the village. Reno was exhibiting symptoms of post-combat stress disorder. On the one hand he sensibly dispatched Lieutenant Hare to ride back to Captain McDougall and cut out two ammunition mules carrying 4,000 rounds of ammunition for re-supply. Hare rode off at 1620 hours and was back in 30 minutes.[1] Meanwhile, Reno bizarrely turned his attention away from defence to recovering 'Bennie' Hodgeson's body. Lieutenant Varnum recalled how he had 'been down to the river and got some little trinkets from Hodgeson's body'.[2] His adjutant was a 'great favourite and friend', he later testified at the 1879 Court of Inquiry. Benteen reluctantly humoured his senior, temporarily assuming command – humanely recognising the mental anguish his failed brother officer was going through.

Lieutenant Weir, a Custer favourite, was increasingly exasperated at the prevailing inaction. Volley fire in the distance indicated that Custer's command was hard pressed. 'We heard two distinct volleys which excited some surprise,' recalled Lieutenant Godfrey with K Company. There was some guilty disquiet. The prevailing conviction was that 'our command ought to be doing something,' Godfrey commented, 'or Custer would be after Reno with a sharp stick'. Whatever was happening, 'Custer was giving it to them for all he is worth'.[3]

The 300-plus force that gathered on Reno Hill moved forward haphazardly to Weir Point. First to arrive at 1700 was Lieutenant Weir, who galloped off on his own accord to observe. He was followed by his second-in-command, Lieutenant Edgerly, who brought up the 47-strong company, but on nobody's order. Benteen did not advance until 30 minutes later, with H, K and M Companies – a further 116 men. By 1745 hours there were four companies in the vicinity of Weir Point, numbering about 163 men. Three of the companies had not yet tasted combat, while the fourth, M Company, had survived the battle in the valley bottom and was weakened, apprehensive and shaken. In no way did this forward move constitute a determined or aggressive cavalry advance. Only half the available force had edged forward.

Captain Thomas Weir stared northwards for some time at the distant ridge that included Calhoun Hill. There were horsemen riding and occasionally the momentary glimpse of a guidon. D Company were dismounted as skirmishers to his right, beneath the promontory that would bear his name. 'That is Custer over there,' he announced to James Flanagan, one of his sergeants. Flanagan passed his binoculars across. 'Here, Captain, you had better take a look through the glasses – I think those are Indians.' There were hundreds, congealing across the whole ridgeline.

What could actually be seen was debated interminably after the event. Binoculars offered little more than three times magnification. It was difficult to identify meaningful activity from so far away. Lieutenant Godfrey later pointed out:

'Persons who have been on the plains and have seen stationary objects dancing before them, now in view and now observed, or a weed on top of a hill, projected against the sky, magnified to appear as a tree, will readily understand why our views would be unsatisfactory.'

It was not clear what was happening to Custer. 'The air was full of dust,' said Godfrey. There were groups of moving and stationary horsemen. 'From their grouping and the manner in which they sat on their horses we knew they were Indians.' As the sun settled lower in the sky they discerned more ridgelines, but the conical hill, later to become Last Stand Hill, was not visible. Weir's men claimed that they could hear firing at 3½ miles' distance, but this has not been verified by modern-day acoustic tests. They were so far away that some soldiers remarked on the reddish-brown burn marks that had apparently scorched the left side of the valley. Only by 'watching this intently for a short time with field glasses,' said Godfrey, investigating its 'changeable' appearance, was it 'discovered that this strange sight was the immense Indian pony-herds'.

Looking toward the Custer field, 'we saw a large assemblage' on a hill 2 miles away. All that was derived from their observations was general impressions. 'We heard occasional shots, most of which seemed to be a great distance off, beyond the large groups on the hill.' This may conceivably have been the Indian assault spilling over Calhoun Hill. 'While watching this group, the conclusion was arrived at that Custer had been repulsed, and the firing we heard was the parting shots of the rearguard.'[4] Private Edward Pigford in M Company claimed that he saw Indians firing from a big circle, which gradually converged into a large black mass on the side of the hill near the river and all along the ridge.[5]

Benteen did not take command of the four companies gathering in the area of Weir Point. Impressions derived from 45 minutes of observation were indistinct, but disturbing. Nobody knew what was going on. There was a mass of Indians to the north and Custer had to be there. Benteen began to realise that things might be going wrong. Despite Custer's attack, the village remained intact. The tepees were up and no Indians were fleeing. Benteen was not thinking offensively, and he was not happy at the present deployment. Reno had rescinded his 'come quick, bring packs' order by directing him to pause with his command. This absolved him of the need to institute the 'do or die' shock action that might be the only solution to Custer's probable dilemma. He was heard to remark that 'this is a hell of a place to fight Indians'. Given ideal circumstances with aggressive and determined leadership, a force of nearly 370 cavalry could conceivably have fallen upon the rear of the Indian advance, or sallied against the village again, launching at 1730 hours.

The Minneconjou Lakota Red Horse acknowledged the threat. 'While this last fight [with Custer] was going on,' he said, 'we expected all the time to be attacked in the rear by the troops we had just left.' Reno, however, dallied with the packs and did not move forward with the remaining 50% of the force until after 1800 hours. Red Horse heard an order given: 'Sioux men, go watch the soldiers on the hill and prevent their joining the different soldiers [ie Reno and Benteen].' With that, groups of warriors began to break contact with the Custer fight and started to move toward Weir Point.

Benteen had made his appreciation even before Reno's contingent arrived. 'I am going back to Reno to propose that we go back to where we lay before starting out here,' he said. Custer's fate was therefore virtually sealed at 1745 hours. There was no other help.[6]

Calhoun's position, 1745 hours

'We formed skirmish lines when we came close to where the battlefield was, so as to find all the bodies that might have been killed. We came across a few bodies about 3½ miles from [Reno Hill]. Each company had orders to bury the dead as they found them and as we came up the first hill … they were all thick.'

Lieutenant Edgerly, D Company, Reno Court of Inquiry

The maximum number of cartridges found near one of the trooper's bodies on Calhoun Hill was 40. It would take 5 to 6 minutes to fire such a quantity at the rapid rate. So desperate and confused was the final fighting that some Indians shot and killed their own people, mistaking them for Rees or Crow Indian scouts. Left Hand, an Arapaho warrior, admitted to one such mistake. In all the shooting and yelling, 'everyone was excited,' he said. As he rode over the position he spotted a wounded Indian on foot. 'I rode at him, striking him in the chest with a long lance which went clear through him.' He collapsed on to a pile of dead soldiers. 'Afterwards I learned he was Sioux.'[7] The battle for Calhoun Hill was not a long one. Standing in the open and subjected to a devastating crossfire from 'Henryville' in the south-east and from the Greasy Grass ridgeline to the south-west, 76 identified weapons made short work of army resistance. More than 200 weapons may have been employed with odds at 20 or 30 to 1.

Marker 128 on the present-day Little Bighorn battlefield is situated just behind the Greasy Grass ridge and about 480 yards from Calhoun's headquarters. Unlike most of the fragmentary skeletal remains excavated following the 1983 prairie fire, that of 'Trooper Mike' was an almost complete skeleton. 'He was between 19 and 22 years old and a healthy specimen,' according to forensic anthropologist Dr Clyde Collins Snow. There was a defect in his fifth lumbar vertebra that would have caused him back pain. 'I'll bet his back was sore that day,' Snow diagnosed, because 'those boys had been riding hard'. Mike, weighing 150 to 160lb and at 5ft 8in tall, was physically average for a 7th Cavalry trooper. He probably falsified his age to join the army. 'I suspect,' conjectured Snow, 'that quite a number of 7th cavalrymen were in their teens.' They were doubtless unworldly and 'green'. Their struggle on the slopes of Calhoun Hill was the most harrowing experience of their lives. Mike had been shot twice in the chest, from two directions – one round entered from the right and another from the left. A bullet fragment was still embedded in his lower left arm. This crossfire either hit the youth three times or the third strike was an exit wound. Whatever, these wounds put him out of the battle. 'My guess,' the anthropologist ventured, 'is that maybe 10% of the men were killed instantly' on the battlefield. This was the likely situation on and around the L and C Company positions on Calhoun Hill. 'The rest lay there wounded but alive. Like Mike.'

> 'If you were to choose an "unknown soldier" of the 7th, he would fit the mould. Here's this young kid, this trooper with a sore back and now lying there with those terrible wounds. What was going through his mind? He could hear the Indians yelling. He knew they were coming. That strikes me as particularly horrible.'[8]

Amid the awful sounds and smells of battle and choking with dust, massive blunt force was applied to Mike's skull at the time of death, fracturing it and breaking off his teeth. The brave who finished him off struck him repeatedly about the head with a rifle butt, stone club or large rock. His scalp was peeled off and probably held aloft with a primeval shriek. Other braves may well have joined in as they hacked off his legs at the hip joint with a war axe or hatchet. These butchery cuts are still apparent on the right thighbone. The warriors were determined that Mike would never ride at them from the spirit world.

The collapse of Calhoun's rearguard opened the floodgates. The 'traffic jam' of Indians on foot and mounted, infiltrating up the side gullies and re-entrants, burst across Calhoun Hill and almost immediately amongst Keogh's company. These were still mounted and waiting, sheltering in the dead ground immediately to the north of the razor-backed ridge connecting Calhoun Hill to Custer's conical hill position.

Keogh received no warning from Calhoun's headquarters. It was not even visible from his position. There was no communication from Custer and now the Indian advance struck his 70-strong contingent in its full force.

Thirty-three or so bodies lay around Calhoun Hill and the ridgeline to the south-west. Only two survivors, Privates Hughes and Tweed, reached Custer's headquarters on the conical hill.[9] Of Private Nathan Short there is no trace. It is conceivable that he may have attempted to escape from the debacle at this point.[10] Scattered markers to the west of Calhoun Hill and around the Greasy Grass Ridge area offer silent testimonial to escape attempts. Some died lonely deaths. Either Private John Duggan from L Company, or possibly Private Darris from E Company, reached the north end of Medicine Tail Coulee, 2 miles from Calhoun Hill. He had ridden with a metal arrowhead embedded within one of his cervical vertebrae. Nobody knew what happened. There may have been a final fight, as numerous cartridge cases were found among the bones. Perhaps he was hidden and then abandoned by a companion, another trooper, such as Private Short, who was also to cover considerable ground. Whatever the outcome, he died alone and in considerable pain. His skeletal remains were not unearthed until 1928. The initials 'J. D.' were still legible inside his rotting boot.[11]

Keogh's Ravine, 1750 hours

Question: 'How far from Calhoun's men were these men found?'

Answer: 'Between Custer and Calhoun's men.'

Question: 'At what distance?'

Answer: 'The first was probably not more than twenty or thirty yards, and they were killed at intervals.'

Question: 'They were scattered along?'

Answer: 'Yes, sir – as they went towards Custer.'

Question: 'After you passed Captain Keogh's men where did you find the next dead men?'

Answer: 'His men occupied the most of the ground well on toward Custer.'

Lieutenant Wallace, G Company, Reno Court of Inquiry

Archaeological research has identified at least seven Indian positions according to cartridge finds and impacted army bullets found around these sites. Two positions are on Greasy Grass Ridge and two others indicate close-in fighting from Henryville Ridge. These four locations suggest that Calhoun Hill lay between their converging advance and crossfire. A further firing point is on a knoll 660 feet north-east of the conical hill where Custer had established his headquarters. Three other locations have been found on the lower south-westerly segment of the Greasy Grass Ridge, clinging on to the flanks of the upper part of Deep Ravine.[12] This mainly Sioux advance converged on Calhoun Hill from the south-west and south-east, then drove on north to Custer's conical hill position. Most of the Indians from the village had been attacking in this northerly direction. Combined Sioux and Cheyenne assaults were at the same time infiltrating up from the village, then attacking from Deep Ravine, heading for the same conical hill from the south. This movement took longer because of the distance to be covered. Crazy Horse's war-band rode up the present-day Cemetery Ravine in a wide northerly sweep, and his warriors began to fire at Custer's over-extended column from the north. The battalions were dispersed and now loosely surrounded. Virtually every gully and covered approach leading to the stricken companies was filled with Indians moving up on foot to be in at the kill. E and F Companies had come under renewed pressure from Indians emerging from the Deep Ravine complex of gullies that snaked up from the village to the south. It was at this stage that Keogh's I Company was unexpectedly exposed to a torrent of braves sweeping over Calhoun Hill. I Company was identified as the weak link in the army 'herd'. The Indians felt that it could be taken now.

'The warriors directed a special fire against the troopers who held the horses,' declared the Sioux chief Gall, 'while the others fought.' 'Keogh's company,' he said, 'were all killed in a bunch.' I Company was unprepared for the action. Foolish Elk, an Oglala, stated that 'those soldiers fortunate to be mounted, did not stop to fight, but instead galloped madly to Custer Hill'. 'As soon as a holder was killed,' continued Gall, 'by moving blankets and great shouting the horses were stampeded, which made it impossible for the soldiers to escape.' Archaeological evidence has identified numerous Indian cartridges on the north-eastern ridgeline overlooking the Keogh area between Calhoun Hill and Last Stand Hill. Indian fire was hitting Keogh's men from three directions.[13]

What happened next is conjecture. Lieutenant Godfrey's experience, retreating under pressure with K Company from Weir Point later that day, provides a parallel for what happened to I Company. Later body finds, as well as Indian descriptions, provide a sketchy outline. In Godfrey's view the 'ping-ping' of bullets flying overhead terrified his men more than the '"swish-thud" of the bullets that [more menacingly] struck the ground immediately about us'. There were never enough soldiers to hold the line and Godfrey 'had a long line and only about thirty or less men to cover it'. These he deployed in squads, each under an NCO. Keogh's I Company was critically deficient in junior leaders, reducing his flexibility to cope with the unexpected. His company was not dissimilar in size to Godfrey's, numbering 37 effectives from a strength of 67. Captain Keogh, Lieutenant James Porter, two sergeants – Varden and Bustard – and three corporals commanded 37 men. Keogh was missing an officer, three sergeants and another corporal.[14]

'According to the old tactics,' explained Godfrey, 'the retreat … was by odd and even numbers moving to the rear alternatively.' Gall described how Keogh's men 'retired step by step' and 'rallied by company'. 'At first there was a semblance of conformity to the drill,' said Godfrey, 'but it was not long till all were practically in one line.' His men at first 'would halt, kneel, and fire deliberately'. But:

> 'After a bit they would stop, fire hastily and move to the rear; and then some men did not stop or fire at all, and of course were far from the rear-most men. In other words I saw that I was losing control.'

Godfrey did his best to maintain cohesion through his officers and NCOs. 'I got them halted,' he said, 'but the tendency was to close into groups.' Body finds confirm that those who died between Keogh and Custer's headquarters came from all five companies and they fell in groups; there are 75 markers reflecting the bunching to which Godfrey alludes. Eight or nine bodies were found on the western slope of the razor-backed ridgeline connecting Calhoun Hill to Last Stand Hill. There is a large group of 18 nearer Calhoun Hill, followed by Keogh's first gravesite with five markers and two others nearby. Substantial additional bunches litter the approach to Custer's position. There are 12, followed by 16, still moving up the hill, then another group of 13. Lying among the latter was press correspondent Mark Kellogg, destined never to profit from his last scoop or see his daughters again. Little Hawk, a Northern Cheyenne warrior, recalled the annihilation of these groups as the Indians charged among them. 'The soldiers ran and went along the straight ridge [Custer Ridge] where they chased them like buffalo and as long as they had their backs toward Indians the Indians rode right in among them.'[15]

It is not difficult to deduce what happened. 'When I ordered the whole line to retire,' stated Godfrey, now under considerable Indian pressure, 'to my amazement some of the men started off like sprinters.' Buffalo hunt analogies constantly recur among Indian accounts. It was accepted frontier lore that Indians would be on the back of a fleeing foe in an instant. 'In running away from an Indian on horseback,' declared Colonel Gibbon, commanding the Yellowstone column, 'the average horseman of the service is almost as much at the mercy of his pursuer as is the buffalo.' Captain Thomas French in M Company voiced a similar opinion. 'To turn one's back on Indians is throwing life away.' Godfrey's heart understandably sank when it appeared that he might be losing control. 'My God!' he exclaimed, 'they are going to run!' Flourishing his revolver and turning the air blue with expletives, Godfrey 'threatened to kill any man who ran away and that he might as well be killed by the Indians as by me'. He regained control. 'Every man turned toward me – it was an awful moment.' They were intimidated into an orderly retreat.[16]

Not so Keogh's men. Control slipped away. 'The Indians acted just like they were driving buffalo to a good place,' said Julia Face, the wife of the Brule Lakota Thunder Hawk, 'where they could be easily slaughtered.' Keogh was a veteran mercenary soldier of fortune, but his Indian fighting experience was limited.[17] 'Left in the rear,' noticed Foolish Elk, an Oglala, 'were the men on foot, shooting their revolvers as they went along, defending themselves as best they could.' Lieutenant Edgerly, examining bodies after the battle, saw that both Keogh's sergeants, Varden and Bustard, were nearby with his trumpeter, John W. Patton, lying across his chest. Keogh's leg had been broken by the bullet wound at stirrup height found in the flank of his horse Comanche, the only living army being to survive the battle. They may have rallied around a dry buffalo wallow with the incapacitated Keogh. Evidence suggests, however, that they were fighting as they retreated. The sergeants were not spread around the men. Perhaps they had been wounded or were seeking direction from their commander. The action appears to have been a debacle. 'I don't know whether they were in skirmish line or not,' stated Lieutenant Wallace at the subsequent Reno Court of Inquiry. 'They were killed at intervals, but, from their position, I don't think they could have been in skirmish line.'[18] They were overcome in a 'line of death' charted by the present grave markers indicating their envelopment as they tried to reach the conical hill.

This was the turning point of the Battle of the Little Bighorn. Custer's main uncommitted combat strength was annihilated in one brief instant. These 75 or so slain troopers represented 35% of his strength, until now held in reserve. They were pinned down in the long re-entrant – Horse Holder's Ravine – behind Custer Ridge, overwhelmed and ridden down. This spelt the end of regimental integration. E and F Companies were out of sight on the other side of Custer Ridge and had no idea that the entire eastern wing of the force had collapsed. The fight now developed into a series of simultaneous 'last stands'.

Custer's men, viewing the catastrophe from their conical hill position, were aghast. Cheyenne chief Two Moons described the dismaying view:

'The smoke was like a great cloud, and everywhere the Sioux went the dust rose like smoke. We circled all round them – swirling like water round a stone. We shoot, we ride fast, we shoot again. Soldiers drop, and horses fall on them. Soldiers in line drop…'[19]

Wounded white soldiers were finished off in full view of their comrades on the conical hill. One of them was Private Phyllis

Wright of C Company. Marker 199, standing near Captain Keogh's, was recently found to contain a white youth aged between 15 and 19 years old. Wright had lied about his age to get into the army. It is assessed that about 15% of the cavalry dead at the Little Bighorn may have been under-age enlistments, compared to about 3% declared on the rolls. Wright's skull, it has been determined, was smashed in about the time of his death.[20]

Conical Hill and the southern salient, 1800 hours

'His [Custer's] body was found surrounded by those of several of his officers and some forty or fifty of his men. We can see from where we are numerous bodies of dead horses scattered along its south-western slope, and as we ride up towards it, we come across another body lying in a depression just as if killed whilst using his rifle there… On the slope beyond others are thickly lying in all conceivable positions.'

Colonel Gibbon's description of Custer Hill[21]

Three hours earlier, Custer had launched his attack with an intact command with every expectation of success. If the battle lasted the 20 minutes associated with the Indian yardstick of as long as it takes 'a hungry man to eat his dinner', then ten of Custer's soldiers died each minute – in short, a massacre. The statement probably referred to the final breakdown. If the end phase lasted about two hours, then Custer was still losing men at the rate of two or three each minute – also a debacle. Extensive research of Indian casualties indicates how few they were, further evidence of tactical failure. Eleven Indians appeared to have died on Calhoun Hill, perhaps three around the conical hill and another two in the area of the salient formed around E and F Companies.[22] This is 16 Indian deaths against Custer's 210 slain.

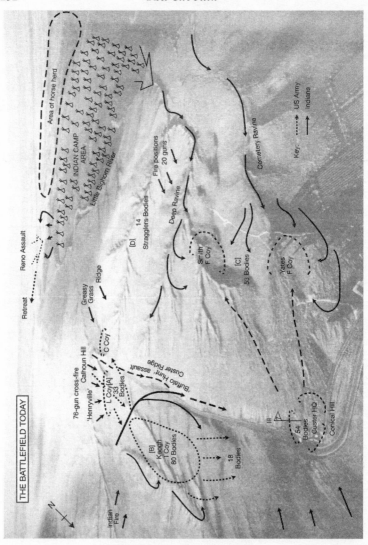

The Battlefield terrain today

Undulating terrain criss-crossed by re-entrants and ravines was unsuited for mobile cavalry operations and tended to break up company skirmish lines in defence. Dismounted companies tended to make their stands on isolated hilltop features, making them even more vulnerable to superior Indian firepower. (See Map 13 [A] to [D].)

A number of explanations have been offered in copious histories over the years to account for Custer's fall. These have included army Springfield carbine extraction failures, but are not sustained by recent archaeological finds. The theory of 'Napoleonic' squadron-like cavalry sweeps led by Crazy Horse, which outmanoeuvred Custer's command to the north,[23] confers a structured command capability on disparate Indian bands that did not exist. They thought and, in consequence, instinctively fought alike, but not in a disciplined or structured US Army way. Suicides among despairing troopers are also cited as an indicator of pending disaster, a catalyst for the impending defeat.

Cheyenne warrior Wooden Leg observed the last moments of troopers surrounded by Indians near the end of the battle. As the warriors 'closed in, the soldiers began to shoot each other and to shoot themselves,' he said. By the time the warriors were among them, 'all were dead'. Friendly fire accidents occurred on both sides during the close-in melees that resulted each time a position was overrun. 'Soldiers were excited and shot wild,' claimed Flying By, a Minneconjou Lakota. Many doubtless despaired. The Minneconjou chief Red Horse described how soldiers were driven 'in confusion' before Sioux charges.

'These soldiers became foolish, many throwing away their guns and raising their hands saying, "Sioux, pity us – take us prisoners." The Sioux did not take a single soldier prisoner, but killed all of them; none were left alive for even a few minutes.'[24]

If soldiers shot each other in despair or by accident in certain circumstances, it appears to be an unusual event and not supported by the general tenor of Indian accounts. Head wounds bordered by powder burns found by the relief force were just as likely to be the *coup de grâce* administered to the unfortunate wounded. 'I have been in many hard fights,' claimed Northern Cheyenne warrior Brave Wolf, 'but I never saw such brave men.' His view was echoed by Soldier Wolf from the same tribe. 'Reno's men were frightened and acted as if they were drunk – as I think they were,' he commented, but 'Custer's men fought well and bravely.' Nobody, white or Indian, records any of Reno's men succumbing to suicide in similar circumstances in the valley bottom or later during the hilltop fight. One explanation for dubious suicide claims may be derived from an examination of Wooden Leg's account. Finding dead soldiers on the eastern end of Custer Ridge, he assumes that 'they too had killed each other or themselves as soon as the Indians had attacked'. Four attempted to flee on horseback, 'but their mounts were jaded, and three of the four were quickly overtaken and killed'. He claims that 'the fourth man, finding that the Sioux were gaining on him, shot himself'.[25] It is possible that the Indians may have confused cavalry pistol-drawing drill, removing the weapon from the holster butt-forward to prevent it falling out, and the final twist of the wrist with the barrel pointing up toward the throat (with the right hand, because the left retained the reins), as shooting himself in the head. Suicides have dramatic film and story-telling potential, but are less credible when compared to other equally desperate frontier actions. Fetterman's men fought to the death. There is no whisper of suicide at the Wagon Box fight, Beecher's Island or the Battle on the Rosebud.

The underlying reason for the rapid collapse of Custer's command was less surprise at overwhelming odds, more the terrific Indian firepower that negated the former '20 against 100' maxim. Custer's low-tech foe had penetrated the comfort zone that the longer-range Springfield carbines had temporarily conferred after the Wagon Box fight. They moved in, taking advantage of the close terrain, bisected by numerous ridgelines, upon which Custer's men chose to expose themselves. Like Royall before them, they were subjected to close-range fire from modern repeater weapons. Even modern Peace Support Operation (PSO) conflicts, like Iraq in 2003, demonstrate how irregulars can down high-tech helicopter platforms using simple hand-held weapons. Custer's men were punished by similarly simple yet lethal equivalents – repeater rifles.

'There were so many Sioux and Cheyennes,' said the Oglala American Horse, 'that the whole country seemed to be alive with them, closing on the troops and shooting.'[26]

At no stage in the battle did Custer seek to establish a consolidated regimental defensive position. E and F Companies were deployed from the conical hill, south towards the village in the area of Cemetery Ravine and Deep Ravine, to find a covered approach to the river or village. This was either an offensive move, or an exploratory breakout attempt. Last Stand Hill was not chosen for its defence attributes. It simply happened to be at the end of the ridgeline linking it with Calhoun's previous position. This knife-edge ridgeline, later Custer Ridge, like others around it, was useful less as a bastion but more for the cover from view that it afforded a mounted column.

The E and F Company 'salient' or southern prong of the 'V' formation into which Custer's command extended itself was a hasty defence position. It coalesced to prevent Indians boiling up Cemetery Ravine and Deep Ravine from the village – two pebbles placed in the path of an irresistible torrent sweeping up the re-entrants. E Company deployed obliquely in and along Cemetery Ravine at the furthest extent of the 'V' and anchored itself on the ridge dividing the northward meandering progress of both ravines. It faced two directions, west and north-west, covering a frontage of 200 yards manned by 38 men in two platoons. With every fourth man holding horses, they were tenuously over-extended with 8 to 10 yards between each man, unsustainable in the face of a massed close-in assault. E Company's right extremity almost connected with F Company, situated nearby on Cemetery Hill with 29 men. On contact with the Indian torrent, braves flowed into the gaps. Moving on foot, they appeared at different points over the ridge-lines and subjected the troopers to a devastating fire.

Initially mounted, the soldiers began to get down and fight on foot to improve fire discipline and accuracy, but were already too late. Casualties began to tumble, creating ragged gaps. Too few commanders could plug the holes. 'I could see the officers riding in front of the soldiers and hear them shouting,' said Minneconjou Red Horse. As more Indians poured out of Deep Ravine and Cemetery Ravine the lines disintegrated into a series of small-unit independently fought actions. 'Five brave stands' were made by 'the different soldiers [in the Custer battalion] that the Sioux killed,' said Red Horse. Unsuitable terrain had spread companies to seek better ground. They were operating as mounted cavalry, seeking to fix targets or envelop area objectives. The Indians refused to be fixed. Instead they dispersed, utilising the advantages conferred by ravine-covered approaches to seek out army weak points. Once identified, they would mass and overrun the position. The so-called 'Southern Skirmish Line' was the consequence of a hasty and, by necessity, dispersed defence by two companies, over-extended into a salient to attempt to block masses of Indians pouring from the ravines having come up from the village. Coordinating a response to this twin re-entrant attack was virtually hopeless, given the distances, weak platoons and too few leaders. 'In the battle I heard cries from troopers,' observed Red Horse, 'but could not understand what they were saying. I do not speak English.'[27] The collapse of Keogh's eastern wing spelled their inevitable doom.

Indian descriptions of the final phase of the Custer battle suggest a simultaneous overall collapse with considerable confusion and frenzied friendly fire incidents at the end. Keogh's demise rendered Custer's conical hill position indefensible. It was completely open to a continuation of the northern Indian assault and the cutting of Custer Ridge that accompanied it. The despairing buffalo-hunt rout that occurred as Keogh's men broke and ran to Custer's hill lapped right up to their position. Custer's headquarters may have been overrun before, or at the same time as, its over-extended companies to the south. Three 'last stands' probably occurred, on the conical hill and at the head of Cemetery Ravine and Deep Ravine.

Long-range rifle fire lashed centres of army resistance into bloody submission. Custer was hit in the right breast, then mortally wounded by a gunshot wound to the temple, as this fire traversed the conical hill. When this occurred is irrelevant. He had already

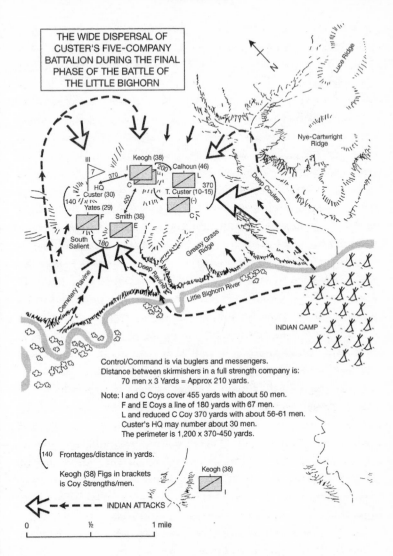

THE WIDE DISPERSAL OF
CUSTER'S FIVE-COMPANY
BATTALION DURING THE FINAL
PHASE OF THE BATTLE OF
THE LITTLE BIGHORN

Nye-Cartwright
Ridge

Luce Ridge

Deep Coulee

Keogh (38)

Calhoun (46)

III
7

HQ
Custer (30)
Yates (29)

T. Custer (10-15)

Smith (38)

South
Salient

Greasy Grass
Ridge

Deep Ravine

Cemetery Ravine

Little Bighorn River

INDIAN CAMP

Control/Command is via buglers and messengers.
Distance between skirmishers in a full strength company is:
70 men x 3 Yards = Approx 210 yards.

Note: I and C Coys cover 455 yards with about 50 men.
F and E Coys a line of 180 yards with 67 men.
L and reduced C Coy 370 yards with about 56-61 men.
Custer's HQ may number about 30 men.
The perimeter is 1,200 x 370-450 yards.

140 Frontages/distance in yards.

Keogh (38) Figs in brackets
is Coy Strengths/men.

Keogh (38)

— — — ▶ INDIAN ATTACKS

0   ½   1 mile

Dispersal into final 'last stands'

Custer so dispersed his companies during the final engagement that the
Indians were able to penetrate his defensive fire zone and close. Indian
superiority in weapons and hand-to-hand combat enabled them to overwhelm
the soldiers with minimal losses.

lost control of the battle when Calhoun and Keogh went down. 'Indians keep swirling round and around, and the soldiers killed only a few, many soldiers fell,' observed Cheyenne Two Moons as the collapse began. The density of incoming fire matched Civil War levels, as captured weapons were turned against those still standing – a storm of fire commented upon again during the Reno hilltop fight. It caused more damage than the charges. Apart from 'bravery runs', the Indian tactic was to rush in and finish off the wounded once the firefight had been won. The paucity of .45 revolver signatures identified by archaeological digs suggests that long-range fire hit the majority of troopers before they could use them. Most of the .45 evidence is of vertical impacts – Indians stood over the wounded and shot them at point-blank range. To fend off the fire, Lieutenant Wallace of G Company later testified, 'They had apparently tried to lead the horses in a circle on the point of the ridge, and had killed them there, and apparently made an effort for a final stand.' Horses, terrified by the noise of battle, were shying, rearing and pulling at reins. It would have been difficult to pacify them sufficiently to lead them into any formation resembling a defensive circle. Young Two Moons, another Cheyenne, noticed that 'the yelling of the Indians seemed to frighten the cavalry horses and they were neighing and plunging so that the men could not handle their guns'.[28] Revolver shots at point-blank range to horse heads, neighing, the smell of sprayed blood and billowing dust as they were haphazardly shot and dropped to the earth provided some semblance of cover. It was a surreal scene.

Last Stand Hill, as it came to be called, was flailed by fire from three directions. Its conical shape was more distinctive at the time of the battle; it and Custer Ridge had 8 feet shaved off to accommodate the later monument site and park road. Incoming fire came from a small hill feature in range to the east, from the Indian advance along the razor-backed [Custer] ridge and the Keogh re-entrant to the south-east. They were also engaged from a small knoll 600 yards to the north. The fight was not completely one-sided. Seventeen-year-old Big Beaver, a Cheyenne boy, saw one war-bonneted Sioux 'jump up and shoot towards the soldiers on the [conical] hill where the monument is, then he would fall down and reload and crawl ahead again'. He did this several times alongside scores of companions also peppering the position with fire. 'At one of these times a soldier bullet hit him exactly in the middle of the forehead. His arms and legs jumped in spasms for a few moments, then he died.'[29] It was not long before 39 horses were felled about the hill in a haphazard defensive pattern. Among them were found 42 dead troopers.

In its final stages the battle was unrelenting and unforgiving. Horned Horse, a Sioux warrior in Crazy Horse's war-band, said that 'the smoke and dust was so great that foe could not be distinguished from friend'. Both sides closed in a savage hand-to-hand melee. Horned Horse intertwined his fingers and said 'just like this, Indians and white men'. The Indians were better equipped with tomahawk, lance, knives and stone clubs for this close-in work. Against this the troopers had no sabres and only a few personal fighting knives. Those still standing had to wield their carbines as clubs. It became a massacre, as two, three or more braves would grapple individual soldiers to the ground. Man against man was challenging for the average Plains Indian – contemporary photographs show their slight stature, with legs and arms that were commonly thin. The Indian disdained hard physical labour, which was regarded as work for squaws; he would ride his pony in preference to moving anywhere on foot. Arrested muscular development was the result and a characteristic noticed by Elizabeth Custer. She observed that 'none of them do any manual labour to produce muscle and their bones are decidedly conspicuous... I never knew but one Indian who worked.'

White Bull, a Minneconjou Lakota, fought a desperate hand-to-hand struggle with a fair, well-built soldier, who had a moustache. Despite the Indian's proficiency in close combat, the white man punched him several times in the jaw and shoulder. He was becoming difficult to handle. At one stage White Bull was seized by his long braids of hair and his face pulled close to that of the white man who attempted to bite off his nose. Two other braves, Bear Lice and Crow Boy, joined in. They pummelled the soldier, who was not letting go of White Bull. Eventually the desperate Lakota pulled the soldier's revolver from his grasp and clubbed him three or four times at last to the ground. He immediately shot him point-blank in the head and heart. 'Ho Hechetu!' White Bull exclaimed. 'That was a fight, a hard fight. But it was a glorious battle, I enjoyed it.'[30]

Lieutenant Algernon Smith's E or 'Grey Horse' Company was the more extended of the two companies fighting astride the two ravines in the southern salient. Keogh's collapse increased the pressure on F Company as braves streamed across Custer Ridge. Both companies were in turn outflanked by hordes of warriors emerging at different points from the two ravines, opening fire on their flanks and rear. E Company was further assailed by 20 or more guns that opened up on it from warriors who had slipped westward along the lower slopes of Greasy Grass Ridge. Driving up from Cemetery Ridge came the 'Suicide Boys'. This bizarre group encompassed young men who had participated in the Dying Dance in the village the night before and pledged to fight to the death in

Custer's tactical battle

Custer took decisions not dissimilar from those of the 2nd and 3rd Cavalry Regiment battalion commanders with Crook at the Rosebud one week before fighting against the same enemy. It was accepted convention to split the force to counter the Indian propensity to scatter if attacked. [A] Custer conducts a 'meeting engagement', committing his force before precisely locating the enemy. [B] He disregards the opportunity to fight his command as a regiment. [C] Not able to see the full extent of the village from Reno Hill, he decides at [D] Weir Point to press on without Benteen and conduct a feint attack against the village with Yates's two companies. Volley fire on Nye-Cartwright Ridge [E] suggests that Indians are starting to close in on Custer. He cannot see the engagement clearly at the ford. A junction is achieved under pressure with Yates [F] and Custer disperses his companies, still anticipating that Benteen will catch up. It is too late and the companies are individually overwhelmed [G].

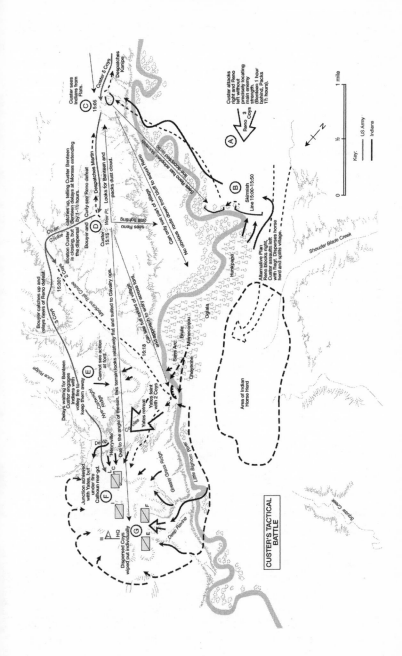

CUSTER'S TACTICAL BATTLE

their next battle. Their savage onslaught stampeded many of the cavalry horses as they careered into the midst of bunched soldiers still standing. Pockets of hand-to-hand fighting developed throughout the remaining area of the battlefield, stretching from Last Stand Hill down to the dogged yet disintegrating lines of resistance crumbling about the twin re-entrants to the south. 'The horses were wild with fright and uncontrollable,' claimed Horned Horse, the Sioux warrior. 'The Indians were knocking each other from their steeds,' he claimed, in the frenzy to close and finish off the white soldiers. 'It is an absolute fact,' he said, 'that the young bucks in their excitement and fury killed each other.'[31]

Lieutenant Thomas McDougall, who previously commanded Smith's E Company for five years, subsequently 'found most of the troop, who had used the upper sides of the ravine for a kind of breastwork, falling to the bottom as they were shot down'. Evidence suggests that they were outflanked, as they 'appeared to have been mostly shot in the side'. Lieutenant Smith was vulnerable during hand-to-hand fighting because a Civil War shoulder wound prevented him from lifting his left arm. Probably wounded again, he was lifted to the conical hill. His company fought back as they retreated along and across the Deep Ravine ridgeline. 'I could see,' said Lieutenant Moylan from A Company after the battle, 'where they had passed down the edge and attempted to scramble up the other side, which was almost perpendicular.'

'We were right on top of the soldiers,' said the Minneconjou Standing Bear, 'and there was no use in their hiding from us.' As the final collapse began on Custer Hill, soldiers ran to where they thought resistance was holding out. This was not easy. Cheyenne Two Moons described how 'once in a while some men would break out and run toward the river, but he would fall'. Resistance south of the conical hill, around the twin re-entrants, may have lasted longer than on Last Stand Hill. Groups of soldiers began to run down the ridge towards E Company. 'As they got down part way toward the Grey Horse [E] Company,' according to the Cheyenne Young Two Moons, 'the latter began to fire and drove Indians off and the soldiers reached the Grey Horse Company.' This E Company resistance caused the Indian advance to falter. They 'shot at Indians so fast that they drove Indians back out of sight over the hill'. But it represented little more than a momentary pause. Young Two Moons soon saw that 'the Indians charged in among them'. 'From this point on, everything was mixed up,' claimed another Cheyenne warrior, Soldier Wolf. 'There was a grand charge and nothing clear could be seen for the dust and the people, until all the troops had been killed.'[32]

Standing Bear, looking down at the group of soldiers who had fled 'into a draw and there was tall grass here', was probably looking into Deep Ravine. Big Beaver, the Cheyenne boy, also observed soldiers fleeing Custer Hill. 'These soldiers were scared as they did not shoot back,' and 'the Indians ran them down'. He suspected that they were out of ammunition and 'were trying to make it to the brush along the river'. Accounts vary between 15 and 25, 30 or even 40 soldiers making this breakout. Good Voiced Elk, a Hunkpapa, said, 'I saw an Indian rush at the men and the Indians killed every soldier, including some of our own Indians who had gone on ahead of the rest.' Lone Man, another Hunkpapa, corroborated the turmoil of the Custer collapse at this point. He noticed the Sioux Indian among 28 soldiers lying dead at the bottom of the 'deep gully'.

'At first thought he was with the soldiers, but later found that he was a hostile who had followed the soldiers too closely. Even his own people had mutilated the body, thinking it was that of the Indian scouts with the soldiers.'

Lieutenant Moylan, later reviewing the scene, saw '20-odd bodies of E Company' in what he thought to be Deep Ravine. He noted the perpendicular sides, which offered no chance of escape. 'The marks were plain where they had used their hands to get up, but the marks only extended halfway up the bank.'[33]

Last stands, 1815 hours

'He [Custer] was dismounted, and doubtless many of his men also, the enemy was pressing, and here was a position on which they could stand and strike back – probably without hope of victory, but at least with the possibility of holding on until Reno or Benteen came, or that relief of dying like brave men. I think no thoughtful and unprejudiced man could have examined the last positions held by Custer, as marked by the dead, without being convinced that he was thinking clearly, fast and courageously. I said to myself, as did others doubtless, here a hero died. That his was the spirit of battle seemed clear from those who chose to die on the knoll with him.'

Sowing the seeds of a legend:
Lieutenant Edward McClernand of Terry's column

Resistance on Last Stand Hill was quickly overcome. Losses had broken the emotional and disciplined cohesion of the command. Adjutant Lieutenant William Cooke, a popular officer, was, according to Indian accounts, one of the last officers to die. Cooke's size and striking side-whiskers gave him a distinctive appearance. He collapsed, riddled with repeater bullets. Indians swarmed over his body and scalped his crown and side-whiskers, producing 'the most fearful sight', according to Lieutenant John Carland with the 6th Infantry Regiment. 'They dug his face all out,' he later testified, 'so as to get at his fine beard it is supposed.'[34] 'Yellow Nose captured from a soldier a flag which had a gilt lance head on the staff,' said Little Hawk, a Northern Cheyenne, 'the only one of this kind taken.'[35] Captain Tom Custer was cut down a few paces from his brother during the last-minute hacking and thrusting. His arm was smashed by the impact of a bullet; someone cut his throat, clubbed his head flat, then disembowelled him. Only the tattooed initials 'T.W.C.' on his arm enabled identification. Lieutenant Godfrey discovered:

'His features were so pressed out of shape as to be beyond recognition, a number of arrows had been shot in his back, several in his head, one I remember, without the shaft, the head bent so that it could hardly be withdrawn; his skull was crushed and nearly all the hair scalped, except a very little on the nape of the neck.'[36]

A generation of Custers died. Boston Custer, having hurried to join his brothers, was shot several times, as also was Harry Armstrong 'Autie' Reed, Custer's nephew, gunned down in the final fighting. General Custer's thigh was gashed open with an 11-inch knife wound. The mortal wound was to the temple. Another gunshot injury to his side probably struck his right forearm as it exited his chest. Like many around, he lay incapacitated until finished off. His thinning hair was not scalped. Excavations at Marker 105 on Custer Hill reveal a soldier lying virtually alongside Custer struck by an arrow in the throat, shot in the ribs and finished off by clubbing to the head. Another corpse investigated at Marker 78, at the base of the western slope, had the left forearm shattered by a bullet and retained lead fragments embedded in the bone; he too was clubbed to death.[37] There are 52 markers on present-day Monument Hill. They include Custer's battalion headquarters staff officers as well as the commanders of E and F Companies. One assumes that the latter, wounded before the final collapse, were carried to Surgeon Lord's First Aid Post and perished when it was overrun.

'When about the last man dropped in the Grey Horse Company,' White Shield, a Northern Cheyenne warrior, said, 'the Indians made a charge and killed the wounded with hatchets, arrows, knives, etc.' Excavations at Markers 9 and 10 at the extremity of the southern salient formed by E Company near Deep Ravine offer a battlefield 'snapshot' of the death of a trooper aged about 25, and 5ft 8in tall. Strong and robust for his height, he was, nevertheless, thrown off his feet when a .44 repeater rifle round thumped into his chest, probably puncturing a lung. Mortally wounded and wheezing for breath,

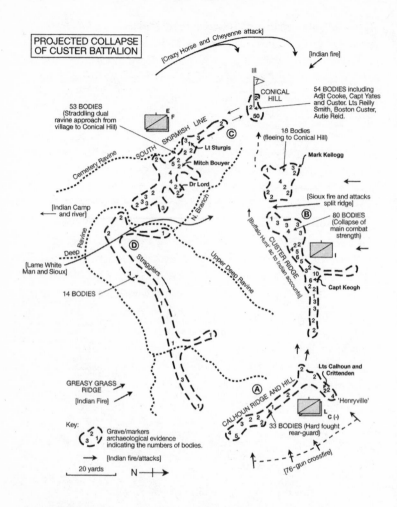

PROJECTED COLLAPSE
OF CUSTER BATTALION

[Crazy Horse and Cheyenne attack]

[Indian fire]

III
CONICAL
HILL

54 BODIES including
Adjt Cooke, Capt Yates
and Custer. Lts Reilly
Smith, Boston Custer,
Autie Reid.

53 BODIES
(Straddling dual
ravine approach from
village to Conical Hill)

SOUTH SKIRMISH LINE

18 Bodies
(fleeing to Conical Hill)

Lt Sturgis

Mark Kellogg

Cemetery Ravine

Mitch Bouyer

Dr Lord

[Indian Camp
and river]

[Sioux fire and attacks
split ridge]

N. Branch

80 BODIES
(Collapse of
main combat
strength)

CUSTER RIDGE

Deep Ravine

(Buffalo Hunt acc to Indian accounts)

[Lame White
Man and Sioux]

Upper Deep Ravine

Stragglers

Capt Keogh

14 BODIES

Lts Calhoun and
Crittenden

GREASY GRASS
RIDGE

[Indian Fire]

'Henryville'

CALHOUN RIDGE AND HILL

L C (-)

Key:

33 BODIES (Hard fought
rear-guard)

Grave/markers
archaeological evidence
indicating the numbers of bodies.

[Indian fire/attacks]

[76-gun crossfire]

20 yards   N

he probably fell on his back as braves swarmed over him. They shot
him in the head with his own Colt revolver and repeatedly brained
him with a war club, shattering his skull. Arrows were shot into his
body and chest. His back was hacked and slashed with knives to
count coup and in order to mark him out as a vanquished foe, before
he set off on his final journey to the spirit world. Nobody bothered
to strip off his shredded uniform. He was left lying on the ridge.[38]

The projected collapse of Custer's battalion

There was a series of forlornly fought company actions rather than an epic 'Last Stand'. Although the collapse of Custer's battalion cannot be charted with any certainty, archaeological information represented on this map offers a projection. [A] Calhoun's L Company, reinforced by elements of C Company, was subjected to a devastating Indian crossfire from 'Henryville' and overrun. The Indian onslaught continued over the hill and [B] surprised Keogh's I Company in the ravine behind, precipitating a collapse. The resulting Indian description of a 'buffalo hunt' broke the remaining uncommitted and primary reserve of combat power still available to Custer. Keogh's soldiers were cut down seeking to join Custer on the conical hill. The southern salient [C] may have survived longer than Custer's headquarters on the hill as evidence suggests that soldiers moved down to join it during the final fighting. Stragglers attempting to escape were picked off in the area of [D].

Markers 33 and 34 are situated near the middle of the southern salient where F Company established its hasty defence at the head of Cemetery Ravine and Deep Ravine. In 1984 bones were discovered indicating a man of Caucasian and Mongoloid mix. He was partly white but with a characteristically Indian face bone structure and was aged between 35 and 45. Clothing fragments indicate that he wore civilian European clothing, not regulation army uniform. Impacted Indian bullets all round identify him as a target, probably a civilian scout attached to Custer's battalion. Two Moons, the Cheyenne chief, recalled a man leading a breakout attempt in this vicinity, which consisted of five mounted men and maybe 40 on foot. 'He wore a buckskin shirt and had long black hair and moustache.' He was shot several times. A bullet-riddled hat was found near this body the following year. 'He fought hard with a big knife,' said Two Moons. A cast was made of the facial bones excavated and superimposed over a life-size full-face photograph of Custer's scout, Mitch Bouyer. It was a strikingly perfect fit – according to one commentary, 'broad face, eye orbit, nasal cavity, teeth and all'. 'If the Sioux kill me,' the half-breed scout reputedly said before his death, 'I have the satisfaction of knowing I popped many of them over, and they can't get even now, if they do get me.' Although repeatedly struck by gunfire, the only injury evident on the remains found was massive blunt force trauma applied to the head at the time of death.[39]

Indian accounts frequently attest to escape attempts by terrified troopers. Cheyenne warrior Wooden Leg remembered the haze of battle obscuring Last Stand Hill, discernible only by 'the dead horses that marked the soldiers' position' which 'was plainly visible'. Escape attempts sought to utilise this cover.

'One mounted soldier broke for the east. Where he came from they did not know, but he too was overtaken and killed.'

One survivor got as far as Marker 174, two ravines east of where Keogh's Company perished. He managed to penetrate 180 yards beyond the 'line of death' that had forlornly grasped at safety on the conical hill. Three spent army .45/55 carbine cartridges, one Colt cartridge, a Colt bullet and an impacted .50/70 bullet were found around the marker. All the carbine cases had been fired from the same weapon, probably as the trooper sought to outrun his pursuers. He was either a lone survivor who had feigned death between Keogh's dead before attempting a final dash or he was perhaps a last messenger. As he sprinted across the ravines he drew fire from the Indians until he reached the side slope upon which he was found. Pausing to fire three rounds, he ran out of ammunition. Discarding his rifle he drew his pistol and was struck by a .50/70 Indian bullet. As he fell his Colt went off, striking the ground nearby.[40]

'When the last soldier was killed,' said Two Kettle brave Runs the Enemy, 'the smoke rolled up like a mountain above our heads, and the soldiers were piled one on top of another dead, and here and there an Indian among the soldiers.' Clearer visibility made escape impossible. One of the last troopers to die may well have been the individual whose remains are at Marker 2. This lone sentinel stands in a small ground depression on the south side of Deep Ravine. There are six impacted bullets scattered within a few feet of the marker, including one .50/70 round from an old batch of Springfield ammunition, a .50 muzzle-loaded ball, an unidentified damaged bullet, one .45 Colt revolver bullet, and two .45/55 rounds. This man was fleeing the final fighting. He was probably seen coming out of Deep Ravine or spotted traversing it. Whatever the case, five or six Indians, each with different weapons, targeted this single individual, also employing captured weapons. Presumably the main battle was over; otherwise so many Indians would not have preoccupied themselves shooting a virtual volley at a fleeting target. After this gauntlet of fire brought down the trooper, they rushed in and smashed in his skull. The body was so hacked at by hatchets and knives that the head was virtually severed from the torso. Marker 2's demise represented a lonely, desperate and forlorn attempt at life.[41]

'Some white soldiers were cut with knives, to make sure they were dead,' said Cheyenne Two Moons, 'and the war women had mangled some.' Custer's battalion was totally destroyed. It appeared that not one man had survived. Crowds of old men, women and young boys, spectators at a distance, now rushed in among the bodies. Cheyenne warrior Wooden Leg saw how 'one wounded officer – a captain – still lived, though in a dazed condition'. As the non-combatants surged forward 'he raised himself upon an elbow, glaring wildly at the Indians, who shrank from him, believing him returned from the spirit world'. An undismayed Sioux warrior 'wrestled the revolver from his nerveless hand and shot him through the head'.

Black Elk, a 13-year-old Oglala boy, walked among the prostrate soldiers at the top of Custer ridge. 'When we got there, some of them were still alive,' kicking, he said. He paused to shoot an arrow into the forehead of one soldier, remaining until he stopped quivering. Other boys shot arrows repeatedly into wounded soldiers, sometimes pushing the protruding quills further in by hand. It was a scene of surreal desolation. Iron Hawk, a Hunkpapa, was attracted by playful laughter and shouting and saw a group of women engaged in a macabre dance with a naked soldier. As they had started to emasculate their hapless victim, he suddenly came to life. He grotesquely plunged around with two of the women clinging to him. A third squaw plunged her knife deep into his body and abruptly terminated the charade. Iron Hawk felt impelled to leave this horrific scene. Another Cheyenne woman, Antelope, called Kate Bighead, noticed a dazed and wounded soldier sitting on the ground rubbing his head. Two Lakotas seized him and held him down and stretched him out on his back while a third cut off his head with a sheath knife.[42]

As the plundering and mutilations continued, discarded green dollar bills began to flutter and blow among the bodies. Custer had insisted on departure from Fort Abraham Lincoln that the soldiers not be paid until their first night in the field. This would avoid the normal drunken excesses associated with pay night at the Post. His men rode into battle with two full months' pay, some $25,000. So far as the Indians were concerned, it could not be eaten and was no use for mending. The money floated away on the breeze.

There was palpable elation in the village at the victory and outrage at the intended white massacre of their families. Revenge manifested itself through the depredations conducted on the hill-sides and ridgelines beyond the village. Yet success was tempered by sadness at losses. Wooden Leg visited Noisy Walking, his dying Cheyenne friend. Passing his distraught mother at the tepee entrance, he could only bring himself to ask, 'How are you?' 'Good, I only want water,' was the laboured response from the dying man. 'I did not know what else to say but I wanted him to know that I was his friend and willing to do whatever I could for him.' He waited through an awkward silence, then said, 'You were very brave.' 'Nothing else was said for several minutes. He was weak. His hands trembled at every move he made.' Noisy Walking asked his father for water, 'just a little of it,' he said. But his father, White Bull, a respected medicine man, could not accede to the request. 'No, water will kill you,' was his choked and emotional response.

'As I sat there looking at Noisy Walking, I knew he was going to die. My heart was heavy. But I could not do him any good, so I excused myself and went away.'[43]

* * *

Back at Fort Rice and Fort Abraham Lincoln, the soldiers' women-folk waited. 'Frank's letters became less and less frequent, because of the increasing distance between us,' wrote Lieutenant Gibson's wife Katherine. He was serving in Benteen's Company. There were few worries at this juncture. The soldiers, she remembered, had left 'feeling secure with such a large command'. Letters received up to now remarked upon few signs of Indians. 'The whole command was taking the adventure as a prolonged picnic,' remarked Katherine Gibson, 'and these bits of news, brought by Indian scouts, were a great comfort to us all.' After the troops left, 'life resumed its usual routine'. There was little to do.

'So time slipped by during the month of June. Our only pleasure after the torrid day was to gather on someone's porch in the long twilight, enjoy what little music we could muster, and try to forget our worries and the devilish mosquitoes.'

Temperatures rose with emotions. 'It was so stiflingly hot that we lingered on our porches until after tattoo,' reminisced Katherine Gibson. The hot weather continued without respite. We drifted day by day,' she wrote, ' – waiting for what?'[44]

There were to be 22 soldier widows left behind after the battle of the Little Bighorn and 32 children without fathers. These families were left with no status in the army, and at this moment were unaware of their plight and that of their loved ones. If there was nobody to support them they were obliged to vacate their quarters and leave the Post. A poignant reminder of this cost was illustrated by the 1984 find at the F Company skirmish line by the entrance to Cemetery Ravine of a silver-plated wedding ring. It still encircled the skeletal left third finger joint of an unknown soldier's hand. Captain Yates's finger had been cut off 300 yards away on the conical hill to take his ring.[45]

'It was the Indian's day,' concluded Corporal Windolph, long after the event. 'Their one and only day.' But the sun had still to run its full course on this, the bloody Red Sabbath.

Chapter 12
'What tomorrow might bring'

'We were a million miles from nowhere.
And death was all around us.'

US Seventh Cavalry Corporal

The hill

Reno's force of 370 soldiers had advanced to Weir Point in three
dispersed groups spread over an hour. Although representing 59%
of the regiment's strength, three of seven companies were intimidated by the mauling they had received in the valley bottom hours
before. Neither Reno nor Benteen appeared to be in overall control
of an advance initiated by Captain Weir, and no one was in charge
now. The Indians were in no way disturbed by their presence at
Weir Point and allowed the force to remain unmolested for two
hours. Firing was audible in the direction Custer was supposed to
have gone. 'All of the officers must have known that Custer was
engaged with the Indians,' recalled Private William Taylor with A
Company, 'and quite nearby for he had not time to go a great way.'
No action was initiated. 'Why don't we move?' surmised Taylor, a
question asked 'by more than one'. 'There was a lot of speculating
going on,' echoed Corporal Windolph with Benteen's company. It
was suspected that Custer had been worsted in the fight because the
tepees remained standing, as also the large assembly of warriors to
their front. Custer had probably retreated northwards to effect the
previously agreed junction with Terry. Lieutenant Francis Gibson
with H Company scanned the area forward with field binoculars

but 'could see absolutely nothing'. He assumed that Custer's battalion 'had gone to the timbers about six miles off and fortified himself'.[1]

'Pretty soon,' said Corporal Windolph, also with H Company, 'it looked as if the Indian masses were coming toward us.' Somewhat deterred by their previous reversal, the force felt vulnerable. 'Here we were stretched out all over the hell's half acre,' said Windolph,

> 'A troop on this hill knob, another in this little valley and over there a third troop. Behind, at a slow walk, came the pack trains, the wounded men and the rear guard.'

They fell back. 'We found our present position hard to defend,' said Lieutenant Gibson, 'so we moved back to where we made our first stand.'

A withdrawal in contact is one of the most difficult phases of war to execute. With nobody in overall command, M and D Companies covered the uncoordinated retirement. The vulnerable packs, sensing the emergency, moved quickly for once. 'Clouds of dust arose from all parts of the field,' observed Lieutenant Godfrey as successive Indian war-bands mounted a pursuit, 'and the horsemen converged toward our position.' Companies dismounted to fight on foot as others galloped by. 'Soon the Indians were pressing hard,' declared Windolph.[2]

'As soon as we had killed all the different soldiers [in Custer's command],' said the Minneconjou Red Horse, 'all went back to kill the soldiers on the hill.' Private Taylor, recalling 'the generally demoralised condition of the command' at this time, reflected that 'it has been to me a great wonder why that strong force of Indians that had swept over and annihilated Custer with his five Troops in such a brief time should have hesitated to pursue the tactics that won for them such a great victory an hour or two before.'[3]

If Reno's movements were uncoordinated, the Indians, lacking centralised command, were even more so. Indians fought as individuals but instinctively acted together as a group. They sensed the vulnerability of the retreating soldiers but were not directed by a single leader. Some remained on the Custer field, exulting in the plunder and magnitude of their achievement. One attacking force had been badly mauled seeking entry into the village, the other totally destroyed. 'The Sioux men took the clothing off the dead and dressed themselves in it,' said Sioux warrior Red Horse. There was no urgency. The crushing victory over the white soldiers foretold by Sitting Bull's prophecy dissipated any compelling need to deal with those who remained. Many Indian accounts predictably linger over Custer's defeat. The coming Reno hilltop fight was a sideshow relative to the carnage that had already been wreaked on Custer Ridge. Red Horse simply recounts that 'the Sioux took the guns and cartridges off the dead soldiers and went to the hill on which the soldiers were, surrounded and fought them with the guns and cartridges of the dead soldiers'. Red Horse grudgingly asserted, 'I don't like to talk about that fight,' a far less glorious episode. 'If I hear any of my people talking about it, I always move away.'[4]

Only Farrier Vincent Charley from D Company was killed during the hastily conducted retirement. Lieutenant Edgerly saw him pitch from his horse after he had been shot in the hips. As he fell he struck his head, which also began to bleed. Edgerly directed him into a ravine to hide until he could return with support. However, Captain Weir, his company commander, refused, despite Edgerly's remonstrations, to deviate from the pell-mell retreat under way to save his trooper. It was symptomatic of lack of confidence and the Indian pressure exerted on the rush to get back.

Taylor, in A Company, encapsulated what was likely to have gone through Charley's mind on being unhorsed. 'One of the thoughts that has often come to me was of the mental agonies as well as the physical sufferings of the seriously wounded.' Custer's troopers suffered the same miserable fate. 'Some were shot,' stated Taylor, 'while the command was in rapid motion, reeling in the saddle and unable to guide his horse which was, freed of its unsteady burden, dashing away.'

Archaeological research suggests that Vincent Charley's skeletal remains were found in 1903 and interred within Grave 455 in the National Cemetery. Charley was struck in the back by a bullet coming from the right. Piercing his hipbone, lead debris exited through the soft tissue of his abdomen. This alone ensured a lingering death from blood poisoning as intestine leaks fouled his system. Such wounds were beyond the best medical care of the era. Hip and pelvis wounds had an astonishingly high 83–85% mortality rate during the Civil War. Charley, according to Private John Fox who paused with Edgerly, pleaded not to be abandoned. Taylor read his thoughts as he painted an image of 'the last of his comrades are rushing by unheeding, for close in the rear comes the swarming Sioux'. Edgerly, joined by Sergeant Thomas Harrison of D Company, was closely pursued by about 200 braves, and they had to shoot themselves out of their close predicament with revolvers. Looking back, Charley was seen with warriors swarming all over him. 'With lightning-like rapidity, many events and scenes of his past life pass through [the] mind' of the blood-spattered trooper, surmised Taylor. He would think of family 'and the earth how beautiful it was, even on that dry dusty plain, and the sky, why, it was never so clear and blue before'. Charley, left behind by his comrades, had 'all these and many more thoughts of a like nature [sweep] over him as the hideously painted and yelling hordes bore down on him'. Whether he had that long to consider is a moot point. Taylor's sentimental account would have struck a chord with his 19th-century audience. When Charley's body was eventually recovered Edgerly found a 'stick rammed down the throat', terminating his screams as he drowned in his own blood.[5]

As Lieutenant Godfrey's K Company held a desperate rearguard on a small knoll beyond, the remainder of the force fell back to the first position held on the bluffs after Reno had been chased from the valley bottom. 'Well, Wallace,' Benteen remarked to the G Company officer, 'this looks like the best place we have passed. No use going any further.' They had to reorganise and fight. 'Deploy your troop, to the right resting there,' he indicated with his hand, 'and stand 'em off. I'll send you help.'[6]

A defensive perimeter was hastily laid out around a relatively high plateau between two ridgelines. Lieutenant McDougall's B Company manned the northern ridge facing the oncoming hostiles. Godfrey's K Company, Weir and Wallace's depleted D and G Companies (the latter with only three men left), and French's M Company faced west. Here the ground fell off sharply into a number of gullies leading down to the river. Moylan's A Company faced east, supplementing D and G covering a flat plain approach. Benteen's H Company formed the handle of the upturned teacup-shaped position, running off from the main position on a ridgeline extending south. Animals and wounded men were gathered within a circular depression in the middle of the position. Godfrey's K Company troopers were the last men to sprint into the position with the Indians in hot pursuit.

'It was now possibly 6.30 in the afternoon,' said Corporal Windolph, 'with three hours of daylight still to go.' The Indians rapidly surrounded the quickly assumed perimeter and commenced long-range sniping. They had retreated 1.2 miles from Weir Point. The perimeter, about 500 yards long by 17 yards wide, incorporated a wide area requiring considerable dispersal by the 370-man force. The conical shape of the end of a ridgeline overlooked it 500 yards to the north, soon named Sharpshooter's Ridge. Slightly right of this and also 300 feet to the north was the small knoll that had protected Lieutenant Godfrey's rearguard action. 'It was impossible,' said Windolph, 'to shield the men and stock from the Indians firing from a hill top off to the east.' Casualties began to mount. 'Animal after animal was killed, and men were hit.' Dust explosions pinged and ricocheted all round the perimeter. 'By this time the Indians had us completely surrounded and opened a furious fire,' said Private Taylor. Godfrey, to the north, felt acutely vulnerable. 'After lying there a few minutes I was horrified to find myself wondering if a small sagebrush, about as thick as my finger, would turn a bullet.' Correctly assuming that it would not, he moved around, seeking to reorganise his men. They were pinned down and hardly able to move, and, as Windolph commented, 'it was tough not to be able to do something about it'.[7]

'We were not very well entrenched,' admitted Private William Slaper with M Company, so 'I used my butcher knife to cut the earth loose and throw a mound of it in front of me upon which to rest my carbine.' Lieutenant Varnum nearby remembered 'a very heavy firing against us'. Little encouragement was needed to get under ground. Slaper was blinded by a storm of dust as a bullet ricocheted off the corner of his earth mound, 'throwing up so much dirt into my eyes that I could scarcely see for an hour or more'. Rounds screeched through the perimeter so long as visibility held out with the approach of dusk. 'While laying face down on the ground,' Slaper ruefully explained, 'a bullet tore off the heel of my boot as effectively as though it had been sawed off!' There were no entrenching tools, but the troopers got to work 'as well as they could,' explained Varnum, 'using tin cups, knives and whatever came to hand to dig into the flinty soil'.[8] Every protrusion of high ground around the teacup-shaped perimeter sprouted little molehills at strategic intervals among tufted clumps of grass and sagebrush, attracting even more Indian fire. Although widely dispersed, the small knots of vulnerable troopers could at least derive comfort from their visibility to each other.

M and B Companies were taunted by the imposing sight of the village below the western ridgeline. It remained intact, a symbol of their failure and proof that Custer had also been driven off. Many a trooper in M Company would have reflected on his terrifying experience in the valley below, where the stripped white corpses of their comrades reflected the dying rays of the sun.

Survivors, previously marooned in the valley bottom, began to make their perilous way to the hilltop after Reno's force returned. They included the civilian scout Herendeen and 12 troopers. Among them was Private Peter Thompson from C Company, left behind with a blown mount when Custer first ascended the ridgeline above the village. Two days later the remaining survivors, Lieutenant de Rudio, scout Frank Gerard and two others, got back.

The Indians were frustrated. Having 'whipped' the whites there was little more they could do. 'All the Sioux watched around the hill on which were the soldiers,' said Minneconjou Red Horse. Army frontier successes were traditionally associated with fights from fortified static positions, such as the Wagon Box fight in 1867 and Beecher's Island the following year. For the first time in this battle Reno and Benteen's troopers were operating within their own comfort zone, a contrast from the terrifying and fluid engagement they had barely survived. Little Hawk, a Northern Cheyenne warrior, blandly stated that 'after Custer was finished [the Indians] went back to Reno to keep him from getting water'. The grim intent was clear, but the entrenchments were the hurdle. 'The soldiers on the hill dug up the ground,' said Red Horse, 'and the soldiers and Sioux fought at long range, sometimes the Sioux charging close up.' 'There was no full-fledged charge,' observed Windolph, 'but little groups of Indians would creep up as close as they could get, and from behind bushes or little knolls open fire.'[9]

A small pile of rocks east of present-day Reno Hill commemorates one such 'bravery run' conducted by Standing Bear, a 15-year-old Minneconjou. As dusk approached, the young Sioux boy tempted fate just too far. Stands in Timber, a Cheyenne warrior, saw that he 'rode too close to the soldiers and was killed'. The horse collapsed in a welter of dust amid army cheers, throwing the warrior to the ground. 'Then the boy was shot,' said Stands in Timber. 'The horse turned over in the air and then got up and ran away.'[10]

As dusk fell, clumps of tufted grass and sagebrush began to glow pink. 'The sun went down that night like a ball of fire,' mused Corporal Windolph. The 'Red Sabbath' was over. Unbeknown to the soldiers on the hill, the stripped and naked bodies of Custer's command were already bathed in its eerie blood-red light. Little had gone well for Benteen and Reno that day, and although entrenched in the relative safety of the new position, 11 more men were killed or wounded. Every time the grass twitched in the fading light, there was an Indian out there. Private Taylor, on the south-east side of the perimeter with A Company, 'scrutinised as carefully as I could all the features of the landscape in front'. He was especially wary of 'the taller growth of sagebrush that might be mistaken in the dark for the stealthy approach of an Indian'. Troopers, starved of proper sleep for days and verging on total exhaustion, struggled against phantoms through the early part of the night. Indians had been trying to reach them crawling through the long grass. 'Firing had gradually died out,' said Windolph. 'Now and again you'd hear the ping of a rifle bullet, but by 10 o'clock even that had stopped.' There was no moon and the chill of the high plains enveloped the hill like a depressing blanket. 'No one ever welcomed darkness more than we did,' admitted the Corporal. Respite brought with it time to reflect and, with that, anxiety.

> 'Welcome as the darkness was, it brought a penetrating feeling of fear and uncertainty of what tomorrow might bring. We felt terribly alone on that dangerous hilltop. We were a million miles from nowhere. And death was all around us.'

Private Taylor recalled that a number of bugle calls were sounded from the perimeter that night, with the hope that they 'might reach the ears of Custer's command and so direct them to our position'. 'Taps' was both a 'last lights' call and the soldier's graveside farewell. The dead were tumbled into shallow scrapes near where they fell. 'No ceremony,' commented Taylor, simply 'a few inches of earth thrown over them, to be washed off by the first rain.' Losses and the recognised 'narrow escape' that day 'had a very sobering effect on all'.[11]

Down in the valley bottom 'the long twilight was prolonged by numerous bonfires,' stated Lieutenant Godfrey, adding to the unearthly red glow permeating all as the sun went down. Not surprisingly the Indians 'were a great deal happier than we were,' Godfrey grudgingly asserted. They continued to intimidate their foes psychologically.

> 'Their camp was a veritable pandemonium. All night long they continued their frantic revels: beating tom-toms,

dancing, whooping, yelling with demonical screams, and discharging firearms. We knew they were having a scalp dance.'

Images of horrific tortures preyed on the mind. 'The long shadows of the hills and the refracted light gave a supernatural aspect to the surrounding country.' Tired men began to hallucinate. At one point during the night 'amidst the savage yells and discordant noise of the Indian drums we heard the sound of a bugle,' remembered Taylor. 'It brought us to our feet at once. "Custer was coming at last" was our first thought.' But it was not so. 'Where was Custer? What had happened to him?' asked Windolph. Private Thompson with C Company thought it 'natural' that the troopers 'should sneer at the idea of Custer getting the worst of any fight'; he had never lost a battle. They 'were greatly puzzled about the whereabouts of Custer', but dismissed pessimistic speculation as 'all bosh'. Questions evoked 'an impatient reply', recalled Godfrey. 'Why had he abandoned us?' appealed Windolph, unable to comprehend that he may have been killed. 'Not lucky Custer.'

It was a depressing night. 'The deep voices of the braves, the howling of the squaws, the shrill piping of the children and the barking of the dogs made night hideous,' said Thompson. Virtually the entire command had not replenished its water bottles for more than 24 hours. Many had drunk them dry early on during the battle. Wounded troopers were distressed. 'You could hear them crying out for water all through the night,' remembered Windolph. They continued to scratch at their shallow earth scrapes, mindful of what would come at dawn. 'Off to the east pink and yellow light began to show.' Dawn was approaching.[12]

At 'about three o'clock just as it was growing light,' observed Private Taylor, 'there came two rifle shots from a low ridge in our front.' It broke the tensions of the night. 'This may have been the Indian's signal to open fire,' he surmised, 'for in less time than it takes to write about it a perfect shower of bullets followed from all along their line.' The Indians commenced long-range sniping interspersed with occasional ground forays. This time, unlike the day before, greater casualties were inflicted. Reno was to lose 48 men killed and wounded this day compared to 11 on the previous. 'The ping of the bullets and the groaning and struggling of the wounded horses was oppressive,' remarked Thompson. The effectiveness of this fire convinced Benteen of the need for limited counter-attacks to dislodge braves who were clearly closing in. Most of H Company's casualties, four men killed and 18 wounded, came from the grey plumes of gunfire spurting out from Sharpshooter's Ridge behind them; this dominated the perimeter but more especially Benteen's exposed southernmost 'tail' nearer the river. Benteen's men had not burrowed down sufficiently during darkness; the men were tired and wishfully assumed that Custer must be on his way.

A flurry of activity accompanied the renewed firing. Lieutenant Gibson, with the exposed H Company, reported that 'the Indians had a clear fire at us from four sides, and my only wonder is that every one of us wasn't killed'. There were only three or four shovels in the whole command, so as Godfrey described 'axes, hatchets, knives, table-forks, tin cups, and halves of canteens were brought into use'. Benteen urgently conferred with Reno. Something had to be done and he wanted reinforcements for H Company in order to do it.[13]

Archaeological research has confirmed that warriors were firing into the perimeter from two primary concentrations to the north, from the north-eastern side of Sharpshooter's Ridge and from around the knoll. Further concentrations have been found in the ravines south of H Company. The majority of bullets that impacted inside the perimeter were Springfield carbine, clear corroboration that captured rifles were used against the Reno-Benteen command. The density of these strikes strongly suggests that incoming fire was indeed heavy. Army cartridges are linear in their distribution whereas the Indians' are bunched or clustered. A mass of Indian cartridge finds also points to extensive fire from folds in the flat plain to the east. 'The bullets fell like a perfect shower of hail,' said

Lieutenant Gibson, 'and every instant I thought I certainly would be the next struck.'[14]

Pressure was indeed building up against the southern side of the perimeter from finger-shaped ravines spreading up from the river above the Indian village. In Gibson's opinion, 'Our position became so desperate and our force depleted so rapidly by killed and wounded that it became absolutely necessary to do something if we hoped to live through the day.' An Indian shot one of Gibson's troopers, then rushed into the perimeter and struck him with his coup stick. He was riddled with bullets as he sped away. Long Road, the Sans Arc youth killed, was, according to the Cheyenne Stands in Timber, despondent over the death of his brother, killed the week before at the Rosebud. 'They knew he did not want to live any more.' Archaeological research has uncovered nine bullets at intervals marking the progress of Long Road's rush up to the commemorative pile of rocks outside the H Company line. It illustrates the courage and conviction of a young brave, who unsettled the troopers that witnessed his lone charge. Lieutenant Godfrey nearby saw that 'he was in such close proximity to the lines and so exposed to the fire that the other Indians could not carry his body away'.

This was also the same day that the junction between Custer and Terry was to be achieved. It was generally thought that Custer must be close by. Even though there was no sign of him, nobody thought of Terry.[15]

'Forward' Terry

At dawn on 26 June Terry's men were 20 miles away and on the verge of effecting the promised junction with Custer. But there was no sign of the 7th Cavalry. Lieutenant Bradley's scouts were exceedingly stiff, trail-worn after the 55 miles they had covered the day before. By 0400 hours they were scouting toward the Little Bighorn, their attention attracted to heavy smoke clouds spiralling into the sky 15 to 20 miles away. While still in the vicinity of the

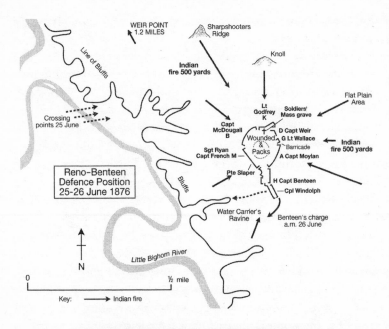

Reno-Benteen defence position, 25-26 June

Reno and Benteen demonstrated that they were able to hold back the Indian onslaught from prepared positions with 60% of the regiment's strength, an argument suggesting that Custer's force might have survived if it had fought together.

Bighorn River, they made contact with a group of three Crow scouts. Bradley's own Crows spoke to them and returned in a state of obvious distress, which Terry's chief of scouts surmised 'boded some misfortune there was no doubt'. As the scouts exchanged news their composure was replaced by visible grief. 'The Crows one by one broke off from the group of listeners and going aside a little distance sat down alone, weeping and chanting that dreadful mourning song, and rocking their bodies to and fro.' Fighting had occurred, Bradley soon discovered, at the point where the smoke was still visible. 'It was a terrible, terrible story, so different from the outcome we had hoped for this campaign,' Bradley later wrote.

According to the frustratingly slow interpretations and halting translations, 'the corpses of Custer's men were strewn all over the country,' Bradley heard, 'and it was probable before this that the last one was killed'. A party who had apparently taken refuge in the hills could not possibly hold out for long 'for the Sioux immensely outnumbered them and were attacking them in dense masses on all sides'. Bradley spotted Terry's column advancing as black dots two miles away and immediately rode back to exchange the doleful news he had received. Terry, now joined by Gibbon, listened 'with blank faces and silent tongues and no doubt heavy hearts', but there was scepticism. 'The voice of doubt and scorning was raised.' It seemed incomprehensible to some members of the staff that a regular cavalry regiment could be worsted by a group of savages, whatever the odds. 'The story was sneered at' by some elements, Bradley explained, 'such a catastrophe it was asserted was wholly improbable, nay impossible'. Even if a battle had been fought, it was 'condescendingly admitted ... then Custer was victorious'. Bradley was uneasy. 'Did we doubt the tale? I could not; there was an undefined vague something about it, unlooked for though it was, that commanded assent.' Terry remained thoughtful. The objective had been to join with Custer and squeeze the Indians in a vice between the commands. Sticking to the plan was the only recourse. The infantry had been on the march all morning and by midday had rejoined the cavalry, achieving a further 12 miles. 'Forward!' cried Terry, his first contribution to the animated discussion.

The whole column advanced together. 'Notwithstanding the stiffened limbs', a factor of 34 miles covered the day before, the likelihood 'of an early arrival at the village and a brush with the Indians imparted a wonderful animation to their movements and urged them on at a rapid gait'. However, nobody was certain whether this was an advance or a rescue mission. Sinister portents of disaster were starting to sap their offensive frame of mind. Terry's column was supposed to be the 'anvil' upon which Custer was to strike the 'hammer' of the 7th. 'If the savages had been able to destroy Custer's noble six hundred,' Bradley considered with some trepidation, 'what can we hope to accomplish with our paltry four?'[16]

Captain Benteen's counter-attack burst over the crest of his exposed southern perimeter position just as the Indians began its steep ascent to reach him. 'I was getting mad,' Benteen had declared to his troopers, and when he gave the word each was 'to yell as if provided with a thousand throats'. Even while forming up, Private Thompson 'could not see how I could possibly get there alive for the bullets of the Indians were ploughing up the sand and gravel in every direction'. 'Are you ready?' Benteen shouted. 'Yes!' was the shouted response. 'Charge down there and drive them out.' They launched themselves over the crest of the ridgeline straight into the unsuspecting Indians. 'With a cheer, away they dashed,' said Thompson, 'their revolvers in one hand and their carbines in the other.' So steep was the slope that the plunging troopers had difficulty remaining on their feet as, shrieking and shouting, they stumbled and tumbled around the sagebrush. Only one man remained behind, who, according to Godfrey, 'lay in his pit crying like a child'.

The Indians had been steadily infiltrating their way up the thin finger-like ravines leading to the river below. They were overwhelmed by the momentum of the charge. Benteen described how:

'We dashed into the unsuspecting savages who were amusing themselves by throwing clods of dirt, arrows by hand, and otherwise, for simply pure cussedness among us; to say that 'twas a surprise to them, is mild form, for they somersaulted and vaulted as so many trained acrobats, having no order in getting down those ravines, but quickly getting; devil take the hindmost!'

Lieutenant Godfrey satisfactorily observed that 'the Indians were driven nearly to the river'. 'Yelling and firing, we went at the "double quick",' said Windolph, 'and the Indians broke and ran.' Presently Reno called out 'Get back, men, back', and the whole line moved back, unscathed, to their scrapes back on top of the hill. A storm of fire began lashing the crest line again and, as Godfrey related, 'the one man who did not go out was shot in the head and killed instantly'.[17]

Long-range sniping had been exacting a lethal toll on Reno's men all day. Lieutenant Varnum recalled fire bursting all around the perimeter at a rapid rate, 'so we just laid still and made no reply to them whatever. We just let them shoot.' Windolph was watching his friend, 'a young fellow named Jones', struggling out of his great-coat as the sun burned off the night chill. As he rolled on the ground working out his arms and shoulder under cover 'I heard him cry out'. He was shot through the heart. Another bullet ricocheted through Windolph's clothing, then his rifle butt exploded as a bullet split it apart. He joined in the universal specu-lation that this sniper 'could shoot too well to have been a full-blood Indian'. Varnum, like his comrades, was intimidated by the intensity and accuracy of fire raining down on their positions. They observed one place in the long grass about 100 yards away where the Indians 'would lie just behind the ridge, and it would be just one ring of smoke from their guns behind the entire range'. They were helpless. 'We would simply lie still and let them shoot away their ammunition,' he said.

Sergeant John Ryan with M Company on the northern side of the perimeter recalled one particularly lethal sniper ensconced on Sharpshooter's Ridge, who 'I must give credit for being a good shot'. Experiences on Reno Hill were to contradict former assump-tions that dismissed Indians as poor shots, and add further credibility to the long-range damage that must have been meted out to Custer's troopers the day before. Ryan described:

'While we were lying in this line he fired a shot and killed the fourth man on my right. Soon afterward he fired again and shot the third man. His third shot wounded the man on my right, who jumped back from the line, and down among the rest of the wounded. I thought my turn was coming next.'

Ryan's organised response was to jump up with Captain French and some half-dozen members of the company and pour a counter volley into the direction of the incoming fire. 'There were no more men killed at that particular spot,' he declared.

The exposed troopers were certainly getting the worse of these long-range exchanges. The Indians, cloaked by the long grass, moved their positions around using the dips and folds in the ground. They were not totally impervious, however, to return fire. One Lakota warrior, Dog's Back Bone, called out to accompanying tribesmen to be cautious as they edged forward. 'Be careful,' he declared, 'it's a long way from here but their bullets are coming fierce.' An incoming round penetrated just above his eyebrow, killing him instantly.[18]

Ever since the fighting had begun the day before, the command had been denied water. There were tantalising glimpses of it for those on the west side of the perimeter, viewing the Little Bighorn River flowing below. 'Excitement and heat made our thirst almost maddening,' declared Lieutenant Godfrey. Private Taylor saw 'a river of clear and cool water' barely a few hundred yards away. Turning aside to avoid the tormenting image, he was treated to the view of 'the snow-topped range of the Bighorn Mountains, seemingly but a short distance' to the south-west. Various expedients were employed to alleviate thirst. 'Chewing lead from a bullet and the inner thick leaves of the prickly pear' gave little succour, observed Taylor. Godfrey described how troopers:

'Put pebbles in their mouths to excite the glands; some ate grass roots, but did not find relief. Some tried to eat hard bread, but after chewing it awhile would blow it out of their mouths like so much flour.'

'The sun beat down on us,' said Private Jacob Adams with H Company, 'and we became so thirsty that it was almost impossible to swallow.' Occupying high ground confers tactical advantage in a siege situation, but rarely water. 'Men began to clamor for water,' claimed Taylor. 'Many of them had not tasted water for 36 hours.' Tongues swelled and many could hardly speak. 'Men tried to eat hardtack, but could not raise enough saliva to moisten them; several tried grass but it stuck to their lips, and not one could spit or speak plainly.' Conditions for the wounded were even worse. 'Many soldiers volunteered to go to the river to get some water,' said Taylor, 'or perish in the attempt.'

An appeal from Dr Henry Porter, the only surviving physician remaining with the 7th, prompted Captain Benteen to seek volunteers to go for water. 'The wounded were crying for water,' stated Porter, 'and ought to have it.' Benteen's counter-attack had opened a tenuous route. 'I had the key,' he said, 'to the beautiful blue water that had been flowing so ripplingly at our very feet for two days.'

A group of 15 volunteers made the first foray, covered by four sharpshooters. Many were subsequently awarded the Congressional Medal of Honor. 'This was extremely hazardous,' recalled Private Slaper of M Company. The Indians dominated the river approaches by fire.

'It was about thirty feet from the mouth of the coulee [ravine], and we had to cover this thirty feet entirely exposed to Indian bullets at short range, fill the canteens or camp kettles from the stream, and go back again under fire.'

Young Two Moons, a Northern Cheyenne, enjoyed the discomfiture of a soldier, stripped to his underclothes, running the gauntlet of fire.

'He carried a quart cup in one hand and a canteen in the other. When he reached [the river] he threw himself in water, filling his vessels and drinking at the same time. Half the time they could not see him because of the water thrown up by the bullets. Then he ran up the hill again and entered the breastworks unhurt though they had been firing at him all this time.'[19]

Several runs were made, including one by Private Thompson from C Company. Coffee kettles were holed on several occasions, spraying the precious liquid as men made their desperate forays. Thompson recalled the situation at Dr Porter's dressing station when he arrived with water. 'Offers of money by the wounded for a drink of water was painful to hear,' he said. "Ten dollars for a drink," said one. "Fifteen dollars for a canteen," said a second. "Twenty dollars," said a third and so the bidding went on as at an auction.' Conditions in the makeshift hospital were fearful: oppressive heat beneath stretched canvas covers, the stench and flies. Corporal Michael Madden, an Irishman in K Company, was carried in to face a leg amputation, his leg having been shattered in two places by gunfire during the water run. Dr Porter's mule carrying the vital medical supplies was lost, including the chloroform. Madden was plied with a quart of whisky for 20 minutes before being held for the surgeon's knife. He allegedly whispered after enduring the trauma that for another quart of whisky – 'Docthor, cut off me other leg!'[20]

Entrenching the hilltop position granted the 7th Cavalry its first stability in a fast-moving battle. They had not planned for anything other than a pursuit and had anticipated no more than a skirmish to eject the Indians from the village. Both sides had adopted static positions and had plenty of ammunition. The Indians had captured theirs alongside a considerable quantity of carbines, and Reno and Benteen could draw on 24,000 rounds from the pack train. Both officers in this static fight began to display the same qualities of courage and resolve that had earned them their distinguished Civil War reputations. Soldiers felt for the first time, despite a dire predicament, that their officers were in charge. Had Custer been informed by Crook what to expect following the Rosebud, he might have occupied a form of bastion to intimidate the village into retreat. Reno subsequently wrote to Sherman a few days after the battle, 'I believe the 7th Cavalry would have whipped them properly handled – if I could stand them off with half the Regiment should not the whole whip them?' The Indians may have been compelled to attack and face the disciplined firepower that had earned the frontier army its rare open battle successes in the past. If not compelled to fight, Custer could have delivered a mass of Indians, encumbered by families, into the waiting and entrenched arms of Terry's column, approaching from the other end of the Little Bighorn Valley.

Reno, to a lesser extent, and certainly Benteen, were lauded by those under command for their conduct during the siege. Private Taylor thought Benteen 'one of the bravest acting men of our entire command', and Windolph 'one of the noblest soldiers who ever lived'. Reno had pulled himself together sufficiently to play a role in what became a joint command of the battle around the hilltop. His frightening setback in the valley bottom, criticised subsequently by armchair commentators, would have taxed any leader of men and overwhelmed a lesser.

By late afternoon, fire directed against the perimeter slackened off. 'Then something happened,' said Corporal Windolph, 'that I'll never forget, if I live to be a hundred.' Huge clouds of smoke began to lift lazily into the air as dusk approached, as the Indians set fire to the prairie grass in the valley bottom. Soldiers anxiously peered over the escarpment to discern what was going on. By about 1800 hours it was apparent that the village was on the move. 'They commenced moving about sunset and they were in sight till darkness came,' Benteen observed. 'It was a straight line about three miles and I think it was at least three miles long and a half a mile wide, as densely packed as animals could be.' Reno likened the column 'to that of a large division of the cavalry corps of the Army of the Potomac' during the Civil War. Beneath the dense clouds of smoke the puzzled troopers caught fleeting glimpses of thousands of Indians on foot and horseback, pony herds, travois, dogs and pack animals. 'It was like some Biblical exodus,' declared Windolph, '…a mighty tribe on the march.' A ruse was suspected. Once the families were out of danger, the warriors would be back to finish them off. They continued to man the perimeter.[21]

At the same time Terry's column was advancing slowly in fighting order. 'It was now sufficiently evident,' said Lieutenant James Bradley, his chief of scouts, 'that we had Indians in our front.' Three companies with the Gatling battery were on the right paralleling a column of four infantry companies on the left. In the centre were the pack mules, guarded front and rear by another infantry company. Groups of Indians were becoming increasingly visible moving down the valley and along the bluffs, from the opposite direction.

Terry had successfully completed his part of the operation and was ready for the junction with Custer. He was within striking distance of the Little Bighorn and able to apprehend Indian moves coming his way. In theory Terry's scheme of manoeuvre had worked, but the outcome was not as countenanced. At the beginning of the campaign, any sign of an approaching Indian mass encumbered by non-combatants would have provoked immediate offensive action. Not so now. Terry's men observed the build-up of this force with some trepidation. The very apparel of the Indians seemed to confirm the sinister reports controversially received from the Crow scouts. Lieutenant Roe, with his 2nd Cavalry contingent on the bluffs, could, according to Bradley, 'see a long line of moving dark objects defiling across the prairie from the Little Bighorn toward the Bighorn [rivers]'. It appeared 'as if the village were in motion retreating before us'. Numerous bodies of warriors seemed to be on the move in the twilight of approaching dusk. There were a few exchanges of shots, but a general reluctance to engage this force. Those nearest to Roe 'appeared to be clothed in blue uniforms, and carrying guidons,' observed Bradley. Although it was probably wishful thinking to assume that they might be from Custer, an attempt was made to communicate with them. It was met with a volley of fire.

Bradley was relieved to hear that camp was being set up as the shadows lengthened. He was convinced that there were a thousand warriors ensconced in the timbers and folds in the ground before them. 'They would have given our whole command a desperate fight had we advanced that evening another mile.' Bradley's view was that 'it was only for the lack of an hour or two more of daylight that we did not come upon them in force'. A battle would have resulted and he would not have been confident of the outcome. 'Their village was retreating,' he concluded, and the warriors to his front 'were there to cover it'. No single column had been able to over-face this force, and when it did disperse, it would be of its own accord.

Terry established camp on the present site of the Crow Agency, near the battlefield. He was within 3 miles of the village and 8¾ miles from Reno Hill.[22]

American Horse, the Oglala chief, had heard that 'a good many' troops were again approaching the village. His warriors left Reno Hill and returned to camp. 'They had fought for two days now and thought that they had fought enough.' The Minneconjou Red Horse said that 'the coming of the walking soldiers was the saving of the soldiers on the hill'. The Sioux had developed a healthy respect for the longer-range infantry Springfield rifle. 'Sioux cannot fight the walking soldiers,' he said, 'being afraid of them, so the Sioux hurriedly left.'[23]

The aftermath

Sheridan's 1876 campaign was a failure. It was a simple scheme of action but the supreme commander chose not to provide the coordination required to achieve a more precise junction of the three columns, which, because of poor communications, might encompass hundreds of square miles. His strongest column had been defeated; the second, more mobile and offensive, was virtually annihilated; and the third was simply deterred from offering combat.

On the morning of 27 June Terry's column finally filed through the Indian village. 'In passing through their camp,' recalled Private Homer Coon, with I Company, 7th Infantry, they began to comprehend with dreadful realisation what they might find. 'We came across a dead cavalry horse which had been cut open and a dead naked soldier was forced head foremost into the horse's belly.' Lieutenant Bradley had located the site of the Custer fight 'when the body of a horse attracted our attention to the field'. It was as suspected, 'the appalling sight was revealed to us of his entire command in the embrace of death'.

Colonel Gibbon, as yet uninformed, riding through the camp, recalled that 'the desire was intense to solve as soon as possible the dread doubt which now began to fill our minds'. The omens were not good. Searching the camp rubbish pile revealed 'a pair of bloody drawers, upon which was plainly written the words, "Sturgis – 7th Cavalry"'. Lieutenant James Porter's buckskin shirt was recognised, 'with a bullet hole passing through it'. Search parties out combing the hills to the east of the camp returned. Gibson listened to the exchange with Terry from the officer in charge:

> 'His voice trembled as he said, "I have a very sad report to make. I have counted one hundred and ninety-seven dead bodies lying in the hills." "White men?" was the first question asked. "Yes, white men." A look of horror was upon every face, and for a moment no one spoke.'

Cheers resounded as Terry's command arrived atop Reno Hill. 'There was scarcely a dry eye; hardly a word was spoken,' said Lieutenant Godfrey. Terry was probably relieved that at least some of the 7th remained alive to be found. 'Quivering lips and hearty grasping of hands gave token of thankfulness for the relief and grief for the dead.' Stunned disbelief met the response to the first question – 'Where is Custer?'[24]

On 28 June the grim clear-up of the battlefield began. 'The early morning was bright,' said Godfrey, 'as we ascended to the top of the highest point whence the whole field came into view, with the sun on our backs.' 'What are those?' asked several, referring to 'what appeared to be white boulders'. Godfrey nervously scanned the field with his binoculars and dully responded, 'The dead!' Captain Weir's anguished response encapsulated the agony that was to remain like a canker with the 7th Cavalry until 1890. 'Oh, how white they look!' he exclaimed. 'How white!'[25] He had been prepared to disregard orders to effect a desperate junction with

Custer and failed. It would haunt him the rest of his days, and they would not be many. Weir would drink himself to death before the end of the year; he was only 38 years old. Lieutenant French, who had distinguished himself throughout the battle, was dismissed from the service as a result of alcoholism within 30 months. He died aged 39, six years after the fight. Reno, although exonerated at the subsequent Board of Inquiry in 1879, was certainly not congratulated. Within four years he had been dismissed from the service, castigated as a 'Peeping Tom', and was drinking heavily. He died in obscurity nine years later.

Both Reno and Benteen were aware of the uncompromising traditional US Army view of failure. They would have some explaining to do, having allowed themselves to be defeated by the savages. Moreover it had been a particularly one-sided affair. Half the 7th Cavalry lay dead or wounded: 210 had been slain with Custer, and Reno lost 53 killed and 60 wounded. Exhaustive research of Indian sources reveal that perhaps 31 males, six squaws and probably four children perished in the battle. R. G. Hardorff,[26] consulting 36 sources, has grouped their casualty ranges within response frequencies. Only three sources identify 61 to 83 Indian casualties, and three fewer than 20; the majority of responses claim a mean average of 30 to 40. This represented a military catastrophe by any measurement. The whites on the battlefield were probably aware of this and exaggerated the odds and casualties suffered on the Indian side, or remained guarded. Only about seven lodge pole burials were found and very few bodies in the vicinity of the Indian village. Interestingly, a *Rocky Mountain News* correspondent dispatch commenting on the battle reported that 'it is the popular belief in Terry's camp that not more than fifty of them [Indians] were slain'.[27] Indian firepower had demolished Custer's companies despite their bravely standing firm. The gross disparity in the outcome suggests, as do Indian commentaries, that this did not take long. Even a conservative estimate of a two-hour fight has Custer's troopers perishing at the rate of two to three a minute. Interestingly the firepower disparities have only recently been unearthed by archaeological digs and only generally alluded to throughout a hundred years of 'Custerama'.

The sight of Custer's corpse personified to Benteen the extent of the 7th Cavalry's failure. 'There he lies, God damn him, he'll never fight any more,' was Benteen's alleged comment. He was the first to identify the corpse. This was not characteristic. Benteen may not have liked Custer, but his personal relationship had no impact on the outcome of the battle. A more plausible description was provided by Private Jacob Adams from Benteen's company, who told Godfrey that Benteen simply stated, 'By God, that's him,' and walked away. Benteen's battlefield responses are more about the awkward military and professional questions that would come his way in the future. The Custer legend was already coalescing because it was claimed that Custer's corpse, unlike those surrounding him, was not mutilated – out of respect. Fifty yards from Custer lay the body of Private Tom Tweed from Calhoun's company. 'His crotch had been split up with an axe and one of his legs thrown up around his shoulder. He was shot with arrows in both eyes.' Private Edwin Pickard, observing his comrades nearby, wrote that 'it made me sick to see my fellow troopers of F Troop lying on the hillside, dismembered, with stakes driven through their chests, with their heads crushed in, and many of them with their arms and legs chopped off'. Custer was stripped and had been shot in the head and side but not scalped. As he was balding and had cut his hair short for the campaign, it was not worth removing.

Why was Custer's body not defiled? Many Indians had assumed that they were fighting Crook, not Custer. Godfrey's idealised description of his 'naked body in a sitting posture', leaning against two fallen troopers, was a heroic posture, probably paying attention to Elizabeth Custer's sensibilities. 'His upper right arm along and on the topmost body, his right forearm and hand supporting his head in an inclining posture like one resting or asleep.' The image might be likened to others of classical antiquity, such as the statue of the 'Dying Gaul'. Custer may have been left alone as a token of respect, but both Godfrey and scout Frank Gerard noticed that an arrow shaft had been forced up the Lieutenant Colonel's penis.[28]

Survivors of the 7th Cavalry were to be haunted by these images for the rest of their days. 'I can never forget the sight,' admitted Lieutenant Godfrey. Lieutenant Gibson, who had exchanged his place in death with the young Lieutenant Jack Sturgis, called it 'the most horrible sight my eyes ever rested on'. Sergeant Ryan declared, 'I served through the Civil War, and saw many hard sights on the battlefield, but I never saw such a sight as I saw there.' It was a picture of unrequited horror and was captured in Captain Walter Clifford's diary account of 27 June:

'Our camp is surrounded with ghastly remains of the recent butchery. The days are scorching hot and still, and the air is thick with the stench of the festering bodies. We miss the laughing gaiety that usually attends a body of soldiery on the battlefield. A brooding sorrow hangs like a pall over every thought. It seems too horrible for belief – that we must wake and find it only a shuddering dream. Every sound comes to us in a muffled monotone, and a dull dogged feeling of revenge seems to be the prevailing sentiment. The repulsive-looking green flies that have been feasting on the swollen bodies of the dead are attracted to the campfires by the smell of cooking meat. They come in such swarms that a pervasive swing of a tree branch is necessary to keep them from settling on the food... They crawl over the neck and face, into eyes and ears, under the sleeves with a greedy eagerness and such clammy, sticky feet as to drive taste and inclination for food away...'

He echoed everyone's sentiments when he declared, 'let us bury our dead and flee from this rotting atmosphere'.[29]

Reno's 60 wounded were transported on improvised litters and travois pulled by mules 15 miles to the paddle-steamer *Far West*. The vessel had amazingly pushed up the Bighorn as far as the mouth of the Little Bighorn. The crew laid freshly cut beds of grass on the deck to receive the casualties. Starting on 3 July, Captain Marsh achieved a navigational first and a speed record on the Yellowstone and Missouri rivers when 710 miles and 54 hours later the paddle-steamer nosed into Bismarck landing. Another trooper died during the journey. That night, 5 July, the first dispatch was tapped out by J. M. Carnahan, the local telegraph operator. It read: 'Bismarck, D. T., July 5 1876: – General Custer attacked the Indians June 25, and he, with every officer and man in five companies, were killed.'

Two Montana newspapers, the *Bozeman Times* and *Helena Herald*, scooped the *Bismarck Tribune* story in Extras on 3 and 4 July. The Centennial Celebration was shattered by the *Helena Herald* headlines of 4 July, which read: 'A Terrible Fight – General Custer and his Nephew Killed – The Seventh Cavalry cut to pieces – The Whole Number Killed 315'. Eastern papers received the news by late editions of 5 July. The nation went into virtual mourning. 'The news received last evening of the defeat of Custer and the massacre of his entire command,' declared the *Helena Herald* editorial, 'fell upon the festivities of the day with a gloom that could not be shaken off.'[30]

On 6 July the *Far West* reached Fort Abraham Lincoln with the surviving wounded of the 7th Cavalry. After the shock of the initial statement, the officers were divided into groups to inform the widows. 'We started on our sad errand a little before seven o'clock on the 6th July morning,' said Lieutenant C. L. Gurley from the 6th Infantry. Elizabeth Custer's maid Maria was woken up. Katherine Gibson and a number of assembled wives recalled the day before. 'It was so stiflingly hot that we lingered on our porches until after tattoo.' Even then there had been a commotion and Horn Toad, an Indian scout, had relayed a disturbing message derived from Indian sources. 'Custer killed. Whole command killed.' 'It couldn't be true,' was the disbelieving response, and 'we sat talking late into the night, stubbornly refusing to accept the Indian's statement.' There was no other recourse but to wait out the night, 'springing up at every distant sound, thinking it might be a courier with messages'. At daybreak the mournful steamboat whistle, 'penetrating as a hunter's horn', brought the news they craved, 'good or bad'.

'All of those from forlorn old Fort Rice were safely accounted for' except for young Jack Sturgis. 'It was with hysterical joy' that Katherine received two letters from her husband Frank written later and describing the massacre. Many of the other wives of the survivors 'were weeping, quietly and reverently'. But, as Katherine Gibson explained, 'on the other hand, practically every house at Lincoln was visited by death'. Lieutenant Gurley, accompanied by Captain McCaskey and Dr Middletown, relayed the news 'of the awful result of the battle on the Little Bighorn' to the ladies of the Custer household in Elizabeth Custer's parlour. 'Imagine the grief of those stricken women,' he later related, 'their sobs, their floods of tears, the grief that knew no consolation.'[31]

There was still campaigning to be done for the survivors of the 7th Cavalry. They were not to return to their start point at Fort Abraham Lincoln until 26 September. 'Tears came unbidden to many an eye,' wrote a correspondent, who witnessed the return. 'The stock was in fine condition, in the main, but the men were sunburnt, worn and dusty.' Many familiar faces were missing. 'Those with whom Bismarck people were best acquainted lie in the trenches on the Little Bighorn.' It was a sad affair. There was no band and the facings and trimmings of the officer's quarters had been painted black as a symbol of mourning. The widows and families of the dead had already left the post.

'The troops that left Lincoln in the spring are now all in,' wrote the *Bismarck Tribune* correspondent, 'except ... those who sleep the long sleep.'[32]

Postscript

'A soldier may have escaped from
General Custer's battle to this point.'

New York Times, 21 August 1876

There is a monument on US County Highway 447 located about
6½ miles south of the Interstate 94 Rosebud Interchange. It is
astride the route Custer's 7th Cavalry travelled on 22 June towards
the Little Bighorn, after leaving Terry's bivouac. Constructed from
local stone on a concrete base, the bronze plaque inscription reads:

GRAVE OF UNKNOWN MAN:
IN 1886, RANCHERS BURIED NEAR HERE WHAT
MANY BELIEVE TO BE THE REMAINS OF PRIVATE
NATHAN SHORT, CO C, 7TH US CAVALRY. SHORT
WAS BELIEVED TO BE CARRYING A MESSAGE
FROM GEN. CUSTER AT THE BATTLE OF THE
LITTLE BIGHORN, 70 MILES S.W. OF THIS POINT
ON JUNE 25 1876.

ERECTED BY:
THE 7TH CAVALRY REGIMENT ASSOCIATION AND
THE 1ST CAVALRY DIVISION ASSOCIATION IN
CO-OPERATION WITH LOCAL RESIDENTS 1983.

The original gravesite was obliterated by the passage of the present
road and is about 100 yards away on the west right-of-way on the

county road. If Private Short managed to elude his Indian pursuers during the battle, his journey to the junction of the Yellowstone River and Rosebud Creek would have been an epic of physical and mental endurance. Sergeant Kanipe, from his company, was convinced that he saw him before setting off to deliver Custer's message to Captain Benteen prior to the collapse of Custer's five companies.[1]

It is perhaps more likely that the trooper concerned was a survivor and not a messenger. Custer would not have dispatched him to the Rosebud Creek, knowing that Terry's final axis of advance would be south along the Bighorn River (see the accompanying map). The significance of Tullock's Fork to Terry's approach may have been known. In any case, the drainages from Tullock's Fork, stretching north, offer the obvious covered escape route in that direction, keeping away from Indians massing in the east and south-east, separating the Custer and Reno battalions.

What was influencing the survivor's choice of direction? Wounded or not, his first desire was to escape the battlefield. Like Curly, the Crow scout, who preceded him and survived the battle, the imperative would be to get away, not pause to review the progress of fighting behind him. Curly, following Mitch Bouyer's advice 'to ride back over the [Custer] trail a ways and then go to one of the high points', followed a stream bed that eventually branched off in a northerly direction. Bouyer was 'pointing eastward over to the high ridge east of the Custer Hill'. Curly stated that 'with glasses he watched the battle a while and then rode away'. He would not have been interested in the tactical niceties of a lost engagement. 'He saw how the Indians circled Custer's men.'[2] A glance was sufficient. All his instinctive Indian sensibilities were focused on escape. He exchanged his clothing for that of a dead Sioux, wrapped himself in a blanket and exfiltrated out, riding toward the Pine Hills. Short may well have followed a similar route, proven by Curly to be achievable.

Plodding northwards, Short would have wanted to put as much distance between himself and the encircling Indians as possible. By sunset he may have covered 15 to 20 miles. This is conjecture, but whatever the case, there was a typical high plains early summer storm recorded in the area. Cold, hard and driving rain would have obliged him, exhausted or wounded, to pause and await daylight. At first light he may have pressed on. There was no sign of the army, because Terry's column would have passed to the west, wending its way southwards along the Little Bighorn River. Short would eventually have emerged at the canyon entrance, where the Bighorn and Yellowstone rivers gradually converge, and stopped. As it was so wide, his only recourse was to continue eastwards along its southern bank and hope to locate the *Far West* paddle-steamer or attract the attention of a passing army supply vessel or civilian steamer. With no evidence of military activity, a dreadful realisation would have dawned. There was no option other than to follow the river's course in the vain hope of finding someone. He continued onwards, covering more than a hundred miles over a number of days after leaving Custer. Near the mouth of the Rosebud stream he may have noticed with some consternation that he had completed a gigantic circle. Moving south along the Rosebud Creek was a well-worn military trail, created by nearly 1,000 mounts – the same route he had ridden with Custer.

Wounded, injured or simply worn out, Short removed the bridle from his horse and tied it to a picket pin to enable it to graze.

On 21 August 1876, seven weeks after the battle, the *New York Times* reported on 'A Mystery of the Rosebud'. Its reporter, writing from a 'camp on the Yellowstone, at Rosebud River, Montana Territory', filed a report written two weeks before:

'A mystery, not reconcilable with any theory, envelops the finding near here of a 7th Cavalry horse shot through the head and a carbine lying beside him, and without other identification. A soldier may have escaped from General Custer's battle to this point; but if he then calculated to go down the river on a raft he would not have abandoned his arms, and as certainly if the Indians captured him they would not have left the carbine.'[3]

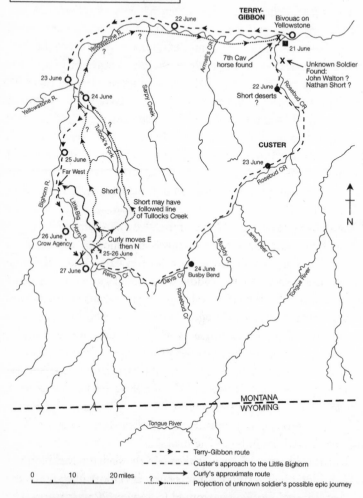

THE MYSTERY OF THE UNKNOWN
SOLDIER FOUND ON THE ROSEBUD

The mystery of the 'unknown soldier' on the Rosebud

Curly, an Indian scout, survived the battle. An unknown soldier – allegedly
Private Nathan Short – may have either deserted, or completed an epic
odyssey before succumbing a short distance from the confluence of the
Yellowstone and Rosebud rivers a few days after the battle. The available
evidence produces more questions than answers.

Shortly afterwards the 'bullet-pierced' body of a trooper was found several miles from the horse, 6 miles down the Rosebud.

The debate about a dead 7th Cavalry horse more than 70 miles from Custer Hill, with a carbine nearby and rumours of a dead soldier in the vicinity, has continued since.[4] It is fuelled by four known historical events. Nathan Short was known to have been present at the battle of the Little Bighorn. A dead sorrel roan 7th Cavalry horse (probably belonging to C Company) was found at the mouth of the Rosebud and an enlisted man's body further upstream. Later, in 1886, local ranchers unearthed a human skeleton adorned with pieces of army uniform. The so-called 'unknown man' was likely to be the same body discovered ten years before. The skull appeared shot through by a bullet. Was the man Nathan Short?

Lieutenant Godfrey, who commanded K Company in the hilltop fight, saw the carcase of the horse 'shot in the head' in August 1876 at a camp at the mouth of the Rosebud. 'Near the horse was a carbine; on the saddle was a small grain sack made of canvas and used by the 7th Cavalry only to carry oats on the march, when detached from the wagons.' His view was that the man escaped, killed his horse for meat and used the saddle straps to construct a raft, to float down the Yellowstone. Lack of ammunition may have caused him to discard the carbine. Apart from this statement, few people definitively saw the body discovered later. Evidence relating to it appears to be primarily based on hearsay or rumour. The story was prevalent among enlisted men but no officer formally linked the horse to the man.

Recent research suggests that although the skeleton had blond or reddish-blond hair – and Short was fair – it is more likely to be the body of Private John Walton from H Company, 22nd Infantry. The 27-year-old Walton went missing in the same area off the line of march on 10 August 1876, between the Rosebud and Yellowstone. His muster roll the following month recorded that he was 'supposed to have died on the trail or to have been killed by Indians'. He was known to be suffering from consumption (TB), and it was suspected that he 'died of exhaustion Aug 11 1876 while trying to make his way back to the camp on the Rosebud'.[5] Descriptions of his appearance fit that of the 'unknown man' found by the ranchers ten years later. Lost and despairing, Walton may have ended his suffering with a bullet.

A 7th Cavalry trooper did reach the Yellowstone, but the intriguing 'who?' may never be resolved. Lieutenant Godfrey noticed when he examined the grain sack on the neck of the dead horse that 'the oats in the bag had not been disturbed'. If Private Nathan Short had completed a circuitous 100-mile route, this could not have been the case. Oats was the only high-energy feed available to cavalry soldiers on the march, and why shoot the horse in any case? However, who is to deny that a canny messenger or resourceful survivor might apprehend a second stray horse or pick up an additional grain bag amid the chaos of abandoned horses and equipment around overrun companies?

It is conceivable that the trooper was a deserter who had slipped from the ranks shortly after Custer's column departed the Yellowstone. The Terry bivouac was completely vacated shortly after the Custer and Gibbon columns departed. An imperative to slip away may have been provided by the intimidating size of the Indian trail wending its way to a difficult fight on grossly unequal terms. Desertions in the field were common to all three columns, and the 7th was no exception – it lost six soldiers during this campaign. Private Charles Anderson from C Company deserted from the Powder River Supply Camp along the Yellowstone 24 hours before Custer set off, and was never apprehended. Three others absconded on 7 July after the battle, again from the supply camp. Privates Hugh Bonner and John H. Littlefield from B Company and Pasavan Williamson from G Company were picked up in 'a starving condition' following a remarkable flight down the Yellowstone and Missouri rivers. Two other veterans of the battle, Privates William Channell and Edler Nees from H Company, deserted on 26 July at the mouth of the Rosebud and were caught two days later near its junction with the Missouri. The 'unknown man' was probably from one of the companies in Custer's doomed battalion, as no officer or sergeant lived to report his absence – that meant from C, F, I or L Companies, and a light sorrel roan suggests C.

The story is an enigma. A deserter, who subsequently perishes riding a fragile raft down the Yellowstone and Missouri? If he survived, he could have lived an anonymous life in safety and civilisation. Likewise he may have been a rugged survivor from the field of honour, who succumbed eventually to wounds and exhaustion. The story of Private Nathan Short, if it was indeed he, encapsulates the results of recent research at the Little Bighorn. The prairie fire of 1983 sanitised many of the heroic myths that had grown around the sensational reporting of a debacle that rocked the American Centennial. Like the story of Nathan Short, it has further fuelled 'Custerama' by posing as many questions as answers.

The fact that the mysterious corpse on the Custer trail was not found until six weeks after the battle indicates the paralysis that news of the disaster imposed on Terry's and Crook's columns – they did not move for a month. A newspaper reporter with Crook wrote, 'General Terry is hopelessly crippled, and now awaits reinforcements.' Crook felt the same. The correspondent assessed that 'an actual consolidation of all the forces in the field would be a good move considering the overwhelming numbers of the Sioux'.[6] Perhaps Custer's legendary luck had rubbed off on Terry and Crook, because they at least survived the battle. As a consequence, they had no intention of taking further risks without reinforcement.

The great Sioux camp dispersed of its own accord, many of the bands withdrawing south-west toward the Bighorn Mountains. After celebrating, they moved north-east on to the prairie. Sitting Bull travelled further north-east, Long Dog's bands north-west, and Crazy Horse's followers eastwards, returning to their sacred Black Hills. Crook and Terry's inactivity encouraged the Indians to assume that overwhelming victory over Custer had settled the issue. The army would give up the campaign. Of course, it had precisely the opposite effect.

Sheridan decided to dispatch every available unit in the Division of the Missouri to assist Crook and Terry, and 18 companies of cavalry and 10 of infantry were soon on their way. The 7th Cavalry received 500 recruits from Jefferson Barracks, raising its strength to 1,205 enlisted men. Only later was it discovered that many were unable to ride! By the late autumn of 1876, 261 officers and 3,482 enlisted men were campaigning against the Sioux and Cheyenne. This represented a large part of the overall US Army total of scarcely 20,000 that could be mustered for combat. Sheridan cabled his superior, General W. T. Sherman, on 5 August: 'I have stripped every post from the line of Manitoba to Texas,' he announced. 'We want more mounted men.'[7]

By the time Crook and Terry received their reinforcements and got under way in August, Indian trails in their respective vicinities were over a month old. They inadvertently combined on 10 August, after mistaking each other for the enemy, and, now numbering 4,000, they proceeded ponderously north-east down the Tongue River Valley. Rain, mud and fatigue sapped their strength and spirits until they halted exhausted alongside the Powder River to await supplies. They never came closer than 100 miles to any sizeable Indian host.

Crook, only partially resupplied, set off on 22 August in a last attempt to salvage something from the lacklustre campaign. His resulting 'Starvation March' resulted in the chance discovery of a small Indian village at Slim Buttes, which was attacked on 9 September. Crook's troopers fought an inconclusive engagement the following day when his 2,000-strong force was counter-attacked by only 200 to 300 warriors from Crazy Horse's band. Still feeling confidently superior, the Indians attacked despite grossly inferior odds. Crook's men destroyed the camp and captured sufficient buffalo meat to alleviate near starvation, but were unable to pursue. His weary, ragged and miserable soldiers fell back to Crook City in the Black Hills. The terrible trek lasted until 13 September. Terry meanwhile pursued a cold trail, which took him north to the Yellowstone, where he gave up the chase. There was no stomach left for a decisive engagement with the Sioux, and with that the summer campaign came to an end.

Having lost the campaign, Congress, shocked by the Little Bighorn setback, proceeded to win the war. The Sioux Appropriation Bill was passed, forcing the Sioux to cede their remaining lands and withdraw to a specified reservation on the west bank of the Missouri. In September a commission visited the Agencies obliging the chiefs to 'touch the pen' and sell the Black Hills. General Sheridan then instituted the measures that ought to have preceded the 1876 campaign. All weapons and ponies were confiscated from the Agency Indians. Although this harsh treatment encouraged newly returned Indians to turn about and rejoin their roaming brethren, denied guns and horses there was no way that Agency Indians could reinforce hostile bands. With food supplies dwindling and amid constant army harassment, the winter campaign of 1876–77 finished the task that had been achievable 12 months before. Colonel Nelson A. Miles pursued the northward-bound Sioux without pause. A temporary cantonment was set up at the mouth of the Tongue River and Miles's 5th Infantry 'Walk-a-heaps', clad in buffalo overcoats and other cold-weather gear, combed the area between the Yellowstone and Missouri rivers. 'Bear's Coat', as the Indians called him, started on 5 November, and by 7 December had succeeded in driving Sitting Bull and Long Dog into Canada.

Crook launched another expedition from Fort Fetterman on 14 November with 400 Indian scouts and 2,000 regulars. Dull Knife's Northern Cheyenne village was sacked during a misty dawn on 25 November 1876 when Colonel Ranald Mackenzie's force of 1,100 horsemen destroyed 183 lodges hidden in a canyon of the Red Fork of Powder River. 'From the hilltops,' announced the Cheyenne squaw Iron Teeth, 'we Cheyennes saw our lodges and everything in them burned.' They lost their ponies, tepees and food. Crook returned to Fort Fetterman secure in the knowledge that starvation and freezing temperatures would do the rest. 'Those were terrible days,' recalled Cheyenne warrior Beaver Heart. 'The nights were alive with the cries of men tortured with wounds and women and children dying of cold.' They travelled on foot for 11 days before finding a camp of Oglala Sioux. 'Children were warmed back to life,' said Beaver Heart, 'by stuffing them into the stomachs of butchered horses.'[8]

Despite his eventual surrender at Fort Buford, Sitting Bull continued to resist passively, demanding fair and dignified treatment for his people. 'If a man loses anything and goes back and looks carefully for it,' he said, 'he will find it, and that is what the Indians are doing now when they ask you to give them the things that were promised them in the past.' He embraced the Ghost Dance, a spiritual panacea to preserve the Indian way of life. 'All Indians must dance, everywhere, keep on dancing,' announced its adherents. 'Pretty soon in next spring Great Spirit come.'[9] He came in another form for the celebrated Sioux Indian chief. On 15 December 1890 Agency tribal police shot and killed Sitting Bull when he and his supporters resisted arrest for supporting the Ghost Dance. Two weeks later, on 29 December, the 7th Cavalry, alongside other units, destroyed the last vestiges of armed Sioux resistance in an untidy skirmish at Wounded Knee. Shot down in the mud and snow, abandoned Indian bodies froze into grotesque shapes parodying the futility of war. Among the few cavalry dead was Lieutenant Wallace, who had survived the Little Bighorn 14 years before. It was the fourth day of Christmas. Custer's troopers got their revenge. The Sioux war was over.

* * *

Nearly 130 years after the event, the Indian wars offer an immediacy of experience still relevant to the modern soldier. Problems faced by the three columns in 1876 are not dissimilar to those faced by peace-keeping armies in the 21st century. Peace Support Operations (PSO) as conducted under the aegis of the UN or NATO or other multi-national organisations are operations of an expeditionary nature, often falling short of high-intensity conventional war. They operate across a spectrum of violence varying from low- to high-intensity operations, ratcheting up or down depending upon circumstances. To be successful a force needs to be 'credible', at least of sufficient strength to over-face conceivable opposition. Despite being the strongest military force to gather on the frontier since the Civil War, the credibility of Sheridan's tri-column 'policing' operation was questionable. A feature of modern peace-keeping is often the extent to which PSO contingents are over-extended. After two 20th-century World Wars and stand-off confrontations like the Cold War, involving the deployment of similar-size armies, nations sought a 'peace dividend' through drastically reducing regular forces. Cut-backs after major conflicts invariably impact on manpower in combat formations. Ironically they often fall to the infantry, the element most in demand for PSO. Massive demobilisations occurred at the end of the American Civil War despite the need for manpower to support operations on the frontier to secure westward expansion against the Indians. General Sheridan's force was required to police an area the size of England and Wales, containing 175,000 Indians, with scarcely 16,000 troops. Artillery was no substitute for manpower operating across such inhospitable terrain.

As is often the case today, Sheridan's troops were neither trained nor structurally configured and organised to conduct low-intensity *gendarmerie* operations. Much of the army's experience was relevant to the Civil War battlefield, where infantry, cavalry and artillery conducted combined operations. This was not appropriate to the conditions on the frontier in 1876. Indians had a low opinion of army fighting competence and refused to be pinned down by the 'fix and strike' conventional tactics employed by the military. Nothing occurred as the 1876 campaign progressed to impress the Indians otherwise. Credible though the three columns may have been relative to 19th-century frontier norms, they did not perform effectively enough to convince the Plains Indians that they should retire to reservations. An inferior force of half-naked but aggressive hostiles beat off Crook's first winter strike at the Powder River in

March 1876. An expanded force was worsted in open battle at the Rosebud in June; one of his battalions was so badly mauled that it was nearly overrun. Terry's column was likewise beaten at the Little Bighorn one week later, and the 7th Cavalry destroyed as an effective fighting unit. At no stage did the three columns demonstrate operational cohesion. The Indians picked them off one by one.

A feature of modern PSOs is the rash complacency that can often influence operations, encouraging risk-taking. None of Sheridan's columns feared or expected an attack. Civilised states have non-violent ways of settling disputes dependent on the assumption of willingness in many circumstances to back down. This is not a feature of the Third World and was not a characteristic of the 19th-century western frontier. Indians belonged to different and misunderstood societies with ingrained rivalries. They did not back down until blood was spilled. Indeed, their whole existence revolved around the warrior's way of life. An element of racism and feelings of pseudo-superiority affected army decisions. Like modern peace-keeping armies conducting expeditionary police operations, the US Army saw itself as restoring 'sanity' and 'civilisation' in its support of continental westward expansion. Complacency often results in the assumption that a low-tech foe will avoid a pitched battle with a superior adversary. All of Sheridan's columns were shocked at Indian willingness to embrace open battle. History is littered with similar examples, such as the French and American experience in Vietnam during the 1950s and '70s. G2 failure, as was the case in 1876, is caused by an inability to perceive different world perspectives, thereby increasing military risk.

All Custer's major decision points prior to the Battle of the Little Bighorn are instructive in leadership terms because alternative judgements might have saved the day. The choice at the Busby Bend to follow the Indian trail rather than scout the headwaters of the Rosebud first – as Terry ordered – reduced the likelihood of a synchronised junction with Terry. Opting for immediate attack on the basis of distant observations from the Crow's Nest, instead of lying up for an intended 24 hours, likewise prevented a combination with Terry. A battle fought in tandem would have reduced the odds. Fragmenting his command at the divide by detaching Benteen, then physically separating from Reno during the initial assault on the village, cost Custer the battle. The final decision at Weir Point to press on with the attack on the village without waiting for Benteen cost the command their lives.

Common to all these decisions was Custer's readiness to split his force to counter assumed superior Indian mobility. Indians would always run. The imperative to spread and disperse units to secure ground, often in support of political initiatives, is very much a characteristic of modern PSO operations. NATO garrisons in the Balkans in the 1990s and Coalition operations in Iraq in 2003 are examples. However, a suicidally brave and aggressive low-tech foe can annul technological superiority with superior numbers. The Chinese demonstrated this in Korea against UN forces in 1950 and the North Vietnamese against the Americans in the early 1970s. Peace-keeping operations in Lebanon in the 1990s and Iraq in 2003 have illustrated the damage that suicide-bomber attacks can inflict on a nation's military and political resolve. Low-tech foes encountered in PSO operations realise instinctively that they must close with their high-tech adversaries to inflict damage. This was no different during Colonial wars in the 19th century: a large British column was wiped out by Zulu warriors at Isandlwana in Natal, South Africa, three years after the Little Bighorn. Such was the case with the Custer column: its feeling of innate invincibility was shattered by a surprise confrontation with repeater rifles deployed in previously unknown quantities. Iraqi irregulars brought down high-tech helicopter platforms in 2003 using rudimentary but simple and modern RPG-7 anti-tank rocket-launchers. Allowing a low-tech foe to close against modern equipped and technically more proficient forces levels the combat playing field. Economics can also play a role. The advantage of the repeater rifle was obvious to the Indian. The US Government was constrained by an economic need to save money and conserve ammunition; it was ready to accept its own military advice that accurate long-range rifle fire would keep Indians at bay. It was the cheaper option.

PSO armies, normally following economic retrenchment, are often over-extended. As a consequence, technology is exploited to improve tactical and operational mobility to even the odds against overstretched forces. Mobility has become crucial in new peace-keeping operational scenarios. Unlike 20th-century World Wars, including the Cold War, there is no front line or rear area. Hostilities can occur at any point. Everyone, including logistic troops, is vulnerable to enemy action, and this has training and organisational implications. Logistics on the frontier were dangerously vulnerable and over-extended. The vulnerability and crucial importance of Custer's pack train, transporting his ammunition reserves, played a decisive role during the Battle of the Little Bighorn; its slow speed and cumbersome defence dogged Custer's offensive potential and weakened the effectiveness of his strike force.

Modern technology produces simple and effective weapons that are not difficult for unsophisticated opponents to master. This characteristic, allied to the high-risk strategies often employed by contemporary PSO contingents against a primitive foe, causes the greatest surprise if battle is offered. Indian warriors were able to close with Custer's columns, already divided to counter dispersion, and inflicted devastating damage. Custer did not configure his units to win a dismounted firepower contest. His troopers anticipated a pursuit. Simple-to-use but technologically advanced weapons have transformed operations in the Third World. No longer can 20 modern soldiers overcome 100 others. Custer was outgunned by his primitive opponents at the Little Bighorn and it was too late to adapt tactics to match. Crook succeeded at the Rosebud – but only just. Vital information regarding Indian firepower and their aggressive willingness to offer open battle was never passed to Custer.

Treatment of prisoners by an unsophisticated enemy in PSO operations is cruel at worse or indifferent at best. This was the situation on the frontier in 1876. To be wounded on the field at the Little Bighorn meant death; to be captured alive was worse. Torture and mutilation of prisoners and the dead encourage 'demonisation' of the enemy. If he is of a different culture or race the hatred engendered is worse. Suicide bombings are incomprehensible to the Western soldier who will generally sanctify life and seek to preserve his own during conflict. Almost suicidal Indian bravery and the seemingly mindless savagery meted out to the captured and fallen influenced the conduct of troopers fighting with Custer. Prospect of failure can quail faint hearts. Either there is determination to sell life dearly, or moral collapse follows. Stories are told of cavalry suicides during the last moments of resistance. Even if true, they were not widespread and did not influence the outcome of the battle. Psychological preparation for war is essential and accepted by most modern armed forces. How mentally prepared or trained the 7th Cavalry was to cope with impending catastrophe is open to conjecture.

Perhaps the primary lesson for PSOs is that it is simply another mode of conflict, like fighting in the desert, woods and mountains, or in cities. The credibility of the force is predicated on its ability to turn the level of violence up or down. Modern armies have learned that it is easier to 'dumb down' from high- to low-intensity operations. It was less demanding to conduct peace-keeping operations in Iraq in 2003 with the same combat troops that had just fought the conventional invasion. NATO forces in the Balkans, particularly Bosnia in the early 1990s, found it difficult to move from a low spectrum of violence to the conventional war-fighting capacity required to intimidate all sides into political agreement at the end of the Yugoslav Civil War. Sheridan's three columns in the 1876 campaign did not anticipate a pitched battle. They expected a police round-up of recalcitrant Indian bands who would meekly allow themselves to be escorted to the reservations. Crook was barely able to cope with the attack on his strong column and retired to await reinforcements. In reality he was shocked and needed to consider what to do next. Poorly trained US Army forces lacked the credibility to over-face their opponents in these operations, which were well short of the high-intensity conflict that characterised the Civil War. Winning was not part of an equation that required a form of military 'posturing' to get the Indians to acquiesce. When the Plains Indians unexpectedly raised the military stakes, Custer had already played all the cards and lost. His force was neither credible nor intimidating in PSO terms to achieve the desired result. Professional skill is needed to over-face the enemy's combat power, in order to deter combat and avoid casualties and thereby achieve the mission. This, Sheridan's campaign of 1876 palpably failed to do.

* * *

The solitary marker casting its shadow on Highway 447 in the United States continues to maintain a lonely vigil on the Custer Trail to the Little Bighorn. Technological and archaeological advances have clarified some of the controversial aspects of Custer's last battle. Despite all this we can still only surmise who lies beneath this stone, and how it became his final resting place near the Yellowstone River in sight of the Wolf Mountains.

Notes

Prologue

1 W. A. Graham, *The Custer Myth*, p11
2 A uniform button impaled by an Indian arrowhead found at the Little Bighorn battle site is exhibited in the Jim Gatchell Memorial Museum at Buffalo, Wyoming, USA
3 White Bull account, J. A. Green (ed), *Lakota and Cheyenne*, p68
4 Red Horse account, ibid, p45
5 Ibid, p45
6 Little Hawk testimony, 5 September 1908, ibid, p64
7 Two Moons oral evidence, 1908, James Welch and Paul Steckler, *Killing Custer*, p294
8 Douglas D. Scott, P. Willey and Melissa A. Conner, *They Died With Custer*, p12
9 K. Hammer, *Men With Custer*, p409
10 The Regimental Marching Song
11 Mark Bowden, *Black Hawk Down*, pp6, 9, 23 and 310
12 The debate is conducted within two articles: R. E. Doran, *The Man Who Got to the Rosebud* (1987), and D. W. Ellison, *Mystery Along Rosebud Creek* (2001)

Chapter 1

1 C. T. Brady, *The Sioux Indian Wars*, p19
2 Dr G. Brown, *Custer and the Centennial Campaign of 1876*, lecture 16 November 2000
3 C. T. Brady, p23
4 Dee Brown, *The Fetterman Massacre*, p187
5 Ibid, p199
6 M. Carrington, *Absarake – Home of the Crows*, quoted in T. Goodrich, *Scalp Dance*, p30
7 Ibid, p29
8 Dee Brown, p203
9 Ibid, p201

10   Ibid, p205
11   Ibid, p215
12   Ibid, p205
13   C. T. Brady, p67
14   Ibid, pp67 and 68
15   Ibid, p54
16   Ibid, pp67 and 56-7
17   Quoted from *Atlas of the Sioux Wars*, Map 7, US Army Command and General Staff College, Fort Leavenworth
18   Dee Brown, *Bury My Heart at Wounded Knee*, p182; anecdotal story, Dr G. Brown

Chapter 2

1   A. Barnitz, ed Robert M. Uteley, *Life in Custer's Cavalry*, diary, November 1868, p218
2   Ibid, 28 July 1867, p90
3   This was Galusha Pennypacker, the youngest Brigadier General, appointed at the age of 20 to Custer's 23 and appointed Major General at 21, one month before Custer at 25
4   M. Merington (ed), *The Life and Intimate Letters of George A. Custer and His Wife Elizabeth*, Custer to Annette Humphry, 12 October 1863, p66. Hereafter referred to as 'Custer Letters'
5   Ibid, p95, Custer to Elizabeth, 1 May 1864
6   J. H. Kidd, *A Cavalryman with Custer*, pXIV
7   Barnitz, Albert to Jennie, 6 May 1867, p45; Jennie to Albert, 3 May 1868, p150
8   Figures quoted from L. Sklener, *To Hell with Honor*, p5
9   Sgt C. Windolph, *I Fought With Custer*, p5
10   J. Russell, *1876 Facts About Custer and the Battle of the Little Big Horn*, p29
11   Windolph, p5
12   Barnitz, 5 August 1867, pp93–4
13   George A. Custer, *My Life on the Plains*, pp5–6
14   D. Rickey Jnr, *Forty Miles a Day on Beans and Hay*, p24
15   Windolph, pp3 and 5
16   Barnitz, pp44 and 86
17   Ibid, letter of 26 February 1867, p15
18   T. Goodrich, *Scalp Dance*, p36
19   *My Life on the Plains*, p48
20   Barnitz, letters of 28 October 1868, p203, and 14 January 1868, p132
21   Rickey, p28
22   Quoted from Sklener, pp16–17

23 Various sources on desertion include G. Brown lecture, Rickey (p305), *My Life on the Plains* (p48) and Barnitz (5 August 1867, p92, and 25 November 1867, p128)

24 Kansas *Daily Times*, 26 September 1868, quoted in Goodrich, p120

25 Goodrich, p58

26 J. Welch with P. Steckler, *Killing Custer*, p36

27 Goodrich, pp41 and 43

28 Barnitz to Jennie, 13 August 1867, p95

29 Dee Brown, *Bury My Heart at Wounded Knee*, p148

30 *My Life on the Plains*, p158

31 Quoted from P. A. Hutton, *Paladin of the Republic*, MHQ, Vol 4, No 3, p90

32 Both quotes from Dee Brown, pp103 and 275

33 *My Life on the Plains*, p103; Barnitz, combat report dated 28 June 1867, p76

34 Welch and Steckler, p99

35 Santana quote from Dee Brown, p241; Barnitz, diary 23 May 1867, p53; buffalo figures from Welch and Steckler, p67

36 Welch and Steckler, p70

Chapter 3

1 Quoted from J. Welch with P. Steckler, *Killing Custer*

2 Sgt C. Windolph, *I Fought With Custer*, p42

3 Ibid, p38

4 Quoted from Dee Brown, *Bury My Heart at Wounded Knee*, p274, and Welch and Steckler, p38

5 Welch and Steckler, p84

6 Windolph, p42

7 Dee Brown, pp284 and 273

8 Peter Thompson, *Peter Thompson's Narrative of the Little Big Horn Campaign of 1876*, p32

9 E. A. Brininstool, *Troopers With Custer*, pp36, 39 and 43

10 K. Hammer, *Men With Custer*, pp275–76

11 Survey of units and force figures extracted from F. B. Taunton, *Sufficient Reason?*, pp7–9

12 F. B. Taunton, *Army Failures Against the Sioux in 1876: An Examination*, p9

13 Quoted in ibid, p9

14 Quoted from Leavenworth, *Atlas of the Sioux Wars*, Map 8

15 Louise Barnett, *Powder River* in *Greasy Grass* Magazine, Vol 16, p8

16 J. A. Green (ed), *Lakota and Cheyenne*, pp4–6

17 Writing for the Denver *Rocky Mountain News*, and quoted in T. Goodrich, *Scalp Dance*, p219

18 Ibid, p220

19   Barnett, p3

20   Ibid, p8

21   Custer Letters, Custer to Elizabeth from Washington, April 1876, p290

22   Green, p7

23   Kate Bighead quotes, ibid pp12 and 14

24   Lt James H. Bradley, *The March of the Montana Column*, pp41 and 43

25   Interview in *The Myth of Custer's Last Stand*, in *Timewatch*, BBC2 TV documentary (UK), August 2002

Chapter 4

1   Letter 5 March 1876, Fort Totten DT, K. Hammer, *Men With Custer*, p98

2   Sgt C. Windolph, *I Fought With Custer*, p49

3   Peter Thompson, *Peter Thompson's Narrative of the Little Big Horn Campaign of 1876*, p38

4   W. Taylor, *With Custer on the Little Bighorn*, p20

5   Thompson, p39

6   He had returned on 10 May. Thompson quotes, pp42 and 45, and Windolph, p50

7   Lt James H. Bradley, *The March of the Montana Column*, pp14, 23 and 50

8   Figures from F. B. Taunton, *Sufficient Reason?*, pp10–11; L. J. Chorne, *Following the Custer Trail of 1876*, p28; Taylor, p18

9   Letter to Sheridan 15 May 1876, quoted in Taunton, p12

10   Ibid, p12

11   Newspaper accounts 2 and 7 June 1876 in R. J. Legoski, *General George Crook's Campaign of 1876*, p74

12   Windolph, p52

13   Elizabeth B. Custer, *Boots and Saddles*, p217

14   Quoted in E. A. Brininstool, *Troopers With Custer*, p43

15   *Boots and Saddles*, p217

16   Windolph, p53

17   Quoted in Chorne, p13

18   *Boots and Saddles*, p218

19   Chorne, p14

20   Letter 8 June 1876, quoted in D. Rickey Jnr, *Forty Miles a Day on Beans and Hay*, p230

21   Chorne, p12

22   Bradley extracts 16 and 17 May 1876, *The March of the Montana Column*, pp99 and 101–03

23   Chorne, pp26–27

24   Letter 29 May 1876, quoted in F. B. Taunton, *Army Failures Against the Sioux in 1876: An Examination*, pp15–16

25 Windolph, p11, and subsequent quote
26 Chorne, p21
27 Thompson, pp44–45, and Windolph, p50
28 Windolph, p11 and subsequent quote
29 All statistics from Scott, Willey and Conner, *They Died With Custer*, pp23 and 33
30 Thompson, pp73 and 56–57; Ewart quote from Chorne, p33
31 Windolph, pp63 and 36
32 Taylor, pp20–21
33 Chorne: De Wolf letters 26 and 29 May 1876, pp79 and 95; Terry letter to sister at home 29 May 1876, p95
34 Bradley quotes 27 May 1876, p124, 28 May 1876, pp126–27
35 De Wolf letter to wife 1 June 1876, Terry 2 June, quoted in Chorne, pp107, 108 and 110
36 De Wolf letter to wife 3 June 1876, Chorne p118, *Peter Thompson's Narrative*, p57
37 Quoted in Chorne, p126
38 Legoski, p74

Chapter 5

1 Foster quoted from J. S. Gray, *Centennial Campaign*, p116; *Cheyenne Daily Leader* 23 July 1876 in R. J. Legoski, *General George Crook's Campaign of 1876*, p132; Grouard, p33
2 Legoski, p30
3 Gray, p119
4 Peter Thompson, *Peter Thompson's Narrative of the Little Big Horn Campaign of 1876*, p67
5 J. A. Green (ed), *Lakota and Cheyenne*: Lazy White Bull account p16, Little Hawk pp24–25, Two Moons p26
6 Analysis based on Gray, p120 and Chapter 27
7 Interview, Dr G. Brown, 2000
8 White Bull, Green, p16; Custer, *My Life on the Plains*, p15
9 Quoted from J. Welch with P. Steckler, *Killing Custer*, p117
10 Bourke, *On the Border With Crook*, p309
11 Finerty, Legoski, p34; T. Goodrich, *Scalp Dance*, p225, Bourke, p311
12 Green, p19
13 Finerty, Goodrich, p225; Towne quoted from C. T. Brady, *The Sioux Indian Wars*, p204; observer is Brady, p194; Byron quoted from D. Rickey Jnr, *Forty Miles a Day on Beans and Hay*, p285; Bourke, p311
14 Brady, p205
15 Legoski, p35

16   Green, p20
17   Legoski, p35
18   Little Hawk's account, Green, p25
19   Ibid, p26
20   Towne quoted from Brady, p206; *Chicago Tribune* report 5 July 1876 in Legoski, p119
21   Correspondent quoted by Legoski, p120, Towne by Brady, p206. Henry was subsequently to survive an epic and difficult evacuation process with his disfiguring wound and eventually achieved the rank of Brigadier General
22   Davenport was from the *New York Herald*. Quoted in Goodrich, pp228 and 229
23   Brady, pp207–08
24   Green: White Bull account, p21; Young Two Moons, pp29–30
25   Bourke, p316
26   Figures from Legoski, p35, and *Leavenworth Atlas*, Map 16; Bourke quote, p316

Chapter 6

1   Peter Thompson, *Peter Thompson's Narrative of the Little Big Horn Campaign of 1876*, p75
2   Quoted from R. H. Nichols, *In Custer's Shadow*, p156
3   Quotations from L. J. Chorne, *Following the Custer Trail of 1876*, pp171–72
4   Custer Letters, Custer to Elizabeth June 1876, p305; Thompson, p78; Sgt C. Windolph, *I Fought With Custer*, p64
5   Orders extract, see Appendix 1
6   Lt James H. Bradley, *The March of the Montana Column*, p143; Windolph, pp64 and 66
7   Thompson, p75; Burkman quoted in Chorne, p183
8   Thompson, p78; Burkman quoted in Chorne, p183; figures from L. Sklener, *To Hell with Honor*, p85
9   Thompson, pp88 and 75
10   Narrative taken from W. A. Graham, *The Custer Myth*, p130
11   See the Prologue and Postscript; based on information researched by D. W. Ellison, *Mystery Along Rosebud Creek* in *Greasy Grass* Magazine 2001, p23
12   Windolph, p66, and Chorne, pp183–84
13   Godfrey narrative, Graham, p130
14   Custer Letters, last letter 22 June 1876 from camp at junction of Yellowstone and Rosebud rivers, p307; Boston Custer letter 21 June 1876, ibid, p306; Dose letter to wife 8 June 1876 quoted in *True West* periodical, May/June 2001, p30
15   Burkman quoted in Chorne, pp183 and 187; Windolph, pp67 and 68
16   Bradley, p148

17 Thompson, p74
18 Godfrey narrative, Graham, p135
19 J. L. Russell, *1876 Facts About Custer and the Battle of the Little Bighorn*, p51
20 Windolph, p73, and Thompson, p71
21 Thompson, p96
22 Quoted in *The Boys of 76* in *True West* periodical, May/June 2001, p30
23 *The Not-So-Romantic Frontier* from D. Scott, P. Willey and M. Conner, *They Died With Custer*, pp301 and 278
24 Frederick William Benteen account in Graham, p178
25 Newspaper account 29 July 1876 in R. J. Legoski, *General George Crook's Campaign of 1876*, p44
26 Thompson, p93
27 Ibid, pp102 and 107, and J. S. Gray, *Centennial Campaign*, p158
28 Godfrey account in Graham, p136
29 Letter to T. W. Goldin 20 October 1891, Graham, p190
30 Katherine Gibson Fougera, *With Custer's Cavalry*, pp250–54 and 234
31 *Men With Custer*, K. Hammer, p232
32 Sklener, p58
33 Mark Kellogg's letters 21 June 1876, Graham, pp234–35 and Hammer, p184
34 Hammer, pp97, 302 and 237
35 Godfrey account, Graham, pp135–36

Chapter 7

1   W. Taylor, *With Custer on the Little Bighorn*, p27
2   Godfrey account, W. A. Graham, *The Custer Myth*, p136
3   J. S. Gray, *Centennial Campaign*, pp313, 318 and 320
4   Quoted in R. H. Nichols, *In Custer's Shadow*, p166
5   Sgt C. Windolph, *I Fought With Custer*, p73; Benteen account, Graham, p179
6   Windolph, p74; Godfrey account, Graham, p136; Benteen account, Graham, p179
7   Taylor, p32
8   Windolph, p75; Benteen, Graham, p179
9   G. F. Michno's estimate in *Lakota Noon*, pp6 and 18–19; Indian byword quoted on p29
10 Benteen account, Graham, p179, Nichols, p166, and note 38, p169
11 Author's experience
12 Nichols, p166, and Windolph, p76
13 Windolph, p76
14 R. G. Hardorff, *Packs, Packers, and Pack Details: Logistics and Custer's Pack Train*, pp226, 228, 236 and 230; also Windolph, p79

15 Letter 24 February 1892, quoted in Graham, p194
16 Windolph, p77
17 Peter Thompson, *Peter Thompson's Narrative of the Little Big Horn Campaign of 1876*, p117
18 Godfrey account, Graham, p137, and Thompson, p115
19 E. A. Brininstool, *Troopers With Custer*, p220
20 Windolph, p80, and Benteen account, Graham, p180
21 Gerard quoted by Gray, p173, Godfrey by Graham, p139
22 Taylor, p35
23 Thompson, p101

Chapter 8

1   Based on J. S. Gray's calculations in *Little Bighorn Battlefield Official National Park Handbook*, p65
2   D. H. Miller, *Custer's Fall*, pp34–35
3   Kill Eagle account, W. A. Graham, *The Custer Myth*, p47
4   Graham: Wooden Leg account, p104, Red Horse, p61
5   Kate Bighead from G. F. Michno, *Lakota Noon*, p24, Red Horse from J. A. Green (ed), *Lakota and Cheyenne*, pp33 and 35
6   Low Dog account, Graham, p75; Pretty White Buffalo, Michno, p23; Two Moons, Graham, p102
7   Soldier, Graham, p38; Varnum, E. A. Brininstool, *Troopers With Custer*, p97
8   Graham: Young Hawk account, p33, and Little Sioux, p42
9   W. Taylor, *With Custer on the Little Bighorn*, pp36 and 37, and Varnum in Brininstool, p98
10 Gall account, Graham, p90
11 Graham: Wooden Leg, p104, Iron Thunder, p79
12 Brininstool: Varnum p100, O'Neal p130, Slaper p48
13 Slaper, ibid, pp48 and 65, and K. Hammer, *Men With Custer*, p352
14 Varnum, Brininstool, p101; She Walks With Her Shawl, Green, p43; Slaper, Brininstool, p48
15 Brininstool, pp102 and 105
16 Ibid, Varnum pp101 and later 102, Slaper, pp48 and 51
17 Green: Red Horse, p33, She Walks With Her Shawl, p43
18 Brininstool, p102
19 Peter Thompson, *Peter Thompson's Narrative of the Little Big Horn Campaign of 1876*, pp119–21; Kanipe account, Graham, p249
20 Kanipe account, Graham, p249
21 Quoted from Neil C. Magnum, *The Civil War Custer*, in *True West*, May/June 2001, p19
22 Graham: Ryan account, p242, Young Hawk, p34

23 Ryan, Graham, p242; She Walks With Her Shawl, Green, p43; Slaper, Brininstool, p51; Soldier Wolf, Green, p51

24 The fight inside the 'timber', Slaper, Brininstool, p51; Koltzbucher's body did subsequently escape mutilation; Ryan account, Graham, p242; Red Bear account, ibid, p41; Taylor, p38

25 Martin account, Graham, p290

26 Martin, ibid; Edgerly quoted from J. S. Gray, *Custer's Last Campaign*, p264 and time chart at p338

Chapter 9

1   O'Neill, E. A. Brininstool, *Troopers With Custer*, p131

2   J. A. Green (ed), *Lakota and Cheyenne*: Soldier Wolf, p51, One Bull, p56

3   Brininstool: O'Neill, p132, Varnum, p108

4   Soldier Wolf, Green, p51; Gerard account, W. A. Graham, *The Custer Myth*, p251

5   The retreat, Brininstool: Slaper p52, Varnum pp108 and 112, O'Neill, pp132–33; Herendeen, Graham, p263; Dorman, G. F. Michno, *Lakota Noon*, p88

6   Pictograph by Sioux Chief Red Horse, National Anthropological Archives, Smithsonian Institution, in *National Geographic*, December 1986, p807

7   W. Taylor, *With Custer on the Little Bighorn*, p41; Darcy, K. Hammer, *Men With Custer*, p82

8   Wooden Leg, Michno, p80; Varnum, R. H. Nichols, *In Custer's Shadow*, p183

9   One Bull and She Walks With Her Shawl, Green, pp56 and 44–45 respectively; Varnum, Brininstool, p108

10 Darcy, Hammer, p82; Two Moons, Graham, p102; Varnum, Brininstool, p108; Spotted Horn Bull's wife, Graham, p84

11 D. Scott, P. Willey and M. Conner, *They Died With Custer*, p174

12 Brininstool, p53

13 Ibid, p109, and Hammer, p89

14 Brininstool, p113, and Taylor, p42

15 Taylor, pp44–45 and 47; Varnum, Brininstool, p113

16 R. G. Hardorff, *Hokahey! A Good Day to Die*, pp13–14 and 52–53

17 Graham: Spotted Horn Bull's wife's account, p84, Crow King, p77

18 Michno, pp24, 85 and 98

19 D. H. Miller, *Custer's Fall*, p82

20 Lt Charles de Rudio's letter, Graham, p254; O'Neill, Brininstool, p134; Ryan, Graham, p243

21 Green, p49

22 Michno: Two Moons, p101; Runs the Enemy, p96; Short Bull, p98; Little Bear, p99

23 Bobtail Horse, Michno, p102; Soldier Wolf, Green, p51; Tall Bull, ibid, p53

24 Artefacts finds map, Michno, p153
25 Graham: Kanipe account, p249, Martin account, pp290–91
26 Sgt C. Windolph, *I Fought With Custer*, pp89–90; Kanipe account, Graham, p249
27 Windolph, pp96 and 98; Martin, Graham, p291

Chapter 10

1   *Custer's Field*, article by F. B. Taunton, pp72–73
2   Martin account, W. A. Graham, *The Custer Myth*, p290
3   There are 252 markers for the 210 dead in Custer's command. D. Scott, R. Fox Jnr, M. A. Conner and D. Harman, *Archaeological Perspectives on the Battle of the Little Bighorn*, pp49 and 88
4   US Smithsonian Institution, National Anthropological Archives, *National Geographic*, December 1986, pp808–11
5   Scott, Fox, Conner and Harman, pp14–15 and 273
6   J. S. Gray, *Centennial Campaign* and *Custer's Last Campaign*
7   J. A. Green (ed), *Lakota and Cheyenne*, p53
8   Soldier Wolf, Green, p52; Henry Dose's body was recognised by Lt de Rudio, Taunton, *Custer's Field*, pp87 and 69 – see Dose's letter on 'flapjacks' in Chapter 4.
9   Green, p50
10 Curly account, Graham, p19
11 Sitting Bull interview, ibid, p72
12 Scott, Fox, Conner and Harman, *Archaeological Perspectives on the Battle of the Little Bighorn*
13 Ibid, pp117–18; Sitting Bull, Graham, p72
14 Scott, Fox, Conner and Harman, p119
15 Green, p61
16 Martin van Creveld, *Command in War*, p107; T. N. Dupey, *The Evolution of Weapons*, p312
17 Scott, Willey and Conner, *They Died With Custer*, Table 1, p34, and Table 2, p37
18 G. F. Michno, *Lakota Noon*, p175
19 Wooden Leg account, Graham, p105
20 Graham: Kill Eagle account, p47, Two Moons account, p103
21 Michno, p177
22 Red Horse, Green, p40; Moylan, Taunton, *Custer's Field*, pp72–73; Eagle Elk, R. G. Hardorff, *Hokahey! A Good Day to Die*, p62; Wooden Leg, ibid, p63
23 Low Dog, Graham, p75; firearms test televised in *Custer's Last Stand*, Channel 5 production (UK) directed by Chris Malone, September 2003;

Sitting Bull, Graham, p72

24 Peter Thompson, *Peter Thompson's Narrative of the Little Big Horn Campaign of 1876*, p178; Sitting Bull, Graham, p71

25 Scott, Fox, Conner and Harman, *Archaeological Perspectives on the Battle of the Little Bighorn*, pp114–15, and Thompson, p151

26 D. Rickey Jnr, *Forty Miles a Day on Beans and Hay*, p325

27 Background material on the Philadelphia World Fair from D. H. Miller, *Custer's Fall*, pp15–31

28 Lt James H. Bradley, *The March of the Montana Column*, pp149, 150, 151 and 152

29 Camp Cloud Peak, 21, 22, 23, 24 and 25 June 1876, newspaper accounts in R. J. Legoski, *General George Crook's Campaign of 1876*, pp42–3

30 25 June reports in Legoski, p43

31 J. L. Russell, *1876 Facts About Custer and the Battle of the Little Bighorn*, Fact 788, p94

32 Quoted in B. C. Johnson, *Weir and the Custers* in *No Pride in the Little Bighorn*, The English Westerners' Society, p11

Chapter 11

1 See F. B. Taunton, *The Enigma of Weir Point*, from which his logically presented timings are taken; *No Pride in the Little Bighorn*, pp16–41

2 E. A. Brininstool, *Troopers With Custer*, p113

3 Godfrey account, W. A. Graham, *The Custer Myth*, p142

4 Ibid, p142

5 Taunton, p32

6 Ibid, p31; Red Horse, G. F. Michno, *Lakota Noon*, p240

7 R. G. Hardorff, *Hokahey! A Good Day to Die*, p64

8 *Ghosts on the Little Bighorn* in *National Geographic*, December 1986, pp798–800, and Scott, Fox, Conner and Harman, *Archaeological Perspectives on the Battle of the Little Bighorn*, pp75–77 and 266–71

9 According to F. B. Taunton, *Custer's Field*, p69

10 See the Prologue

11 Scott, Fox, Conner and Harman, p246

12 Ibid, p121

13 *Archaeological Finds and Historical Locations Little Bighorn Battlefield Map*, produced by M. Bonafede, 1999; Gall account, Graham, p89; Foolish Elk, Hardorff, p69

14 Scott, Willey and Conner, *They Died With Custer*, derived from tables on pp34 and 36

15 Gall account, Graham, p89; E. S. Godfrey, *Cavalry Fire Discipline*, article in *Journal of the Military Service Institution*, September 1896, quoted from Taunton, *The Enigma of Weir Point*, p35; Little Hawk, J. A. Green (ed),

Lakota and Cheyenne, pp62–64

16　Godfrey; Gibbon and French quote, Michno, p239
17　Julia Face, Michno, p239. Keogh missed the 1867 Washita campaign and battle, the 1873–74 and the Yellowstone and Black Hills expeditions. In fact he was only in one short 'fight' in Kansas in 1867 out of 31 7th Cavalry skirmishes; Michno, p240
18　Foolish Elk, Hardorff, pp69–70; Edgerly, Taunton, *Custer's Field*, p77
19　Two Moons account, Graham, p103
20　Scott, Willey and Conner, *They Died With Custer*, p245, and Scott, Fox, Conner and Harman, *Archaeological Perspectives on the Battle of the Little Bighorn*, pp80 and 69
21　Taunton, *Custer's Field*, p75
22　Hardorff, p82 summary list
23　Stephen E. Ambrose, *Crazy Horse and Custer*, 1996
24　Graham: Wooden Leg account, p105; Flying By, p61; Red Horse, p37
25　Brave Wolf and Soldier Wolf, Green, pp48 and 52; Wooden Leg, Graham, p105
26　Green, p50
27　Ibid, pp40, 37 and 45
28　Two Moons, Graham, p102; Wallace at the Reno Court of Inquiry, Taunton, *Custer's Field*, p75; Young Two Moons, Green, p70
29　Hardorff, p72
30　Horned Horse account, Graham, p63; Elizabeth B. Custer, *Boots and Saddles*, pp134 and 237; White Bull, Michno, p234
31　Graham, p63
32　Young Two Moons and Soldier Wolf, Green, pp68 and 52
33　Hardorff: Big Beaver and Standing Bear, p75, Good Voiced Elk, p76, and Standing Bear, p78; Moylan from Taunton, *Custer's Field*, p75
34　McClernand quoted in T. Goodrich, *Scalp Dance*, p263; Carland quoted in Steve Arnold article, *Cooke's Scrawled Note*, in *Greasy Grass* Magazine, Vol 14, May 1998, p25
35　Green, p64
36　Taunton, *Custer's Field*, p85
37　Scott, Fox, Conner and Harman, pp61–62, 64, 262 and 272
38　D. D. Scott and R. A. Fox Jnr, *Archaeological Insights into the Custer Battle, 1984 Field Season*, 1987, p124
39　Interestingly, Bouyer does not have a moustache on his photograph. J. S. Gray, *Custer's Last Campaign*, pp396 and 398–99, and Scott, Fox, Conner and Harman, pp73–74
40　Scott and Fox, p124
41　Ibid, p125; Two Kettle, Michno, p276
42　Two Moons account, Graham, pp105–106; Black Elk, Michno, p287, and Miller, p115; Iron Hawk, Michno, p287; Antelope, ibid, p289

43   Hardorff, pp77–78
44   Katherine Gibson Fougera, *With Custer's Cavalry*, pp258, 260 and 261–63
45   Scott, Fox, Conner and Harman, p93

Chapter 12

1   W. Taylor, *With Custer on the Little Bighorn*, p48; Sgt C. Windolph, *I Fought With Custer*, p98; Gibson letter 4 July 1876, Katherine Gibson Fougera (KGF), *With Custer's Cavalry*, p269

2   Windolph, p99; Gibson, KGF, p269; Godfrey, from W. A. Graham, *The Custer Myth*, p142

3   Red Horse, J. A. Green (ed), *Lakota and Cheyenne*, p37; Taylor, p50

4   Red Horse account, Graham, pp62 and 60

5   Taylor, p82; Scott, Willey and Conner, *They Died With Custer*, pp197–201

6   T. W. Goldin account, E. A. Brininstool, *Troopers With Custer*, p224

7   Windolph, pp99 and 101; Taylor, p49; Godfrey account, Graham, p143

8   Brininstool: Slaper, p55, Varnum, p116

9   Red Horse, Green, p37, and Graham, p62; Little Hawk, Green, p64; Windolph, p101

10   R. G. Hardorff, *Hokahey! A Good Day to Die*, p86

11   Windolph, p102; Taylor, pp53 and 51

12   Godfrey account, Graham, p144; Taylor, p53–54; Windolph, pp102–103; Peter Thompson, *Peter Thompson's Narrative of the Little Big Horn Campaign of 1876*, pp189 and 193

13   Taylor, pp54–55; Thompson, p195; Gibson, KGF, p269; Godfrey, Graham, p144

14   Scott, Fox, Conner and Harman, *Archaeological Perspectives on the Battle of the Little Bighorn*, pp136–141; Gibson, KGF, p269

15   Gibson, KGF, pp269–70; Stands in Timber, Hardorff, pp89–91

16   Lt James H. Bradley, *The March of the Montana Column*, pp152–56

17   Benteen account, Graham, p182; Thompson, p197; Godfrey, Graham, p145

18   Varnum, Brininstool, pp116–17; Ryan account, Graham, p244; Dog's Back Bone, Hardorff, p91

19   Taylor, pp59 and 167; Godfrey, Graham, p145; Porter and Slaper, Brininstool, p57; Benteen, Graham, p182; Young Two Moons, Green, p72

20   Brininstool, pp57–59; Thompson, p215; Taylor, p60

21   Windolph, p106; Benteen and Reno quotes in R. H. Nichols, *In Custer's Shadow*, p203

22   Bradley, pp157–61

23   Green: American Horse, p50, Red Horse, p37

24   Bradley, letter to the *Helena Herald*, 25 July 1876, p172; Gibbon, T. Goodrich, *Scalp Dance*, pp257–58; Godfrey, Graham, p146

25 F. B. Taunton, *Custer's Field*, p78
26 Hardorff, p130
27 Newspaper accounts, 25 July 1876, Denver, Colorado, in R. J. Legoski, *General George Crook's Campaign of 1876*, p135
28 Taunton, *Custer's Field*, pp87 and 83, and Goodrich, p262
29 Ibid, p88
30 R. Uteley, *LBH Battlefield National Official Park Handbook*, p75, and Graham, pp349–351
31 KGF, pp261–66; Gurley quoted in Nichols, pp219–20
32 Nichols, pp334–35 and 239–40

Postscript
1 See Chapter 8
2 Curly account, W. A. Graham, *The Custer Myth*, pp18–19
3 Quoted from D. W. Ellison, *Mystery Along Rosebud Creek* in *Greasy Grass* Magazine, 2001, p17
4 R. E. Doran, *The Man Who Got to the Rosebud*, 1987, and D. W. Ellison, *Mystery Along Rosebud Creek*, 2001, are only two examples of this output
5 Ellison, p25
6 *Rocky Mountain News*, Denver, Colorado, 25 July 1876, in R. J. Legoski, *General George Crook's Campaign of 1876*, p135
7 F. B. Taunton, *Army Failures Against the Sioux in 1876*, pp20–21
8 J. A. Green (ed), *Lakota and Cheyenne: Iron Teeth*, p114, Beaver Heart, p120
9 Sitting Bull quoted in Dee Brown, *Bury My Heart at Wounded Knee*, p415, as also Wovoka, the Paiute Messiah of the Ghost Dance, p416

Bibliography

General

Arnold, Steve *Cooke's Scrawled Note* (*Greasy Grass* Magazine, Vol 14, May 1998, pp18–26)

Barnett, Louise *Powder River* (*Greasy Grass* Magazine, Vol 16, May 2000, pp2–8)

Bowden, Mark *Black Hawk Down* (Penguin, 1999)

Brady, C. T. *The Sioux Indian Wars* (Doubleday, 1904)

Brown, Dee *The Fetterman Massacre* (Pan Books, 1972)

Brown, Dr Jerold E. *Custer's Vision* (*Studies in Battle Command*, Faculty Combat Studies Institute, US Army Command and General Staff College, Fort Leavenworth, Kansas, pp75–78)

Custer and the Centennial Campaign of 1876 (Lecture, Wilton, UK, 16 November 2000)

Campsey, William M. *Intuitive Vision Versus Practical Realities: Custer at the Battle of the Little Bighorn* (*Studies in Battle Command*, Leavenworth, pp71–74)

Creveld, Martin van, *Command in War* (Harvard University Press, 1985)

Doran, Robert E. *The Man Who Got to the Rosebud* (Papers of the Custer Battlefield Historical and Museum Association Symposium, June 26, Crow Agency, Montana, 1987, pp19–33)

Ellison, Douglas *Mystery Along Rosebud Creek* (*Greasy Grass* Magazine, 2001, pp17–28)

Gray, John S. *Centennial Campaign – The Sioux War of 1876* (University of Oklahoma Press, 1910/1988)

Custer's Last Campaign: Mitch Bouyer and the Little Bighorn Reconstructed (University of Nebraska Press, 1991)

Goodrich, Thomas *Scalp Dance: Indian Warfare on the High Plains 1865–79* (Stackpole Books, 1997)

Hardorff, Richard G. *Packs, Packers, and Pack Details: Logistics and Custer's Pack Train*, from *Custer and his Times*, Book 3, ed Gregory J. Urwin and Roberta E. Fagan, pp225–48 (UCA Press, 1987)

Hutton, Paul A. *Paladin of the Republic* (*MHQ*, Vol 4, No 3, Spring 1992, pp82–91)

Jordan, Robert P. *Ghosts on the Little Bighorn* (*National Geographic*, Vol 170, No 6, December 1986)

Kraft, Louis *Separating the Man and Myth* (*Greasy Grass* Magazine, Vol 11, May 1995, pp39–45

Krott, Rob *Was Custer Outgunned? Firepower at the Battle of the Little Bighorn* (Military Illustrated, December 1999)

Legoski, Robert J. *General George Crook's Campaign of 1876. Newspaper Accounts of the Day* (private publication, Sheridan, Wyoming, 2000)

Longstreet, Stephen *War Cries on Horseback: The History of the Indian Wars* (Sphere, 1972)

Michno, Gregory *The Mystery of E Troop: Custer's Gray Horse Company at the Little Bighorn* (Mountain Press Pub Co, Montana, 1994)

Nichols, Ronald H. *In Custer's Shadow – Major Marcus Reno* (University of Oklahoma Press, 1999)

Pohanka, Brian *Custer and the Little Bighorn* (Lecture, Wilton, UK, 2 May 2001)

Rickey, Don Jnr *Forty Miles a Day on Beans and Hay* (University of Oklahoma Press, 1963)

Robertson, Dr William G., Brown, Dr Jerold E., Campsey, William M., and McMeen, Scott R. *Atlas of the Sioux Indian Wars* (US Army Command and General Staff College, Fort Leavenworth, Kansas)

Russell, Jerry L. *1876 Facts About Custer and the Battle of the Little Bighorn* (Savas Pub Co, 1999)

Sklener, Larry *To Hell with Honor: Custer and the Little Bighorn* (University of Oklahoma Press, 2000)

Taunton, Francis B. (ed) *No Pride in the Little Bighorn* (English Westerners' Society, 1987)

Army Failures Against the Sioux in 1876: An Examination (Westerners' Publications Ltd, 2000)

Sufficient Reason? (English Westerners' Society, 1977)

A Scene of Sickening, Ghastly Horror: The Custer battlefield – 27–28 June 1876 (Johnson-Taunton Military Press, London, 1983)

Uteley, Robert M. *Sitting Bull* (*MHQ*, Vol 5, No 4, Summer 1993, pp48–59)

Crook and Miles, Fighting and Feuding on the Indian Frontier (*MHQ*, Vol 2, No 1, Autumn 1989, pp81–91)

Welch, James, with Steckler, Paul *Killing Custer. The Battle of the Little Bighorn and the Fate of the Plains Indians* (Penguin, 1995)

Personal accounts and diaries

Bourke, John *On the Border with Crook* (Rio Grande Press 1969)

Bradley, Lt James H., ed E. I. Stewart *The March of the Montana Column* (University of Oklahoma Press, 1961/1991)

Brininstool, E. A. *Troopers With Custer* (University of Nebraska Press, 1952/1989)

Chorne, L. J. *Following the Custer Trail of 1876* (Trails West, 1997)

Custer, Elizabeth B. *Boots and Saddles* (1885) (University of Oklahoma, 1961)

Custer, George A. *My Life on the Plains* (1875) (Star Book, 1982)

Fougera, Katherine Gibson *With Custer's Cavalry* (University of Nebraska Press, 1986)

Graham, W. A. *The Custer Myth* (Stackpole Books, 1953/2000)

Hammer, Kenneth *Men With Custer. Biographies of the 7th Cavalry June 25 1876* (Custer Battlefield Historical Museum Association, 1995)

Kershaw, R. J. *Battlefield Tour Notes* (unpublished, 2000 and 5–10 May 2001)

Kidd, J. H. *A Cavalryman With Custer* (1908) (Bantam, 1991)

Merington, Marguerite (ed) *The Life and Intimate Letters of George A. Custer and His Wife Elizabeth* (University of Nebraska Press, 1950/1987)

Taylor, William O. *With Custer on the Little Bighorn* (Penguin, 1996)

Thompson, Peter, ed Daniel O. Magnussen *Peter Thompson's Narrative of the Little Big Horn Campaign of 1876* (The Arthur H. Clark Co, California, 1974)

Uteley, Robert M. (ed) *Life in Custer's Cavalry: Diaries and Letters of Albert and Jennie Barnitz, 1867–1868* (Yale University Press, 1977)

Windolph, Sgt *I Fought With Custer: The Story of Sgt Windolph, Last Survivor of the Battle of the Little Bighorn as told to Frazier and Robert Hunt* (Bison Books, 1987)

Indian accounts

Brown, Dee *Bury My Heart at Wounded Knee* (Vintage, 1970/1991)

Green, Jerome A. (ed) *Lakota and Cheyenne: Indian Views of the Great Sioux War 1876–7* (University of Oklahoma Press, 1994)

Hardorff, Richard G. *Hokahey! A Good Day to Die: The Indian Casualties of the Custer Fight* (Bison Books, 1993/1999)

Michno, Gregory F. *Lakota Noon: The Indian Narrative of Custer's Defeat* (Mountain Press Co, 1999)

Miller, David H. *Custer's Fall* (Bantam, 1957/1963)

Morelock, J. D. *Native American Accounts of the Little Bighorn Battle: Charting Custer's Last Moments From Eye-Witness Testimony* (Leavenworth)

Archaeological accounts

Scott, Douglas D. and Fox, Richard A. Jnr *Archaeological Insights into the Custer Battle: An Assessment of the 1984 Season* (University of Oklahoma Press, 1987)

Scott, Douglas D., Fox, Richard A. Jnr, Conner, Melissa A. and Harman, Dick *Archaeological Perspectives on the Battle of the Little Bighorn* (University of Oklahoma Press, 1989)

Scott, Douglas D., Willey, P. and Conner, Melissa A. *They Died With Custer* (University of Oklahoma Press, 1998)

Index

American Horse, Oglala Sioux 192, 202, 216, 255, 293

Amos Bad Heart Bull. Pictograph 195

Archaeological evidence
Arrows – effectiveness 231–2
Forensic studies, bodies 134, 196, 212, 213, 276
Forensic studies, firearms xiv, xvii, xviii, 205, 213, 219, 225, 231, 247, 253, 258, 282, 295
Prairie fire xvii, 212, 213, 219, 243, 307

Barnitz, Albert, Capt. 7th Cav. 29, 30, 33, 38, 39, 41, 44, 46, 47

Barnitz, Jennie 37, 38

Beecher's Island, Battle 1868 24, 26, 104, 255, 279

Belknap Case 1876 70, 234

Benteen, Frederick William, Capt. H. Coy. 7th Cav.
Early career 34, 35, 80, 139
Relationship with Custer 81, 152
'Left oblique' move 147, 148, 154, 156, 159, 161, 162, 164, 178, 179, 184, 185, 302, 313
Dilemma of delayed arrival 187, 203, 205, 207, 209, 212, 215, 219
Relieves Reno 199, 221, 224, 238
At Weir Point 240, 243, 264, 271, 273
Hilltop Fight xiii, 277, 278, 282, 288, 290, 292, 295

Big Beaver, Cheyenne boy 258, 263

Black Elk, Oglala Sioux youth 200, 269

Black Hills, Dakota 27, 46, 51, 52, 53, 54, 82, 88, 155, 301, 308

Black Hills Expedition, 52, 56, 82, 155

Black Kettle, Southern Cheyenne chief 43

Bloody Knife, Custer's Arikara Indian Scout 136, 149, 183, 191

Botzer, Edward, Sgt. G. Coy. 7th Cav. 74, 195, 216

Bourke, John, Lt. Aide to Brig Gen Crook 63, 99, 100, 103, 113, 236, 237

Bradley, James, Lt. Army Scout / Montana Column 75, 76, 84, 86, 95, 122, 127, 144, 235, 283

Brisbin, James S., Maj. 2nd Cav. 58, 121, 127

Bouyer, Mitch, Civilian Scout with Custer 94, 117, 129, 145, 184, 186, 187, 203, 218, 267, 302

Brown, Frederick H., Capt. Quartermaster, Fort Phil Kearney 4, 12, 13, 15

Bozeman Trail 2, 14, 26, 28, 88

Buffalo Calf Road Woman, Cheyenne squaw 108

'Buffalo Jump' at Rosebud 103

Burkman, John, Pte. Custer's orderly 74, 76, 87, 88, 122, 123, 126, 127

Busby Bend, Rosebud Creek 144, 146, 312

Byron, H. S., Maj. 3rd Cav. 103

Calhoun, James, Lt. Coy Comd L Coy. 7th Cav. xi, xiii, 77, 124, 211, 216, 218, 219, 221, 222, 223, 224, 225, 226, 227, 232, 238, 239, 244, 255, 258

Calhoun Hill 216, 218, 223, 224, 225, 230, 242, 243, 244, 247, 248

Carrington, Henry, Col. Comd Fort Phil Kearney 1, 2, 5, 8, 14, 16, 18, 24

Casualties at Little Bighorn
Indian vii, 199, 254, 295
US Army vii, 253, 282, 295, 296

Centennial Celebrations Washington 1876 77, 137, 140, 164, 233, 234, 298, 307

Chambers, Alexander, Major. Infantry with Crook 93, 100, 104

Charley, Vincent, Farrier. D Coy. 7th Cav. 275, 276

Conical or 'Last Stand' Hill 106, 112, 241, 247, 248, 252, 271

Comes-in-Sight, Cheyenne warrior 106

Cooke, William, Lt. Adjutant 7th Cav. 42, 186, 264

Crazy Horse, Sioux chief 6, 26, 49, 51, 54, 66, 109, 168, 176, 223, 247, 253, 259, 307, 308

Crittenden, John, 2Lt. L Coy. 7th Cav. 139, 140, 211, 222, 232

Crook's Column
  Departure 29 May 1876 72, 75, 77, 78, 86, 88, 89
  Rosebud battle vi, 91, 115, 128

Crook, George, Brig Gen.
  Early career 35, 58, 60
  Character 92, 94, 290, 295
  At Powder River 62, 65, 69, 157, 311
  Does not act at Little Bighorn 117, 123, 144, 236, 237
  Campaign after Little Bighorn 307, 308

Crow King, Sioux warrior 168, 200

'Crow's Nest' Feature 145, 150, 151, 152, 156, 161, 312

Crow Scouts ix, 45, 66, 67, 71, 76, 88, 92, 100, 102, 103, 109, 111, 126, 145, 150, 188, 193, 235, 243 284, 292, 302

Curly, Indian scout 184, 186, 187, 203, 218, 302

Custer, Elizabeth 'Libby' xi, 31, 37, 72, 77, 209, 259, 296, 298

Custer, George Armstrong, Brevet Maj Gen. Comd 7th Cav.
  Civil War experience 30, 35
  Character and early life 30, 31, 37, 39, 43, 44, 46, 52, 65, 69, 86, 98, 120, 129
  Command competence 33, 59, 71, 82
  Embarks on Bighorn campaign 71, 77, 83, 87
  Decision points 93, 94, 120, 122, 123, 128, 130, 133, 143, 154, 159, 164, 312, 316
  Message 'Bring Packs' 187

Divides Forces 154, 166
Tactical battle v, xi, xix, 167, 263
Death 256, 264, 265, 296, 299

Custer, Boston 77, 125, 180, 187, 264

Custer, Thomas, Capt. Coy Comd C Coy. xii, 55, 77, 80, 124, 178, 226

Dakota Column (Terry)
  Departure 17 May 1876 71, 79
  Journey to operations area 77, 89, 93, 98

Davenport, Reuben. Correspondent with Crook's Column 111

Deeds, Sans Arc youth 171

Deep Ravine Feature 246, 255, 256, 262, 263, 265, 267, 269

De Rudio, Charles, Lt. A Coy. 7th Cav. 201, 278

De Wolf, James, Dr. Surgeon, 7th Cav. 83, 86, 120, 197

Divide Ridgeline 145, 147, 153, 157, 160, 236, 313

Dorman, Isaiah. Civilian Black interpreter with Reno 191

Dose, Henry, Sgt. Bugler 7th Cav. 74, 125, 134, 216

Eagle Elk, Oglala warrior 201, 227, 228

Eagon, Thomas, Cpl. E Coy. 7th Cav. 69

Edgerly, Winfield Scott, Lt. 7th Cav. 186, 238, 239, 243, 249, 275, 276

Elliot, Joel, Maj. 7th Cav. 43, 44, 80

Far West Steamboat 88, 120, 121, 124, 126, 151, 235, 237, 297, 298, 303

Fetterman Massacre, 21 Dec 1866. v, 1, 17, 19, 22, 24, 26, 29, 98, 109, 111, 226, 254

Fetterman, William J, Capt. 3, 5, 6, 8, 13, 14, 15, 16, 18, 24, 26, 67, 226

Fisher, Isaac. Army Scout with Fetterman 4, 9, 13, 26

Finerty, John. Press correspondent with Crook's Column. 94, 99, 100, 103, 105, 135, 236, 237

Finlay, Sgt. L Coy. 7th Cav. xiv, 140

Finkle, Sgt. C Coy. 7th Cav. 178

'Flats' Feature 8, 9, 162

French, Thomas H., Capt. M Coy 7th
   Cav. 55, 182, 184, 249, 288, 295
Force Marches
   Dakota Column 86–9
   Custer's Column 128–41, 154
Fort Abraham Lincoln 53, 55, 56, 58,
   59, 65, 70, 71, 76, 123, 125, 146,
   233, 270, 271, 298
Fort Phil Kearney 2, 17, 23, 24,
Foster, E. H., 2nd Lt. 3rd Cav. 92, 94

Gall, Hunkpapa chief 168, 171, 226,
   228, 247, 248
Gerard, Frank. Interpreter and scout,
   Custer's Column 148, 162, 190, 278,
   297
Gibbon, John, Col. Comd Montana
   Column xv, 66, 71, 76, 77, 78, 84,
   86, 89, 91, 94, 95, 118, 122, 128,
   129, 136, 144, 151, 249, 251
Gibson, Francis, Lt. M Coy. 7th Cav.
   138, 271, 273, 282
Gibson, Katherine 138, 271, 299
Gravestone markers xii, 212, 213, 216,
   248, 251, 265, 268, 301, 316
Godfrey, Edward S, Lt. K Coy 7th Cav.
   124, 129, 137–47, 152, 157, 161, 240,
   241, 247, 248, 276, 280, 283, 286,
   288, 294, 296, 297, 305
Gold – Black Hills discoveries 51, 52
Goldin, Theodore. D Coy. 7th Cav. 161
Goose Creek 89, 93, 114, 236
Grant, Ulysses S., General and US
   President 31, 35, 53, 54, 65, 70, 75,
   233, 234
Grouard, Frank, Army Scout with Crook
   62, 88, 92, 236
Grummond, George, Lt. 2nd Cav. 3, 5,
   8, 10

Henry, Guy V., Capt. Bn Comd 3rd Cav.
   100, 103, 111
'Henryville' Ridge, Calhoun Hill.
   224–32, 244–6
'Hilltop fight', Little Bighorn 257,
   273–90
Hodgeson, 'Bennie', Lt. Aide to Reno. 7th
   Cav. 194, 240
Horner, Jacob, Pte. K Coy. 7th Cav. 79

Horses – 7th Cav. x, xiii, 4, 9, 12, 13,
   29, 36, 72, 94, 104, 122, 123, 128,
   133–48, 160, 162, 170, 172, 178, 183,
   193, 194, 206, 208, 216, 226–8, 247,
   255, 257, 258, 262

Indians
   Atrocities 2, 13, 16, 39–42, 43–4, 54,
      112, 192–4, 202, 245, 269, 297–8
   Firepower and accuracy xii, xix, 13,
      46, 97, 132–3, 213, 219–20, 231–2,
      254, 259–62, 282, 287, 295, 314
   Intelligence on Indians vii, 57, 59,
      69–72, 84, 87, 94, 97, 103, 114
   Sioux 2, 3, 5, 7, 24, 26, 28, 45,
      47–59, 66, 72, 89, 91, 143, 145, 167,
      203, 307, 309, 310
   Tribes 2, 6, 45–54, 56–9, 145, 168,
      233, 310
   Way of life 25, 44, 47–50, 52–6, 66,
      129, 150, 310
Iron Hawk, Hunkpapa warrior 203, 269
Iron Thunder, Sioux warrior 172

Kanipe, Daniel, Sgt. C Coy. 7th Cav. xv,
   177, 178, 206, 302
Kate Bighead, Northern Cheyenne. 66,
   168, 270
Kellogg, Mark Henry, Newspaper
   correspondent with Custer's Column
   74, 139, 249
Keogh, Myles, Capt. Coy Comd I Coy 7th
   Cav. xi, xiv, 226, 239, 245, 246, 248,
   250, 256, 258
Kill Eagle, Sioux warrior 168, 225
Kollmar Creek, Rosebud 105, 108, 109

Laramie Treaty, 26, 29, 42, 54
Little Hawk, Northern Cheyenne xiv, 97,
   106, 109, 249, 264, 279
Little Bighorn
   River ix, xvii, 121, 122, 128, 144,
      150, 163, 167, 235, 237, 284, 292,
      303
   Odds against Indians xvi, 125, 129–32
   Searching for Indian village 75–89,
      117–28
   Force march to village 128–54
   Custer sub divides Comd 154

Advance to Contact 154–66
    Reno's attack 170–82
    Reno's retreat 182–202
    Yates feint 202
    Calhoun Hill 211–46, 273–94
    Custer overwhelmed 244–71
    News of massacre 293–9
Lodge Trail ridge 1, 3, 14
Low Dog, Oglala Sioux chief 167, 169,
    172, 228

McDougall, Thomas M., Capt. B Coy. 7th
    Cav. 155, 158, 179, 181, 187, 206,
    240, 262, 277
McIntosh, Donald, Lt. G Coy. 7th Cav.
    139, 201
Marsh, Grant, Capt. of *Far West* 126,
    237, 298
Martin, John, Bugler, Custer's staff 7th
    Cav. 138, 185, 187, 206, 208, 211
Meador, Thomas, Pte. H Coy. 7th Cav.
    140
Medicine Tail Coulee 150, 185, 187,
    202, 215, 254
Metzger, Adolph, US Army bugler 163
Mills, Anson, Capt. M Coy. 3rd Cav. 62,
    63, 100, 104, 108, 109, 112, 113,
    236, 237
Mogadishu, Somalia xvii, 221
Montana Column (Gibbon)
    Departure 1 Apr 1876 65, 71
    Discovers Indian camps 75, 79, 84,
        86, 94
    Moves with Terry to Little Bighorn xv,
        89, 94, 96, 118, 120, 121, 127, 144,
        285, 306
'Morass' Feature 206
Moylan, Myles, Capt. A Coy. 7th Cav.
    77, 211, 227, 262, 263
Mules 19, 43, 61, 71, 87, 92, 100, 122,
    128, 148, 157, 158, 177, 240, 290

Noyes, Henry E., Capt. 2nd Cav. 62, 63,
    100, 104
Nye-Cartwright Ridge Feature 187, 202,
    204, 205, 215, 229

One Bull, Lakota Sioux 189, 193
O'Neill, Thomas, Pte. G Coy. 7th Cav.

    183, 189–92, 201
'Packers and Miners' at Rosebud 106
Pack Train, Custer's Column 123, 128,
    148, 151, 155, 157–8, 178, 181, 184,
    186, 187, 207, 209, 238, 242, 290
Peace Support Operations. (PSO). Modern
    warfare xvii, xviii, 34, 57, 254, 311,
    313, 314, 316
Pretty White Buffalo, Hunkpapa squaw
    169
Porter, Dr. Surgeon, 7th Cav. 83, 289, 290
Powder River battle. 16 March 1876. v,
    60–7, 69, 75, 77, 78, 88, 94, 108,
    115, 131, 157, 311
Powell, James W., Capt. 27th Inf. 5,
    18–19, 20

Rain-in-the-Face, Hunkpapa Sioux chief
    26
Red Cloud, Oglala Sioux chief vi, 6, 19,
    23, 26, 29, 45, 52, 67, 72, 98, 131,
    138, 169, 203
Red Horse, Minneconjou Sioux xii, 168,
    176, 212, 220, 227, 253, 256, 274,
    275, 279, 293
Reed, Harry Armstrong 'Autie'. Custer's
    nephew 265
Reno, Marcus Alfred, Maj. Second-in-
    Command, 7th Cav.
    Reno's Reconnaissance 80, 94–6,
        117–20
    Attack on village 156, 162–85
    Combat stress 184
    Retreat 183–202
    Hilltop Fight 237–44, 273–94
Reno Court of Inquiry, 1879 xvi, 211,
    239–51, 295
Reynolds, Charley, scout 183–4
Reynolds, Joseph J., Col. Comd Powder
    River Column 61–7, 130, 145
Rosebud, Battle, 17 Jun 1876
    Surprise Indian attack 91–104
    Crook's counter measures 102–6
    Fighting withdrawal and stalemate
        108–15
Rosebud River xiv, xix, 77, 84, 91–4,
    94–102, 108, 117, 120, 128, 133,
    143–8, 157–9, 237, 301–3, 305–7,
    312

Royall, W. B., Lt Col. 3rd Cav. 104–9,
    109–14, 156, 226, 254
Ryan, John, Sgt. M. Coy. 7th Cav. 173,
    181, 183, 201, 287–9, 297

She Walks With Her Shawl. Lakota squaw
    173, 176, 181, 194
Sheridan, Phillip N., Dept of Missouri
    Comd 31, 40, 44, 50, 52, 56–8, 60,
    65, 67, 70, 74–9, 96, 121, 155, 234,
    308–16
Sherman, William T., Gen. in Chief US
    Army 31, 37, 40, 44, 71, 78, 290,
    308
Short, Nathan, Pte. C. Coy. 7th Cav.
    Early career/recruitment x–xvi,
    xviii–xix, 54, 139–41
    Journey to Little Bighorn 94–6,
    123–4, 178–9
    Riddle of fate xi–xii, 228–33, 244–6,
    301–8, 316
    Grave marker 301–2, 316
Sitting Bull, Sioux chief 47–9, 51–4, 59,
    66–76, 87–92, 96–8, 126, 131, 136,
    139–41, 143–4, 150, 166, 168, 176,
    193, 200, 219, 229–31, 275, 310
Slaper, William, Pte. M Coy. 7th Cav.
    55, 73, 138, 172–5, 182–4, 190, 196,
    278, 289
Slim Buttes battle, 9 Sep 1876 308
Smith, Algernon E., Lt. E Coy. 7th Cav.
    262
Smyth, R.J, mule driver, Wagon Box fight
    19, 22
'Snow Camp' 1 Jun 1876 86
Soldier Wolf, Northern Cheyenne warrior
    182, 190, 205, 216, 254, 263
Southern Skirmish Line or 'Salient' 256
Springfield Allen M-1866 .50-70 breech-
    loading rifle 17, 42, 269
Springfield .58 muzzle loader 4, 12, 18,
    25
Springfield 1873 Cavalry Carbine xii–xiv,
    132, 213, 229–31, 253–4, 282
Standing Bear, Minneconjou Sioux 228,
    262–3, 279
Sturgis, Sam, Col. Comd 7th Cav. 38–9,
    121, 139
Sturgis, James 'Jack', 2Lt. E Co 7th Cav.

139, 294, 297–9
Sun Dance 91, 131, 136, 141
'Suicide Boys' 259–62

Tactics
    Firepower v–xiv, xvi–xvii, 13, 24, 26,
        47–9, 69–70, 102–4, 111–12, 130–2,
        154–6, 220–2, 224–6, 226–7, 254–6,
        289–91, 295–8
    Indian vi–vii, 6–8, 24, 47–9, 104–6,
        109–10, 114–15, 128–32, 136–7,
        150–1, 181–3, 226–7, 248–9, 256–8,
        275–6
    US Army v–vi, 24–5, 44, 49–50,
        60–3, 92–4, 128–32, 143–4, 154–8,
        160–1, 164–6, 172–4, 174–5, 179–81,
        185–6, 203–4, 222–4, 251–4, 288–9,
        310–15
Taylor, William, Pte. A Coy. 7th Cav
    69–70, 82, 143–4, 146–8, 163, 170,
    183–4, 192–6, 197–9, 273–81, 288
Ten Eyck, Tenodor, Capt. 12–17
Terry, Alfred, Brig Gen. Dakota Column
    Comd.
    Dakota Column 52, 58–60, 69–79,
        85–9, 96–8, 117–21, 126–30, 137–9
    Orders to Custer 81–4, 92–6, 120–2,
        143–6
    Moves to relieve Custer 219, 233–6,
        283–5, 291–4
    Discovers battlefield 293–9
Thirst – US Army 135, 148, 154, 163,
    205–6, 235–6, 288–91
Thompson, Peter, Pte. C. Coy. 7th Cav.
    55, 70, 80, 87, 95, 120, 128, 133,
    158, 160, 166, 177, 230–1, 278–83,
    286, 290
'Timber' fight, Little Bighorn 176–9,
    179–84, 190–2
'Trooper Mike' on Calhoun Hill 244–6
Towne, Phineas, Pte. F. Coy. 3rd Cav.
    103, 109–11
Tongue River 62, 84, 89, 91–3, 95–6,
    236, 308–9
Two Moons, Northern Cheyenne 97,
    113, 169, 195, 203, 225, 258, 262–3,
    267, 289

Ultimatum to Indians, 6 Dec 1875 54–6

US Army
  Desertion 36–9, 70–2, 130–2, 139–41
  Frontier Army 24–7, 29–43, 70
  Lessons from Fetterman Massacre
    16–28
  Post Civil War reductions and
    experience 6–8, 30–7, 40–1, 79–81,
    102–4, 154–6, 172–4, 179–8, 220–2,
    222–4, 228–9, 310–12
  Service life 36–9
  Training 8–9, 36–7, 54–6, 130–2,
    222–4, 228–9
  3rd Cav Regt. 58–62, 77, 92, 103–4,
    111, 131, 236
  7th Cav Regt. xiv–xx, 29, 30, 32–9,
    41–2, 47–9, 52–5, 58, 69–73, 79–83,
    121–3, 126, 130–2, 139–40, 155–8,
    180, 237–8, 244, 293–6, 298–303,
    305–12

'Valley bottom' fight, Little Bighorn
  180–8
van Vliet, Frederick, Capt. C. Coy. 3rd
  Cav. 100, 104, 108–9
Varnum, Charles, Lt. Custer's Chief Scout
  145–6, 149, 172–5, 189–90, 208, 240,
  276–8, 287
Villages – Plains Indian 29–30, 42–3,
  43–5, 49–50, 56–8, 65–7
  Discovery, 16 May 1876. ix–x
  Size of 92–4
  Initial attack on 145–6, 148–72

Wagon Box Fight, 2 Aug 1867 19–23
Wallace, George, Lt. G Coy. 7th Cav.
    129, 141, 227, 246, 250, 258, 277,
    310
Washita, Battle of, 25 Nov 1868 29,
    42–5, 43–5, 77, 80–1, 130, 150,
    155–7, 162, 180–1
Weapons
  Indians 10–12, 12–14, 47–9, 96–9,
    132–3, 218–20, 220–2, 224–6, 233–5,
    254–6
  US Army 8–12, 12–14, 16–19, 22–5.
    36–7, 70–2, 130–2, 220–2, 224–6
Weir Point Feature 184
Weir, Thomas B., Capt. D Coy. 7th Cav.
    207, 238–41, 273, 277, 294–5
Wheatley, James S., Army Scout 4, 14
White Bull, Lakota Sioux warrior x–xiii,
    96–7, 102, 105, 113, 261–2
Windolph, Charles 'Dutchy', Cpl. H Coy.
  7th Cav. 34–6, 51–3, 70–2, 79–82,
    126–7, 132–3, 136, 146–7, 154,
    156–9, 162, 207–8, 220, 272–4,
    277–81, 286–7, 291
Wright, Phyllis, Pte. C. Coy. 7th Cav.
    251
Wooden Leg, Cheyenne warrior 63, 65,
    168, 171, 193–6, 224, 228, 253–4,
    268–70

Yates, George W., Capt. F. Coy. 7th Cav.
    187, 202–5, 218, 272
Yellowstone River xiv–xvi, xviii–xix, 59,
    65, 70, 76, 118, 121, 127–8, 131,
    166, 218, 237, 298, 302–3, 305–9,
    316